STEAM
at sea

STEAM
at sea

Two centuries of steam-powered ships

DENIS GRIFFITHS
BEng MSc PhD CEng FIMarE

CONWAY MARITIME PRESS · LONDON · 1997

© Denis Griffiths 1997

First published in Great Britain in 1997 by
Conway Maritime Press,
9 Blenheim Court,
Brewery Road,
London N7 9NT
www.conwaymaritime.com

A member of the Chrysalis Group plc

Reprinted 2000

British Library Cataloguing in Publication Data
Griffiths, Denis 1943-
      Steam at Sea: two centuries of steam-powered ships
      1. Marine engines – History   2. Steam-navigation – History
      3. Marine engineering – History
      I. Title
      623.8'722'09

ISBN 0 85177 666 3

All unattributed illustrations are from the author's collection.

Jacket designed by Ken Wilson
Book designed by Nicholas Jones
Typeset in Monotype Ehrhardt by Strathmore Publishing Services, London N7
Printed and bound in Great Britain by Butler and Tanner Ltd, Frome

This book is dedicated to the memory of

my brother
Arthur James Griffiths
whose passing I still grieve

and to the memories of

Harold *and* **Madeleine Russell**
my parents-in-law

and my very good friend
Stan Wakefield

Contents

Acknowledgements

This book follows from the chapters on marine engineering contributed by the author for two volumes in the series *Conway's History of the Ship* and thanks must go to Robert Gardiner, editor of that series, for encouraging and commissioning this volume. The author is indebted to many individuals and organisations for the provision of information, photographs, facilities and encouragement; if any are omitted from the following list the author sincerely apologises.

Facilities and information have kindly been provided by Liverpool City Library, Merseyside Maritime Museum, Cammell Laird Archive at Birkenhead Town Hall, The National Maritime Museum Library, Lloyd's Register of Shipping Record Centre, The Institute of Marine Engineers, The Mitchell Library, Glasgow, Tyne & Wear Archive, Newcastle-upon-Tyne, the Submarine Museum, Gosport and the library at Liverpool John Moores University. The author expresses his thanks to the staff at these establishments.

David Carter and David Strawford at P&O Cruises have been most helpful, as have the engineers aboard the steamship *Canberra*. Thanks are due to the US Department of Defense, the Public Relations Officer at the MOD, and to Mitsubishi Heavy Industries. Shipping companies, many now defunct, have over the years provided the author with information and photographs and these include French Line, Cunard, Ellermans, Manchester Liners, Clan Line, British Petroleum, Esso and Furness Withy. Engineering companies who have been useful in the same respect include Weirs, Cammell Laird, Babcock & Wilcox and Foster Wheeler.

Two individuals to be thanked are Fred Walker for his constant encouragement and Peter Gee for his enthusiasm concerning all matters relating to marine engineering. Professor Tom Ruxton, John Banks and Mike Diggle of Liverpool John Moores University have been most helpful during the years of research and writing. Particular thanks must also go to the late Stan Wakefield who helped the author cope with the problems of word-processing and with many other trials. The late Harry Weston provided the author with many valuable photographs, considerable information and much encouragement when he was setting out on a marine engineering career. Harold E. Philpot of the RMS *Queen Elizabeth* Historical Society has been most useful with respect to information concerning that ship. Marine engineers Keith Corlett, Martin S. Harrison and Enda Cadwell have been most helpful and informative about current practice.

Thanks must go to my family; my wife Patricia and children Sarah and Patrick have tolerated my obsession with marine engineering, while my mother Elizabeth E. Griffiths has, as always, enthused about everything her son has undertaken. My brother Arthur died before the book was completed but, as usual, he offered encouragement throughout my efforts.

Finally I would like to thank all of those marine engineers with whom I have sailed or have taught over the years; I have gained much from their experience.

Units and Conversions

Throughout the book imperial units have been used as most of the machinery discussed was constructed using such units; even though later engines and boilers were constructed using SI units these have been converted to imperial units in order to ensure consistency and to allow for direct comparison between machinery. Conversion factors are given below for those who wish to make the conversion to modern practice.

Mass
1kg = 2.2lbs; 1 lb = 0.4545kg
1 ton = 2,240lbs = 1,016kg
1 tonne = 1,000kg (i.e. one metric ton)

Area
1in^2 = 645mm^2 = 0.645 x 10^{-3}m^2 1ft^2 = 0.0929m^2

Power
1 horse power = 746 watts = 0.746kW

Pressure
Unless otherwise stated, all pressures are gauge pressures, which means that they are pressures above that of the atmosphere. Atmospheric pressure = 14.7psi = 101.325 kN/m^2; 1psi = 6.9 kN/m^2

Length
1in = 25.4mm = 0.00254m
1ft = 2048mm = 0.3048m

Volume
1ft^3 = 0.0283m^3
1 gross ton = 100ft^3 = 2.83m^3

Consumption
1lbs/hp/hr = 0.609kg/kW/hr

Introduction

The ship is the largest moving object devised by man and for the past 200 years steam has been applied to its propulsion. Over these two centuries the size and type of plant has changed but the basic use of a vapour produced by heating water has not. However, just as sail gave way to steam, the internal combustion engine has all but replaced steam as the means of propelling the world's ships. Technical development has brought about the demise of steam at sea just as it heralded steam propulsion in the late eighteenth century. Over those years steam has been no more than an intermediary in the production of power from the combustion of fuel. The logical, and more economic, process is to develop power direct from the combustion gases, as is done in the reciprocating diesel engine or the gas turbine; but the use of steam was, for many years, the only practicable option for a number of reasons, not least because of the fuel available. Coal and steam power are almost synonymous but fuel oil has played a significant part in the development of steam plant. Internal combustion engines operating on the principle devised by Rudolf Diesel soon showed that they were much more fuel-efficient than any steam plant and in 1924 the eminent naval architect Sir Westcott Abell expressed the view that the 'disappearance of the steam engine from overseas trade is largely a matter of time.'[1] In that view he was correct, but some seventy years later there are still steam-powered ships on, and below, the oceans of the world. Steam is now confined to a few vessels such as the liquefied-gas carrier, where boil-off gas from cargo tanks can be effectively burned in boilers, and the nuclear-powered naval ship. Its future at sea may be limited but its history is rich in achievement.

Steam set ships free from the vagaries of wind and wave but it imposed limits of its own. Although the steamship could battle against head winds or make progress in still air it could only do so if sufficient fuel was carried for the intended voyage. That fuel, and the machinery itself, occupied valuable space within the ship; freedom had its price, but as trade increased and the demands of naval warfare changed it was a price which had to be paid in order to stay ahead of the competition. Once steam had become an established means of ship propulsion, no matter how inefficient at first, its development and progress were inevitable; the power of steam was its own driving force. Neither the ship operator, whether of the commercial or the naval type, nor the engine builder could become complacent, competition ensured that. Ashore, new industries

evolved to support the steamship both in terms of equipment and operation, while steam fleets offered prospects of employment to skilled engineers and unskilled stokers and coal trimmers.

It is no accident that Britain took a lead in the adoption and development of steam propulsion; her seafaring tradition and growing manufacturing industry ensured that. Being in at the start of the Industrial Revolution gave Britain a lead in the manufacture of steam plant, but it was on the rivers and coastal waters of the United States of America that much early progress was made. Not all early ventures were successful and it says much for those early entrepreneurs and engineers that they persevered against seemingly overwhelming odds to justify their faith in the power of steam at sea.

This is not a book about steamships; it is the story of the machinery which powered those ships. However, it aims to tell the story of marine engineering development through the steamship and the job it did both in commercial and naval terms. It is a story of triumph and ingenuity as well as technical achievement, for marine steam engineering is not simply a tale of machines it is the story of those who designed, built and operated those magnificent dinosaurs of an age now fast drawing to a close. The development and decline of steam power at sea was a gradual thing, an evolution not a revolution. Although there were significant stages in that evolution the changes were not as rapid as might be imagined. The introduction of the turbine was certainly significant, but Charles Parsons and others had been working on turbine design long before *Turbinia* made her dash through the fleet at Spithead in 1897; it took many years before the turbine became an established means of steamship propulsion[2] and steam reciprocating engines were still being constructed during the 1950s. At times the pace of change was apparently slow, but the transition of an idea into a practical piece of equipment required manufacturing processes and materials to improve at the same pace and that was not always the case; steam power at sea was part of the continuing industrial revolution and at times progress had to wait for that revolution to catch up.

The book aims to cover the development of steam power at sea and will look at the successes and some of the failures. There will be omissions which some might have considered worthy of inclusion but it is impossible to deal with every type and design of marine engine and boiler in a book of reasonable length; to do so would be simply to produce a marine engine catalogue and this book aims to be more than that. The story of the marine steam engine and boiler is an important part of man's history for it tells not only of technological achievement but also of the spirit of adventure and ingenuity which have subsequently taken man to the moon and will eventually take him to the far reaches of space.

References

1 Sir Westcott Abell, I.Mar.E. Presidential Address, *Trans I.Mar.E.*, vol. 37, 1924–5, p. 780–81.

2 A review of Parsons's turbine development work is given in 'An Almost Unknown Great Man' by J. F. Clarke, Newcastle-upon-Tyne Polytechnic Occasional Paper in the History of Science, No. 4, 1984.

I
Steam Goes to Sea

There was no single inventor of the steam engine, but over the years many individuals played a part in its development; in fact it is not easy to define its origins. Most people consider the steam engine to be a device which has a cylinder containing a piston, but the application of steam to the production of motion or the pumping of liquids came long before that time. Hero of Alexandria produced a steam-driven reaction turbine over 2,000 years ago although it was merely a toy which produced no useful work. A number of inventors proposed the use of steam for pumping water, including Denis Papin who in 1690 produced a machine which contained a moving piston; Papin even suggested that several such engines could be arranged to drive paddles on a boat but he did not follow up the idea.[1] Thomas Savery is given credit for the first practical steam pump, outlined in his patent of 1698, but this had no piston and operated because condensing steam created a vacuum.

The real breakthrough came with Thomas Newcomen who, in 1712, erected a pumping engine at a colliery near Dudley Castle in Staffordshire. This beam engine was powered by a single, open-topped, steam cylinder while the pump situated in the mine was of the reciprocating type and so was independent of the effects of atmospheric pressure. The steam cylinder did, however, require atmospheric pressure in order to force the piston downwards as steam in the cylinder below the piston was condensed. That downwards movement of the piston acting through the beam pulled the pump piston upwards. Over the succeeding years many Newcomen engines were constructed and modifications made but the engine remained much as Newcomen had devised it.[2]

The influence of James Watt on the steam engine has often been misunderstood. He did not invent the steam engine but he did improve it thereby making it a more useful tool for the Industrial Revolution. Watt fitted a separate condenser to the Newcomen engine and so improved its efficiency, but he also made the engine double-acting and devised a form of hemp packing for the piston which acted as a seal. During the 1870s Watt went into partnership with Matthew Boulton and established a steam engine manufacturing company which set the standard by which others would be judged. In 1876 blast-furnace blowing engines were constructed for John Wilkinson, the Shropshire iron founder, but Watt was also aware that rotative power was the key to industrial steam application and as early as 1774 a rotary engine, known as a 'Steam Wheel' was built at the Soho works of Boulton & Watt. This machine was not a

success, but at Boulton's suggestion Watt modified the reciprocating engine to produce rotary power. James Picard took out a patent for a crank in 1780 and applied this idea to an atmospheric reciprocating engine at a mill at Snow Hill, Birmingham and rather than make use of this device Watt designed a sun-and-planet mechanism to convert reciprocating to rotary motion.

Other Watt ideas applied to the rotary engine included double-action, a parallel-motion mechanism for the piston rod and a conical governor for regulating speed. The double-acting engine required four valves, two for steam and two for exhaust, but in 1799 William Murdock, an employee of Boulton and Watt who subsequently became a partner, patented a slide valve worked by a crankshaft-driven eccentric. At the beginning of the nineteenth century there was available an effective rotary beam engine which could be applied to many areas of industry and the marine field was but one area.[3]

The pre-eminent position of Boulton and Watt was in no small part due to the efforts of John Wilkinson for whom the firm had built steam engines. Efficient operation of the steam engine depended upon an accurately bored cylinder and in 1774 Wilkinson, without doubt the greatest iron master of the time, had obtained a patent for the casting and boring of guns and cannons. The patent was challenged by the Board of Ordnance and revoked in 1779, but Wilkinson's boring machine was also set to work boring steam engine cylinders for James Watt. Later developments of the boring machine enabled larger cylinders to be accommodated with greater accuracy but Wilkinson failed to patent these subsequent ideas and he gained little financial reward from them. However, British industry did, and many competitors constructed boring machines based upon the Wilkinson pattern.[4] Britain thereby gained a lead in the production of accurate steam cylinders which enabled enterprising people to apply the steam engine to many situations.

Throughout the eighteenth century there were many proposals for the application of steam power to drive ships and claims have been made on behalf of individuals concerning the title 'father of the steamship'. As with the steam engine itself, it is difficult from this distance to decide who had the idea first and who produced the first application; in reality it does not really matter as many had a hand in subsequent developments and it was these developments which resulted in the commercial application of steam at sea. In the words of John Scott Russell, renowned naval architect and builder of Brunel's *Great Eastern*, 'the creation of the steamship appears to have been an achievement too gigantic for any single man'.[5]

A successful steamship must have three basic systems which operate satisfactorily together and failure in any one means failure of the venture. The hull of the ship must be adapted to operation on the water for a particular purpose. But there must also be an effective means of propulsion which has to be powered by a steam engine; even then there is a problem in that the steam engine must be supplied with steam and that has to be generated on board the vessel. Over the years a number of systems for propelling ships had been devised using an assortment of means including oars, paddles and even screw propellers. Manual labour was generally the means of driving these devices but some did advocate the use of fire to drive an engine. Space precludes discussion of such schemes. This book aims at charting the progress of marine steam engineering and not the development of the steamship itself; for that reason many of the early experimental ventures are not covered as they were effectively blind alleys.[6] Significant early steamship and marine engineering developments took place in America and Britain and the operational needs on opposite sides of the Atlantic resulted in a divergence in machinery design.

In its extensive array of East Coast rivers the USA had the basis of a transportation system to the interior but the rivers flowed from west to east and so it was necessary to drive any vessel against the flow; steam was the obvious choice but in the newly independent United States there was a shortage of steam engineers and manufacturing facilities. Among the early advocates of steam in America was John Fitch, a Connecticut farm boy who had served as a soldier in the Revolutionary War and subsequently found employment as a surveyor, engraver and silversmith. He had no engineering understanding nor any practical experience but he had a dream of propelling a boat by means of steam power. To provide technical understanding he enlisted the help of Henry Voight, a Philadelphia clock and watch maker and the pair set about their task. A small steam engine was built but failed to operate and a second with a 3in diameter cylinder was then constructed; simultaneously propulsion systems using paddles and oars were developed. In 1786 the steam engine operated successfully and the oar propulsion system, using manpower, also proved itself capable of driving a small skiff. Fitch never claimed that the steam engine drove the oars.[7]

Fitch and Voight continued with development work and in 1787 actually built an engine having a 12in bore and 36in stroke; the interesting thing about the engine was that it had wooden cylinder covers and trials showed this material to be totally unsuitable. By August that year a 45ft long craft had been fitted out for trial on the Delaware River but performance proved to be poor. In an attempt to improve matters the craft was redesigned to reduce resistance and the twelve vertical oars were replaced by three rectangular paddles at the stern. Even with modifications to the engine and boiler the new craft proved too slow when tested in October 1788. Eventually, in 1790, following many modifications to the machinery, vessel and propulsion system, a successful trial was achieved and the vessel went into commercial service on the Delaware.[8] The single cylinder beam engine for this vessel had an 18in bore and although a speed of 7 knots was achieved the service proved a commercial failure. A 25-ton craft was built by Fitch for service on the Mississippi but this was wrecked before completion. In 1796 attention turned to screw propulsion with a small 18ft long boat on Collect Pond, New York. A two-cylinder beam engine drove the propeller shaft by means of connecting rods and cranks but the interesting thing about the engine was that the cylinders were made from wood with iron hoops for reinforcement.[9] Fitch made little impact on the development of marine engineering but his enthusiasm for the steamboat attracted the interest of many.

James Rumsey, another enthusiastic American with no engineering experience, was a contemporary of Fitch who shared the same vision for steam power on water. Whereas Fitch possessed a personality which tended to repel potential patrons, Rumsey was of milder manner and articulate. Rumsey's first idea was for a vessel which could be worked upstream by means of poles pushed against the river bed and a small model did function but not with the aid of steam power. Appreciating his own lack of engineering expertise Rumsey employed a mechanic, Joseph Barnes, to seek out sources of good castings and engineered parts. His first steam driven vessel was ready for trials in April 1786 but boiler failure delayed these until December 1787 when a third boiler proved capable of generating steam. Details of this vessel do not exist but the propulsion system was probably similar to that for a craft proposed in 1788. Rumsey was an advocate of water-jet propulsion and his second vessel called for a single-cylinder pump driven by a single-cylinder steam engine positioned directly above, with the steam and pump pistons being attached to the same rod. Water was drawn into the pump through an opening in the bottom of the hull about one-third of the length from the bow and pumped through a rectangular trunking before being discharged at the stern to produce a drive. The second water-jet-powered boat was never built.[10]

Rumsey probably realised that his lack of success was due to the low efficiency of the engine and pump he was using and he possibly felt that better machinery was available in England. With financial aid from the Rumsean Society, formed in Philadelphia in 1788, he took ship to London where he obtained a British patent for his propulsion plant.[11] He also had sufficient backing to order a 101-ton experimental vessel, subsequently known as

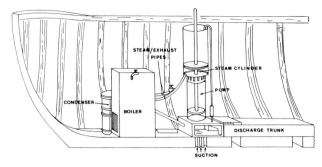

1.1 Arrangement of water jet propulsion system devised by Rumsey (1788)

Columbian Maid, from a shipyard in Dover. During trials in December 1792 the ship worked well but the water-jet plant proved to be a failure.[12] Rumsey's efforts also headed up a blind alley in terms of marine engineering as it existed during its formative years. However, modern high-speed catamaran ferries employ a system of water-jet propulsion with the use of diesel engines.

In Scotland progress was also being made in the application of steam to marine propulsion. Three men, Patrick Miller, James Taylor and William Symington, applied their collective talents and produced a small steamer which operated on Dalswinton Lake in 1788. Miller was an Edinburgh banker who had previously experimented with manual paddle propulsion, while Symington was an experienced mechanic who had patented a steam engine design in 1787. The pair were brought together by Taylor, the tutor of Miller's sons, who had suggested that steam might usefully be employed to drive the paddles of the boat Miller proposed. Symington's engine, made of brass by George Watt of Low Carlton, Edinburgh, had two open topped Newcomen type cylinders, 4in diameter and 9in stroke, the pistons of which brought about the rotation of the two paddle shafts via a system of chains and ratchets. These paddles were positioned between the twin hulls of the 25ft long boat.[13]

Successful operation of the first boat, which achieved a speed of 5 miles per hour[14] prompted the trio to construct a second boat at Carron in 1789. This 60ft long vessel had an engine of similar design to that used for the first boat but the bore was increased to 18in. Although a speed of 7 miles per hour was achieved after paddle modifications the vessel was not suitable for commercial traffic and experimentation ceased.[15] Symington continued his interest in the steam engine and its application to marine propulsion but it was not until 1801 that he succeeded in finding a backer. Lord Dundas agreed to sponsor construction of a steam tug to be used for towing barges on the Forth and Clyde Canal and the 56ft long *Charlotte Dundas* was constructed of wood by Alexander Hart of Grangemouth Dockyard for that purpose. Propulsion was by means of a single paddle wheel

fitted in a recess at the stern, the wheel being driven by an engine constructed to a design patented by Symington in 1801.[16] A double-acting cylinder of 22in bore and 48in stroke was placed horizontally on the port side of the paddle wheel which it drove via a connecting rod and a crank arm; a crosshead worked in guide slides thus keeping the piston rod horizontal. A condenser was fitted below deck level, the air pump being driven by a bell-crank lever from the crosshead. Towing two barges loaded to 70 tons, *Charlotte Dundas* covered 19.5 miles in six hours; while working alone she could maintain a speed of six miles per hour. Although the boat proved to be economical and successful there were canal company directors who had financial interests in horses normally used for towing on the canal and they convinced their fellows that steam barges would cause damage to the canal banks. The first practicable British steamer was taken out of service.[17]

On the other side of the Atlantic the cause of steam at sea was also progressing despite the failures of Fitch and Rumsey. The diplomat Robert R. Livingston had faith in steam propulsion but, like others before him, he had no engineering knowledge. However, in 1797 he joined with his brother-in-law John Stevens and the foundry owner Nicholas J. Roosevelt to build a steamship. Following a disagreement Roosevelt left the partnership and the two wealthy businessmen were without an engineer until Robert Fulton agreed to join them. The partnership agreement signed with Livingston in 1802 indicated that an operating steamboat would be ready in five years but it also allowed for construction of an experimental boat in England. Fulton had contacts in France, having previously constructed an unsuccessful submarine with the aid of money from the French Navy, and work on the experimental boat was undertaken in France rather than England. After initial problems, including a sinking, the experimental boat demonstrated its ability on the River Seine in August 1803. The 74ft 6 in long hull was propelled by paddle wheels positioned near mid-length, the paddle shaft being driven by a vertical cylinder acting through a crosshead, bell-crank lever and connecting rod. This engine was designed by Fulton although the parts were constructed in France.[18]

It is possible that the partners may have believed that financial help could have come from French sources but that was not the case and in 1804 Fulton moved to England. While in Paris during 1803 he enquired of Boulton & Watt concerning a 24-horsepower engine and supplied a drawing showing the arrangement he required for the condenser and air pump. He also asked many questions including methods of boiler construction, the use of coal and wood in furnaces, problems with salt water in condensers, delivery dates and costs. The correspondence must have continued as in July 1804 Fulton instructed Boulton & Watt to proceed with an engine, 24in bore by 4ft stroke, based upon their standard

20 nominal horsepower (nhp) unit. Fulton provided drawings for the modifications he wanted; these included the repositioning of the condenser and the use of brass for the air pump; modifications were needed as space was limited. Thus Fulton must already have had the dimensions of his steamboat in mind. In his earlier letter from Paris Fulton requested that only the steam cylinder, piston, piston rod, air pump condenser and connecting pipes be made in England the remainder constructed in New York, 'as it will save on the expense of transport, and they require particular arrangement which must be done while I am present'.[19] For the basic engine Boulton & Watt quoted a price of £386 but in its modified form the same firm wanted, and received, £548. That increased cost far outweighed the higher price for materials and additional labour but it does show what could be charged by an established concern with a near monopoly. In order to minimise the risk of corrosion and allow for ease of repair Fulton stipulated copper for the boiler and this was constructed by the London firm of Cave & Son to a sketch he supplied.[20]

Fulton had visited England during the 1790s and his ideas for a steamship were already established since in 1794, from the Bridgewater Arms in Manchester, he approached Boulton & Watt concerning the price and dimensions for a 3- or 4-horsepower engine. He did inform the engine builders that the intention was to place the engine in a boat; however, nothing came of the enquiry.[21]

Various matters delayed Fulton's return to America and it was not until early 1807 that work on the hull for the steamer commenced. The 133ft long vessel was ready for trials during August of that year and these proved an unqualified success, enabling the backers to establish a steamer service between New York and Albany. Steam was supplied to the single cylinder at a pressure a little above atmospheric and the condenser was of the jet type with river water being injected into the condenser shell to condense the exhaust steam and produce a vacuum. A lever-driven air pump extracted air and water from the condenser, thus maintaining the vacuum, and discharged the hot water on to a hot-well which surrounded the condenser. A separate lever-driven pump was used to force some of this hot water into the boiler. The levers, connecting rod, gear wheels, flywheels and paddles were all manufactured in the USA. The steamer was officially known as *North River Steam Boat* but more recently she has been referred to, incorrectly, as *Clermont*.[22]

Construction of this vessel is important not only because she established the first commercial steamship service in American waters but because her success spawned other ventures which made use of local engineering firms for machinery construction. Fulton and others moved away from the basic Boulton & Watt engine design by using ideas of their own and thus establishing an American marine engineering industry which satisfied local needs. Any industry can only survive if it receives regular orders and orders for marine steam plant were only forthcoming after Fulton and his partners, with the help of Boulton & Watt, showed that a river steamship service was a commercial proposition. The year 1800 was an important one for steam engine development as it saw the expiry of the patent extension granted to Watt with respect to his engine incorporating a separate condenser. Up to that time it was impossible for anybody to

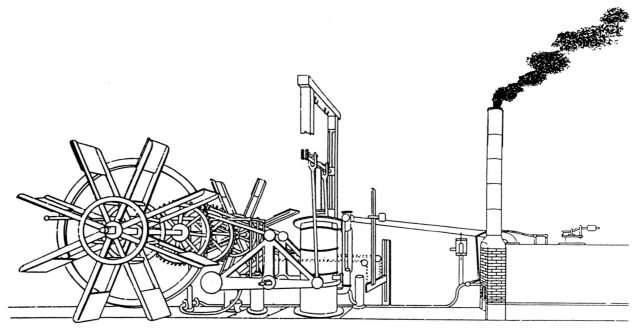

1.2 Machinery arrangement for the North River Steam Boat

produce an economic steam engine without infringing Watt's patent, while the firm of Boulton & Watt refused to grant licences for others to make use of the idea. The original patent was granted in 1769 and would have expired in 1783 had not the British Parliament granted the extension in 1775. That action created a monopolistic situation which had the effect of stifling steam engine progress for many years. Progress from 1800 was rapid and particularly in the application of steam power to the propulsion of ships. In Britain that advance in marine engineering was probably more rapid than anywhere else.

As in America, application of steam to British shipping was centred upon major rivers and the Clyde was the first to see extensive steam operations. Henry Bell of Helensburgh had noted the efforts of Symington and believed that he could make a steam venture pay. In 1812 he contracted John Wood of Port Glasgow for construction of a 42ft long wooden vessel and also John Robertson of Glasgow for a small steam engine capable of developing 4 nominal horsepower. This 11in bore cylinder had a stroke of 16in and was originally arranged to drive two pairs of paddle wheels via spur gearing. When this arrangement proved unsatisfactory a single pair of paddles was substituted and the vessel achieved a speed of 6.7 knots.[23] The machinery of Bell's steamer, known as *Comet*, was of novel form and peculiar to the builder as were most marine engines of the period. The success of *Comet* between Greenock and Glasgow encouraged others and by 1814 there were five steamers operating on the Clyde while a total of ten had been built by yards on the river.

This period saw the evolution of an engine type which was to become standard for most paddle steamers for many years, namely the side-lever engine. This was based upon the Watt beam engine but positioning the beam above the cylinder resulted in a tall engine which was unsuitable for all but the smallest of vessels. It is not known who originally had the idea of placing two levers low down on either side of the cylinder instead of a single beam above but what is certain is that once the idea evolved it was rapidly taken up by many engine builders. At least three steamers built on the Clyde in 1814 had side-lever engines, the machinery for one of these, *Industry*, was built by George Dobbie of Glasgow, while James Cook of Tradeston near Glasgow provided engines for *Margery* and *Thames*. The Dobbie engine, 16in bore and 32in stroke, drove the paddle shaft through spur-gear wheels. Both Cook-built engines had a cylinder of 22in diameter but the strokes differed; that fitted in *Margery* had a 2ft stroke, the side levers connecting direct with the paddle shaft while the engine for *Thames* had a 3ft stroke and a flywheel was fitted to the paddle shaft.[24]

Side-lever engines differed slightly from builder to builder but the same basic form remained and the design became a favourite with Clydeside shipyards. By 1818

steamers were considered safe enough to venture away from rivers and David Napier of Glasgow built a 30 nominal horsepower engine side-lever engine (30in diameter cylinder by 3ft stroke) for *Rob Roy* which operated between Greenock and Belfast. The Thames also saw the development of steam services and a number of marine engine builders became established along its banks. Maudslay, Sons & Field had an established reputation as mechanical engineers and the firm produced some very good steam engines including Maudslay's 'table engine' of 1807 which was used extensively for driving workshop machinery. In 1818 the 315-ton paddle steamer *London Engineer* was built by Daniel Brent of Rotherhithe and Maudslays supplied two bell-crank engines to drive a pair of paddle wheels contained in a casing within the hull. The paddle floats projected below the hull and were protected by three keels running the length of the ship. Two engine-driven air compressors supplied air to the paddle casing thus lowering the water level in the casing so that the floats were only immersed during the lower portion of their rotation. Engine cylinders were of 36in diameter and 3ft stroke, being capable of developing 88 horse power when turning at 28 revs. per minute with steam supplied at a pressure of 5psi (pounds per square inch) above atmospheric pressure.[25]

American marine engineering progress was no less rapid than that in Britain, with Fulton's partners taking the lead. John Stevens experimented with screw propulsion when in 1804 he equipped the launch *Little Juliana* with a small steam engine operating at a pressure between 20 and 40psi. In 1808 Stevens built the 95-ton paddle-driven *Phoenix* which was initially fitted with two 16in by 3ft steam cylinders; she was subsequently fitted with a single cylinder engine of 24in bore and the same stroke and operated on the Delaware River until wrecked in 1814.[26] Fulton continued working with the Livingston family and in 1809 produced the *Rariton* for them. She had machinery similar to that installed in the *North River Steam Boat* but it was manufactured in America, the ship itself being built by Charles Browne of New York. Increasing profits on the Albany route prompted construction of another ship in 1809, the 295-ton *Car of Neptune* being ordered from Charles Browne, but Fulton designed her machinery using his own ideas. In order to construct the power plant, and undertake winter overhauls, he established an engine shop in Jersey City with a former Boulton & Watt employee, Charles Stroudinger, as foreman. No records of the engine design exist but it is probable that it was of a bell-crank form outlined in Fulton's 1809 patent.[27]

American East Coast river services expanded during the second decade of the nineteenth century but the Livingston family's monopoly on the Hudson tended to restrict developments there. However, other waters offered potential. The British blockade imposed during the Anglo-American war

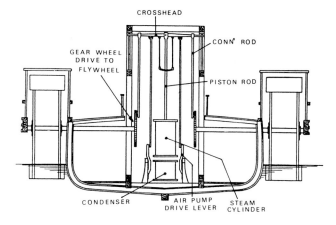

1.3 Geared single-cylinder engine system fitted in Chancellor Livingston

(1812–15) prevented steamers from making coastal journeys to other rivers, but when the war ended Hudson-built steamers moved as far south as Washington while new vessels were ordered, amongst them the 496 gross ton *Chancellor Livingston*. This proved to be Fulton's last ship for he died in February 1815 by which time he had developed his own crosshead-type engine for paddle propulsion. Return connecting rods from the crosshead above the single cylinder drove the paddle shaft, while a lever system operated the air pump and valves with a set of gear wheels driving a flywheel to ensure that the piston operated past the ends of its strokes. Fulton's engine works supplied

machinery for a number of other steamers built around New York and it is likely that the crosshead engine was used for these.[28]

A significant event in terms of steam navigation, if not marine engineering, took place in 1819 when the auxiliary steam ship *Savannah* crossed the Atlantic from the port whose name she bore to Liverpool. She was effectively a sailing ship with a small steam engine driving a pair of collapsible paddle wheels and during the 27.5-day crossing her steam plant operated for a total of 85 hours only. Her single cylinder engine, 40in bore by 5ft stroke, could develop about 90 horsepower. As was the general case at the time steam was applied for the full piston stroke, no expansion being used; thus the engine was inefficient and so the ship could not have carried sufficient fuel for a crossing under continuous steam power. The engine was inclined at about 20° and the piston rod acted direct on the paddle shaft crank via a connecting rod. The air pump, extracting air and water from the jet condenser, was driven from the engine crosshead.[29] In marine engineering terms the power plant fitted in *Savannah* was basic but her voyage showed what steam could do, even for auxiliary propulsion purposes, and others were bound to follow.

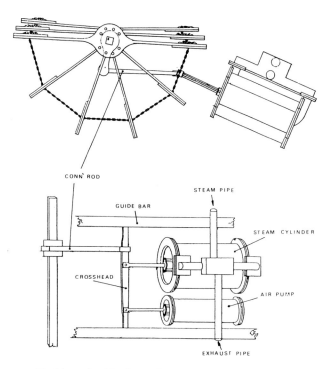

1.4 Machinery fitted in the auxiliary steamship Savannah

References

1 R. J. Law, *The Steam Engine*, HMSO, London 1965, p. 5.

2 A complete history of the development of the Newcomen engine may be found in: L. T. C. Rolt, *Thomas Newcomen, the Prehistory of the Steam Engine*, David & Charles, Dawlish, 1963.

3 The influence of James Watt and the engines he developed are covered in great detail in H. W. Dickenson and R. Jenkins, *James Watt and the Steam Engine*, Encore Editions, London, 1981.

4 L. T. C. Rolt, *Tools for the Job*, HMSO, London, 1986, pp. 60–62.

5 Henry Dyer, 'The First Century of the Marine Engine', *Trans I.N.A.*, vol. 30, 1889, p. 87.

6 Detailed information regarding early steamships may be found in H. P. Spratt, *The Birth of the Steamboat*, Charles Griffin, London 1958.

7 C. Ridgely-Nevitt, *American Steamships in the Atlantic*, University of Delaware Press, Newark, 1981, p. 14.

8 Ibid., pp. 14–16

9 H. P. Spratt, *The Birth of the Steamboat*, pp. 40–42.

10 C. Ridgely-Nevitt, *American Steamships*, pp. 16–18.

11 British Patent No. 1738 (1790), 'Applying water and steam power to machinery, to the propulsion of vessels'.

12 H. P. Spratt, *The Birth of the Steamboat*, pp. 45–8.

13 H. Sandham, 'On the History of Paddle-Wheel Steam Navigation', *Proc. I.Mech.E.*, 1885, p. 125.

14 H. P. Spratt, *The Birth of the Steamboat*, p. 49.

15 H. Dyer, 'First Century of the Marine Engine', p. 88.

16 British Patent No 2544 (1801), 'Constructing steam-engine'.

17 H. Dyer, 'First century of the Marine Engine', p. 88; also *Marine Engineer & Motorship Builder*, vol. 53, Sep. 1930. pp. 356–7.

18 C. Ridgely-Nevitt, *American Steamships*, pp. 18–9; H. P. Spratt, *The Birth of the Steamboat*, pp. 64–9.

19 Letters and drawings are published in the discussion of the paper by C. H. Haswell, 'Reminiscences of Early Marine Steam Engine Construction in the USA from 1807 to 1850', *Trans. I.N.A.*, vol. 40, 1898, pp. 111–13.

20 C. Ridgely-Nevitt, *American Steamships,*. p. 20.

21 Letter reproduced in *Trans. I.N.A.*, vol. 40, 1898, p. 111.

22 C. Ridgely-Nevitt, *American Steamships*, pp. 21–24.

23 *Marine Engineer*, 1 Apr. 1890, p. 19.

24 H. P. Spratt, *The Birth of the Steamboat*, pp. 91–97.

25 T. Tredgold, *The Steam Engine*, London, 1838, vol. 1, p. 316; *Engineer*, vol. 87, 15 Oct. 1897, p. 368.

26 C. Ridgely-Nevitt, *American Steamships*, pp. 26–28.

27 Ibid., p. 33.

28 Ibid., pp. 37–47.

29 The full story of the ship is related in, F. O. Braynard, *S.S. Savannah, the Elegant Steam Ship*, University of Georgia Press, Athens, Georgia, USA, 1963.

2
Merchant Ships and Paddle Wheels

The 1820s saw rapid growth in the application of steam to ship propulsion although vessels so powered were generally confined to rivers and coastal waters. As confidence grew in the reliability of the steam engine and, perhaps more importantly, the safety of the boiler it was natural that ship owners would turn to steam power but there also had to be sound commercial reasons for doing so. The advantages of steam power for moving a vessel against the flow of a river were obvious to the early protagonists, but for coastal and deep sea operations there were also sound reasons for using steam. A steam-powered ship could operate in adverse wind conditions and against the tide thus allowing the operator to publish a timetable. Ships which could offer arrival and sailing times could attract better rates and if a shorter passage could be guaranteed they were likely to find favour with passengers susceptible to seasickness. Steam freed the shipowner from wind or tide and the enterprising owners took advantage of it.

Although experiments had been carried out with crude forms of screw propulsion during the latter years of the eighteenth century the paddle wheel was the only effective and reliable means of driving a ship during the first three decades of the nineteenth century. Industrial development in Britain, together with the increasing demand for steam-powered ships, resulted in an expansion of the steam engine manufacturing industry, with a tendency for workshops to be established in port areas. The expiry of Watt's condenser

and other patents freed manufacturers to use these innovations and a variety of engine designs were developed for land and marine applications. For paddle propulsion the side-lever engine became a favourite with manufacturers and steamship owners because of its simplicity and ease of operation. The design was based upon the Watt beam engine and most builders followed the same basic pattern with minor modifications or to introduce improvements such as the expansive working of steam.

Early steam engines had steam admitted to the cylinder for the entire stroke but this represented a waste of energy even with low pressures as that steam was then released to the condenser at almost boiler pressure. By the early part of the nineteenth century a number of engineers realised that steam supply to the cylinder could be cut off part way through the piston stroke and the steam in the cylinder then allowed to expand for the remainder of the piston stroke; this resulted in some loss of power but a considerable saving in steam, and hence coal consumption. Such ideas were applicable to all steam engines whether stationary, railway or marine and initially steam cut-off would have been arranged at the same part of the piston stroke no matter what the engine load. However, by the mid-1830s the advantages of the variable expansive working of steam were obvious enough for the more enlightened engineers to fit expansion gear to their engines. Brunel insisted that the side-lever machinery built by Maudslay, Sons & Field for *Great*

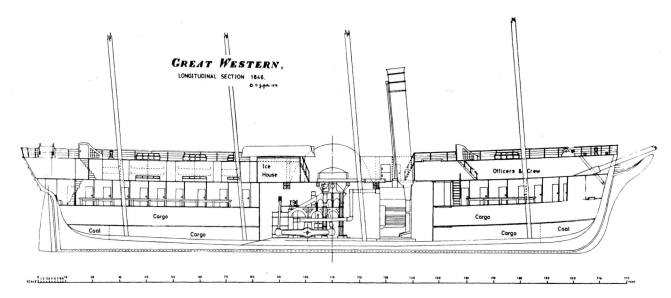

2.1 Section through the paddle steamship Great Western *(1837)*

Western in 1837 be fitted with such equipment which allowed for nine grades of expansive working. This essentially consisted of a steam expansion valve fitted in the steam supply line to the engine, the valve being controlled by a linkage from the paddle shaft. A follower on the end of that linkage could be moved to any one of the nine cams on the paddle shaft, each of these cams allowing the expansion valve to be open for a different period of time. The slide valve which directed steam to and exhaust from the top and the bottom of the cylinder had its own actuating mechanism and a system for controlling the direction of rotation.[1] In later years both systems were combined in the valve gear such as the Stephenson link motion.

The basic side-lever engine had a single, vertical cylinder containing a double-acting piston, the top end of the piston rod being attached to a crosshead; two side rods, passing on either side of the cylinder, connected the crosshead with the side levers positioned on each side of the engine. These side levers were pivoted at about mid-length and were connected at their other end by a crosstail, to the centre of which was attached a connecting rod. The connecting rod attached to the crank-pin on the paddle shaft which was supported on columns or an elaborate structure of cast Gothic arches depending upon the artistic ideas of the designer. As the piston reciprocated through the action of steam, the side rods would cause the side levers to rock and these in turn would bring about the rotation of the paddle shaft through the connecting rod. Steam supply to and exhaust from the cylinder were regulated by means of a slide valve actuated from the paddle shaft through an eccentric-driven system of linkages.

In order to reduce wear on the piston, cylinder, piston rod and cylinder-cover gland, it was necessary to ensure that the piston moved parallel to the cylinder and, as the side lever engine cylinder was vertical, the piston had to have a vertical motion. James Watt appreciated this problem with his beam engines and devised a parallel-motion mechanism which consisted of a number of linkages connecting with the side rods, side levers and fixed parts of the engine frame. Similar parallel-motion mechanisms were fitted to all side-lever engines, the actual arrangement of linkages differing depending upon the designer.[2] Most side-lever engines had a jet condenser fitted between the cylinder and the connecting rod, with the engine base plate acting as part of the condenser and water-collecting chamber. The water-spray injection was fitted about half way up the condenser with provision being made for water injection from the engine room bilge as well as from the sea. That engine room connection provided a convenient means of pumping out the engine room in an emergency. An air pump, driven by rods attached to the side levers, extracted air and water from the condenser and discharged it to the hot-well; warm feed water for the boiler was generally taken from the hot-well

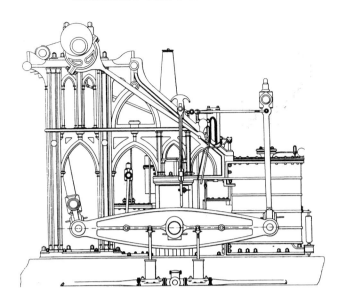

2.2 Side-lever engine fitted in the Cunard 'Britannia'-class vessels

with the surplus being pumped overboard. Boiler feed pumps, engine room bilge pumps and pumps for other duties were generally actuated by the side levers, but other engine builders had different ideas as to the actual arrangement.

The side-lever engine did not change much in essential arrangement from the early types until the last one constructed for deep sea operations, but there was a considerable increase in size and power output. Robert Napier built a side-lever engine for the coastal steamer *Leven* in 1823 and this had a cylinder of 31.5in bore and 3ft stroke;[3] forty years later his cousin, David Napier, constructed two engines for Cunard's *Scotia*, these having cylinders of 100in bore and 12ft stroke, the total power output being 4,570 indicated horse power (ihp) from steam at a pressure of 25psi.[4]

In many respects the side-lever engine was ideal for merchant paddle steamer propulsion as it had a low centre of gravity and could permit a long piston stroke while also allowing a long connecting rod to be used. It was, however, heavy and required a long engine room. The long connecting rod allowed for an effective turning action at the crank without excessive fore' and aft' reaction thrusts at the engine or paddle shaft. Positioning of the paddle shaft had a considerable influence on the length of the connecting rod, but the location of that shaft was dictated by the size of the ship and the paddle wheels. Factors such as engine power, operating speed, size of paddle floats, number of floats and diameter of paddle wheel were interrelated and care was required in deciding upon the size and arrangement of the paddle wheels to suit the engine power and service speed. Too many floats could cause propulsion problems as a paddle would enter water disturbed by the preceding float while alteration in width or depth of float

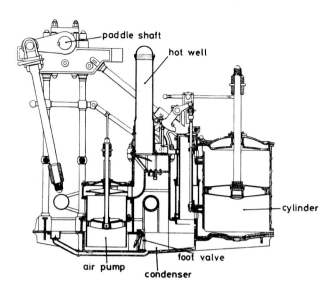

might change rotational speed and hence speed through the water; in many cases the optimum condition was arrived at by trial and error. The paddle shaft axis had to be positioned such that the floats were correctly immersed but the length of the paddle arm could not simply be changed to suit as that would alter the power transmission effect from the engine. Immersion of the paddle float changed during a passage, particularly a long passage, and it was important that the floats remained immersed to provide the required drive. In many respects paddle propulsion was a problem and an effective drive a compromise. Raising or lowering the paddle shaft axis was not an acceptable proposition for obtaining a long connecting rod and the ideal arrangement was to position the drive end of the connecting rod as low in the ship as possible – which is what could be achieved with the side-lever engine. Sometimes engine builders would accept the problems caused by a short connecting rod in order to save weight or space or to simplify the engine arrangement.

Side-lever engines found their way into most steamers built during the 1820s and 1830s with engine builders on

2.3 Section through the side-lever engine fitted in the steamship America

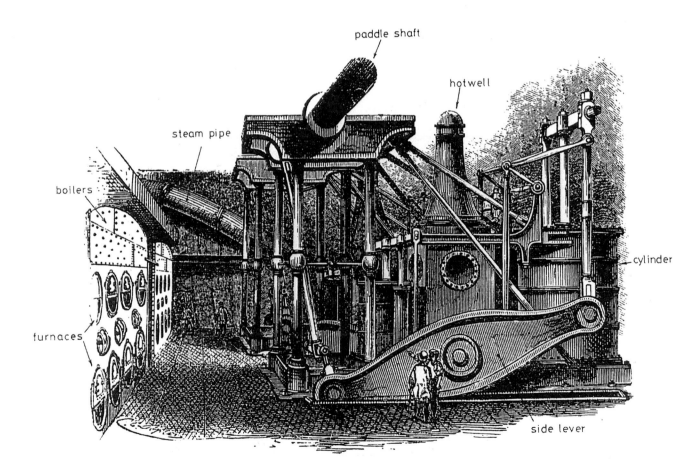

2.4 Engine room of the Collins liner Atlantic, *showing side-lever engine and boilers*

the Clyde, the Mersey and the Thames taking up the design and installing such engines in commercial and Admiralty-sponsored steamers. Maudslay, Sons & Field built side-lever engines for many early steamers and earned a deserved reputation for craftsmanship, so much so that Brunel advised the directors of the Great Western Steamship Company to fit Maudslay engines in their first ship *Great Western*. 'I think you will be safest, in the peculiar case of the first ship, in the hands of the parties who have most experience, and that Messrs. Maudslay are those persons.'[5] That company had constructed some of the earliest side-lever engines for the Admiralty and the efficiency and reliability of those in operation must have advanced the cause of steam propulsion in naval circles. In 1823 two engines were constructed for HMS *Lightning* and these were still operational when the ship ended her useful life in 1872 although the boilers had been replaced three times.[6] The same company also provided engines for *Enterprize* (1825) which made the first steam-powered voyage to India, and for many other commercial steamers, including some early members of the Royal Mail fleet in the 1840s. But it was work for the Admiralty which established and maintained Maudslays' marine engineering reputation.

Other builders constructing side-lever engines included Messrs. Caird & Co. (who also built engines for the early Royal Mail steamers), Fawcett & Preston of Liverpool (builders of engines for early P&O steamers), George Forrester of Liverpool, Scott & Sinclair of Greenock, Miller & Ravenhill of Blackwall, and Seawards of Poplar. Although there were minor differences in design the engines produced by all these followed the basic side-lever pattern, although the engines fitted in the Atlantic steamer *British Queen* (1839) and the coastal vessel *Sirius* (1837) differed in that they had surface condensers rather than jet condensers.

The idea of a surface condenser was not new when Samuel Hall took out his patent No. 6556 in 1834, but he did not claim originality for the concept, rather the combination of at least three of five different pieces of equipment, namely tubular surface condenser, circulating pump, air

pump, evaporator and a steam saver.[7] Despite the other devices covered by the patent it was essentially the surface condenser which attracted interest and it was that which Hall publicised whenever he could. In 1837 he approached Lord William Bentinck, chairman of the Parliamentary Select Committee on Steam Communication with India, laying before him papers concerning the operation of his condenser or, as he preferred to call it, his 'improvement in the steam engine'. Later he made a similar approach to Sir John Hobhouse, President of the Board of Control (the body which oversaw the East India Company), giving him four advantages of his engine improvement. These were: a great saving in wear and tear of the boiler, a great saving in wear and tear of engine internal parts, an important saving in fuel, and a considerable increase in power, particularly during stormy weather and heavy seas.[8] How all the claims were justified is difficult to explain but there was certainly considerable merit in using hot, fresh water in boilers as it reduced scale and so improved fuel consumption. At the time, however, the problems of corrosion arising from the use of fresh water containing oxygen were not understood and salt scale in boilers did actually reduce corrosion. Hall arranged his condenser so that steam from the cylinder passed through small diameter tubes while sea water circulating around these tubes condensed that steam. The basic

2.6 *Steamer* Sirius *(1837) fitted with an early surface-condensing, side-lever engine*

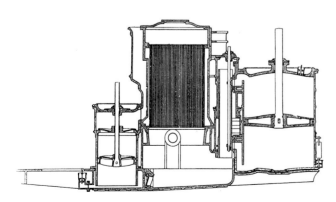

2.5 Hall's surface condenser located in a side lever engine

design was suitable for any engine, not just those of the side-lever type.

In 1834 the St. George Steam Packet Co. fitted Hall's equipment in its steamer *Prince Llewellyn* with three other small steamers being similarly equipped during the next year. In 1837 the St. George Steam Packet Co. had Hall's condensing equipment fitted to its steamers *Sirius* and *Hercules*. After its representatives inspected *Hercules*, the Admiralty, in 1837, adopted Hall's condensers for the paddle sloop HMS *Magaera* and later for HMS *Penelope*. Other owners, including the East India Company, also fitted the equipment to some of their steamers while the British and American Steam Navigation Company decided upon Hall's condensers for *British Queen* having operated *Sirius* for two Atlantic voyages in 1838.[9]

Performance of the surface condensers was variable and seemed to depend, among other things, upon the quality of the engineers and the operating area of the ship. In the mid-1840s HMS *Grappler*, fitted with surface condensing engines by Maudslays, returned to Woolwich after three years abroad; the machinery had performed above expecta-

tion and inspection of her boilers showed them to be in excellent condition. A vessel trading between Hull and London had her surface condensers removed when the outside of the tubes became coated with mud. In other cases grease from cylinder lubrication formed deposits in the tubes causing blockage.[10] At the time surface condensers were not effective owing to material and basic design problems. Improvements in materials and a design change so that cooling sea water passed through the tubes and steam flowed around them allowed the surface condenser to prove its merits in later years.

The procedure for starting a side-lever engine, or any other early marine engine with a jet condenser, was straightforward but required several engineers in order that the controls and valves might be actuated in the correct sequence. The entire engine system, cylinders, air pump and condenser, would be flooded with steam by opening the main supply valve and moving the cylinder valve manually so that steam would be present above and below the piston; this could be achieved at the valve drive cams on the paddle shaft or at some intermediate position on the linkage if that

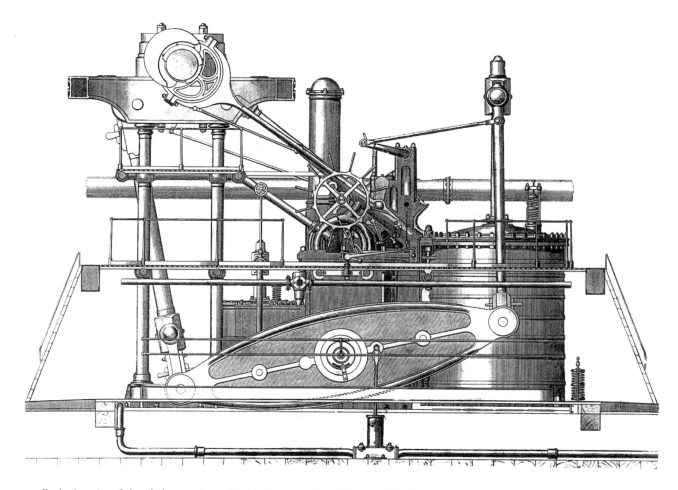

2.7 Evolved version of the side-lever engine as fitted in the Cunard liners Persia *and* Arabia *during 1850–60*

had been arranged. The cylinder slide valve would be positioned for the correct direction of engine rotation by engaging the gab at the end of the valve linkage on the ahead or astern cam. For later engines, some builder used a single cam with a slotted link in which was positioned a block attached to the valve drive; movement of this block set the cylinder valve for ahead or astern running. With the cylinder slide valve positioned for the desired direction of rotation, injection water to the jet condenser would be turned on in order to create a vacuum in the condenser, air pump chamber and on the side of the piston connected to the condenser via the slide valve. The engine would begin to rotate in the required direction and speed would be adjusted by regulating the steam supply valve together with the expansion cam settings if that facility was provided.[11]

During operation of a side-lever engine, or any engine fitted with a jet condenser, it was important that the water supply to the condenser was correctly regulated in order to ensure effective operation. If too little water was injected for the amount of steam being used complete condensation would not be achieved and a back pressure would build up in the condenser and cylinder causing loss of power. Should excessive water be supplied at a particular engine operating speed the air pump might not be able to remove it all from the condenser which would consequently flood and this might result in cylinder damage if water found its way in during the exhaust period.

Side-lever engines were relatively simple to construct and operate, features which suited conditions during the formative years of steam navigation and many marine engine builders started by constructing such machinery before they graduated to designs of their own. Although each engine builder incorporated his own ideas, the engine was essentially the standard British marine steam engine of the 1820s, 1830s and even 1840s. In later years other designs became popular but for mail paddle steamers, particularly on the rough north Atlantic, it was retained because of its simplicity, reliability and ruggedness. In the gigantic pair of engines constructed in 1862 for the mail steamer *Scotia* the side-lever design reached its zenith but its real usefulness was long past as simpler, smaller and more fuel-efficient engines were then available. It is difficult to understand why Cunard persevered with antiquated machinery which consumed 350 tons of coal each day for a speed of 14.5 knots,[12] but possession of a mail contract allowed the company to be less fuel efficient than its more commercially-oriented competitors.

The side-lever engine did survive a little longer in modified form, the most common being the 'Grasshopper' type with side-lever pivots at the opposite end of the levers from the cylinder drive. Air pump and paddle wheel connecting-rod attachments were towards the middle of the levers. Engines of this type were fitted in smaller craft, generally tugs, a pair going into the tug *Old Trafford* built for the Manchester Ship Canal Company in 1907 by Joseph Eltringham of South Shields. These surface condensing side-lever engines were made by Hepple & Co., also of South Shields, who supplied the engines for three sister

2.8 *Paddle tug* Old Trafford *fitted with a 'Grasshopper' engine, a modified version of the side-lever engine (Manchester Liners Ltd)*

tugs built around the same time; in 1903 two sister tugs were built and engined in South Shields by J. P. Reynolds & Sons.[13] *Old Trafford* worked for over forty years on the canal before being sold for service on the Tyne and now, as *Reliant*, survives on display in the National Maritime Museum, Greenwich.

The side-lever engine came late to America probably because the Fulton design of crosshead engine satisfied most needs of the river boats and coastal craft during the first three decades of the nineteenth century. That does not, however, mean that there were no developments. American engineers were great innovators and improved the machinery which served their purpose. In the 1820s James Allaire, who had taken control of the engine works established by Fulton,[14] introduced compounding to the Fulton crosshead engine and fitted engines of this type in six small steamers, but owing to the low steam pressure of 25psi the design was not a success. Allaire also introduced the steam chimney which was effectively a steam dryer using the heat in the boiler gases passing up the funnel. It consisted of a chamber surrounding the lower part of the funnel into which steam from the boiler was directed, a diaphragm in the chamber leading the steam first downwards through the outer part of the chamber then upwards past the funnel casing.[15]

By the 1840s side-lever engines were being installed in coastal steamers and Atlantic liners, the Allaire Iron Works and the Novelty Iron Works favouring this design. Both were based in New York which was the centre for marine engineering in the USA at that time. In 1847 the Novelty Iron Works fitted a single 70in bore by 8ft stroke side-lever engine in the 1,012 ton coastal steamer *Northerner* and two 72in bore by 10ft stroke side-lever engines in the Atlantic liner *Washington*. In general, this type of engine did not appear to find popularity with American owners, almost certainly because by the time it was introduced there were superior designs available. The coastal steamer *Columbia* received a single Novelty-built engine, 86in bore by 9ft stroke, in 1857,[16] and that was probably the last such large engine built in America. American liners built for Atlantic service during the 1840s and the early 1850s all had side-lever engines, probably because of the success of such machinery aboard British liners crossing that ocean. Some were lost at sea but the surviving ships failed to make any commercial impact on the route, resulting in their early withdrawal, and the cause of the side-lever engine disappeared with them.

By contrast America took to the beam engine which was essentially a marine version of the Watt engine and this had a long history in American and Far East waters. The first engine of the type was probably constructed by Daniel Dod in 1820 for the auxiliary steamship *New York*, but apart from the fact that gearing was used to transmit the drive to the paddle shaft little is known about the machinery.[17]

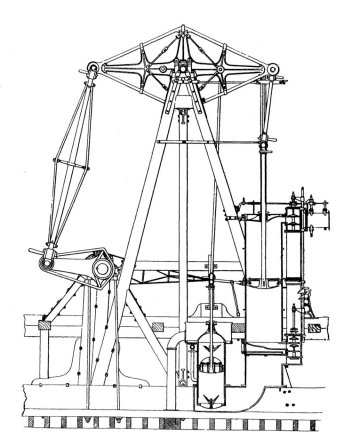

2.9 *Arrangement of the walking beam engine*

Robert Stevens fitted a walking beam engine (originally known as working beam) in the small ferry *Hoboken* during 1822,[18] while James Allaire supplied two independent engines each for the steamboats *Benjamin Franklin* (1828) and *President* (1829). These engine could drive their own paddle shafts independently or a single engine could drive both paddles if necessary, but this idea was not perpetuated. Engines for *President* had a bore of 48in and stroke of 7ft, allowing some 320ihp to be developed.[19] The more usual arrangement for river and coastal steamers was a single beam engine driving both paddles and the engine fitted in *North America* (1827) by Robert Stevens was typical of the period. This 200ft long steamer had a jet condensing engine with a 43in diameter cylinder and 11ft stroke; air pump, feed pump and bilge pumps were driven by levers from the overhead beam which was supported on a wooden tower frame. The walking beam had a cast iron frame with wrought iron trussing while the cranks and connecting rod were also trussed with iron rods. Instead of the parallel-motion mechanism common in British practice, this engine, as with other walking beam engines, had a guide system for the piston rod crosshead. Steam supply to and exhaust from the cylinder were regulated by double poppet-type valves rather than the slide valve used in British engines of the period.[20]

Large walking beam engines were constructed for ocean steamers, particularly the Atlantic but later for Pacific routes. *Vanderbilt* (1856) was a comparatively large vessel of the period, 331ft long and 3,360 tons, and was the only vessel fitted with two walking beam engines to cross the Atlantic regularly. Her engines, built by the Allaire Iron Works of New York, could develop 2,800ihp from their 90in diameter by 12ft stroke cylinders burning between 80 and 100 tons of coal per day.[21]

Over the years the walking beam engine did not change much apart from a few refinements such as the fitting of surface condensers; many engines fitted to steamers operat-

ing on southern and western rivers such as the Mississippi did not have condensers owing to the problems of silt in the rivers. In 1882 the Morgan Iron Works of New York supplied a walking beam engine for the 3,500-ton river steamer *Pilgrim* and this differed little in form from those of *North America*. The 110in bore by 14ft stroke cylinder could develop 6,500ihp at full power when supplied with steam at a pressure of 50psi. Double-beat poppet valves directed steam to and from the cylinder, operation being by means of cams on a rocking shaft driven by an eccentric from the paddle shaft. A centrifugal pump, driven by its own engine, supplied cooling water to the surface condenser.[22]

Although walking beam engines had their origins in America they were not all constructed there; some were actually built in Scotland. A. & J. Inglis of Pointhouse, Glasgow fitted walking beam engines in four Yangtze River steamers built for the China Navigation Company, *Pekin* (1873), *Shanghai*, (1873), *Ichang* (1873), and *Hankow* (1874).[23] Operations on the Yangtze required shallow-draft vessels and at the time the type of paddle steamer operating on American rivers appeared most suitable. The engines were of similar design but that fitted in *Hankow* was the largest having a single 72in bore by 14ft stroke cylinder of 400 nominal horsepower. In 1884 Inglis constructed machinery for the 286ft long sister ships *Saturno* and *Olympo* which were designed for service on the River Plate; both had compound beam engines with the 36in diameter high-pressure and 66in diameter low-pressure cylinders connecting to the same end of the walking beam; the stroke was 10ft.[24]

Even while they were profitably engaged in constructing side-lever engine many builders engaged themselves with designs which would overcome the problems of weight and

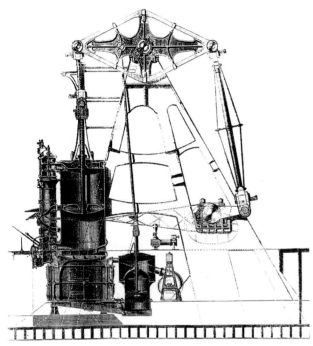

2.10 (Above) Walking beam engine as fitted in the American river steamer Pilgrim (1882)

2.11 (Below) Burnt-out Yangtze River steamer Shanghai (1873) showing the arrangement of the walking beam engine (John Swire & Son)

size which afflicted that engine. In the early 1830s David Napier introduced the steeple engine which occupied little fore' and aft' space in the ship but did require considerable head room. In this design the cylinders were placed immediately below the paddle shaft with the piston rods being attached to the lower part of a triangular crosshead. The upper part of the crosshead ran in a guide and located the upper end of the connecting rod which drove the paddle shaft located below the guide. The crosshead, which operated several pumps, had to be triangular in order to clear the cranked paddle shaft. The engine design was taken by other builders and modified to suit particular situations, but the basic arrangement remained the same even when compounding was introduced. The compactness of the design and its relative accessibility made it popular over many years.[25]

This type of engine was being fitted as late as 1891, for during that year the London & North Western Railway Company had its Holyhead to Dublin paddle steamers *Violet* and *Lily*, originally built in 1880 with compound oscillating engines, fitted with triple-expansion steeple engines built by Laird Brothers of Birkenhead. The company wished to increase the speed of the ships and decided upon re-engining and re-boilering but insisted that the new ma-

chinery should occupy the same space as the old but develop 30 per cent more power. Lairds installed three engines on the paddle shaft, a total of nine steam cylinders, giving a total output of 4,200ihp with steam at a pressure of 150psi. A separate surface condenser was installed in the forward part of the engine room, and, because of the space limitation, no pumps were driven by the main engine.[26] Other designs of steeple engine had pumps driven via levers from rods attached to the lower part of the crosshead. Although the steeple-engine concept remained the same other builders used their own ideas to save space and weight or to make the installation fit particular needs.

Maudslays developed the double piston, or Siamese, engine as a means of saving space and introduced the design in the paddle frigate HMS *Retribution* (1844). Each engine had two cylinders which were placed in a fore' and aft' direction with the rods from both pistons, which moved up and down together, connecting with the ends of a double crosshead shaped in the form of a T. The crosshead worked in guides positioned between the two cylinders while the connecting rod, attached to the lower part of the T, swung between the plates of that crosshead. Air and feed pumps were driven by levers connecting with the crosshead while the valve gear (there being one piston type valve for each pair of cylinders)

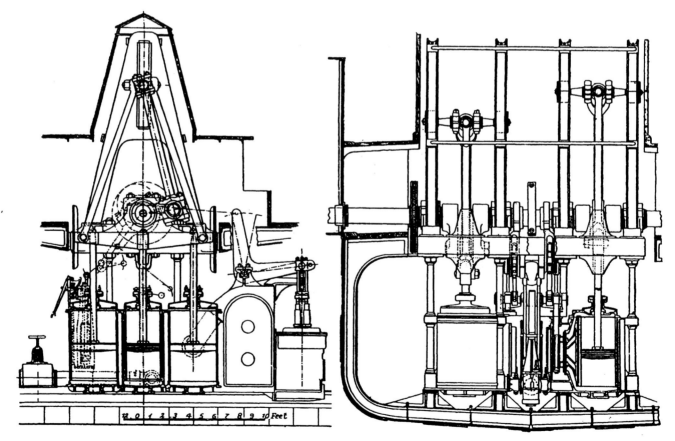

2.12 Arrangement of a three-cylinder, compound steeple engine built in 1861

was operated by an eccentric on the paddle shaft working through linkages.[27] *Terrible* had two engines with cylinders 72in diameter and 8ft stroke and took steam at 7psi. The engine appears to have been popular initially as within ten years of its introduction there were fifty-five sets at sea, mainly for warships, [28] but according to John Bourne they were not a success. He believed that they did not save much space or weight and that there were considerable radiation losses owing to the use of two smaller diameter cylinders rather than a single, large one.[29] Shortly after the Siamese engine Maudslays introduced the annular engine which effectively served the same purpose of allowing for a long connecting rod but the design was more suited to screw propulsion and will be discussed later.

A variation on the Siamese was developed by Forrester & Co. of Liverpool and fitted in the North Sea steamer *Helen McGregor* built by Laird Brothers in 1843. This engine had two cylinders, 42in bore by 4ft 6in stroke, positioned athwartships below the paddle shaft. However, the cylinders were inverted and the piston rods connected with a crosshead which worked below the cylinders. A parallel-motion system of levers maintained the crosshead working in a vertical plane while the connecting rod, which was attached to the crosshead, swung between the cylinders. Levers on the parallel motion mechanism were also used for

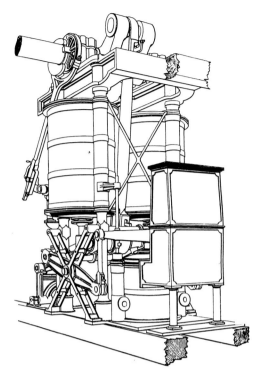

2.14 Inverted Siamese engine fitted in the steamer Helen McGregor *(1843)*

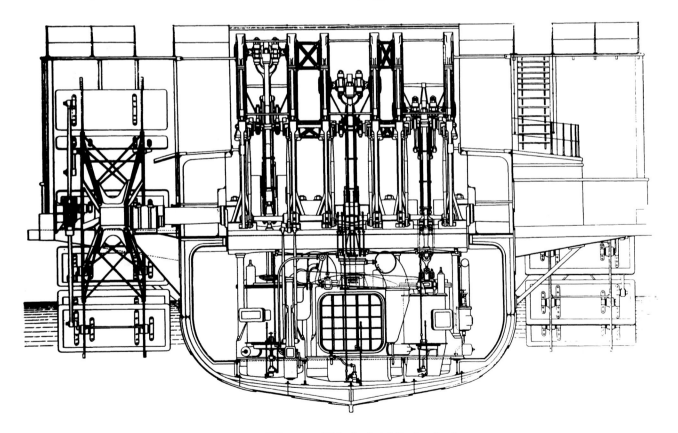

2.13 Triple-expansion steeple engine fitted in the L&NWR steamer Violet *by Laird Brothers in 1891*

driving the air, feed, bilge and brine pumps. The condenser was positioned immediately below the valve chest; each cylinder had its own slide valve and both were actuated by a single eccentric. The air pump, connecting with the condenser by means of a passage in the foundation plate, expelled water into a rectangular hot well from where what was not taken by the feed pump was discharged overboard through a pipe in the side of the ship.[30]

Because the indirect-acting paddle engine presented problems with respect to size, weight and complexity, the aim of most designers was an engine which had no need for lever drive systems. Positioning the cylinders directly below the paddle shaft had a major advantage in that it saved space but the resulting short connecting rod introduced additional fore' and aft' thrusts on the paddle shaft and particularly on the piston rod. In order to minimise such problems at the piston rod and retain its motion in the vertical plane, the firm of Seaward & Capel of Limehouse introduced an engine which had a novel parallel-motion mechanism for its pistons. Attached to the piston rod crosshead was one end of the air pump twin lever, the other end driving the pump via a connecting rod, crosshead and guide. The pivot for the air pump lever was provided by a vertical link which was itself pivoted at its lower end and thus the lever pivot could rock

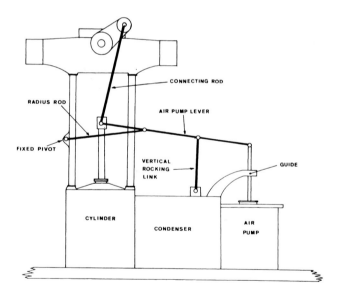

2.15 Arrangement of the 'Gorgon' engine

back and forwards. Twin radius rods were also attached, by means of pivot pins, to the air pump levers at a point between the lever pivot and the piston crosshead; the other ends of the radius rods were attached by means of pivot pins to the engine framing. This arrangement provided a substantial linkage which kept the piston rod moving in the vertical plane and overcame the fore' and aft' thrusts which resulted from the use of the short connecting rod.

Each cylinder had a single eccentric operating its valve gear which consisted of four valves, two steam inlet and two exhaust. Individual valves were actuated by a system of levers and this arrangement allowed for individual control of steam and exhaust valves at each end of the cylinder. A jet condenser was placed in the centre of the bedplate between the cylinder and the air pump.[31]

The first of these engines, which became known by the name of the ship in which they were first fitted, was constructed by Seaward in 1837 and installed in the frigate HMS *Gorgon*, this engine having two 64in diameter by 5ft 6in stroke cylinders operating at 18 revolutions per minute; the engine weighed some 60 tons less than a side-lever engine of equivalent power.[32] Despite this saving in weight Gorgon engines were not popular with engineers owing to the short connecting rod and it was claimed that this caused wear at the crosshead and paddle shaft bearings; excessive wear at the parallel motion pin bushes was also a problem.[33]

In an attempt to provide a direct acting engine with long connecting rod Seawards designed an engine with open-topped pistons, the connecting rod being attached to the piston rather than a piston rod. In 1839 a three-cylinder engine (74in bore by 3ft stroke) was installed in the 238-ton steamer *Sapphire* but the objection to the engine was that it was single acting and although two cross-Channel steamers, *Alliance* and *Havre*, were fitted with similar engines in the 1850s the design was not popular.[34] A variation on this idea was the trunk piston engine in which the connecting rod operated in a trunk attached to the upper part of the piston, thus allowing the cylinder to be double-acting. Several designs were introduced by builders but the main problem tended to centre around the provision of an effective gland for the trunk. A great enthusiast of the trunk engine was Francis Humphreys who was appointed Engineer-in-Charge by the Great Western Steam Ship Company when

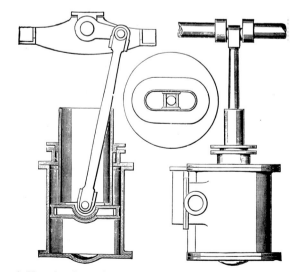

2.16 Humphrey's trunk engine for paddlewheel drive

that company was building its second vessel in Bristol during the late 1830s. Humphreys had convinced the directors that his trunk engine would be suitable for driving the company's new vessel *The Great Britain* which was then still to be propelled by paddles. For this ship Humphreys had proposed a two-cylinder engine, the cylinder bore being 110in, but with the later change to screw propulsion the machinery was never built.[35] Before the company took an interest an engine to Humphreys' patent had been built and installed in the steam packet *Dartford* but excessive wear in the cylinder subsequently proved the design to be unsatisfactory.[36]

The direct-acting paddle engine which attracted considerable attention was the vibrating cylinder engine, more generally known as the oscillating engine. As with most machines the concept was not new but it took a good engineer to translate the idea into a practical engine. That engineer was Joseph Maudslay, son of Henry Maudslay and hence one of the sons in Maudslay, Sons & Field, who took out a patent for an oscillating engine in 1827. In this type of engine the piston rod was attached direct to the paddle shaft crank without the use of a connecting rod. In order to compensate for the crank rotation the cylinder and piston were allowed to vibrate or oscillate as the engine operated. Each cylinder in an engine was mounted on a pair of pivots or trunnions through which steam and exhaust were directed to and from the cylinder. Apart from the fact that it saved space, the oscillating engine also had other advantages not least being the reduction in working parts through the omission of crossheads, parallel-motion mechanisms and beams.

Maudslay's fitted their first oscillating engine in the Thames pleasure steamer *Endeavour* during 1828, this having two cylinders of 20in bore and 2ft stroke; a similar

engine was later fitted in seven other steamers including the cross-Channel packet *Dover Castle*. Although these engines worked successfully, many ship operators and engineers of the day believed, erroneously, that the rolling and pitching of a ship would result in trouble at the trunnion and in the cylinders. Considerable prejudice built up against the engine and few orders were forthcoming during the 1830s.[37] In 1838 John Penn introduced an improved version of the oscillating engine and this found greater favour with the shipping companies which, by then, appreciated the limitations of the side-lever engine upon which they had relied for so long. The reluctance to put faith in the oscillating engine during the 1820s and early 1830s is understandable as the success of any new venture relied upon effective engines and boilers. The side-lever engine may have had its faults but it was rugged and generally reliable, such factors being important to any new steam-powered service.

Penn replaced the cast iron frame of the Maudslay oscillating engine with wrought iron columns and altered the way in which the valves were operated. Each Maudslay engine cylinder had a single 'D' pattern slide valve operated by a single eccentric, the valve being positioned at a trunnion through which the inlet steam flowed. Penn removed the valves from the trunnion region and mounted them on the sides of the cylinders thus making the engine more compact; early designs had a single valve on one side of the cylinder balanced by a weight on the other but later engines had two valves, one on each side of the cylinder. A single eccentric was used to actuate the valves through a system of linkages. However, with the advent of valve actuating systems such as the Stephenson link motion, oscillating engines built by Penn and other manufacturers were so equipped. Steam supply to the engine cylinders was by

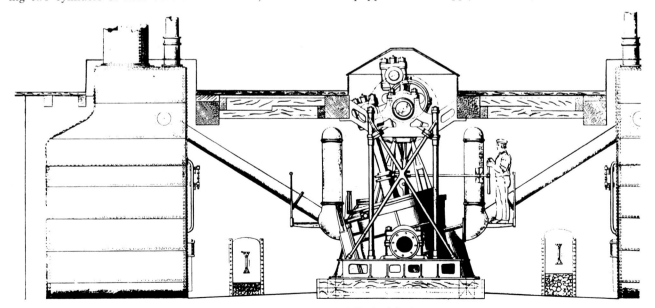

2.17 Penn oscillating engine as fitted in the re-engined Admiralty yacht Black Eagle *(1844)*

means of throttle valves generally mounted on the trunnions. For engines having two cylinders a condenser would be mounted between them as would the air pump; this pump's cylinder would be fixed with the piston operated by a crank from the paddle shaft.[38]

Among the early successful Penn oscillating engines was a series built during the early 1840s for eleven of twelve Thames steamers owned by the Waterman Steam Packet Company. These engines were small, 24in bore by 2ft 3in stroke, but they were very reliable and the steamers operated successfully.[39] That success and the compact design of the engine interested the Admiralty which entrusted Penn with the re-engining of the 540-ton official yacht *Black Eagle* which by 1843 was proving to be too slow for her duties. The Admiralty consulted Boulton & Watt with regard to the replacement of the original 130nhp side-lever engines with more powerful machinery occupying the same space, but the reply was not favourable.[40] In 1844 oscillating engines of double the power were fitted in the same space occupied by the original engines, and that proved to be the first of many Admiralty contracts received by John Penn & Sons of Greenwich.[41]

The success of the oscillating engine prompted other

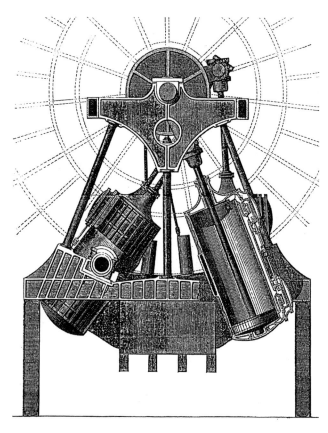

2.18 (Right) Oscillating paddle engine built by John Scott Russell for the Great Eastern

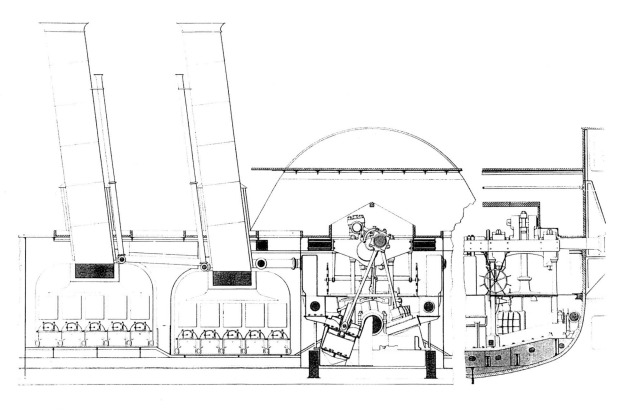

2.19 Ravenhill & Salkeld oscillating engine as installed in the Irish Sea packets Leinster *and* Connaught *(1860)*

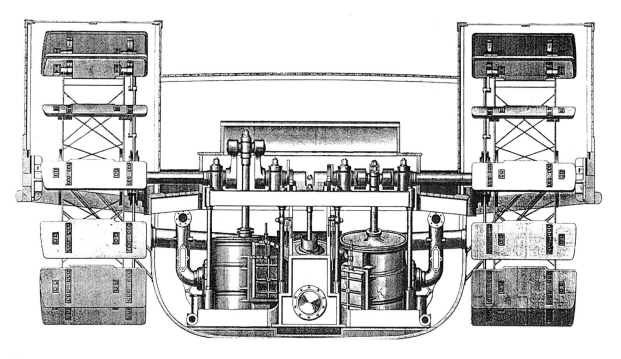

2.20 *The 46in bore by 4ft stroke oscillating engine built by J. & G. Thomson for the steamer* Iona *during the 1860s*

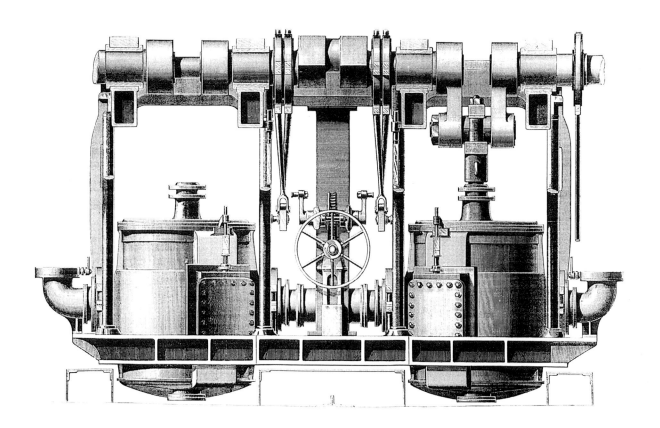

2.21 *Typical Penn oscillating engine of 1860–70; built for a paddle steamer operating on the Bosphorus*

2.22 *Side view of the Penn oscillating engine installed in Bosphorus steamers*

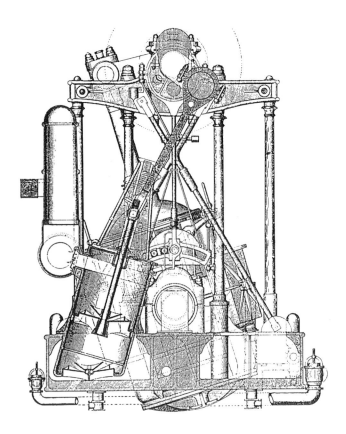

2.23 *American-built oscillating engine; constructed by Murray & Hazlehurst in 1849 for the steamer* Illinois

builders to adopt the design and each incorporated modifications to suit his own ideas or the requirements of clients. When built by John Scott Russell & Co. in 1858 the paddle machinery for Brunel's giant *Great Eastern* attracted considerable interest; it weighed some 836 tons and developed about 3,400ihp with steam supplied at 24psi. The engine had four cylinders and the paddle shaft two cranks, there being two inclined cylinders connected on each crank. The use of a fork and blade arrangement for the bottom end connections of each opposing pair of cylinders enabled the cylinder centres to be kept in line in a fore' and aft' direction thus minimising the space occupied by the engine. The cylinders were of 74in bore and 14ft stroke, slide valves being fitted to the cylinder sides facing outwards.[42]

In 1860 Ravenhill and Salkeld of Blackwall constructed a two-cylinder oscillating engine of more conventional form for the Irish Sea packet steamer *Leinster*, but this was more powerful than that installed in *Great Eastern*. Some 4,750 ihp could be developed from the 98in bore by 6ft 4in stroke cylinders when turning at 25 revolutions per minute with steam supplied at 20psi; the nominal horse power of the engine was only 720. Each cylinders had two valve chests on opposite sides of the cylinder, both valves being operated by a single eccentric which drove a sliding rod. The lower end

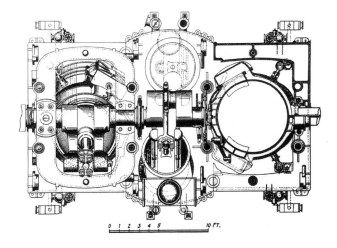

2.24 *Plan view of the oscillating engine fitted in* Illinois

of that eccentric rod terminated in a curved, slotted arm which accommodated sliding blocks attached to the valve-rod linkages. This arrangement permitted the valves to be independent of the oscillations of the cylinder and enabled the engine to be reversed by moving the slotted link; this was achieved by means of a rack and pinion gear worked by a large hand wheel.[43]

Although the early Penn engines had the air pump positioned vertically between the cylinders, most builders, including Penn, moved it from below the paddle shaft but still kept it and the condenser positioned with one cylinder on each side. This necessitated the air pump's being inclined slightly, but the new arrangement made the engine less crowded while allowing the cylinder centres to be moved closer together.

The oscillating engine proved popular with overseas builders both in Europe and America but the design remained fundamentally the same as that developed by Penn. Two of the earliest large oscillating engines to be built in America were installed in the almost identical, 2,000-ton ships *Illinois* and *Golden Gate*, the former being built in 1851 by Smith & Dimon for the New York to Chagres service, while the latter was constructed in the same year for the route between Panama and California. Engines in both ships were practically identical, 85in bore by 9ft stroke, working at 15rpm with steam at a pressure of 12psi. Instead of ordinary slide valves these engines were fitted with American-pattern balanced valves with Allen valve gear

using two eccentrics. The engine for *Illinois* was built by Allaire and that for *Golden Gate* came from Stillman, Allen & Co. at the Novelty Iron Works, both engine builders achieving high power from an engine only some 18ft long.[44]

The success of *Illinois* and *Golden Gate*, as well as the 852-ton *Republic* fitted with the first American built oscillating engine, constructed by Murray and Hazlehurst of Baltimore in 1849, prompted others to follow. Novelty built an engine of 65in bore and 10ft stroke for the Havre Line's *Arago* in 1865 and the same year the Morgan Iron Works built an engine of similar cylinder size for the same owner's *Fulton*. This engine, however, had its two cylinders inclined at an angle of 45° to the vertical, both driving a single crank in a similar manner to that of the paddle engines installed in *Great Eastern*. In 1856 the Novelty Iron Works built a large oscillating engine for Collins Line's 4,145-ton *Adriatic*. This had two 100in bore by 12ft stroke cylinders and could develop 3,300ihp when working at 14rpm, the cylinders being inclined at 45° to the vertical and their centres offset about 12in from the centre line of the ship. This enabled the opposing cylinders to drive

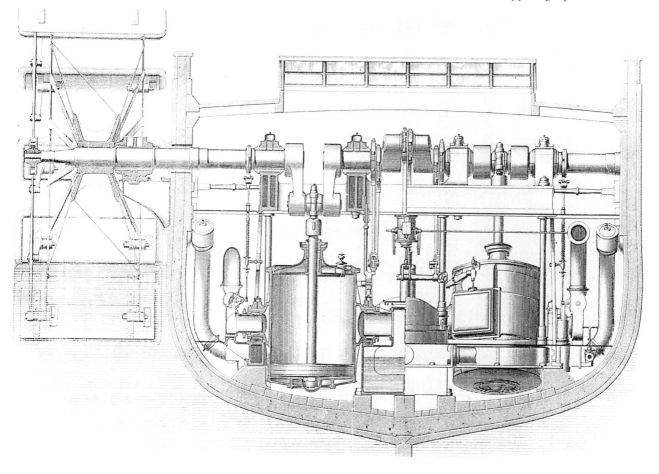

2.25 French-built oscillating engine; constructed in early 1860s by Mazeline & Co. for the yacht L'Aigle

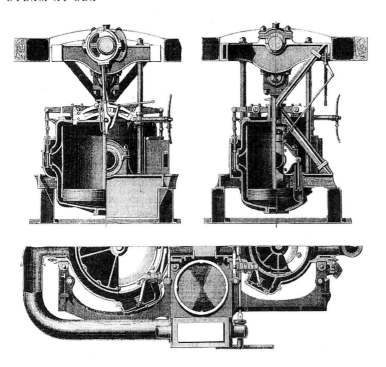

2.26 Compound oscillating engine built in 1866 by Escher Wyss of Zurich for the Danube Steam Navigation Company

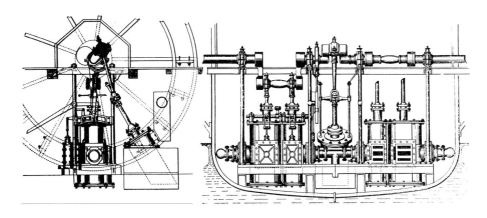

2.28 Compound oscillating engine of the 1840s; built by Joyce & Co. of the Greenwich Iron Works for the Thames steamer Cricket

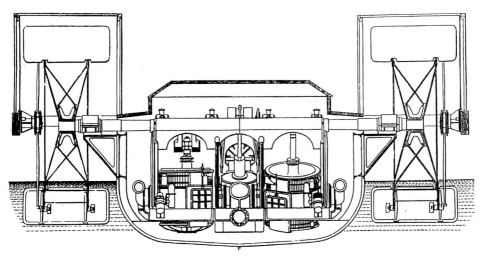

2.27 Penn surface condensing engine built in 1882 for the cross-Channel steamer Mary Beatrice

2.29 Diagonal engine arrangement for a tug as proposed by Alex Wilson & Co. during 1880

separate cranks which were at 18° to each other; a type of flexible coupling was provided between the crank pins by way of a loose fitting link. The original design of surface condenser failed during trials and had to be substituted. Several different arrangements of valve gear were tried with the engines before one was produced which functioned reasonably well; however, the engines never performed to expectation.[45]

By the 1850s the days of the large seagoing paddle steamer were fast drawing to a close but paddle-driven vessels still had a role to play in the shallow waters around coasts and in rivers. Many builders became involved in the construction of paddle engines for such steamers, a number in the industrialised areas of Europe. MM Mazeline & Co. of Havre built an oscillating engine for the yacht *L'Aigle*, this being displayed at the 1862 International Exhibition.[46]

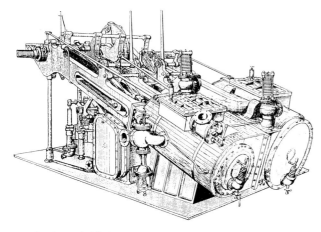

2.30 Ranken & Blackmore 500ihp diagonal compound engine for paddle-driven tug of the 1880s

The only other non-British company displaying marine machinery at that exhibition was Messrs. Escher, Wyss & Co. of Switzerland who had on show a double inclined engine for driving a small paddle boat. Over the years it had

built many two-cylinder oscillating engines of conventional form for paddle steamers operating on the Danube. By 1866 the Danube Steam Navigation Company operated ninety-five paddle boats and twenty-five steamers, the company's routes covering some 3,000 miles. It also possessed its own workshops for repairing its ships and their machinery but always obtained new engines from outside firms such as Escher, Wyss. The Swiss engine builder modified his standard type oscillating paddle engine for compounding and supplied a number for new ships for the Danube fleet. Engines supplied in 1866 had a 38in diameter, high-pressure (HP) cylinder and a 57in diameter low-

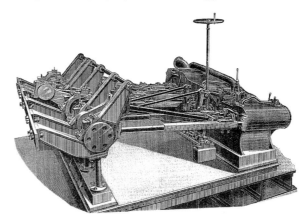

2.31 Triple-expansion diagonal engine of low height devised by the Southampton Naval Works in 1891 for use in shallow draught Nile steamers

pressure (LP) cylinder connected to their own cranks on the paddle shaft. Between the trunnions of the HP and the LP cylinder the builder fitted a steam reservoir in order to ensure that steam flow to the LP cylinder would be maintained. The need for this type of feature is considered in Chapter 6. In order to minimise steam loss through the condensation of incoming steam on the cylinder walls, Escher, Wyss adopted a form of steam jacketing (see Chapter 3) by passing exhaust steam from the LP cylinder through a passageway around that cylinder; a jacket around the HP cylinder had steam supplied from its valve chest.[47]

John Penn and Son remained at the forefront of oscillating engine construction almost until the design ceased to be built. In 1882 a surface condensing engine was built for the cross-Channel steamer *Mary Beatrice*, claimed at the time to be the fastest ship afloat with an average trials speed of 19 knots. Her two 72in bore by 5ft stroke cylinders could develop some 3,000ihp in order to produce that speed.[48] As late as 1890 Penns were constructing simple expansion surface-condensing oscillating engines, as in that year the company built such a unit for a Turkish steamer designed to operate on the Bosphorus. This small engine, 37in bore by 3ft stroke, had all the features of the earlier giants and

2.32 Denny compound diagonal engine as fitted in the steamers Princess Victoria *and* Clacton Belle

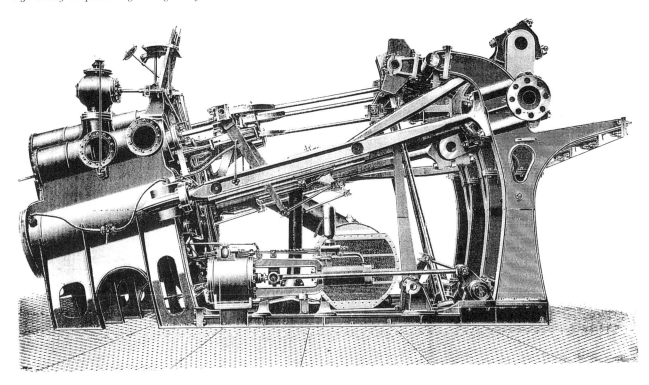

2.33 Denny triple expansion engine of 1897 as fitted in the pleasure steamer Walton Belle

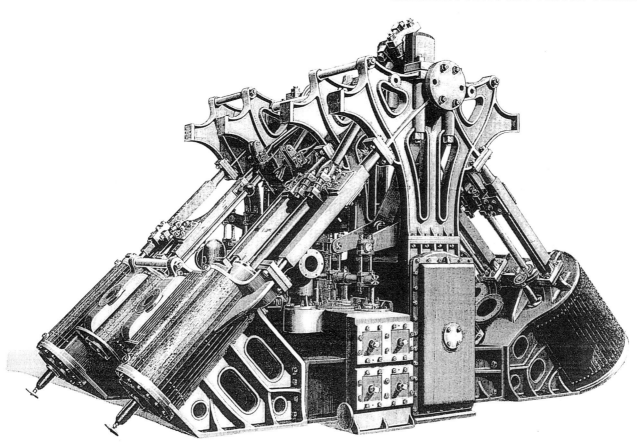

2.34 Triangular form of diagonal engine; compound triangular engine fitted in the tug Mana *during the 1880s*

although rather antiquated in design was ideally suited to the type of vessel and trade upon which she was engaged. Over the years since 1865 the same owner had built and engined some twenty-three similar vessels on the Thames.[49]

Although the oscillating engine was ideal for simple expansion, a number of compound oscillating engines were developed the earliest of which was probably that fitted in the little steamer *Cricket* which operated on the Thames between Hungerford and London Bridges. This four-cylinder compound engine was built and installed by Messrs. Joyce & Co. of Greenwich Iron Works during the mid-1840s, there being a high and a low pressure cylinder bolted together with their piston rods driving the same crank. Sets of slide valves regulated the steam flow to and from the cylinders, these valves being actuated by eccentrics working through rocking shafts and linkages. Although the engine functioned satisfactorily, the steam supply pressure of 20psi was not really high enough for compounding and the absence of a steam receiver between the high and the low pressure cylinder limited the effectiveness of the compounding. In September 1847 a boiler explosion killed seventeen people and curtailed any thoughts of employing higher-pressure steam.[50]

The diagonal or triangular engine for paddle propulsion

was patented by Sir Marc Brunel, father of Isambard Kingdom Brunel, in 1822 and an engine of this form was originally considered for propelling the steamship *The Great Britain* when she was to be paddle driven.[51] The triangular concept was revived in later years but mainly for small ship propulsion, particularly ferries and tugs which still employed paddle wheels, the compact design saving a considerable amount of space when compared with other engines. A triangular arrangement was particularly suited to compounding, as four cylinders, two high and two low pressure, could be conveniently connected to a single paddle shaft.

The main problem with the triangular engine was that the space below the crankshaft was rather cluttered by the condenser, air pumps and pump rods, thereby limiting accessibility and where engine room space was not so limited the half triangle or diagonal engine found favour. Although oscillating engines were still constructed towards the end of the nineteenth century the diagonal engine was considered more suitable for compounding and triple expansion owing to its simpler arrangement for valves and steam passages and because of the absence of trunnions which presented problems with high-pressure steam with oscillating engines.

The compound or triple expansion diagonal engine with

2.35 The paddle steamer **Princess Elizabeth** *(1927) fitted with a two-cylinder diagonal compound engine, 23in + 48in by 4ft 3in stroke; the ship survived in commercial service until the 1960s*

2.36 Denny-built Isle of Wight paddle steamer **Sandown** *(1934) fitted with a triple expansion diagonal engine; 16in + 25.5in + 41in by 5ft 3in stroke.*

surface condenser became popular for paddle propulsion from the mid-1870s and remained so until the final steam paddle vessels were constructed. Designs differed but the basic arrangement of cylinders, crankshaft and valve gear remained relatively simple and accessible. The surface condenser and air pump, driven from the crankshaft by a crank or eccentric, were positioned below the connecting rods. Diagonal engines were the favoured means of propulsion for tugs and other shallow-draught vessel, including Nile paddle steamers. In 1891 the Southampton Naval Works built a triple expansion three-crank diagonal engine for the light-draught, paddle-driven pleasure vessel it was constructing for service on the Nile. This engine had cylinders 12.5in, 20in, and 30in diameter, the stroke being 3ft; piston valves were used for all cylinders, Stephenson link motion operated the valves. The ample beam of the vessel allowed the surface condenser to be positioned well to the side of the engine, the low angle of inclination resulting from the shallow draught leaving little room beneath the connecting rods. Locomotive-type boilers provided steam at 160psi.[52]

Some of the largest and most powerful compound diagonal engines were built by Messrs. Denny & Co. of Dumbarton for service in pleasure and railway steamers built by themselves. During 1888 they built and engined the 300ft long *Princess Henriette* and *Princess Josephine* for the Belgian government's cross-Channel service between Dover and Ostend, both vessels being fitted with two crank compound diagonal engines of 59in and 104in bore and 6ft stroke. With steam at 110psi these engines could develop some 6,500ihp giving the ships a speed of 21 knots.[53] Engines of similar design were fitted in other vessels although the size of cylinder and power developed varied with installation. *Princess Victoria* (1890) had cylinders of 51in and 90in diameter with a 6ft 6in stroke, while the cylinders for *Clacton Belle* (1890) were of 28in and 50in diameter with a 6ft stroke. The surface condenser and air pump were, as usual, located beneath the connecting rods.[54]

In 1893 Dennys adapted the diagonal engine for triple expansion and continued its application mainly to pleasure steamers as the cross-Channel and railway ferries had generally turned to screw propulsion. Belle Steamers Company, which operated pleasure vessels on the Thames between London and Clacton, had been regular customers since 1890, and in 1893 the *London Belle* was fitted with the first triple expansion diagonal engine built by Dennys. This had cylinders of 24.5in, 44in, and 64in bore with a stroke of 6ft. In 1897 the *Walton Belle* received a similar but slightly smaller engine, 20.5in, 30in, and 43in bore by 5ft stroke.[55]

By the twentieth century paddle propulsion was essentially limited to pleasure steamers and ferry services where shallow-draught vessels were required. In Britain paddle vessels were constructed for services between the mainland and the Isle of Wight until the 1930s but the last British passenger paddle steamers were not constructed until 1947. *Bristol Queen* was built in 1846 for the Bristol Channel fleet of P.& A. Campbell and *Waverley* was built in 1947 by A.& J. Inglis for the London & North Eastern Railway. Both had triple-expansion, diagonal engines built by Rankin & Blackmore with that of *Bristol Queen* being the larger and more powerful; 27in, 42in, and 66in bore by 5ft 6in stroke developing 2,700shp (shaft horse power) compared with 24in, 39in, and 62in bore by 5ft 6in stroke developing 2,100shp for *Waverley*.[56] Fortunately *Waverley* survives and operates regular pleasure cruises from ports around the coast of Britain.

Over the years the paddle engine changed considerably, but that was also true of other marine and land-based engines. Improved workshop techniques and materials allowed the designer to make engines larger, stronger, lighter and more efficient, as well as make use of higher steam pressures through compounding in two or more stages. In engineering nothing remains the same and the approach of the engineer is always one of improvement on what has gone before. However, anything produced by the engineer has to have commercial application and in that respect the marine engine was no different from any other engine. Ultimately the shipowner decided upon the success or otherwise of a particular type of engine and the development of efficient screw propulsion heralded the end of the paddle steamer although, as has been shown there was a niche market for the paddle steamer until the middle of the twentieth century. At sea change was inevitable and advances in machinery design had to meet the developing demands of the military and commercial operators. Just as paddle gave way to screw propulsion so the quest for higher efficiencies saw simple expansion give way to compounding, triple expansion and even quadruple expansion. The steam turbine eventually ousted the reciprocating engine but was subsequently displaced by the internal combustion engine, such is the nature of improvement. However, it all began with the paddle wheel and the story of marine engineering has its heart in the chronicle of paddle machinery development.

References

1 A description of the steam expansion gear for the side-lever engine fitted in *Great Western* is to be found in D. Griffiths, *Brunel's Great Western*, Patrick Stephens, Wellingborough, 1985, pp. 71–5.

2 J. Bourne, *A Treatise of the Steam Engine*, Longmans, Green, London, 1876, pp. 142–7.

3 H.P. Spratt, *Science Museum Catalogue: Marine Engineering*, HMSO London, 1953, p. 20.

4   *The Engineer*, vol. 75, 3 Mar 1893, pp. 181–2.

5   Brunel *'Facts Book'*, p. 5, Brunel Collection, Bristol University.

6   E. C. Smith, *A Short History of Marine Engineering*, Cambridge University Press, 1937, p. 19.

7   E. C. Smith 'Samuel Hall and His Inventions', *Trans. Newcomen Society*, vol. 19, 1938–9, p. 91.

8   Hall publication relating to the surface condenser, pp. 18–21, Hall documents, Science Museum Library.

9   E. C. Smith, 'Samuel Hall and His Inventions', pp. 92–4.

10 E. Humphrys, 'On Surface Condensation in Marine Engines', *Proc. I.Mech.E.*, 1862, pp. 99–100.

11 R. S. Robinson, *The Nautical Steam Engine Explained*, Saunders & Otley, London, 1839, pp. 96–105.

12 *The Engineer*, vol. 75, 3 Mar 1893, pp. 181–2.

13 H. C. McMurray, *Old Order, New Thing*, National Maritime Museum, Greenwich, 1972, pp. 18–38.

14 C. Ridgely-Nevitt, *American Steamships, on the Atlantic*, University of Delaware Press, Newark, 1981, p. 39.

15 C. H. Haswell, 'Reminiscences of Early Marine Steam Engine Construction in the USA from 1807 to 1850', *Trans. I.N.A.*, vol. 40, 1898, p.106

16 C Ridgely-Nevitt, *American Steamships*, Appendixes J and L, pp. 98–154.

17 Ibid., pp. 68–72.

18 *The Engineer*, vol. 54, 28 July 1882, p. 61.

19 C Ridgely-Nevitt, *American Steamships*, pp. 47–8 and Appendix E.

20 J. Bourne, *A Treatise on the Steam Engine*, pp. 336–7.

21 *Marine Engineer & Motorship Builder*, June 1927, p. 221.

22 *The Engineer*, vol 54, 28 July 1882, pp.61–2.

23 H. Sandham, 'On the History of Paddle-Wheel Steam Navigation', *Proc. I.Mech.E.*, 1885, pp. 155–6; also C. Havilland, *The China Navigation Company*, Butterfield & Swire, London, 1994, pp. 9–15.

24 H. Sandham, 'On the History of Paddle-Wheel Steam Navigation', p. 156; ship details from *Lloyd's Register of Shipping*, 1885.

25 G. E. Barr, 'The History and Development of Machinery for Paddle Steamers', *Trans. I.E.S.S.*, vol. 95, 1951, p. 108.

26 *The Engineer*, vol. 71, 17 Apr 18901, p. 296.

27 J. Bourne, *A Treatise on the Steam Engine*, p. 304.

28 *The Engineer*, vol. 87, 5 Apr 1897, pp. 446–8.

29 J. Bourne, *A Treatise on the Steam Engine*, p. 304.

30 H. P. Spratt, *Science Museum Catalogue*, p. 24.

31 *The Engineer*, vol. 87, 10 Dec. 1897, p. 565.

32 H. P. Spratt, *Science Museum Catalogue*, p. 22

33 J. Guthrie, *A History of Marine Engineering*, Hutchinson, London, 1971, pp. 85–6.

34 H. P. Spratt, *Science Museum Catalogue*, p. 22.

35 E. Corlett, *The Iron Ship*, Moonraker Press, Bradford-on-Avon, 1975, pp. 14–6.

36 *The Engineer*, vol. 87, 12 Nov. 1897, p. 470.

37 Ibid., vol. 87, 22 Oct. 1897, p. 394.

38 J. Bourne, *A Treatise on the Steam Engine*, pp. 305–9.

39 *The Engineer*, vol. 87, 29 Oct. 1897, pp. 415–6.

40 E. C. Smith, *A Short History of Marine Engineering* , p. 60.

41 *The Engineer*, vol. 87, 5 Nov. 1897, p. 446.

42 J. Bourne, *A Treatise on the Steam Engine*. pp. 322–5.

43 R. Mallet (ed.), *Scientific Record of the International Exhibition of 1862*, Longman, Green, London, 1862, pp. 207–8.

44 *Marine Engineer & Motorship Builder*, Aug.1929, pp. 346–7; Jan. 1931, pp. 30–31.

45 *The Engineer*, vol. 9, 27 Apr. 1860, p. 267; C. Ridgely-Nevitt, *American Steamships*, pp. 167–183, 358.

46 R. Mallet, *Scientific Record*, p. 219.

47 *Engineering*, vol. 2, 5 Oct. 1866, p. 261.

48 *The Engineer*, vol. 54, 25 Aug. 1882, p. 145.

49 Ibid., vol. 70, 7 Nov. 1890, pp. 371, 378.

50 Ibid., vol. 87. 12 Nov. 1897, p. 471.

51 British Patent No. 4683 (1822); see E. Corlett, *The Iron Ship*, pp. 67–70.

52 *The Engineer*, vol. 71, 13 Feb. 1891, p. 125.

53 D. J. Lyon, *The Denny List*, Part II, National Maritime Museum, Greenwich, 1975. pp. 291–2, 301.

54 *The Engineer*, vol. 70, 1 Aug, 1890, pp. 85–6.

55 Ibid., vol. 84, 16 July 1897, p. 64: *Denny List*, Part II, pp. 355, 412.

56 *Birth of a Legend*, Paddle Steamer Preservation Society, Glasgow, 1987, pp. 16–19.

3
Screw Propulsion

Screw propulsion had a significant impact on shipping both of the commercial and the naval type. With hindsight the advantages of the screw propeller appear obvious, but 150 years of continuous development have brought us to our present state of knowledge and even now propellers are the subject of detailed research in order that further improvements in performance might be obtained. Compared with the basic and crude screw-propeller designs of the 1830s and 1840s the modern propeller is a piece of high technology equipment resulting from complex mathematical analysis and testing. It is, however, a device which the nineteenth century proponents of screw propulsion would still recognise. As with many other inventions which seemed to appear suddenly the real story of the screw propeller is somewhat different and many years of hard work were required of a number of 'inventors' before the screw became the accepted means of propelling ships. A detailed account of screw propeller development has been related in *The Advent of Steam*, a volume in Conway's 'History of the Ship' series,[1] and need not be repeated here. This chapter will be confined to the engineering changes brought about by the use of the screw and to the machinery used for rotating it.

Even though the screw propeller had many advantages it should be borne in mind that during the 1840s and the 1850s most ships were still constructed from wood and that form of construction did not lend itself to such a method of propulsion. The flexing of a wooden hull in a seaway presented problems with respect to the propeller shaft and its bearings, while vibration induced by the propeller could have an adverse effect on the hull structure. In terms of machinery there were few vibrational problems arising from unbalanced masses with the slow-speed paddle engine, but for higher rotational speeds of the propeller engine even slight imperfections in the balance of rotating and reciprocating machinery could be significant.

The use of a screw propeller at the stern of the ship necessitated an opening through which the propeller tailshaft could pass and as this opening was below the water line some form of gland had to be provided. It was also important to support the shaft and that meant the provision of a bearing. The length of the stern tube depended upon the design of the ship at its after end and early designs essentially consisted of a brass tube located in an aperture at the stern, a packed stuffing box being provided at the inner end. In some designs the bearing brass was not continuous but only present for a part of the length of the tube at each end, the tailshaft seating on these sections. The fit between

tailshaft and bearing brasses was not very good and with only sea water, often containing sand, as a lubricant, wear was a constant problem. Even the use of soft metals failed to prevent the problem of stern tube wear and it was only with the introduction of the water-lubricated, lignum vitae-lined stern tube by John Penn in 1854 that the problem was overcome.[2] With the success of this invention screw propulsion became a practicable commercial proposition, but over the years there were still problems. Tailshafts were made from steel and as the lignum vitae bearing surface was sea water-lubricate, a corrosion risk existed. To avoid such problems the tailshaft was surrounded by a brass bush which, because of the size of the shaft, was made from rolled brass plate. Should the joint between the edges of the brass fail those edges would part and the projecting edge would act like a cutting tool when the shaft rotated with that edge facing the direction of rotation. Lignum vitae would be planed away and the tailshaft would drop through the effective lowering of the bearing surface. In such circumstances fatigue failure of the propeller shaft could result and in 1890 the large Atlantic liner *City of Paris* suffered such an incident which resulted in the engine collapsing by its racing out of control.[3]

With a paddle steamer the thrust exerted by the action of the paddle floats on the water was transmitted to the ship through the paddle-shaft bearings. A number of such bearings were arranged to support the shaft and to allow for effective transmission of the thrust to give the ship its motion through the water. Bearing load could be kept within reasonable limits by making the bearings larger while an ample supply of grease for lubrication kept frictional wear and the temperature low. Screw propulsion thrust was transmitted along the axis of the screw shaft and some way had to be found to transfer the axial force in the shaft to the hull of the ship without restricting the rotation of the shaft. In Brunel's screw steamship *The Great Britain* a 2ft diameter, circular, gunmetal plate was attached to the end of the screw shaft and this acted against a steel plate of similar diameter supported by the engine bedplate. Water under pressure was forced through a hole in the centre of the plate and escaped radially, this water acting as a lubricant and coolant.[4] This arrangement appeared to function well but with the increase in engine power more efficient systems were needed and by 1850 the collar type thrust had been introduced. The first section of propeller shaft from the engine had a number of collars machined on it and these fitted into grooves in the thrust bearing housing, each collar forcing against the front face of its groove when running ahead and the rear face when operating astern.[5]

Early thrust blocks had a cover which also contained grooves giving a full 360° surface upon which the collars could act; later blocks were of horseshoe shape with only the lower half of the collars transmitting thrust. Grooves were lined with a soft metal, white metal or a similar material, and lubrication was supplied from an oil box fitted above the thrust block. Rigid attachment of the thrust block to the hull of the ship was essential in order to give correct thrust transmission and to ensure that the axial force in the propeller shaft did not act on the engine and result in alignment problems. The collar-type thrust block remained standard until the early years of the twentieth century when a more compact block with floating thrust pads was introduced by A.G. Michell.

The pioneers of screw propulsion experimented with an assortment of propeller designs before commercial application of the concept began. In 1838 Captain Stockton of the US Navy had a screw-propelled tug boat, *R.F. Stockton*, built in Liverpool, the direct acting engine being designed by the Swede John Ericsson who was also responsible for the propeller design. After successful trials the tug sailed to America without making use of her powered propulsion and her achievements there encouraged the US Navy to adopt screw propulsion for the frigate *Princeton* in 1842.[6]

In Britain Sir Francis Pettit Smith was a major champion of the screw propeller and, following trials with small boats, he succeeded in interesting backers in sponsoring a large screw propelled vessel. The 200-ton *Archimedes* was built by Henry Wimshurst of Limehouse and engined by George Rennie, both members of the consortium established to build and operate the screw-driven steamer. Screw propeller trials had shown that efficient propulsion could only be achieved if the propeller were driven at speeds higher than those required for paddle propulsion, but engines of the period were slow turning to suit paddle operation. The solution lay in some mechanism to increase the propeller shaft speed and Rennie chose two-stage gearing. The engine, with two vertical 36in diameter by 3ft stroke cylinders, was positioned on the ship's centre line in a fore' and aft' direction, driving an overhead crankshaft which, in turn, drove the propeller shaft through a double system of gears which increased shaft speed in the ratio 5.5:1.[7]

The performance of *Archimedes* encouraged Brunel to adopt screw propulsion for his second ship, *The Great Britain*, but no engine of sufficient power to drive the ship's screw was then available and it was decided that the Great Western Steamship Company would build the engine from the design of the triangular engine patented by Sir Marc Brunel. To propel the ship at the desired speed 2,000 horse power would be required and four cylinders of 80in diameter by 6ft stroke were chosen, but as his son was aware of

the advantages of the expansive working of steam the bore was increased to 88in. In order to increase the propeller shaft speed from the 18rpm of the engine, Brunel adopted a chain drive after having discounted the idea of using straps or belts because of the high power output of the engine; he considered the geared drive of *Archimedes* to be noisy and crude. A four-chain system was required with the primary chain wheel driven by the crankshaft being 18ft diameter by 38in wide and the secondary wheel on the propeller shaft being of 6ft diameter; these sizes gave a speed increase ratio of 2.95:1.

Cylinder valves were operated by eccentrics on the overhead crankshaft, but expansive working, six grades, was provided for by a slide valve situated in the steam passageway to the cylinder valves. Reversing was achieved by moving the eccentric on its drive shaft and locking it in the new position. The engine used a jet condenser situated between the cylinders and below the crankshaft, the air pumps being driven by cranks.[8] For the time this engine and the use of a chain drive were significant advances, particularly in view of the power being transmitted and the experimental nature of oceanic screw propulsion.

In terms of screw propulsion the requirements for fighting ships differed in one important respect from merchant ships: the machinery had to be kept below the waterline; as naval requirements will be considered in Chapter 5 only merchant ship screw machinery developments will be discussed here.

The failure of *The Great Britain* through its grounding at Dundrum Bay was a setback for the cause of the screw but it did not deter others from pursuing what was a superior method of ship propulsion compared with the paddle. Technology was much the same in terms of engine design and construction but the final drive to the propeller shaft taxed the engineers of the day. As with the engines themselves, different people had different ideas but screw propulsion engines of the early 1850s were still much like paddle engines with some means of speed increase incorporated in the final drive. Although Brunel had a preference for a chain drive the gear wheel system was adopted by most engineers because it was simpler to construct.

In 1845 the Admiralty ordered the screw propelled yacht *Fairy* from Ditchburn of Blackwall to replace the former paddle-driven Royal Yacht which was then considered too slow. Initially the Admiralty raised objections to Ditchburn's proposal for the use of a screw but he was eventually ordered to 'do things his own way, but to keep the matter a secret.' The need for secrecy is difficult to understand as screw propulsion was a fact even if it had not been widely adopted. Ditchburn employed a two-cylinder oscillating engine driving an overhead crankshaft which connected to the propeller shaft by means of gearing, the large diameter main gear wheel being cast with five radial arms.[9]

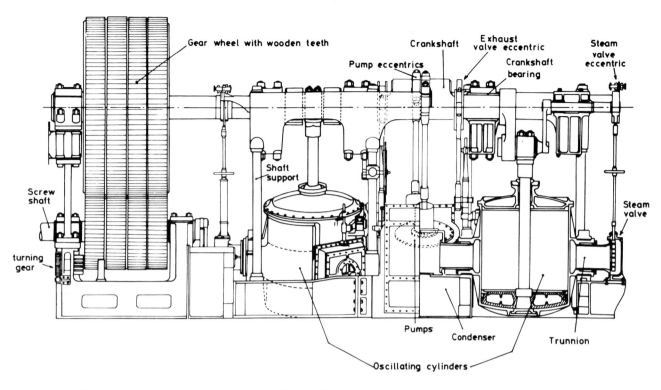

3.1 Geared oscillating screw engine fitted in the Cunard ship China *(1862)*

A similar engine system was adopted for the Cunard screw steamer *China* in 1862, Robert Napier building the ship and fitting a two-cylinder geared oscillating engine. The cylinders were 80in diameter and the stroke 5ft 6in, the engine differing little from the geared oscillating engines fitted in screw steamers by a number of builders up to that time. The gear wheels contained four rows of wooden teeth these being less noisy, easier to cut and less of a problem to lubricate than metal teeth; chain drives were never particularly popular with large engines even though the system had worked satisfactory aboard *The Great Britain*. Teeth were fashioned individually and bolted to the gear wheels but those fitted in *China* did wear at an alarming rate and had to be replaced frequently. Such problems with transmission systems prompted development of direct-drive engines in merchant ships; direct-drive horizontal engines had been employed in naval ships for many years because of the need to keep the engine below the waterline (see Chapter 5).

The main difference, apart from size, in the machinery for *China* compared with that built by Ditchburn was the reintroduction of the surface condenser. As the use of steam power at sea increased during the 1850s it became obvious that a reduction in coal consumption was required in order that vessels could make longer voyages, increase their carrying capacity, or both. Expansive working of steam had shown that improvements were possible and experiments with compound operation had been tried without great

success thus a number of engineers felt that coal could be saved by blowing down the boilers less frequently. With salt water feed the salinity of the water in the boiler had to be controlled in order to minimise scale formation and this was achieved by frequent blow down, the water in the boiler being replaced by water of lower salinity from the hot-well. Jet condenser operation relied upon sea water spray to condense the exhaust steam and so feed water, taken from the hot-well, contained salt. Hall had shown that the surface condenser allowed fresh water to be used in the boiler with consequent improvement in thermal efficiency owing to the fact that hot fresh water from the hot-well was pumped into the boiler with none being discharged overboard. There was less need for boiler blow down, but a reserve supply of fresh water had to be carried on board to serve as make-up feed in order to make good for the leakage of steam and water from the system.

During the late 1850s a number of engine builders re-invented the surface condenser, with Edward Humphrys of Humphrys, Tennant & Dykes being a driving force. In 1859 he decided to fit surface condensers in the 1,734ihp two-cylinder, direct-acting, horizontal engine his firm was building for the P&O steamer *Mooltan*, the primary intention being to improve fuel economy. Additional advantages were expected from increased boiler durability and a reduction in time required for boiler cleaning. The boilers in the ship had a total heating surface of 4,800ft^2 while the condenser had a cooling surface of 4,200ft²; the large cooling surface area and the consequent large capacity of the circulating pumps were considered essential as the ship would be operating in the Indian Ocean where sea temperatures were relatively high. Humphrys arranged his condenser in the same way as Hall had with steam passing through the tubes and water surrounding them, packed glands being used at the ends of the tubes in order to seal them into the tube plates and so minimise the risk of leakage. After steaming 30,000 miles the condensers in *Mooltan* were inspected and showed no signs of leakage with only a slight build-up of grease deposits on the tube surfaces.[10]

During the 1860s surface condensers became increasingly popular, but the design changed to one where water passed through the tubes and exhaust steam surrounded them, this arrangement proving less prone to blockage by grease contained in the steam. The reasons for boiler corrosion when fresh water was used were not fully understood until later in the nineteenth century when effective chemical treatment was introduced. However, the problem of corrosion was recognised during the early 1860s and there were many who preferred to stay with the jet condenser for that reason.[11]

Another popular form of geared engine was based upon the beam engine turned sideways in the ship and, again, the idea was used by a number of builders. One of the first such installations was by the Clydeside shipbuilder Todd & MacGregor who in 1849 laid down a 1,600-ton iron steamer on their own account in the hope that a buyer would be forthcoming before its completion; this was a common practice when orders were difficult to obtain as it kept the shipyard's skilled workforce together. *City of Glasgow* did not find a buyer and the builder put her on the Greenock to New York service in 1850 until she was sold to the then recently established Inman Line later that year. The ship's overhead beam engine had two 66in bore by 5ft stroke cylinders, each connected to its own beam, the other end of which drove the crankshaft by means of a connecting rod. The piston rod crosshead ran in a guide of similar form to that used for steeple engines and the cylinder connecting rod was rather small. In addition to transmitting power from the cylinder to the propeller shaft via the gear wheels, the overhead beams also operated a number of pumps including the air pump. Cylinders were positioned on the starboard side of the ship and the crankshaft on the port, the propeller shaft with its gear wheel was situated slightly to port of the column supporting the beam bearings. A system of levers drove each of the cylinder slide valves, these being actuated by a crankshaft driven eccentrically. At this time the jet condenser was still the accepted means of dealing with exhaust steam and for this engine it was fitted within the support structure for crankshaft, propeller shaft and beam bearing column.[12]

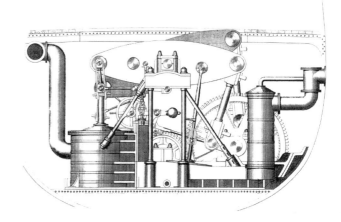

3.3 *Geared beam screw engine, 76in bore by 5ft 5in stroke, built by J. & G. Thomson for the steamer* Jura *(1855)*

The geared beam engine was popular with a number of builders and shipping companies who, in general, preferred to standardise on a particular type of engine in order to ensure that as many engineers as possible were familiar with the installed machinery. Cunard had a number of its early screw steamers fitted with these engines, the first being *Andes* of 1852 which had a single cylinder engine (66in bore by 4ft 6in stroke) constructed by the shipbuilder William Denny & Co. of Dumbarton. One of the last of the type installed in a Cunard ship went into the 2,241-ton *Jura* built in 1855 by J. & G. Thomson & Co. of Glasgow, this two-cylinder engine (76in bore by 5ft 5in stroke) being similar to the type built by Tod & MacGregor except that a parallel motion mechanism was used to guide the piston rod crossheads.[13]

Geared oscillating and beam engines were essentially

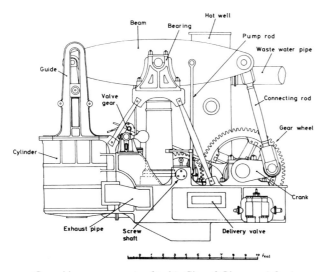

3.2 *Geared beam screw engine fitted in* City of Glasgow *(1849)*

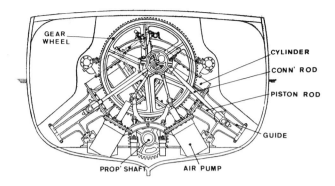

3.4 Trunk geared engine with inclined cylinders built by Scott & Sinclair in 1853 for the steamer Clyde

paddle engines turned through 90° with the result that the engine room length was larger than might otherwise be required for a differently designed engine of similar cylinder size. A design produced by Scott & Sinclair of Greenock in 1853 was different from most others of the period and showed a saving in length compared with other engines of similar power. Designed by George W. Jaffey and installed in the 1,190-ton iron screw steamer *Clyde*, this two-cylinder engine was only 12ft 6in long although the cylinders were 52in diameter with a stroke of 3ft 9in. The inclined cylinders were positioned close to the crankshaft with their piston rods acting downwards thus allowing for the fitting of long connecting rods. Each cylinder had two piston rods which bolted to a long crosshead running in two guides mounted at the sides of its cylinder cover. There was no actual crankshaft but the connecting rods, one at each end of the crosshead, attached to crankpins fitted in the ends of a pair of large spur gear wheels; these were located at each end of the engine with their centres along a common axis. The forward connecting rods from each cylinder were attached to the crankpin in the forward gear wheel while the after pair had a similar connection to the after main gear wheel. Main gear wheels drove the propeller through small pinions keyed to the screw shaft situated between and below the cylinders, the gear ratio being 2.5:1.

Trunk-type air pumps, bolted at their lower ends to the engine sole plate and at their upper ends to each other, were driven from an extension of the forward gear wheel crankpin. Because the air pump stroke was less than that of the main pistons an eccentric drive system was used for the air pumps in order to reduce the effective crank throw. Levers connected to the air pump rods operated bilge and feed pumps. The jet condenser occupied a position between and below the cylinders, acting as a support for the cylinders. Positioned between the cylinder and the gear wheels were the valve mechanisms for each cylinder, the drive for these being by means of eccentrics attached to the main gear wheels. Following a few voyages to New York *Clyde* became

a troopship during the war in the Crimea and then returned to the north Atlantic but was lost on the coast of Labrador in 1857.[14]

As already mentioned, the problem of gearing wear and the difficulty encountered in cutting effective gearing, together with the loss of efficiency owing to the gearing, encouraged the development and installation of direct-acting engines in commercial ships. Initially horizontal engines of the type used for naval steamers were also fitted in merchant ships because they were readily available from engine builders who made such machinery for Admiralty vessels. John Penn of Greenwich and Humphrys, Tennant & Dykes of Deptford were favoured suppliers of horizontal screw engines but they, and others, also produced the same type of machinery for mercantile steamers. P&O obtained a number of the horizontal, simple expansion, direct-acting type. Penn supplied an 84in bore by 3ft 6in stroke two-cylinder engine of this type for *Himalaya* (1853) and the 2,500ihp developed at 55rpm gave the ship a speed in excess of 13 knots making her one of the fastest steamers of the day. Originally the ship was fitted with a cast iron stern tube but wear was so excessive that within a few months lignum vitae bearings were adopted, these having been patented by John Penn only a few months earlier.[15] Among the last such engines ordered for a P&O ship were those from Humphry, Tennant & Dykes for *Mooltan* and *Rangoon* (1863). After this time vertical direct-acting engines became more popular as did compounding.

Horizontal engines were an interesting concept in terms of merchant shipping because there was generally no height restriction. However, they had been proved in naval ships and they were direct acting which avoided the use of gearing or chain drives. Brunel had certainly had no height restriction in *Great Eastern* (1858) but the power required, about 7,500ihp, to drive the ship at its design speed was far in excess of any engine then in service. By adopting a

3.5 Horizontal screw engine built by James Watt & Co. for the Great Eastern

combined screw and paddle propulsion system with the screw machinery developing about two-thirds of the power it was possible to design engines of reasonable size; the idea of employing twin screws was considered impracticable. James Watt & Co. built the four-cylinder screw engine for *Great Eastern*, the cylinders being 84in diameter and 4ft stroke, opposing cylinders having their connecting rods attached to the same crank pins in a rather unusual way. All pistons had single piston rods and crosshead; the starboard side cylinders had single connecting rods but those on the port side had twin connecting rods with a port side connecting rod attached to the crank pin on each side of the opposing starboard connecting rod. Stephenson link motion was used to actuate the slide valves, allowing for expansive working and for reversing. Each cylinder had it own jet condenser mounted adjacent to it and alongside the companion cylinder on that side of the ship. The engine weighed 500 tons and took steam at a pressure of 25psi, developing about 5,000ihp at a speed of 39rpm although the designed maximum speed was 45rpm.[16] Interesting though this machinery is it was unique and not part of mainstream marine engineering development; engines of this type taxed the skills of the designer and the resources of the manufacturer but they added little to marine engineering evolution apart

from any new or enhanced processes they may have required the builder to develop.

Brunel had intended to employ steam jacketing of the cylinders in order to reduce steam loss through condensation, but the engine builder objected on the grounds that it would be difficult to core the cylinder casting to provide for a steam jacket space. The concept of steam jacketing was becoming popular at the time from the belief that it saved steam and so increased operating efficiency when working expansively. As steam expanded in a cylinder the temperature of the steam and the cylinder walls fell: the greater the degree of expansion the lower the temperature. When steam was admitted to the cylinder on the other side of the piston it would encounter cylinder walls much colder than itself and steam in contact with the wall would condense thus being unavailable to produce power. A number of engineers believed that by supplying steam to a space surrounding the cylinder wall the temperature of that wall could be maintained high enough to prevent condensation and so maintain power development. The concept was certainly correct but the potential for saving energy depended upon a number of factors, including the temperature range in the cylinder (governed by the degree of expansion used), the initial steam pressure, the cylinder diameter and the

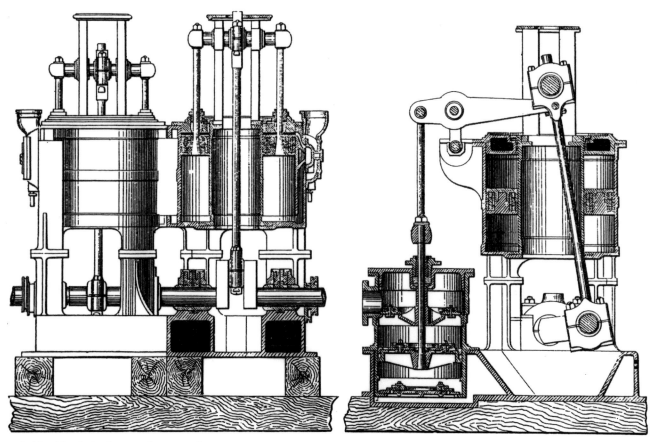

3.6 Maudslay design for a trunk screw engine

amount of lagging around the cylinder. Over the next four decades engineers argued about the effectiveness or otherwise of steam jacketing, but eventually opinion favoured no steam jacketing but adequate lagging and even the use of superheated or 'dried' steam.

The limited width of many merchant ships presented problems with respect to the fitting of direct-drive, horizontal engines and the real solution as far as most engine builders were concerned was the vertical arrangement. Some paddle engine designs could be readily modified to such an arrangement and in 1845 Joseph Maudslay proposed an annular screw engine based upon his paddle design. Because of the annular arrangement of the cylinder each piston had two rods which attached to the ends of a crosshead running in vertical guides mounted on the upper cylinder cover. Attached to the centre of the crosshead was the upper end of the connecting rod, the lower end connecting with a crankpin on the crankshaft. To allow for this arrangement there was a fixed trunk down the centre of the cylinder, hence the annular piston. Cylinders were erected on a cast bedplate which also supported the crankshaft. In theory, any number of cylinders could be mounted in line on the bedplate but generally there were only two. A lever attached to one of the piston crossheads operated an air pump and other pumps mounted alongside the cylinder and above the jet condenser. Advantages claimed for this engine design were the use of long connecting rods and accessible piston-rod glands placed in the top cylinder cover.[17]

A small, two-cylinder engine of this type was fitted in the 330-ton yacht *Hebe* in 1856[18] but there appear to have been few other installations despite the advantages of the design. Due to the annular design, the cylinder diameter had to be larger than in other engines of similar power, which possibly led to casting difficulties with the high-powered engines needed in the 1850s.

Tall engines presented no installation problems for merchant ships and as the 1850s progressed a number of engine builders produced designs for inverted direct-drive engines. Cylinders of an inverted engine were mounted on supports bolted to the bedplate, the piston rod of each cylinder passing through its lower cylinder cover and connecting with a crosshead running in guides attached to the cylinder supports. Single connecting rods from each crosshead transmitted power to the crankshaft below the cylinder. Levers from crossheads actuated several pumps while the condenser was generally located alongside the bedplate. This arrangement remained much the same for subsequent direct-drive reciprocating screw engines until the type ceased to be employed at sea.

In 1846 Caird & Co. of Greenock constructed an engine of this type for the coastal steamer *Northman* but details of the design are unknown. However, the advantages of the vertical inverted engine for mercantile work were easy to see

and many other builders produced similar designs over the next decade. J. & G. Thomson were to the fore in this and during the early 1850s installed a two-cylinder engine, 40in bore by 2ft 9in stroke, in *Frankfort*, the machinery design being described by John Bourne as 'simple, compact, and substantial, and on the whole a very eligible class of engines for merchant vessels.' For this installation the square condenser was fitted between the cylinders with the air pumps, driven by levers from the cylinder crossheads, and the hot well located alongside the engine.[19] By the time Thomsons had built a similar but larger engine, 56in bore by 3ft stroke, for *Laconia* in 1856 the design was well established because it was 'easily made and has few working parts'; those engines in service had given satisfactorily results.[20]

By the late 1850s most of the large marine engine builders were constructing inverted direct-acting screw engines, with the Scottish builders particularly establishing a reputation for this type of machinery. Many engine builders, especially those on the Thames, still offered and sold horizontal and geared engines for which there was a continuing market in commercial shipping as well as for naval steamers.[21] In 1854, at about the same time that Thomsons were working on their design, Scott and Sinclair made a three-cylinder inverted, direct-acting engine for the Canadian Steamship Company's 305ft long *Oneida*. Cylinders were 58in diameter by 3ft stroke with slide valves worked by a link motion driven by eccentrics. Controversy remained as to which was the better type of engine, geared or direct drive, and after only a short while *Oneida* was re-engined by A. & J. Inglis with a two-cylinder geared trunk

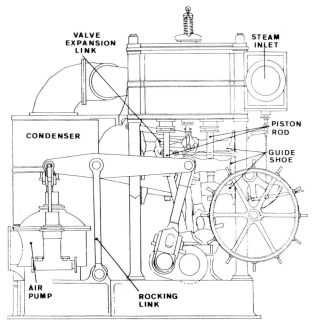

3.7 Three-cylinder inverted screw engine built by Scott & Sinclair in 1854 for Oneida

engine, the cylinders being of 82.5in bore and 4ft 6in stroke. It is not known whether the original engine developed defects, but Ebenezer Kemp, who worked at Scotts as a draughtsman when it was constructed and as chief draughtsman with Inglis when the replacement was ordered, considered that re-engining was the result of prejudice against the inverted direct-acting type. Kemp believed that seagoing engineers of the time preferred the slow rotating geared engine to the higher speed, direct-acting type and it was this partiality which ensured that geared engines were built until the mid-1860s.[22]

Despite the fact that some owners insisted upon geared engines builders still continued with the design of inverted, direct-acting engines, confident that the future of marine engineering lay with this form. In 1857 the Glasgow ship-

developed with early compound machinery. Many of the problems related to the boilers generating steam at higher pressure. Even the shipowner and marine engineer Alfred Holt, an early advocate of compound engines, had his doubts about their use in certain trades. In 1877 he stated that simple expansion beam engines still used in American paddle boats were almost as fuel efficient as the best compound engines made in Britain, adding 'it is matter of reasonable speculation, whether the compound engine may not yet be abandoned, and a return made to the single cylinder engine modified in details to suit high-pressure steam.'[23]

Britain remained the major shipbuilding and marine engineering nation throughout the 1860s, and, although European countries were developing such industries of

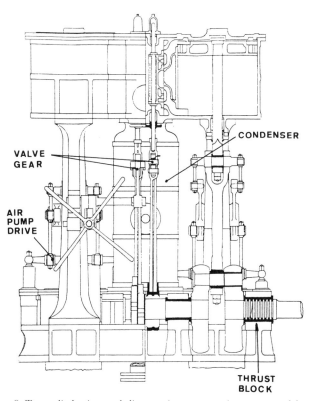

3.8 Two-cylinder inverted direct-acting screw engine constructed by John Barr of Glasgow for Sligo *(1857)*

builder John Barr constructed a two-cylinder, inverted direct-acting engine for the screw steamer *Sligo* but by that time expansion of steam in two stages had been accepted and the days of the simple expansion engine were numbered; however, the inverted, direct-acting arrangement was to prove the most suitable for use with compounding.

Although the fuel saving advantages of compound expansion were evident some owners still insisted upon simple expansion engines because of problems that

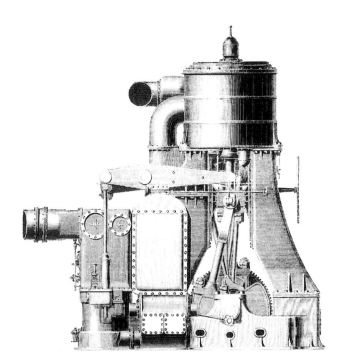

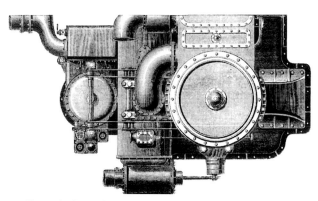

3.9 Two-cylinder surface condensing engine built by Robert Napier in 1866 for the French liners Pereire *and* Ville de Paris

3.10 Front view of the Napier engine for Pereire

their own, most still came to British yards for ships and engines. In 1866 the Compagnie Generale Transatlantique placed an order with Robert Napier & Sons for two 3,227-ton screw steamers *Pereire* and *Ville de Paris*. Two-cylinder, inverted simple expansion engines with surface condensers were fitted, these being among the last large engines of the type installed in passenger liners for service on the Atlantic. The 84in diameter by 4ft stroke cylinders were supported on hollow 'A'-frames which also located the guide bars. The large box-shaped surface condenser extended the whole length of the engine, cooling water passing through the condenser tubes and steam surrounding them. Air and other pumps were driven by levers from the crossheads, a feature which became standard with the inverted engine.[24]

Britain turned to iron steamship construction before the USA for a number of reasons including the shortage of

suitable timber. But wooden ships remained the norm in American waters and there was thus a tendency for paddle drives to be retained. Some ship and engine builders did make moves towards the use of the screw propeller but the advances were not as rapid as in Britain while the Civil War limited much development during the 1860s and the succeeding decade. Where screw propulsion was employed machinery tended to be of the same general type as that produced by British builders, although the use of geared machinery died out sooner as the direct-acting engine found favour. The American shipbuilding and marine engineering industries expanded to meet local demands but occasionally ships were still built in Britain if American yards were unable to supply them for some reason. In 1857 Randolf & Elder of Govan supplied a two-cylinder, geared beam engine, 60in bore by 4ft stroke, for the auxiliary screw steamer *Circassian* which had been built in Belfast.[25] Generally, however, American-owned vessels were constructed in the USA and fitted with machinery designed and built in American workshops.

Inverted direct-acting engines became popular during the early 1850s with Reaney, Neafie & Co. of Philadelphia being early builders. The vertical trunk engine was designed by C.W. Copeland for the West Point Foundry which installed two-cylinder versions in the wooden steamers *Pioneer* and *City of Pittsburg* during 1851. This engine was based upon the Penn horizontal trunk engine extensively used in Britain for naval screw steamers; cylinders were 85.5in bore with the trunk bore 39in while pistons had a stroke of 4ft 3in.[26] This arrangement allowed the cylinders to be arranged vertically but enabled the height to be kept low, although for merchant ships tall engines were not a particular problem. Even with horizontal engines, cabins or cargo could not be located above the engine room as there had to be an opening above the machinery for ventilation and, especially, illumination through a skylight. When owners realised that the inverted cylinder engine saved on engine-room floor space, thus allowing for more cargo, cabins or coal, and when prejudices against the design were overcome, inverted cylinders arranged vertically above the crankshaft were the norm for screw propulsion until the advent of the turbine.

References

1   R. Gardiner and B. Greenhill (eds.), *The Advent of Steam*, Conway Maritime Press, London, 1993, Chapters 4 and 7.

2   E. C. Smith, *A Short History of Marine Engineering*, Cambridge University Press, 1937, pp. 78–9.

3   D. Griffiths, *Power of the Great Liners*, Patrick Stephens, Sparkford, 1990, pp. 65–7.

4   T. Guppy, 'The Steamship *Great Britain*', *Proc. Inst. of Civil Engineers*, No. 4, 1845, pp. 160–61.

5   J. Bourne, *A Treatise on the Steam Engine*, Longmans, Green, London, 1876, p. 323.

6   E. Corlett, *The Iron Ship*, Moonraker Press, Bradford on Avon, 1975, p. 54.

7   *The Engineer*, vol. 87, 24 Sept. 1897, p. 298.

8   T. Guppy, 'The Steamship *Great Britain*', pp. 151–85.

9   *The Engineer*, vol. 87, 29 Oct. 1897, p. 416.

10 E. Humphrys, 'On Surface Condensation in Marine Engines', *Proc. I.Mech.E.*, 1862, pp. 99–104.

11 J.F. Spencer, 'On the Mechanical and Economical Advantages and Disadvantages of Surface Condensation', *Trans. I.E.S.S.*, vol. 5, 1861–2, pp. 74–6.

12 A. J. Maginnis, *The Atlantic Ferry*, Whittaker, London, 1893, pp. 46–9.

13 J. Bourne, *A Treatise on the Steam Engine*, p. 319.

14 E. Kemp, Presidential Address, *Trans. I.E.S.S.*, vol. 34, 1890–91.

15 *Marine Engineer & Motorship Builder*, vol. 52, Sept. 1929, p. 384.

16 R. G. Fuller, 'The *Great Eastern*' Canadian Supplement to *Transactions I.Mar.E.*, vol. 6, 1961, p. 136.

17 *The Engineer*, vol. 87, 5 Nov. 1897, p. 448.

18 H. P. Spratt, *Marine Engineering Science Museum Catalogue*, HMSO, London, 1953, p. 40.

19 J. Bourne, *A Treatise on the Steam Engine*, p. 314.

20 Ibid., p. 319.

21 S. Rabson and K. O'Donoghue, *P&O: A Fleet History*, World Ship Society, Kendal, 1988, pp. 53–64. Ships built between 1857 and 1863 for this major shipping company were fitted with a wide variety of simple expansion engines from several manufacturers.

22 E. Kemp, I.E.S.S. Presidential address, pp. 8–10.

23 Alfred Holt, 'Review of the Progress of Steam Shipping during the Last Quarter of a Century', *Proc. Inst. of Civil Engineers*, vol. 51, Part 1, 1877–8, p. 5.

24 *Engineering*, vol. 2, 31 Aug. 1866, p. 156.

25 C. Ridgely-Nevitt, *American Steamships on the Atlantic*, University of Delaware Press, Newark, 1981, pp. 286–7.

26 Ibid., p. 192.

4
Compound Marine Engines

Early steam engines used steam essentially as a means of obtaining a vacuum, atmospheric pressure acting on the opposite side of the piston effectively producing the work. All that was required in such cases was a steam supply which would force air from the cylinder and any steam pressure just above atmospheric would do that. During the latter part of the eighteenth century and the early decades of the nineteenth little theoretical study into thermodynamics or the properties of steam took place and steam engines were generally developed in the absence of this knowledge. The idea of expanding steam in a number of stages, compounding, goes back to the time of James Watt and one of the first advocates of the idea was Jonathan Hornblower who in 1781 increased the output of an atmospheric beam pump by fitting a high-pressure cylinder alongside the normal, but by now low-pressure, cylinder.[1] The idea found no support until in 1803 Arthur Woolf developed the concept and erected compound engines in both England and France.

Woolf's method of compounding had the exhaust steam from the high-pressure cylinder pass direct to the low-pressure cylinder and required the pistons to reciprocate together, i.e., crank angles had to be 0° or 180° apart. This system lent itself to the tandem arrangement of pistons with the high-pressure (HP) piston directly above, or in some cases below, the low-pressure (LP) piston; as steam exhausted from one side of the HP piston it passed direct to act on the LP piston. The need to have a particular arrangement of crank angles presented problems in some cases and forced the fitting of a large flywheel in order to obtain an even turning of the engine. It was also considered that problems in starting would result if the engine came to rest with the pistons at the top or bottom of their strokes. An alternative compounding arrangement which overcame these problems was to fit a steam receiver between the HP and the LP cylinders into which HP exhaust steam passed before being directed to the LP cylinder. In most cases the receiver was simply the steam pipe connecting the two valve chests, but it acted as a reservoir for the steam which could be used by the LP cylinder as required; this enabled cranks to be positioned to give the best turning moment while also allowing for smoother operation and easier starting.

Now that we have looked at the two general systems of compounding it is worth spending some time considering what compounding is and why it was employed. In Chapter 3 it was shown that as steam expanded the cylinder temperature fell and some of the steam on the next stroke condensed on the cylinder wall thus reducing efficiency.

Compounding reduced the degree of expansion which would take place in a cylinder, hence it also reduced the temperature range and so minimised losses due to condensation. With low-pressure steam there was a limit to how far the steam could expand but for higher pressures, above about 50psi, the expansion range increased thus making multiple expansion an economic necessity; at higher pressure more energy is stored in a unit mass of steam hence less water is needed for the same amount of work output and boilers can be smaller. Theoretically the same amount of work should be obtained by expanding steam from the same pressure in a single stage or a number of stages provided that condensation can be avoided. If expansion from higher pressure took place in a single cylinder either steam would have to be cut off from the cylinder very early to get the required degree of expansion or the length of piston stroke would have to be increased. The former could present problems in terms of valve control while the latter would result in a tall engine and crankshaft manufacturing difficulties. By arranging for the steam to expand in a number of stages construction and operational problems may be reduced, although the cost of the engine will increase owing to the additional parts required.

From the initial application of compounding to ship propulsion during the 1830s until the late 1870s, when Alfred Holt speculated that the compound engine might even then be abandoned in favour of simple expansion, there was considerable discussion among marine engineers and shipowners as to the effectiveness or otherwise of compounding. In 1881 Holt actually abandoned his design of single crank tandem compound engine and used a single cylinder engine with high-pressure steam to drive one of his ships but he soon returned to compounding.[2] Unfortunately, the efficiency of a compound engine does not depend just upon the engine; the boiler and condensers are important parts of any steam plant. Compounding is only efficient when steam at pressures in excess of about 40psi are available and such pressures required strong boilers which were unlikely to fail in service. Salt scale from the use of jet condensing caused boiler problems and the use of fresh water feed, made possible by the reintroduction of the surface condenser, allowed the internal surfaces of boilers to be kept scale-free. Boilers will be discussed in Chapter 5 but it should be appreciated here that higher pressures were only possible through the availability of stronger materials and better design, but corrosion problems took some time to overcome.

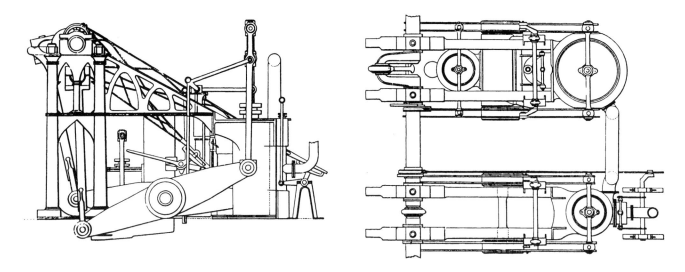

4.1 *Roentgen compound engine design of 1834, based upon a patent granted to Wolff*

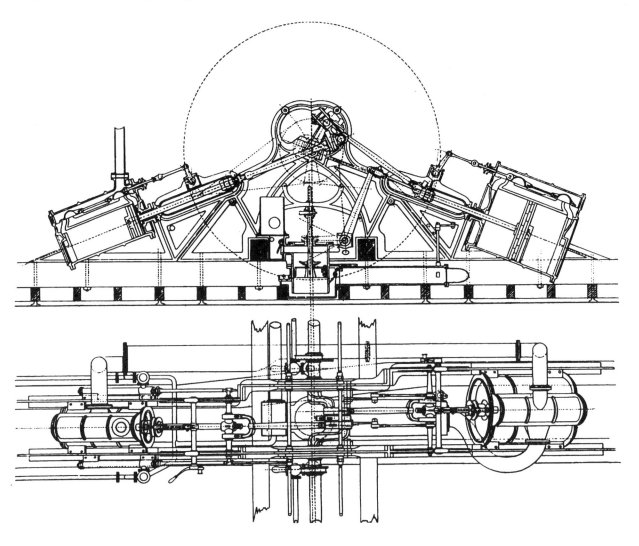

4.2 *Compound engine installed in the* Kronprinz von Preussen *(1835)*

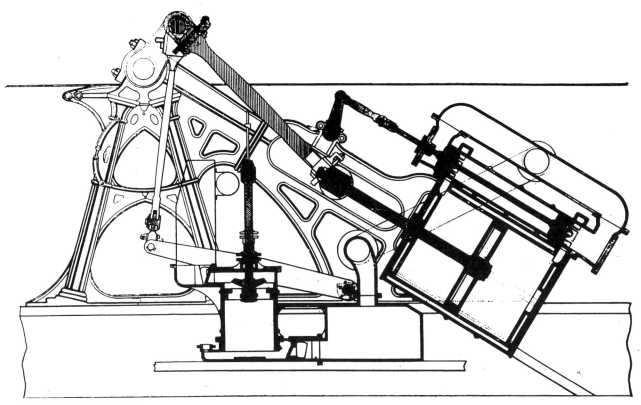

4.3 Diagonal compound engine installed in Batavia *(1840)*

Possibly the first compound marine propulsion engine in service was that fitted in the paddle steamer *James Watt* when she was re-engined in 1829 and named *Stad Keulen*. Her original two-cylinder, geared lever engine was replaced by a two-cylinder, compound, direct-acting engine, the diagonal HP cylinder being positioned in the engine room and the horizontal LP cylinder on deck. The 54in diameter LP piston also powered the air pump piston, connected to it in tandem.[3] Another steamer re-engined with compound machinery at about the same time was *Hercules*, originally built in 1826 for service on the Rhine and the Maas and owned by the Nederlandsche Stoomboot Maatschappij (Netherlands Steamboat Company). Conversion to compounding saw the retention of the original pair of 20in diameter horizontal cylinders, which drove the paddle shaft through gearing, now the high-pressure cylinders, and the fitting of a direct-drive, low-pressure cylinder, 54in diameter, directly beneath the paddle shaft. Steam at pressures between 70 and 80psi was obtained from a drum-type boiler.[4]

Several other Dutch steamers were fitted with compound machinery during the 1830s, the machinery being devised by Gerard Maurits Roentgen, a Dutchman of German origin and founder of the Netherlands Steamboat Company, the engines being constructed at the company's works. Roentgen obtained a number of European patents but Ernst Wolff , Roentgen's British agent, took out British

Patent No. 6600 (1834) for a compound engine. All of the patents dealt with improvements in the basic compound engine operation, but Roentgen introduced the use of a receiver, under the name of a reservoir, and admission of high-pressure steam to low-pressure cylinders to assist starting. Compound engines fitted to Dutch vessels of the period include the two-cylinder diagonal arrangements installed in *Kronprinz Von Preussen* (1835) and *Batavia* (1840).[5]

One of the earliest Woolf compound marine engines constructed in Britain went into the small Thames steamer *Cricket* as referred to in Chapter 3. It is not necessary to repeat the description but mention should be made of the steam generating plant. Two tubular boilers supplied steam at a pressure of 20psi, there being between 60 and 70 tubes, about 2in in diameter. Boiler shells were made from iron plate 0.375in thick, while tube plates were 0.75in thick. During a trip at the end of September 1847, after the vessel had been in service for a year, the starboard boiler exploded killing seventeen people and injuring a further sixty. The cause was attributed to an overloaded safety valve which resulted in excessive pressure causing a badly fitted longitudinal stay to fail.[6] Incidents like this did not endear the public to steamships and certainly put back the cause of higher steam pressures.

While boiler explosions were spectacular demonstrations

of the power of steam it was not these alone which held back development of the compound engine; economics were just as important, perhaps more so. Compound engines cost more per unit of output power because they required two-cylinders and associated fittings to develop the same power as could be produced by a single, simple expansion cylinder. That additional capital cost, together with the additional operating and maintenance costs, could only be recovered from savings in coal consumption, but if coal was relatively cheap it took a long time for the shipowner to break even. Ships operating around British or European coasts could obtain supplies of cheap coal while steamers operating around or on the American coasts or rivers had ample supplies of wood or coal. Oceanic operations offered a better prospect for cost recovery but Atlantic steamers could also obtain plentiful supplies of coal on each side of the ocean. Compound marine engines were only likely to be an economic proposition if fuel was difficult to obtain and its cost was high or if compounding could show large savings compared with the simple expansion engine of equivalent power. It was in the former regard that compounding obtained its main breakthrough but it was not simply a case of wishing for an idea to be realised, practical engineering was involved.

Higher powers and compounding required larger diameter LP cylinders and their casting posed problems, particularly if steam jacketing was to be incorporated. Castings with steam jackets were complex as a great many cores had to be provided for in the mould and the more complex the mould the greater the risk of a defect in the final casting. In order to reduce the risk of defective castings and simplify the making of patterns and moulds a number of engine builders adopted the idea of the separate cylinder liner sitting in a cylinder block. Component manufacture was easier and less problematic and the steam jacket was provided by the space between the cylinder liner and the block in which it sat. There was an additional advantage in that excessive cylinder wear required only the liner to be replaced and not the entire cylinder casting. In 1855 the Ramsbottom piston ring was introduced and that provided a much more satisfactory means of sealing the piston in the cylinder than packed hemp or the methods previously employed. Adoption of these piston rings allowed higher steam pressures to be employed as they sealed the piston against the cylinder wall much more effectively than earlier methods had and with less rubbing.

In 1853 Charles Randolf and John Elder, partners in the Govan shipbuilders Randolf & Elder, patented a compound engine for screw propulsion, and the following year fitted a compound engine of the Woolf type in the steamer *Brandon*. The real breakthrough came two years later when the Pacific Steam Navigation Company (PSNC) decided to have two of its new paddle steamers *Inca* and *Valparaiso*

fitted with compound machinery. These engines were of the four-cylinder diagonal type, two HP and two LP opposite cylinders connecting with the same crankpins. Although the steam pressure was only about 25psi fuel consumption was good, 2.5 to 3lbs per ihp per hour, so good that it encouraged the owners to bring three of their other steamers, *Lima*, *Bogota* and *Callao*, back from the west coast of South America to be fitted with compound engines. These had jet condensers and relatively low-pressure but the fuel consumption of *Bogota* fell by some 50 per cent following re-engining. When surface condensers were adopted by Elders in 1860 and steam pressure was raised to 40psi coal consumption fell to about 2.25lbs per ihp per hr.[7]

Similar problems with respect to the availability and cost of coal were to be found in the Indian Ocean and P&O became the second major steamship operator to adopt compounding for its new construction and re-engining. Samuda Brothers of Poplar built *Carnatic* in 1863, but her 2,442ihp four-cylinder compound engine was constructed by Humphreys, Tennant & Dykes. Cylinders were arranged in a tandem manner, each 43in diameter HP cylinder being positioned above a 96in diameter LP cylinder thus requiring a crankshaft with two cranks. Steam jackets were used for all cylinders but only two sets of valve gear were fitted, one for each tandem pair. Steam pressure was 26psi, typical for the period, although a form of superheating was used to dry the steam and this arrangement proved effective as coal consumption amounted to only 2lbs per ihp per hr.[8] Evidently the company was happy with compound engine operation on its long haul service, particularly in the Indian Ocean, as by 1866 there were ten compound engined steamers in the fleet.

The concept of compounding had been known for many years and so could not be protected by patent; however, particular component designs and cylinder arrangements could, and builders adopted their own ideas in order to avoid the infringement of patents. The connecting of cylinders in tandem was free from patent protection and engine builders could make use of the idea in whatever way they liked, provided that they did not infringe patents which might exist on individual components. During the 1860s and the 1870s many patents were taken out by individuals in order to protect the designs of engine parts but the blanket coverage of a general concept, such as existed when Watt held the patent for a separate condenser, was no longer available. This period saw the rapid development of designs and improvements in performance as the advantages to be gained from higher steam pressures were appreciated. A number of designers adopted tandem cylinders as this enabled the engine length to be minimised and output power could be increased by adding another tandem pair rather than by increasing cylinder bores or stroke. A limiting factor on engine power during those early years of compounding was

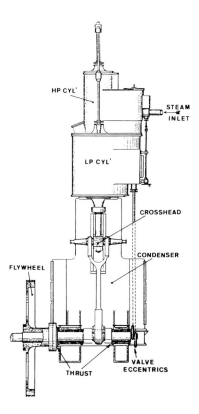

4.4 Holt's single-crank compound engine of 1864

the strength of the crankshaft and it was only with the introduction of higher quality steel that high output powers became possible.

Alfred Holt was a shipowner but he was also an engineer and understood the advantages to be gained from compounding on long voyages. If less coal was consumed the ship could go further on a particular tonnage of bunkers or more cargo could be carried for a particular length of voyage; in addition it would be possible to reduce the engine room complement if less coal was burned with the consequent savings in ship operation. Holt also believed that he could design a compound engine which would suit his needs rather than accept what a builder had to offer and in 1864 he fitted his own tandem design of engine in *Cleator*, the only ship he and his brother Philip retained after selling their West Indies trade ships. Operation of this ship convinced Holt that ships of that size fitted with compound machinery could operate successfully in the China trade, which before the opening of the Suez Canal involved a long 8,500-miles trip around Africa before bunker supplies could be obtained at Mauritius. The engine fitted in *Cleator* had its HP cylinder located below the LP, piston rods attaching to a common crosshead located between the cylinders. Two connecting rods, running each side of the HP cylinder and joined at their lower ends, attached to a single crankpin on the crankshaft.[9] Successful operation of *Cleator* encouraged

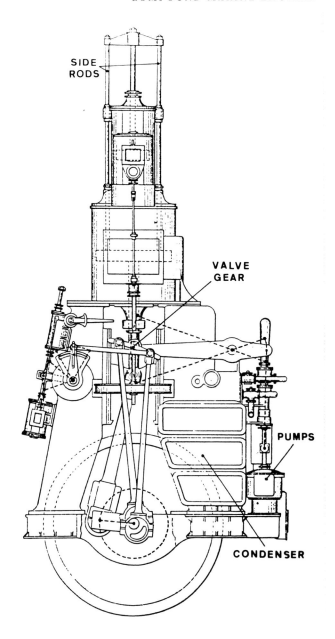

4.5 Holt's tandem compound engine used for Agamemnon-*class ships in 1864*

Holt and later in 1864 he ordered three 2,280-ton ships *Agamemnon*, *Ajax* and *Achilles* and had them fitted with tandem compound engines to a modified design and operating with a steam pressure of 60psi. The ships were designed for a speed of 10 knots, their engines developing 964ihp on a daily coal consumption of about 22 tons or 2.25lbs/ihp/hr.[10]

These three Holt iron steamers were built by Scotts of Greenock who also constructed the engines (30in bore HP and 62in bore LP by 4ft 4in stroke). The HP cylinder was positioned above the LP, its piston rod passing upwards to a beam from which two side rods extended down to connect with the LP piston. This arrangement required two glands in the upper LP cylinder cover, but it allowed the HP cylinder to be mounted direct on the LP and avoided the need for a piston rod gland between them. A piston rod attached the LP piston to the crosshead, a single connecting rod then driving the crankshaft. Two bearings were provided for the crankshaft and the edges of these acted as thrust bearings, crank web faces and a collar fitted on the propeller shaft transmitting the thrust. The surface condenser contained 420 tubes, 1.5in diameter, the seawater circulating pump being connected at the condenser outlet so that water was effectively sucked through the tubes rather than being forced through.[11, 12]

Without doubt Holt's engine was of good design and well made but others were also making compound engines and the advantages of 'the coal pile' were evident for any shipowner to see. Prejudice still existed but as boilers were pushed to higher pressures those advantages were even more evident. However, economy had to be paid for by increased complexity and, as already mentioned, in the late 1870s and the early 1880s even Alfred Holt had cause to question the continued development of the compound engine. His change of mind regarding compounding centred on a belief that fuel costs were relatively small in relation to total ship operating costs, the additional complexity and cost of the compound engine not being justified for the small improvements obtainable in that area. The opening of the Suez Canal reduced coal consumption for a voyage between Britain and China and so fuel costs as a portion of total operating costs did fall where ships could make use of it. Obviously Holt had figures from his own ships to back his

case and he believed that a simple expansion engine operating at the steam pressures then being used would burn coal at the rate of 2.3lbs/ihp/hr. While that may have been the case, contrary to Holt's opinion, improvements in economy were possible with compound engines and any savings were worth having as, in general, fuel costs amounted to about 18 per cent of total operating. In 1881, arguing against Holt's opinion, F. C. Marshall estimated that a new 2,500-ton cargo steamer would have an annual fuel bill of about £3,000 but ten years earlier, at equal coal prices the bill would have been £750 higher, the saving being equal to a dividend of 3 per cent on the value of the ship.[13]

Over the next ten years Holt's Blue Funnel Line built further steamers with two-cylinder, tandem, compound engines to the same basic design, except that a modified form of crankshaft was employed. In fact, there was no crankshaft as such, merely a cranked axle on the end of the propeller shaft to which was also fitted a shaft for driving the valve gear eccentrics.

Other engine builders favoured the tandem arrangement of cylinders as it allowed for a shorter engine. In 1871 Maudslay, Sons & Field provided a four-cylinder engine of this type for the White Star Line's first Atlantic steamer *Oceanic*, the builder, Harland & Wolff, of Belfast, at that time having no engine building facilities. Maudslays constructed further engines to the same design for two other members of the *Oceanic* class while a fourth was constructed by Forrester & Co. of Liverpool. These propulsion units consisted of twin tandem units comprising a 41in bore HP cylinder above a 78in bore LP, the stroke being 5ft. Unlike the Holt engines, a distance piece separated LP and HP cylinders allowing access to the piston rod glands. Slide

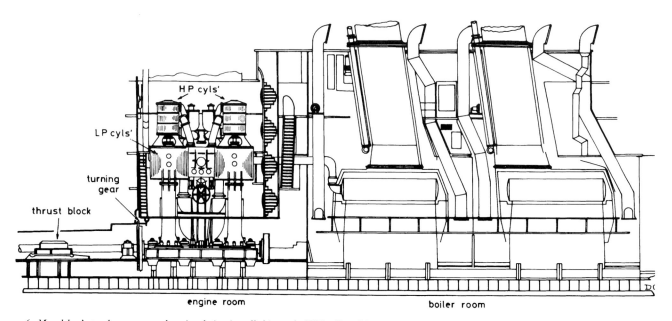

4.6 Maudslay's tandem compound engine design installed in early White Star Line steamers

valves controlled the steam supply to and the exhaust from the cylinders, movement of the link motion for reversing being by means of a steam cylinder. Steam pipes were provided with bellows in order to minimise stress through expansion and contraction. A cylindrical surface condenser was positioned between the cylinders, sea water being provided by an independent pump, driven by a small steam engine, rather than by an engine-driven pump. These engines were capable of developing 2,000ihp from steam at a pressure of 65psi; daily coal consumption was about 60 tons.[14]

The success of the first four liners prompted White Star to construct two larger ships *Britannic* and *Germanic* in 1874, these also receiving Maudslay-built four-cylinder tandem engines but of greater power than the earlier group. HP cylinders were 48in diameter and LP 83in but the stroke remained the same at 5ft. With steam at 70psi these engines could develop more than twice the power of the previous engines, 4,971ihp. Apart from the size, however, and a few minor details the basic engine design was the same as that fitted in *Oceanic*.[15]

The Barrow Shipbuilding Company also favoured the tandem cylinder arrangement on the grounds that power could still be generated with a multiple unit engine, should one group fail for some reason. During the late 1870s the company developed an engine of this type with six cylinders in three tandem groups, each group being considered as a separate engine. In order to allow for this, each pair of cylinders had its own condenser, lever-driven air pump, condensate pump and valve gear. The 43in diameter HP cylinder sat upon the 86in LP (6ft stroke) with access being provided to the piston rod glands between the two cylinders. The first large engine of the type was installed in the Inman Liner *City of Rome* (1881) and worked satisfactorily although the ship itself was not a success on the Atlantic service owing to the fact that she was heavier than intended, having been constructed from iron because of the shortage of steel. Steel was actually used for the engine crankshaft, this being Whitworth compressed steel which was subjected to hydraulic pressure while still molten in order to exclude gases which could produce weak spots. The three engine cranks were positioned at 120° in order to give a smooth rotation with minimal vibration from unbalanced forces. The engine failed to develop the planned 10,000ihp although steam was supplied at the intended 90psi pressure and the ship could not achieve the 18-knot service speed. Inman Line returned *City of Rome* to her builders, who made modifications and eventually sold her to the Anchor Line.[16]

Despite the failure of this ship to achieve her design speed the engine was looked upon as successful particularly

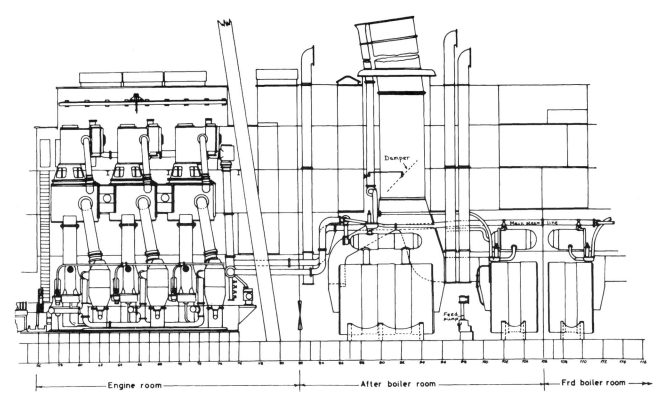

4.7 *Tandem compound engine devised by the Barrow Shipbuilding Company and installed in liners such as* City of Rome *(1881) and* La Normandie *(1883)*

in terms of its relatively high power to length ratio and the apparent security derived from the fact that there were three identical engine units connected to the single crankshaft. In 1883 a similar but slightly smaller, six-cylinder engine was installed in *La Normandie*, built in Barrow for the Compagnie General Transatlantique while four others of the same design were constructed under licence in France. The French engines had 1,007mm bore HP cylinders, 2,003mm bore LP and a stroke of 1,776mm with a power capability of about 9,000ihp from steam at 85psi.[17]

Other builders also adopted tandem designs of their own but they would also build whatever a shipowner wanted. In 1881 Palmers Shipbuilding & Ironworks of Jarrow built engines to a patent of George Allibon, superintendent engineer of the Liverpool shipowners F. Leyland & Co., the engines going into two 4,081-ton Leyland Line ships *Virginian* and *Valencian*. The patent was not new, an engine to the design having been installed in the steamer *Kirkstall* some ten years earlier, and in many respects it was similar to

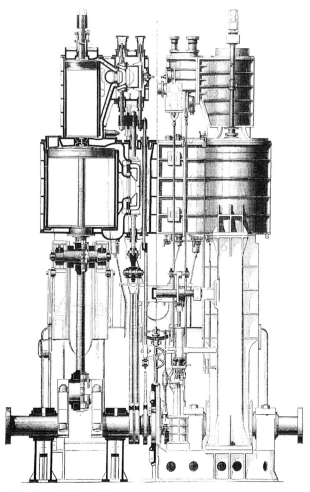

4.8 Palmers-built tandem compound engine to the design of George Allibon and fitted in the Leyland Line vessels Valencian *and* Virginian *during 1881*

that devised by Alfred Holt. HP (29in bore) and LP (62in bore) cylinders were bolted together and the HP piston rod passed upwards to a beam from where two side rods passed through glands in the upper LP cylinder cover to the LP piston. In Allibon's engine these rods continued through glands in the lower LP cylinder cover to the crosshead which was located in two guides. A single connecting rod transmitted power to the crankshaft; the stroke was 5ft and the engine was designed to develop 3,000ihp. The condenser was at the back of the engine and several pumps were operated from the crosshead via levers, the system common to most engines of the period. The steel, double-ended Scotch boilers were provided with cylindrical steam receivers which acted as dryers, thus giving a degree of superheat.[18]

The Barrow-built engine for *City of Rome* was probably the most powerful tandem engine constructed, but in time it appeared that triple-expansion machinery was becoming established and the tandem compound had evolved as far as it would go. The same could also be said for all compound engines, for as soon as Kirk's triple expansion engine proved itself during 1881 in the cargo steamer *Aberdeen* the end was in sight for compounding. The story of the compound engine is not, however, confined to the tandem arrangement for there were other forms which proved themselves equally as effective, if not more so.

The two-cylinder, two-crank tandem engine was probably the simplest arrangement to construct, and most marine engine builders produced machinery to that form between the 1860s and the 1880s. Over the years modifications would have been made by individual manufacturers to suit particular circumstances, but the basic design was the same whoever built the engine. Invariably engines of this type operated on the receiver system of compounding, exhaust steam from the HP passing to the LP via a receiver, which was usually just the connecting steam pipe; many engineers considered the receiver system superior to the Woolf system and it certainly allowed for greater flexibility in the positioning of the cylinders and cranks. Positioning cranks at 90° to each other allowed for a more even turning moment than when they were at 0° or 180° and meant that the engine could be started from any crankshaft rotational position.

The longevity of the two-crank compound stemmed from its simplicity, relatively low cost and ease of maintenance. Economy of operation was important to the shipowner but so was engine length as the saving of a few feet could increase the cargo capacity by several hundred tons and for this reason the two-crank compound remained popular with the cargo ship operator well into the 1880s. Typical of the design was the engine constructed by Adam & Millar of London in 1879 for the steamship *Lord of the Isles*, this having a 44in diameter HP cylinder and a 76in diameter LP with a stroke of 4ft. Using steam at a pressure of

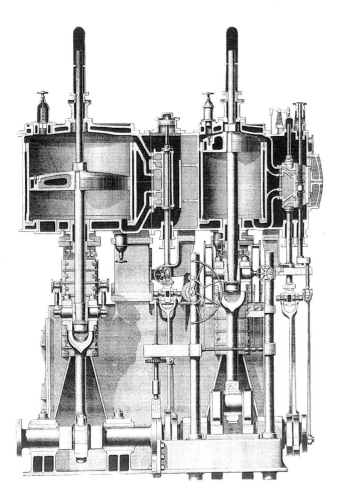

4.9 *Two-crank compound engine designed by Adam & Millar and fitted in* Lord of the Isles *(1879)*

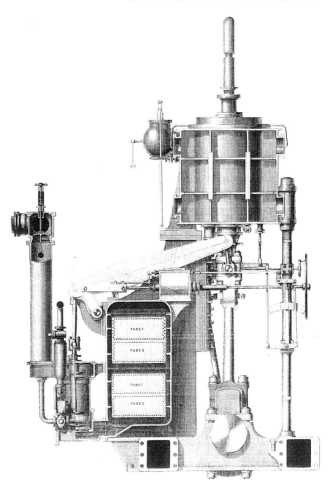

4.10 *End view of the engine fitted in* Lord of the Isles, *showing lever-driven pumps and the surface condenser*

65psi the engine could develop 1,750ihp at 63rpm; under these conditions the receiver pressure was 12psi. A feature found in this engine and common to single-piston designs

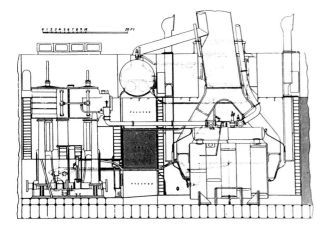

4.11 *Two-cylinder compound engine designed by Earles of Hull and fitted in the steel vessel* Assyrian Monarch *(1880)*

of the period and later was the extended piston rod passing through a guide and gland in the upper cylinder cover. This arrangement helped to keep the piston central in the cylinder thereby reducing wear. Cylinders and covers were steam jacketed, steam being taken direct from the boiler, while a layer of papier mâché was used for insulation. Each cylinder had its own slide valve actuated through a link motion system from a pair of crankshaft-driven eccentrics and it was possible to supply the LP valve chest with high-pressure steam should that be required for any reason.[19]

Earle's Shipbuilding & Engineering Company of Hull built the 3,317-ton steel-hulled *Assyrian Monarch* in 1880 for the Atlantic emigrant and cargo trade. Her two-cylinder compound engine, 46in HP, 87in LP by 4ft 9in stroke, developed 2,300ihp at 56rpm with 80psi steam supply. The HP cylinder had a separate liner but not the LP, the space between the casing and the liner being used for steam jacketing, although the covers were not jacketed. All main pumps (air, circulating, bilge and boiler feed) were worked by levers from the LP crosshead.[20]

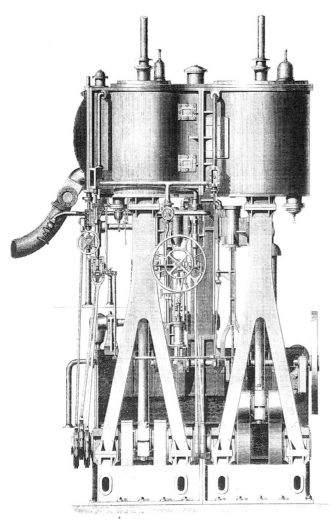

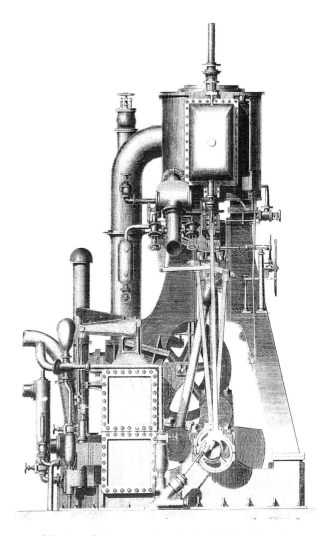

4.12 American design of in-line compound engine built by J. Roach for the steamer Rio de Janeiro *(1881)*

4.13 Side view of the compound engine fitted in Rio de Janeiro

As may be seen from the engines of *Assyrian Monarch* and *Lord of the Isles* cylinder dimensions differed considerably for similar powers. Naturally the initial steam pressure had a considerable influence on such dimensions but there was much discussion among engineers as to the degree of expansion which should take place in each cylinder and about the size of steam receiver which was required for efficient operation. *Lord of the Isles* had a receiver capacity 2.5 times that of the HP cylinder volume, but that was by no means typical and whenever engineers discussed the expansion of steam in two, three or four stages there was often disagreement as to the optimum cylinder and steam-receiver sizes for a particular duty.[21]

American engineers also constructed some fine two-cylinder compound engines, the design and arrangement being much like those of the British builders. In effect, there was no reason to do otherwise apart from minor details and the engine constructed by John Roach & Son of New York

in 1881 indicates little difference from the type built on the other side of the Atlantic. This engine, 42.5in HP plus 74in LP by 5ft stroke, was installed in the cargo vessel *City of Rio de Janeiro*.[22]

The two-crank arrangement did cause problems with higher-powered engines not only because of the large diameter of the LP cylinder but also with respect to balancing in order to minimise vibration. The three-crank arrangement overcame these difficulties, the low-pressure stage comprising two cylinders positioned either side of the HP cylinder. As with the two-crank design engineers had different ideas with respect to cylinder proportions, but most followed the basic pattern of passing the HP exhaust to a receiver and then directing this to the LP cylinders. Setting of valves became critical, for not only would inaccurate setting influence the power developed by the HP it would also affect steam conditions in the receiver and hence power developed in the LP cylinders. Each LP cylinder had its own valves

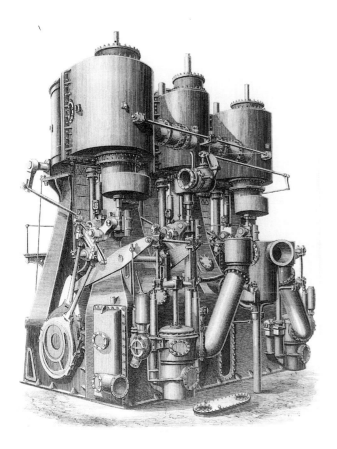

4.14 View of engine fitted in Parisian showing lever-driven pumps

4.15 Three-crank compound engine built by Napiers for the Allan liner Parisian *(1881)*

and accurate setting of these was crucial to power balance and performance; if one LP cylinder took less or more steam than the other this could have an adverse effect on those cylinders and upon the HP cylinder. Although the general three-crank arrangement was adopted by most engine builders there were a number of variations and one patented by William MacNab in 1861 is worthy of mention as it had the usual two LP cylinders driving outer cranks but there were two HP cylinders arranged in a transverse direction. HP piston rods were bolted to the same crosshead which then connected with the central crank. What practical advantages the arrangement had is difficult to imagine as both HP cylinders exhausted into the same receiver space which surrounded them.[23]

John M. Rowan of Glasgow developed a three-cylinder compound engine during the late 1850s, the single HP and twin LP cylinders driving the single crank of a paddle steamer steeple engine.[24] Application of this cylinder arrangement to screw propulsion must have taken place about the same time and MacNab's engine was obviously a means to avoid the infringement of any patents. Randolf & Elder built many three-cylinder, three-crank compound engines with that constructed for the Atlantic liner *Arizona* in

1879 being particularly impressive. On trials the engine developed some 6,357ihp from steam at 90psi, giving the 5,147-gross ton steamer a speed of over 17 knots. The HP cylinder was 62in diameter and the LP cylinders 90in, the stroke being 5ft 6in. All cylinders were steam jacketed and had piston valves at the back thus allowing for a reduction in engine length. Levers attached to the crossheads drove an assortment of pumps while each LP cylinder had its own condenser.[25]

Such was the competition on the Atlantic and the progress in marine engineering that ever bigger and faster liners were demanded and builders had to develop their manufacturing techniques and facilities in order to compete. In 1881 Napiers built *Parisian* for the Allan Line and fitted a three-crank compound engine designed by the A. C. Kirk. This was smaller than that built for *Arizona*, having 60in + 85in × 5ft cylinders but could develop 6,000ihp with steam at only 75psi. The single condenser was supplied with circulating sea water by centrifugal pumps.[26]

John Elder & Co. built what were probably the most powerful engines of the type in 1884 when they constructed Cunard's *Etruria* and *Umbria*. With steam at 110psi the engines of these ships (71in + 105in × 6ft) could develop

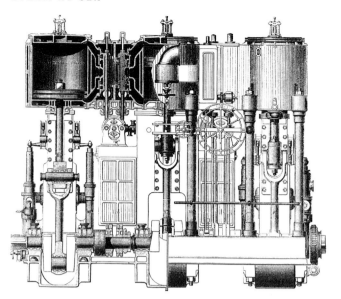

4.16 *French-built compound engine for the steamer* La France *(1882), all cylinders being the same size*

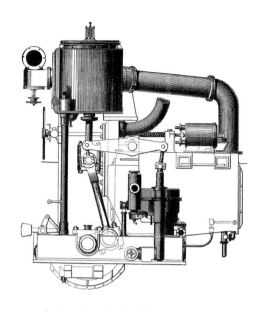

4.17 *Section through the three-cylinder compound engine fitted in* La France

some 14,500ihp but in terms of design they differed little from others of the type built by Elders and others. The compound had effectively come to the end of its development and had to give way to triple-expansion machinery.

By the 1880s the shipbuilding and marine engineering industries on the European continent were developing as France and Germany in particular expanded their overseas trade. Although ideas were taken from British builders they were modified to suit local manufacturing facilities and skills. In many cases the production of large castings was difficult and that limited the size of cylinders and other components which could be used. The three-cylinder compound engine built in 1882 by La Société Nouvelle des Forges et Chantiers de la Méditerranée of Marseilles for the steamer *La France* is interesting and shows how good design could be used to overcome certain manufacturing difficulties. All the cylinders were 1,520mm diameter (1,250mm stroke) and supported on forged columns rather than cast 'A'-frames. There were two condensers, one for each LP cylinder, with air, bilge and feed pumps being driven by levers from the LP crossheads. The steam pressure employed was only 40psi,[27] rather low for the time, possibly reflecting caution on the part of the builders as boilers capable of handling a pressure of 85psi had been built in northern France for the sister ships of *La Normandie*.

The compound engine presented marine engineers with a challenge, which was fundamentally one of obtaining maximum power from the smallest size without infringing the patent rights of others. The improved fuel efficiency of the compound put economic steam power at the command of any shipowner and its use brought about a revolution in

4.18 *Typical two-cylinder compound engine of the 1880s as fitted in the steamer* Auric

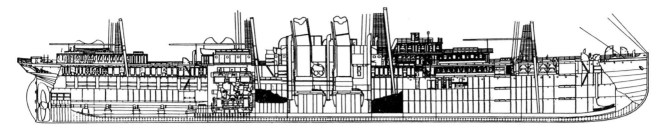

4.19 Section through the compound-engined liner Orient *showing the machinery layout of this typical 1870s liner*

commercial shipping. Naval engineering developments will be considered later and the impact there was no less revolutionary although not primarily for economic reasons. Other factors influenced the change from sail to steam power including the adoption of iron, and then steel construction, while the opening of the Suez Canal gave steam a shortcut to India, the Orient and Australia, one not available to the sailing ship. No one factor alone is ever responsible for any major change but had the compound engine not been available when it was the sailing ship would have been more difficult to oust from many trades. Increased demand for steamships resulted in more shipyards and larger engine building establishments, generally attached to shipyards but not always. The 1870s and the 1880s saw an expansion in the industries supplying auxiliary equipment, such as pumps and electrical generators for marinue purposes, and because Britain had the lead in world shipbuilding those industries tended to be centred in Britain, particularly in Scotland and the northeast of England. Each stage in marine engineering development has been significant, whether it be the introduction of the triple-expansion engine, turbine or diesel engine but it can be argued that the compound engine was of greater significance than any other.

The main types of compound engine have been discussed above but there were other forms that were significant because of their novelty or because they were designed for specific purposes. Horizontal compound engines for screw propulsion developed from the horizontal machinery constructed by several manufacturers to suit the height restriction imposed by naval authorities and,

although a number of this type were installed in commercial steamers, they will be discussed as a group in Chapter 6. One installation is, however, worthy of consideration here and that involves the 1,850-ton *Ruahine*, built in 1865 for the Panama, New Zealand & Australian Royal Mail Company by Dudgeons of Poplar. *Ruahine* was one of the first twin-screw vessels to put to sea and she had twin direct-acting, horizontal compound engines of the annular type, the machinery being constructed by her builder. Cylinder dimensions were 27in HP, 62in LP and 2ft stroke, the short stroke being particularly useful because of the horizontal positioning of the engine. Total power output was about 1,620ihp at 93rpm giving the ship a speed of over 14.5 knots. The condensers, one for each engine, were of the surface type.[28]

Combined horizontal and vertical compound engines were constructed for a number of ships of the Guion Line during the 1860s to a design developed by the company's superintendent engineer John Jordan. Engines for *Wisconsin* and *Wyoming* had two cylinders connected to the same crank, the 60in diameter HP cylinder being positioned vertically and connected via a crosshead with the 120in diameter LP cylinder of the trunk type having its piston directly connected to the crank. Both pistons had a stroke of 3ft 6in and cylinders had Corliss drop valves rather than slide

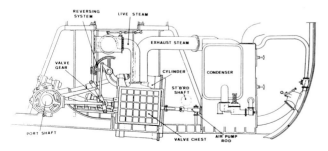

4.20 Horizontal compound engine as fitted in the twin-screw steamer Ruahine *(1865) by Dudgeons of Poplar*

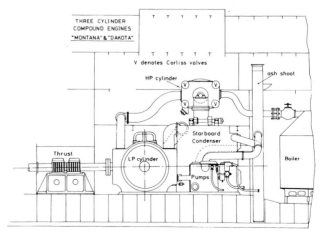

4.21 Palmers-built compound engines for the Guion liners Montana *and* Dakota

valves. The main advantage of this hybrid design seems to have been that it was short and so required little engine room length. Despite the machinery's novelty it appeared to work well and encouraged the owner to build further ships with more powerful engines. *Montana* and *Dakota* had similar engines but the 60in diameter HP cylinder was connected to the forward crank while the two 113in diameter LP pistons were attached to the after crank. LP cylinders were not of the trunk type but a return connecting rod arrangement was employed, two piston rods being used to attach each piston to the crosshead which was located to the port side of the crankshaft. Engines for the earlier pair of ships used steam at 70psi but for the later pair 100psi was intended. However, failure of the water tube boilers resulted in reboilering and operation at lower pressure with consequently reduced power.[29]

Novel engine designs were typical during the compound era and most failed to make any mark on the industry, the simple two- or three-crank arrangement being subsequently found to be ideal. Compound paddle engines have already been discussed but in conclusion it should be mentioned that some of the best compound designs were for paddle propulsion. One of the largest and most powerful compound paddle engines ever built in Britain was the three-cylinder, diagonal engine constructed by the Fairfield Shipbuilding and Engineering Company in 1897 for the Isle of Man Steam Packet Company's 2,140-gross ton *Empress Queen*. The centrally-positioned 68in diameter HP cylinder exhausted steam to the 92in diameter LP cylinders located alongside; all cylinders had the same 7ft stroke. Piston valves were fitted to the HP cylinder while LP cylinders had slide valves, all positioned above their cylinders and controlled by eccentric drive-link motion. With steam at a pressure of 140psi, 10,000ihp could be developed by the engine, itself a fitting tribute to the compound era at sea.

References

1 F. J. Bramwell, 'On Progress in Economy of Fuel in Steam Navigation', *Proc. I.Mech.E.*, 1872, p. 135.

4.22 Compound diagonal paddle engine built by Fairfields for the Isle of Man steamer Empress Queen *(1897)*

2 J. Guthrie, *A History of Marine Engineering*, Hutchinson, London, 1971, p. 131.

3 *The Engineer*, vol. 69, 27 June 1890, pp. 524–6.

4 Ibid., vol. 69, 21 Mar. 1890, pp. 232–4; 11 Apr. 1890, pp. 294–6.

5 Ibid., vol. 70, 8 Aug. 1890, pp. 103–6; vol. 71, 3 Apr. 1891, pp. 267–70.

6 Ibid., vol. 87, 12 Nov. 1897, p. 471.

7 F. J. Bramwell, 'On Progress in Economy of Fuel', p. 52.

8 H. P. Spratt, *Marine Engineering Descriptive Catalogue*, HMSO, London, 1956, p. 41.

9 A drawing of the engine fitted in *Cleator* is shown in Sir Stewart MacTier and W. H. Falconer, 'The Development of Marine Machinery', *Trans. Liverpool Engineering Society*, 1961, p. 100, with a description in the manuscript 'Information on Engines of Alfred Holt's Early Steamships', para. 4; Blue Funnel Archive, Liverpool Maritime Records Centre.

10 S. MacTier and W. H. Falconer, 'Development of Marine Machinery', pp. 100–101.

11 Scotts of Greenock, *Two Hundred and Fifty Years of Shipbuilding*, 1961, pp. 43–4.

12 The Holt engine is discussed by Adrian Jarvis in *The Advent of Steam*, Conway, London, 1993, Ch. 9, 'Alfred Holt and the Compound Engine'.

13 F. C. Marshall, 'On the Progress and Development of the Marine Engine', *Proc. I.Mech.E.* 1881, pp. 463–5.

14 C. C. Pounder, 'Some Notable Belfast-Built Engines', *Trans. Belfast Ass. of Engineers*, 1948, p. 8.

15 H. P. Spratt, *Marine Engineering*, p. 41.

16 *The Engineer*, 7 Oct. 1881, pp. 349–52.

17 *Engineering*, 18 Jan. 1884, p. 65; 1 Feb. 1884, pp. 103–4; 5 May 1891, p. 593.

18 *The Engineer*, vol. 52, 9 Sept. 1881, pp. 185, 188, 191, 242.

19 Ibid., vol. 47, 7 Feb. 1879, p. 96.

20 *Marine Engineer & Motorship Builder*, vol. 52, Dec. 1929, p. 494.

21 Several contributors make such comments during the discussion of many engineering papers of the period, including F. J. Rowan, 'On the Introduction of the Compound Engine', *Trans. I.E.S.S.*, 1880, and J. P. Hall, 'Compound versus Triple Expansion Engines', *Proc. N.E.C.I.E.S.*, 1886–7.

22 *The Engineer*, vol. 52, Dec. 1881, pp. 402–4.

23 Ibid., vol. 11, 17 May 1861, p. 306.

24 F. C. Marshall, 'Progress and Development of Marine Engineering', pp. 543–4.

25 *Engineering*, 3 Sep. 1880, pp. 196–7.

26 Ibid., 16 Sept. 1881, pp. 278–9.

27 *The Engineer*, vol. 53, 10 Feb. 1882, pp. 99–101.

28 *Marine Engineer & Motorship Builder*, vol. 55, Nov. 1932, pp. 380–381.

29 D. Griffiths, *Power of the Great Liners*, Patrick Stephens, Sparkford, 1990. pp. 32–5.

5
Low-Pressure Marine Boilers

What constitutes low pressure is not easy to define as it depends upon the range of pressures being considered. The chapter title is used, however, to represent boilers in general use up to 1880. This is an arbitrary choice, it is true, but it does define a distinct period in marine engine and boiler development culminating with the general adoption of the triple-expansion engine and boiler pressures reaching about 100psi.

Early engines operated because atmospheric pressure acted on one side of a piston while a vacuum was developed on the other. That vacuum was produced when steam or water vapour was condensed and so early boilers needed only to generate steam at very low pressure as it was simply going to be condensed anyway. Boilers for the first steamships followed land practice to a great extent and were often just enclosed kettles sitting upon a brick furnace; pressures were very low, no more than 5psi, as it was the condensing effect of the steam which mattered not its pressure. Even by the beginning of the nineteenth century matters had not progressed much as there was still a need only for small amounts of steam at very low pressure. The boiler fitted in *Charlotte Dundas* was just a cylinder, containing water, which sat upon a brick base built in the form of flues so that the hot furnace gases passed under and around the boiler shell before entering the chimney.[1] The boiler for Fulton's *North River Steam Boat* was of similar form, the dimensions being 20ft long, 7ft high and 8ft wide. Copper was originally used for the construction of the pressure vessel but when the boat was reconstructed after a period in service iron was used and this burst in service.[2] Tall chimneys or funnels were employed in order to create an adequate draught and so ensure satisfactory combustion in the furnace.

Copper was the only material available in large enough sheets to allow for the construction with the minimum number of joints, such joints being looked upon as potential sources of leakage. Engineers understood some of the problems of boiler construction but they were limited to the materials available and the methods of fastening which could be employed. A tubular boiler was patented by Nathan Read in America in 1790, but turning a concept into a steam-generating device proved more difficult than the inventor imagined. Such was the case with many designs and boiler development was slow, designs being aimed more at steam storage rather than strength for increased pressure. Haystack-type boilers found application at sea because they were more compact than the wagon type, but there was no

common design until about 1820 when the box boiler containing flat-sided flues gained the ascendancy. Management of boilers during those early years was neither efficient nor effective in many cases, resulting in explosions due to neglect, poor materials or defective construction. Public opinion was so disturbed by the frequency of boiler explosions aboard ships that the British government ordered an enquiry in 1817 which resulted in a regulation that all steamships must be registered. Rules were published which stated that boilers had to be constructed from wrought iron or copper, had to be tested to three times their normal working pressure and that two safety valves needed to be fitted. Twice each year the boilers had to be inspected internally and externally by a competent master engineer who would issue a certificate regarding their condition; similar rules applied to the inspection of the engines.[3] Initially safety valves were of the dead-weight type but spring-loaded safety valves became normal during the 1850s following their general adoption on railway locomotive boilers.

The box-type flue boiler became popular because of its ability to generate large quantities of steam and the relative ease with which it could be kept clean. Rectangular flues wound their way from the furnace to the funnel uptake, the pathway being chosen in order to ensure the maximum heating surface area. The shape and the size of the flues were dictated by the size of the boiler but they were always of sufficient size to allow a man to crawl through in order to facilitate cleaning and undertake any minor repairs. Often the flue would taper inwards towards the top so that steam bubbles generated on the sides of the flues would break away readily. Early flue boilers had flues on only a single level, that of the furnace, but by the late 1830s double levels of flues were employed since that increased the heat-transfer surface area and made for greater efficiency. Such improvements were only possible with the increasing availability of larger copper and iron plates from which boiler shell and flues were constructed.

Copper was considerably more expensive than iron but copper boilers lasted much longer, an iron flue-type boiler having an expected working life of about five years at most because of the problem of corrosion. The use of salt water as boiler feed caused scale formation in the water spaces. That reduced effective heat transfer from flues to the water but it did form a protective layer on the iron surfaces and so reduced the risk of corrosion in those areas, but the steam spaces were not so readily protected. At the time the cause of corrosion was not known, but deep corrosion pits

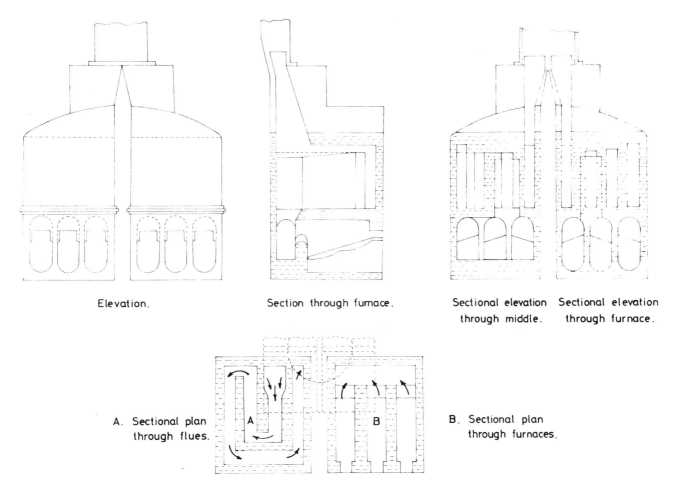

Elevation.

Section through furnace.

Sectional elevation through middle.

Sectional elevation through furnace.

A. Sectional plan through flues.

B. Sectional plan through furnaces.

5.1 Arrangement of flue-type boilers as originally fitted in Great Western *(1837)*

occurred in the steam space near the water level and such pits were generally covered by a scab of iron oxide. The presence of oxygen, liberated from the sea water during heating, resulted in this pitting and it was not until years later when effective chemical treatment and feed-water deaerators were introduced that some degree of control could be exercised over corrosion. Boilers were generally mounted upon wooden platforms and set in mastic cement in order to ensure that they stayed in position, the mastic being a mixture of sand, powdered stone, lead oxide and oil. In wooden ships water in the bilges could become very acidic and that too caused severe corrosion of iron boiler plates which were not protected by the mastic cement. Levels in boiler room bilges were generally high through water leakage, but bilge water provided a useful means of cooling the ashes which were raked from the furnaces. It was not unknown for boilers to corrode from the outside inwards under such circumstances.[4]

Rivets were used to join boiler plates whether they were made of copper or iron and even when the standard of workmanship was good, which was not always the case, a

considerable number of leaks would be evident when the boiler was filled. Only the most severe leaks were attended to by caulking the leaking seams as the corrosion which occurred with iron boilers and the salt scale which formed soon attended to the minor leaks. With low boiler pressures, no greater than about 5psi, leaks did not present a major problem and even when pressures increased to about 12psi measures were adopted to plug those leaks that did develop in service by introducing compounds which would find their way into the leaks and form seals. Sawdust, oatmeal and other substances, including potatoes and dung, were used from time to time and in most cases were effective provided that the boiler pressure was relatively low;[5] the same principle is used today as a temporary measure for stopping leaks in automobile radiators.

The actual design of a flue boiler differed with the manufacturer but all types followed the same basic arrangement of a number of furnaces in which the coal was burned and a system of flues through which the hot gases passed to the funnel. The boilers built by Maudslay, Sons and Field for *Great Western* in 1837 were among the best of their type and

59

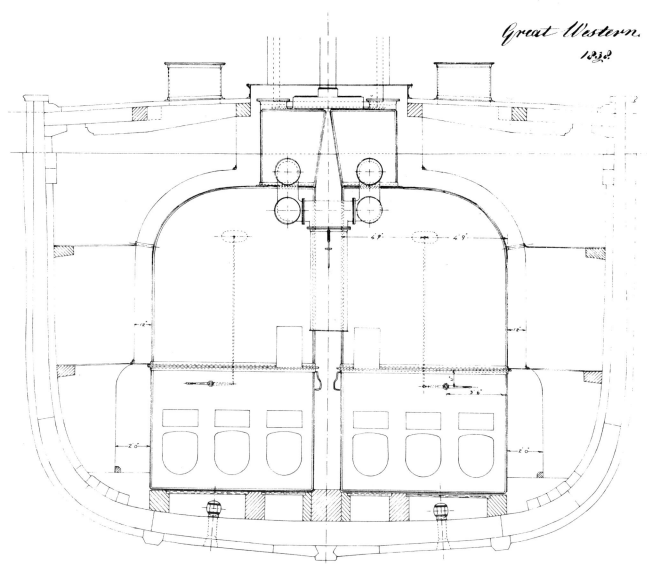

5.2 Flue-type boilers located in Great Western

incorporated a number of novel devices. There were four boilers operating at a pressure of 5psi, the boilers being arranged in pairs back-to-back with combustion gases passing to a single funnel. Flues were on two levels, the total area being 2,850ft² and the grate area 202ft². The water level in the boiler was indicated by means of a float-operated pointer device, a feature used in land engines but not common at that time in marine practice; gauge glasses for indicating the boiler-water level were not introduced until many years later.

In order to minimise the formation of salt scale within the boiler frequent blowdown was required so that the density of the water could be kept below the level at which serious precipitation would occur. The usual practice was to take a sample of water from the boiler and test it with a hydrometer, although before introduction of such devices the water would be boiled and the temperature of boiling used to assess the salinity; the higher the salinity the higher the temperature of boiling. Blowing water from the boiler was wasteful as that hot water had to be replaced by relatively cold feed from the hot-well but *Great Western* was fitted with a heat-recovery system patented by Joshua Field. Water blown from the boiler did not pass direct to the sea but went to a refrigerator where it transferred heat to feed water being pumped to the boiler. The refrigerator was essentially a tubular heat exchanger with incoming feed-water passing through the tubes and hot water from the boiler surrounding them, a feed-water temperature increase of some 70°F being possible. Because the boiler pressure was only 5psi at most and the refrigerator induced a further pressure loss, it was necessary to pump the blowdown water overboard by engine-driven brine pumps.[6] In some

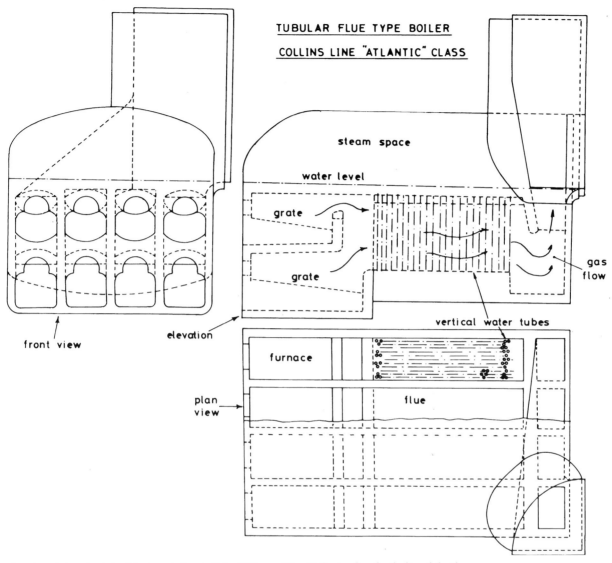

5.3 American designed tubular/flue type boilers built by Stillman Allen & Co. in 1850 for the liner Atlantic

installations blowdown water passed to the bilge from where it was pumped overboard, but as boiler pressures increased it became possible to pass blowdown water direct to the sea.

The power developed by any engine depended upon the ability of the boiler plant to supply sufficient steam, and the rate at which steam could be generated depended upon the amount of coal which could be burned, and that in turn was governed by the grate area. Increasing the number of boilers allowed more steam to be generated but boilers occupied space in the ship which could be used for bunkers or cargo. The solution adopted by a number of engineering companies, including Scott, Sinclair & Co. of Greenock and Stillman Allen & Co. of New York, was to increase the total grate area by providing a double tier of furnaces. Although such an arrangement increased the area and saved upon the

total number of boilers, there were many disadvantages, not least of which was the problem of firing and serving the upper tier of furnaces. Cold air entering the upper furnace also tended to interfere with steam generation by the lower furnaces. Scotts fitted boilers of this type in the Royal Mail Line steamers *Dee* and *Solway* during the early 1840s, while Stillman Allen built them for the American passenger ships *Humbolt* (1851) and *Atlantic* (1850). Boilers for the Collins Line *Atlantic*-class ships operated at 17psi and were designed by the company's superintendent engineer John Faron and were of a novel, tubular form. Each of the four boilers in the ships had eight furnaces grouped in four vertical pairs. Both furnaces in each pair fed hot combustion gases to a chamber through which passed 1,406 vertical tubes containing water, these 2in diameter tubes connected

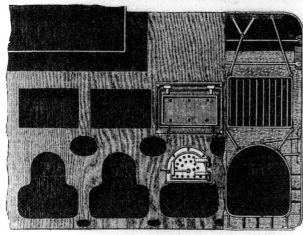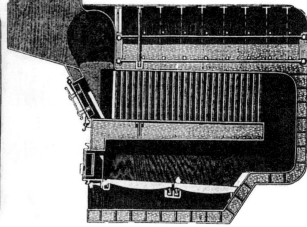

5.4 Tubular/flue boilers fitted in the US Navy sloop Hassalo *(1866)*

the water space at the bottom of the boiler with the water and steam space at the top.[7]

Boilers of similar design were fitted in the American sloop *Hassalo* during 1866, the design being to a patent by a Mr Martin. The four steam-generating boilers in the vessel had rectangular flues above the furnaces and these contained vertical seamless brass tubes which connected the water spaces above and below the flues. A door at the front end of each flue gave access to the vertical tubes for cleaning purposes but the cleaning of those tubes at the middle of the pack must have presented difficulties. All surfaces were stayed in order to withstand the working pressure of 40psi. In addition to the steam-generating boilers the ship had two single-furnace superheating boilers with horizontal iron flue tubes.[8]

Stillman Allen developed a fire-tube boiler and fitted this design of cylindrical boiler in the steamer *Franklin* (1850), the large diameter tubes effectively being circular flues.[9] Such boiler designs would indicate that American marine engineers were attempting to improve the specific output of their boilers but at the expense of increased complexity. Certainly steam pressures did not increase much as the boilers fitted in *Franklin* operated at only 15psi. In 1837 Scotts of Greenock fitted double-tier furnace boilers in the 743-ton P&O steamer *Tagus*, these boilers also containing 14 fire tubes or pipes instead of an upper row of flues. These 10in diameter pipes were 10ft long and were made from rolled boiler plate with turned rings at their ends, the rings being inserted into holes in the smokebox plates and then riveted over.[10]

By the 1840s the disadvantages of the flue boiler were evident and most builders moved towards the development of tubular-type boilers which not only had the potential of being more efficient generators of steam but were also more compact for the same generating capacity, that saving in space being particularly important for the shipowner. During that decade many of the early paddle steamers required new boilers and the adoption of the tubular type offered not only savings in coal but also in space. In 1844 it became evident that the steam-generating equipment in *Great Western* was no longer fit for service and her owners decided on its replacement by a tubular boiler designed by its engineer Thomas Guppy and built by the company itself in Bristol. The design followed a pattern which had become established during the early 1840s this being essentially a return tube arrangement. Most tubular boilers at that time had a single bank of tubes through which hot gases flowed from a combustion chamber at the back of the boiler to a smokebox at the front, the smokebox being located above the furnaces. From the smokebox gases passed to the funnel, but in the case of the boiler fitted in *Great Western* the gases flowed through a second bank of tubes to the back of the boiler and then into the funnel. The new boiler was essentially three units connected together, the outer units having three furnaces each and the centre unit two, and being only 12ft long with a stokehold at one end only, there was a considerable saving in space compared with the original boilers fitted in the ship.

In total there were some 750 tubes, with the upper banks having fewer than the lower banks which must have restricted the flow of hot gases. Although the new higher-pressure (12psi) steam-generating plant was more efficient than the old and showed savings on fuel of about £275 per voyage, steaming performance was defective with trouble being experience in maintaining pressure at times. Brunel advocated the use of a steam blast up the chimney, just as in a steam locomotive, in order to improve the furnace draught, but a simpler option was adopted. This involved cutting a hole through the water space at the back of the boiler so that hot gases could pass direct from the combustion chamber to the funnel and so promote a better draught.[11] John Bourne believed that the problem with the boiler was caused by cold funnel gases because heat transfer from gases to water was too efficient owing to the large tube area; the ratio of total heating area to grate area was 49.5:1 while for the original boilers it was 19.2:1. Like Brunel he advocated use of a steam blast.[12]

Throughout the 1840s and into the 1850s the tubular boiler evolved into a type which became almost standard, this being the box form with a bank of tubes returning hot gases from the combustion chamber at the back of the boiler to the smokebox at the front. The box shape remained as it was relatively easy to construct but it also fitted conveniently into the hull of the ship giving a large capacity. Flat surfaces were stayed in order to withstand pressure forces but pressures remained relatively low rising to only about 20psi with this type of construction. The large return-tube boilers fitted in *Great Eastern* during 1856 had a maximum working pressure of 25psi and these had to have a substantial system of stays. Use of this relatively low pressure allowed for the fitting of atmospheric feed heaters, these consisting of a 6in wide water jacket around the base of each funnel with a standpipe at the jacket upper casing extending to the top of the funnel in order to provide a water-pressure head. Water was pumped into the heater and then allowed into the boiler as hot feed, with no further

pump action as the static pressure head was greater than the boiler pressure. Unfortunately, failure to open the stopcocks on the paddle engine boilers and the by-passing of the feed heaters on these boilers resulted in the generation of steam in the jackets when the boilers operated, with a resultant pressure increase which caused a fatal explosion.

This type of feed heater had been patented by Robert Napier and was fitted to a number of steamers, although the consequences of operation never seemed to be as catastrophic as in the case of *Great Eastern*. The boilers of this ship were also fitted with superheaters on the recommendation of James Watt & Co., the idea being to dry the steam rather than increase its temperature, thereby reducing the risk of boiler priming. These superheaters took the form of steam chests built into the base of the funnel, hot furnace gases passing through a number of vertical tubes located in the chests on their way to the funnel. Each superheater had its own set of safety valves while steam stop valves were fitted in the steam lines before and after the superheater.[13]

The concept of superheating or steam drying was not new and one of the earliest arrangements was developed in 1827 by the American James Allaire who invented what he referred to as the 'steam chimney'. His original design consisted of an annular casing constructed from boiler plate, boiler gases passing up the centre of the casing and steam flowing through the annular space. Steam entered the dryer at the top and was forced to move downwards through the presence of a vertical diaphragm within the annular space,

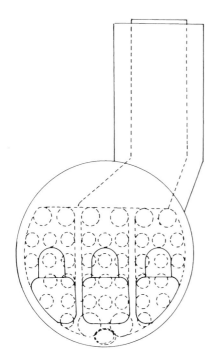

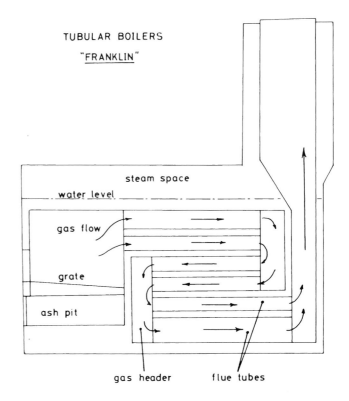

TUBULAR BOILERS
"FRANKLIN"

steam space
water level
gas flow
grate
ash pit

gas header   flue tubes

5.5 Tubular/flue boiler built by Stillman Allen & Co. for the steamer Franklin *(1850)*

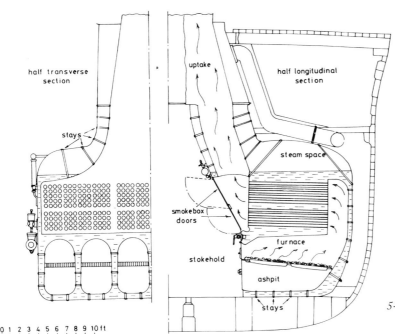

half transverse
section

uptake

half longitudinal
section

stays

steam space

smokebox
doors

furnace

stokehold

ashpit

stays

0 1 2 3 4 5 6 7 8 9 10 ft

RETURN TUBE FLUE TYPE BOILER   S.S. ARABIA

5.6 Typical box-type tubular boiler design of the 1850s

this diaphragm extending almost to the bottom of it. As steam flowed around the diaphragm any remaining water droplets were deposited in the casing to be vaporised by the funnel gases. As in the case of *Great Eastern* the device was essentially intended to prevent boiler priming.[14] Many early boilers had the facility for steam drying simply because the hot uptake gases passed through the large steam space at the top of the boiler; this arrangement may be seen on the drawings of the flue boilers of *Great Western* and the return tube boilers of *Arabia*.

Superheaters became accepted boiler fittings during the 1860s when the problem of cylinder condensation was appreciated and they found favour for compound engines, particularly those operating at relatively low pressures; superheating of the steam limited condensation on the cylinder walls. Superheaters gradually evolved from the wall-contact type to the Napier type, in which flue gases passed through tubes in the steam chamber, to a generally accepted form in which steam flowed through the tubes while hot flue gases heated them. Lamb & Summers of Southampton and Robert Napier introduced superheaters of this type in 1860, the design finding favour as it allowed for control over the degree of superheat.[15] With steam at a pressure of 20psi it was usual to raise the temperature by about 100°F above that at which it left the boiler and this produced a fuel saving of about 20 per cent. While pressures did not exceed about 40psi, superheating was considered effective, but when pressures reached about 60psi there were problems due to the high temperatures involved. At such pressures the superheat temperature could reach

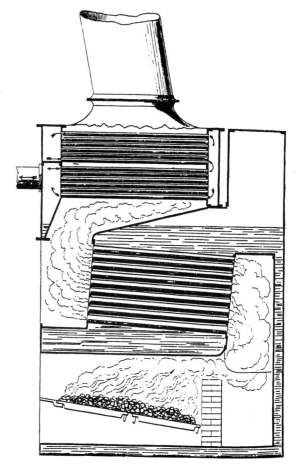

5.7 Beardmore boiler with superheating apparatus at the base of the funnel (c. 1860)

400°F and that caused trouble at the engine and within the superheater; the fuel savings did not compensate for the problems caused. At high temperatures wear in the cylinders, at the piston-rod glands and in the valve chests became excessive owing to the lack of an effective lubricant film; water droplets acted as a lubricant when condensation occurred but no condensation took place at the HP stage and the temperature was too high for the animal-based lubricants used at the time to be effective. As superheaters wore out, particles of corroded iron were carried into the valve chests and cylinders resulting in additional damage.[16] As steam pressures increased, superheating became an even less attractive proposition and it was not until many decades later with the development of high-quality lubricants for high temperature work that it again found favour.

The effectiveness of compounding depended upon higher steam pressures but increasing steam pressure presented difficulties for boiler designers and builders: it was not simply a case of making the boiler plates thicker. By the 1860s it was well known that flat surfaces were less able to resist steam pressure than curved surfaces and required many support stays to be fitted in order to operate at even moderate pressures. Box-type boilers were used because they fitted into the box-shaped stokeholds of ships, providing a large steam storage capacity with little waste of space; their flat sides, however, needed substantial support and operating pressures were still limited. A cylindrical-shaped container is stronger than one with flat surfaces and by using such a shape the pressure vessel may be made thinner for the same strength or stronger for the same thickness and the message was not lost on boiler designers. However, at the same pressure cylindrical boilers of a given diameter

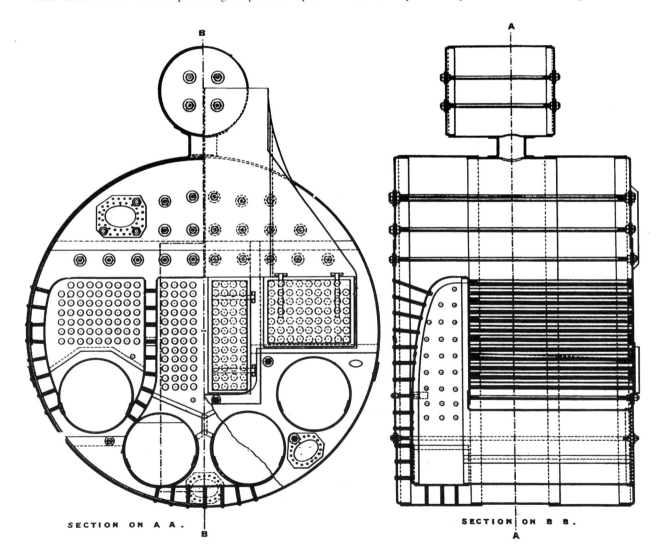

SECTION ON A A.

SECTION ON B B.

5.8 Cylindrical boiler with steam collector drum (c. 1870)

5.9 Scotch boiler installation of City of Sydney *built by Risdon Iron Works, San Francisco, during the 1890s when the ship was reboilered*

offer less steam storage capacity than a box boiler of the same external dimensions and for that reason they met with resistance from the shipping industry. An interim design was the oval boiler which had flat sides but hemispherical tops and lower sections; this shape allowed more of the stokehold space to be actually occupied by the boiler while at the same time giving some of the advantages of the cylindrical boiler. Maudslay, Sons & Field supplied oval boilers for many of the early White Star liners, *Britannic* (1874) and *Germanic* (1875) each having eight double-ended oval boilers working at a pressure of 75psi. Such a pressure was at about the limit of the design and by that time the advantages of the cylindrical boiler had been amply demonstrated.

As with many engineering ideas, it is difficult to say who was responsible for the cylindrical boiler concept and the truth is that a number of individuals probably had similar ideas at the same time. However, credit for the first Scotch boiler at sea goes to Randolf & Elder. Two four-furnace, double-ended Scotch boilers, using common combustion chambers, were installed in the steamer *McGregor Laird*

during 1862.[17] The Scotch boiler is essentially a multi-furnace, cylindrical fire-tube boiler in which the fire tubes, positioned above the furnace, bring hot gases from a combustion chamber located at the rear of the furnace to a smokebox positioned at the front of the boiler. Over the years there have been minor modifications but the design has always remained essentially the same, the number of furnaces varying from two to four if the boiler is single ended. Double-ended boilers offer a saving in materials and weight compared with two single-ended boilers of the same total output. In some such boilers combustion chambers backing on to each other are completely separate while in others pairs of furnaces use the same combustion chamber; the Scotch boiler was a type not a rigid design.

Priming was still a problem and the Scotch boiler design did not lend itself to a solution; in fact, some authorities considered that the cylindrical shell actually made matters worse. Steam bubbles bursting through the water surface carry droplets of water upwards and it was believed that the relatively small water-level surface area at the top of the

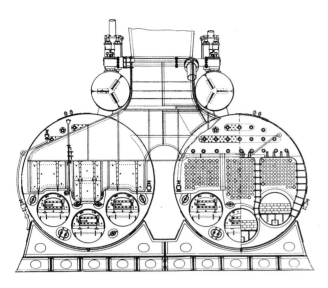

5.10 Scotch boilers and supports fitted in Hannoverian

Scotch boiler compared with the large heating surface resulted in increased priming compared with the box-type boiler. Some Scotch boilers were fitted with annular superheaters around the base of the funnel in order to minimise the carry over of water droplets, but the more usual arrangement was to fit a cylindrical steam reservoir at the top of the boiler.[18] This feature became common as pressures increased and the application of superheating fell; in some cases the reservoir was located in the flue-gas uptake

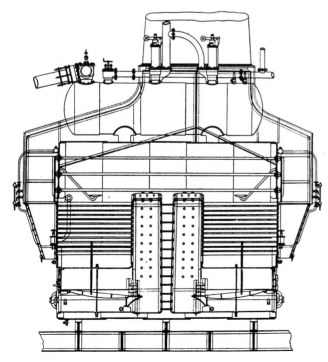

5.11 Double-ended Scotch boilers with separate combustion chambers and steam collectors; installed in the steamer Hannoverian

to give a degree of steam drying but more usually it was outside the gas flow and provided with good insulation.

The number of furnaces fitted to a Scotch boiler depended upon its diameter and that in turn depended upon the steam generating rate required. During the 1870s two or three furnaces were normal but by the 1880s some large boilers were being fitted with four. During the 1860s wrought iron plates were used for boiler construction as this was the most suitable material then available, but wrought iron was not particularly strong and to withstand higher pressures the plate thickness had to be increased; that in turn caused difficulties in punching holes to accommodate the rivets. Steel has a higher carbon content than wrought iron and, if of good quality, few inclusions of slag and other impurities. Early steels were not, however, of high quality nor was the quality consistent from batch to batch thus the boiler designer could not rely upon the steels which were available during the 1850s. This is not the place to discuss the relative merits of steel and iron nor to go into their particular properties save to say that a good consistent steel has a higher tensile strength and better elongation characteristics than iron thus making it more suitable for boiler construction. Steel, however, is more susceptible to corrosion. As early as 1857 the Admiralty authorised tests on steel in order to determine its suitability for boiler construction, but the results were not satisfactory and costs were higher than for iron.[19]

Over the following years experiments continued as metallurgists developed steels of better and more consistent quality, but it was only with the introduction of Henry Bessemer's steel-making process during the 1860s that material of consistent quality became available at reasonable cost and in sufficient quantity for general adoption. The London & North Western Railway's locomotive works at Crewe built its first steel boiler in 1863 and marine practice followed soon afterwards. Bessemer steel quality improved as practitioners became familiar with the process and as techniques for analysing and testing steels developed. By the end of the decade the rival Seimens-Martin open hearth process was introduced with the result that high-quality, low-cost steels in large quantities were available to boiler and ship designers. By the 1870s no boiler designer would consider using anything other than steel for construction; the greater strength of this material allowed for higher steam pressures and by the end of that decade pressures up to 100psi were regularly being used. The higher strength of steel compared with that of iron also allowed for a reduction in plate thickness which not only reduced boiler weight but increased heat transfer at the furnace, combustion chamber and flues and also made for easier construction in terms of the drilling and punching of rivet holes.[20]

A limiting factor in the ability of the Scotch boiler, or

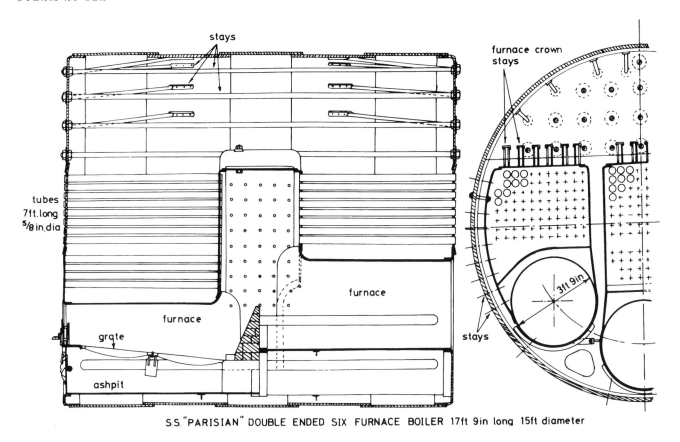

stays

furnace crown
stays

tubes
7ft.long
⁵⁄8 in.dia

furnace

furnace

grate

ashpit

stays

3ft 9in

S.S. "PARISIAN" DOUBLE ENDED SIX FURNACE BOILER 17ft 9in long 15ft diameter

5.12 Double-ended Scotch boiler with combined combustion chamber

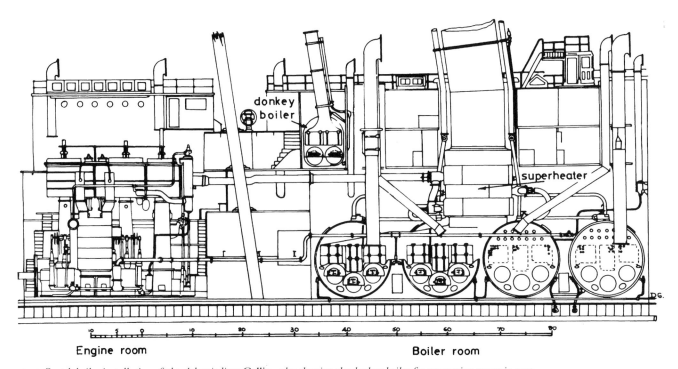

donkey
boiler

superheater

Engine room

Boiler room

5.13 Scotch boiler installation of the Atlantic liner Gallia *, also showing the donkey boiler for generating steam in port*

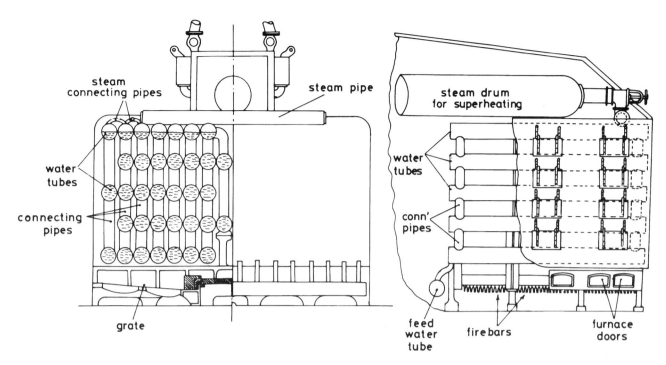

5.14 Water-tube boilers as constructed for the liner Montana *(1873)*

any boiler for that matter, to withstand pressure was the strength of its furnaces. A cylindrical furnace was stronger than a rectangular one but the pressure it could withstand was limited to about 80psi for a number of reasons, including its unsupported length. Making the diameter of the furnace smaller would increase its stiffness but also reduce

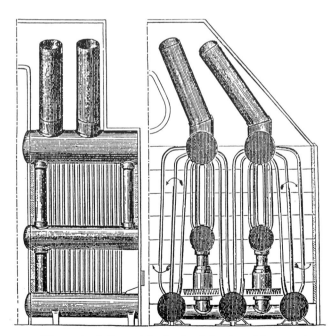

5.15 Water-tube boilers originally fitted in the triple-expansion-engined Propontis

the steam-generating rate while little scope existed for strengthening by way of stays as rivet heads were likely to be damaged and weakened by the fire. The attaching of strengthening rings and flanges was not successful for similar reasons. Several methods of strengthening boiler furnaces were developed but the most successful and one which lasted until the end of Scotch boiler production in the latter half of the twentieth century was the corrugated furnace. Although a number of designers arrived at the same idea at about the same time it was Samson Fox who took the lead and convinced many boiler makers to adopt his design and method of construction. Fox was a machine-tool maker who had a number of patents for machinery which could be related to the construction of boilers, but it was his 1877 patent, No. 1097, concerning corrugated boiler flues which attracted most attention. Not only did he devise the flue, as he called it, but he also designed the machinery for its construction and in 1877 convinced the Barrow Shipbuilding Company to make use of his design in boilers then being constructed for a small steamer. The successful operation of that and other steamers satisfied many sceptical engineers and the design became widely accepted. By the 1880s most boilers were fitted with corrugated furnaces either with Fox corrugations or one of the many similar designs which soon followed.[21]

Before leaving the discussion of low-pressure boilers it is worth looking at some of the water-tube boilers which evolved in the period up to 1880. As has already been mentioned, the design of the fire-tube boiler limited the pressure which could be developed but the introduction of compound engines prompted some engineers to attempt the production of higher pressure steam. Water-tube boilers constructed for the Guion Line steamers *Montana* and *Dakota* during 1873 were novel and unsuccessful. They operated at a pressure of 100psi and each boiler contained 35 tubes which were 15ft long and 15in diameter; in addition to the steam-generating tubes the boilers contained superheating drums. Failure of tubes occurred during the delivery voyage of *Montana* with cracking taking place from overheating resulting from poor circulation; the design was fundamentally unsound.[22] A year later the steamer *Propontis* was fitted with a triple-expansion engine and given water-tube boilers to a patent of Rowan & Horton, the design working pressure being 150psi. It took a number of weeks for defects in these boilers to become evident, corrosion resulting in leakage at a number of points. After repairs the boilers operated successfully, but in 1875 a series of explosions resulted in the pressure being reduced to 60psi for the sake of safety.[23] J. M. Rowan of Glasgow and T. R. Horton of Birmingham were enthusiastic collaborators and advocates of the water-tube boiler, first patenting such a boiler and the accompanying compound engine in 1858. This boiler consisted of a series of vertical water tubes which surrounded the furnace while other vertical tubes were positioned above the furnace.[24] Modified boilers to the patent were constructed by Scotts of Greenock in 1858 for the compound-engined steamer *Thetis*, these boilers operating at a pressure of 115psi and being capable of evaporating 11lbs of water per pound of coal, which was 30 per cent better than other boilers of the period. Corrosion and erosion soon resulted in tube leakage.[25]

Development of the steel Scotch boiler with corrugated flues allowed the generation of steam at pressures of up to 150psi which proved suitable for most mercantile purposes during the remaining years of the nineteenth century, and it was to be many years more before the water-tube boiler found general application in merchant ships. Naval needs differed and water-tube boilers were developed to meet these but even then there were similar problems.

References

1 *Marine Engineer & Motorship Builder*, vol. 53, Sep. 1930, p. 356.

2 Ibid., vol. 53, July 1930, pp. 280–81.

3 G. Blake, *Lloyd's Register of Shipping 1760–1960*, Lloyd's Register, 1960, p. 39.

4 J. Bourne, *A Treatise on the Steam Engine*, Longmans, Green, London, 1876, pp. 212–3.

5 E. C. Smith, *A Short History of Marine Engineering*, Cambridge University Press, 1937, pp. 128–9.

6 D. Griffiths, *Brunel's Great Western*, Patrick Stephens, Wellingborough, 1985, pp. 69–70; 78–82.

7 B. H. Bartol, *Treatise on the Marine Boilers of the United States*, Philadelphia, 1851, pp. 40–48.

8 *Engineering*, vol. 2, 21 Sep. 1866, p. 217.

9 B. H. Bartol, *Marine Boilers*, pp. 52–3.

10 J. Bourne, *Treatise on the Steam Engine*, p. 221.

11 D. Griffiths, *Brunel's Great Western*, pp. 82–4.

12 J. Bourne, *Treatise on the Steam Engine*, Artisan Club, London, 1846, pp. 63–4.

13 R. G. Fuller, 'The *Great Eastern*', Canadian Supplement to *I.Mar.E.Transactions*, 1961, pp. 135–6.

14 C. H. Haswell, 'Reminisces of Early Marine Steam Engine Construction in the USA from 1807 to 1850', *Trans. I.N.A.*, vol. 40, 1898, p. 106.

15 J. Bourne, *Treatise on the Steam Engine*, 1876, pp. 239–40.

16 *Shipping World*, 1 Sep. 1887, p. 150.

17 J. F. Clarke and F. Storr, 'The Strength of Marine Boilers and the Design of the Furnace', Newcastle-upon-Tyne Polytechnic, Occasional Paper in the History of Science and Technology, No. 2, 1983, p. 1.

18 J. McGregor, 'Construction and Efficiency of Marine Boilers', *Trans. I.E.S.S.*, vol. 23, 1879–80, pp. 103–7.

19 Quoted by J. Ravenhill, *Trans. I.N.A.*, 1878, vol. 19, p. 185.

20 Details concerning the application of steel in marine engineering and shipbuilding are given in J. F. Clarke and F. Storr 'The Introduction and use of Mild Steel into the Shipbuilding and Marine Engineering Industries', Newcastle-upon-Tyne Polytechnic, Occasional Paper in the History of Science and Technology, No. 1, 1983.

21 The full story of the Fox corrugation is related in G. A. Newby, *Behind the Fire Doors*, published by the author in 1979.

22 J. F. Flannery, 'On Water-tube Boilers', *Trans. I.N.A.*, 1876, vol. 17, pp. 263–5.

23 Ibid., pp. 266–8.

24 *The Engineer*, vol. 10, 28 Sep. 1860, p. 210.

25 Scotts of Greenock, *Two Hundred and Fifty Years of Shipbuilding*, 1961, pp. 41–2.

6
Steam Power and the Fighting Ship

Adoption of steam propulsion by naval authorities was somewhat slower than by commercial interests but there were far-sighted individuals at the British Admiralty who could see where the future of maritime power lay. The problem with the Admiralty was that it was a large and bureaucratic organisation where seniority commanded influence and power rather than intellect and ingenuity; it took much persuading to convince anybody in authority to adopt steam propulsion in any vessel, let alone a fighting ship. To some extent the reluctance to embrace steam power was understandable as naval ships had to do more than simply get from port to port, they were for the most part fighting vessels with different operating criteria from merchant ships. Similar situations existed with the naval authorities of other countries and during the early years of the nineteenth century it would have been foolhardy for any admiral to advocate dependence upon a largely untried and certainly unreliable technology for his country's defence. The power of steam, however, could not be ignored: early naval vessels powered by steam served mostly in support roles, but there were people who could see where the future lay. The battle to introduce steam power to Britain's fighting ships has been admirably recounted in *Steam, Steel and Shellfire* in Conway's 'History of the Ship' series.

It is reasonable to consider steam developments in the Royal Navy during the first half of the nineteenth century for it was Britain which possessed the largest fighting and commercial fleets, as well as an undoubted lead in terms of steam-engine manufacturing capabilities. The other major European naval powers, Russia and France, relied on British technology either in the form of complete engines or the machinery to produce them and it was left to British engineers to be the innovators. American naval engineering fully developed only after about 1840.

During the 1820s a number of vessels were constructed for support purposes and for the carriage of mails, and the machinery installed in them was the same as that fitted in commercial steamers, being ordered from commercial engine and boiler builders. Side-lever engines drove paddle wheels with the steam being supplied by rectangular flue-type boilers; the ships were virtually merchant ships but they were operated by the Admiralty. By 1829 a decision had been taken to construct steam-powered fighting ships and the first of these, HMS *Dee* was launched in 1832. Four other vessels *Rhadamanthus*, *Salamander*, *Phoenix* and *Medea* soon followed and all had paddles driven by jet-condensing, side-lever engines, the standard means of ship propulsion at that time. There was, in fact, no reason for any other type of machinery, the design having proved itself successful in commercial service. Maudslay, Sons & Field supplied the engines for all of these ships as well as for five other Admiralty steamers built during the 1820s, the quality of that company's work being appreciated by the naval authorities.[1] The Admiralty took engines only from approved builders who could demonstrate skill and quality of workmanship, the only other contractor on the approved list during that period being Boulton & Watt. After 1830 other builders gained approval but Maudslays remained the leading supplier for many years.

The machinery fitted in *Dee* was less powerful than that of the other ships, 200nhp compared with 220nhp, but in terms of general design the installations were the same. Cylinder dimensions for the more powerful engines were 55.5in bore by 5ft stroke with a weight of 165 tons; the two iron boilers weighed 35 tons and held 45 tons of water. Coal bunkers stowed 250 tons and at full power the boilers consumed 18 tons per day or 8lbs/nhp/hr.[2] A drawing of *Salamander* shows a typical merchant-ship machinery installation with a large double-ended boiler positioned aft of the engines, the width of the ship at deck level being reduced where the paddle wheels were located.[3]

Expansion of the British steam-powered fleet took place during the 1840s with the construction of a number of paddle frigates giving scope for other engine builders to take their share of the market. Although side-lever engines were satisfactory, their weight and the space they occupied prompted the Admiralty to encourage engine builders to find alternative arrangements. A number of the designs produced have been considered in Chapter 2, including Seaward's 'Gorgon' engine and the Siamese engine developed by Maudslays. The Seaward engine was originally to have been fitted in the paddle frigate *Cyclops* and machinery from Boulton & Watt was intended for *Gorgon* but a change in plans saw the two 150nhp Seaward engines and the four copper boilers installed in *Gorgon*, after which ship the engine type was subsequently named; *Cyclops* also received Seaward engines.[4] During the early 1840s Maudslays supplied Siamese or twin-cylinder engines for a number of frigates including *Devastation* (1841), *Retribution* (1844) and *Terrible* (1845); but other builders also obtained their share of what was becoming a steady market. Boulton & Watt, Rennie, Miller & Ravenhill and Fairbairn also supplied direct-acting engines to their own design, while Penn, Rennie and Miller & Ravenhill built oscillating engines for

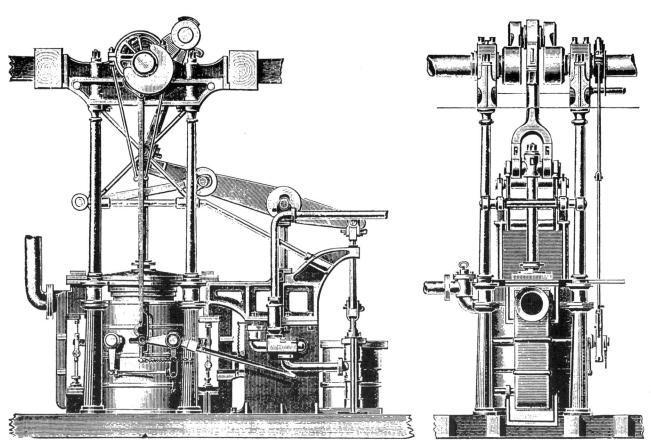

6.1 The 'Gorgon' paddle engine as developed by Seaward

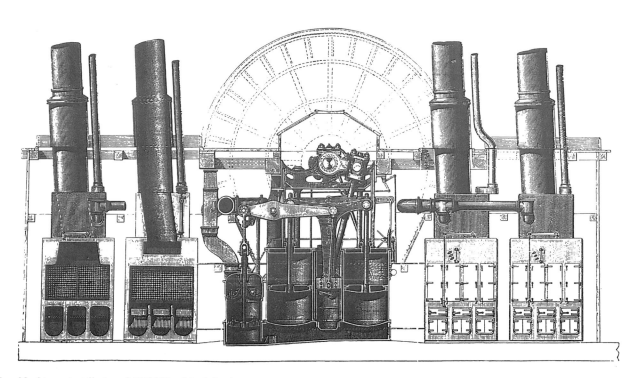

6.2 Machinery installation of HMS Terrible (1845)

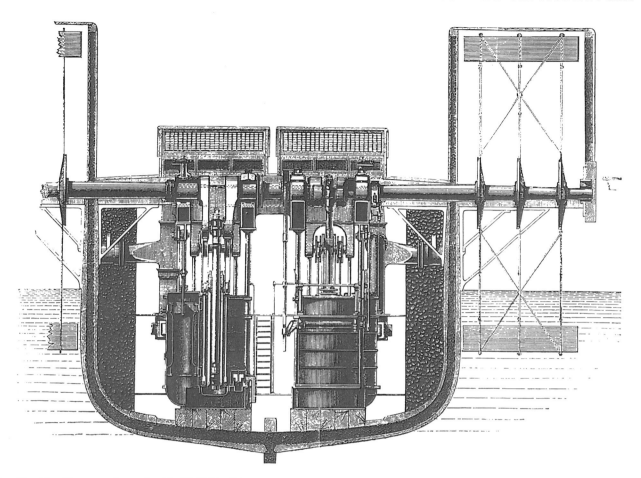

6.3 Maudslay Siamese engine as fitted in HMS Terrible

naval duties.[5] Engines varied little from their commercial counterparts, only the duties of the ships in which they were installed differed. The growth in demand and the competition it produced encouraged higher workmanship and innovation to meet the particular demands of the military; the marine engineering industry as a whole benefited from the naval adoption of steam propulsion.

Although not under the same commercial pressures as mercantile steamship operators, naval authorities did have to work within tight budgets and value for money was important; but quality and reliability were the overriding considerations. The commander of a naval steamer had to be certain of his ship before he could commit her to any action and unreliable machinery could mean the loss of the ship and her crew. Quality construction and the use of the best available materials helped to ensure reliability but they did not guarantee it; the engineers and stokers also had their role to play. During the 1830s naval vessels were usually fitted with copper boilers[6] rather than iron even though the latter material had proved reasonably satisfactory in merchant steamers. Corrosion was the problem with iron but with care iron boilers might be made to last five years,[7]

while copper boilers could last double that time. Copper boilers for the 720-ton, 120nhp HMS *Volcano* (1836) cost £5,000 while iron boilers of similar capacity would have cost £1,500, but when scrapped the iron boilers would be virtually worthless whereas scrap value of copper boilers might be as high as £3,000.[8] At the time there was, however, a further advantage in favour of copper and that centred around its potential reliability. Copper could be obtained in much larger plates than iron thus allowing furnaces to be constructed without any riveted seams above them. Riveted joints were a potential source of leakage and failure, particularly when rivet heads were exposed to direct furnace heat; the avoiding of riveted joints eliminated a possible cause of unreliability.

The paddle frigate reached its zenith with the construction of *Retribution* (1844) and *Terrible* (1845), these ships being fitted with 2,059ihp Siamese engines which gave them the capability of towing a large, three-deck battleship at 8 knots. By this time, however, the naval disadvantages of paddle wheels were becoming evident and at the same time the screw propeller was proving itself to be a much more efficient means of driving a ship. In addition to its higher propulsive efficiency, the screw remained fully immersed when the ship rolled, it was not so vulnerable to damage by enemy shot, nor did it hinder the armament of the ship and thus the paddle propulsion of fighting ships came to a rapid end. Other paddle-driven warships were built in Britain, France, America and other countries up to 1850 but they were the end of the line, paddle machinery for warship propulsion was a blind alley. British naval authorities recognised that fact relatively early but it was only from the service experience of so many paddle-driven warships that the defects of that means of propulsion could really be appreciated. The maintaining of a lead in any technology requires the exploration of many blind alleys if progress is to be maintained. The money spent was not wasted as it enabled British marine engineers to develop design and machinery-production techniques which set them apart from most of their competitors for many years to come.

Screw propulsion may have seemed a logical choice for warship propulsion but even some advocates of a steam navy were not convinced of its effectiveness. In the late 1830s, after John Ericsson had demonstrated the practicability of screw propulsion, Sir William Symonds, Surveyor of the Navy, argued against it on the grounds that it would be impossible to steer a screw vessel since the power was applied at the stern.[9] Ericsson had better luck with the American Navy and in 1843 a propeller to his design was fitted in the new frigate *Princeton*. Despite the initial scepticism there was movement in Britain towards the use of the screw for warships and the first screw steamer built to order by the Admiralty was the 60ft long HMS *Bee* in 1842. This ship was unusual in that she had a single side-lever engine driving conventional paddle wheels and a screw through a 5:1 gearing system. Unfortunately there is no detail as to the nature of that gearing nor of the arrangement of the screw shaft. Maudlays supplied the 20in diameter by 2ft stroke engine and the boiler which generated steam at 10psi. Originally the ship was intended for officer instruction at the Naval College in Portsmouth but her early years were spent engaged on experimental work on different types of screw propellor and other engineering components. The dual method of propulsion appears to have been unsuccessful as the vessel was criticised as being unmanageable by those who had charge of her.[10]

The merits of the screw could not be ignored and during the early 1840s a number of screw-propelled vessels were constructed, machinery from several manufacturers often being of the same type as that used for paddle vessels. Although the more enlightened would have understood the benefits of the screw propeller, others were less convinced and some shrewd individual convinced his masters that a series of trials would demonstrate the better form of propulsion. During 1844 the screw sloop HMS *Rattler* was tried against the similarly-sized paddle-driven *Alecto* with the

former winning handsomely, even towing the paddle steamer backwards at 2.8 knots although her paddles were working at full power. *Rattler* had a four-cylinder Siamese engine built by Maudslays, a gear drive being used to rotate the screw shaft. Further back-to-back trials were organised in 1849 when the screw corvette *Niger* had a similar effect on the paddle sloop *Basilisk*. As with most such trials they proved nothing that the well-informed did not already know but they did demonstrate the effectiveness of the screw to the public in general and politicians, who controlled the purse strings, in particular.[11]

Even at the time of the first trial plans had been made for the construction of screw-driven steamers and by the time *Niger* pulled *Basilisk* there were several such ships in naval service and a number of old wooden battleships had been fitted with screws. In addition to the advantages already mentioned, the screw was more readily taken out of service than the paddle wheel thus allowing the ship to proceed under sail alone. Lifting screws proved to be the best means of achieving this, the two-bladed screw being raised into a opening in the stern of the vessel by a rack arrangement; the propeller shaft had to be turned so that the dog clutch drive between shaft and screw was positioned to enable the screw to be disengaged. Boilers were provided with telescopic funnels so that they could be lowered when the vessel was not steaming in order to allow for easier control of the sails. When reverting to steam power the process would be reversed, prompting the call 'Up funnel, down screw'.

HMS *Ajax*, a wooden, two-deck battleship built around 1809, was one of the first large vessels to be converted to screw propulsion when she was fitted with a two-cylinder, horizontal engine in 1846. Maudslays built the engine for this ship and others which were similarly fitted at about the same time. Some ships simply had the machinery installed in their after holds while others were lengthened in order to improve the flow of water around the stern and into the propeller. The French ordered similar conversions at the same time, steam propulsion being an evident part of the mid-nineteenth-century arms race. One of the first battleships built with steam propulsion from new was the 91-gun *James Watt*, originally ordered to be laid down at Devonport in 1847 as HMS *Audacious*. Delay in construction resulted in the order being changed to Pembroke Dockyard with design changes to incorporate steam propulsion. James Watt & Co. supplied the machinery (hence the change in name), this consisting of a four-cylinder, horizontal engine, 52in bore by 3ft stroke, and iron tubular boilers. The cylinders were arranged two on each side of the ship, opposing pairs connecting with one of the two cranks placed at 90° to each other; there were two jet condensers and two opposing air pumps driven by a crank positioned between the two sets of power cylinders.[12]

The year 1848 saw the completion of the screw frigates

Arrogant and *Encounter* at Portsmouth, their two-cylinder engines being of the trunk-piston type patented by John Penn, William Hartree and John Matthews. Cylinders were both on the same side of the engine with the jet condenser, air pumps and hot well located on the opposite side, the air pumps being driven by rods attached to the pistons below the trunks. The design became standard for naval installation but the engine fitted in *Arrogant* was relatively small (bore 6oin, trunk diameter 24in and stroke 3ft) compared with later requirements.[13] The trunk engine was ideally suited for use in early screw warships owing to the relatively small space it occupied in the hull. Screw machinery was a problem particularly for ships of narrow beam and a number of designs evolved in order to allow for a relatively long connecting rod, but at the same time, meet naval requirements for the engine to be completely below the water line. Penn's trunk engine was just one design but it was favoured by the British naval authorities not only because it met the height requirements but also because of the quality of workmanship. *Arrogant* initially had box-type tubular boilers, also built by Messrs. Penn, the total cost of her machinery being £22,432.[14]

Although the Admiralty appeared slow in adopting new ideas, steam power gradually took over from sail during the 1840s. However, there could not be a wholesale change to steam because of Britain's world role. Coaling stations did not exist in many parts of the world and steam plant was not then considered reliable or efficient enough to make long voyages, particularly for battleships. Smaller vessels provided valuable experience in terms of steam operations as did the converted older battleships and by 1850 it was generally accepted, at least in Britain, that the sailing warship was a thing of the past. The radical change of attitude on the part of the Royal Navy was significant both in terms of Britain's maritime role in the world and also for her shipbuilding and marine engineering industries. Other nations had to follow if their fleets were not to be made obsolete, indeed France had reached the same conclusion with respect to steam power at about the same time,[15] while the demand for high quality, reliable steam plant of ever increasing power stimulated the British manufacturing sector for the next two decades and beyond.

Machinery failure in a fighting ship was potentially more catastrophic than in a merchant ship and British naval authorities took steps to ensure that, as far as possible, any machinery purchased for warships would be to the highest standard. An Admiralty committee was established during the late 1850s and reported on its findings in 1858 after considering the machinery available from many manufacturers and looking at the records of engines already installed. The committee recommended three types of engine for future use as they were far superior to all others then available, adding that no engines of an older make should ever again

be put on board naval ships. The approved engine types were:

1. Single piston rod direct-drive engine with a single flat crosshead guide;
2. Trunk engines of the type patented by Messrs. Penn;
3. The double piston rod engine (also known as the return connecting rod engine).

For small ships the single piston rod engine of Humphrys, Tennant & Dykes was recommended, but in terms of the other machinery no particular supplier was specified although the Admiralty had its own list of approved engine builders. The committee stated that only machinery of the highest quality should ever be purchased and urged that '... all engines furnished to our men-of-war should have all that modern knowledge of steam machinery can produce'.[16] Obviously the members of the committee believed in progress and desired to see that only the most modern machinery ever went into naval ships.

An important step was taken during the late 1850s with an order for the construction of the iron screw steam frigate *Warrior*. Although she was beaten into service as the first major ironclad warship by the French *Gloire* she was the real innovator, the French ship being effectively a poor relation. In terms of construction *Warrior* was a significant step forward and her machinery was also the most powerful then built for any warship. Penn's two-cylinder jet condensing trunk engine (112in bore by 4ft stroke) developed 5,469ihp at 54rpm with a steam pressure of 22psi, giving the ship a speed of 14.3 knots during her trials. Each cylinder had its own expansion valve and piston-rod glands were

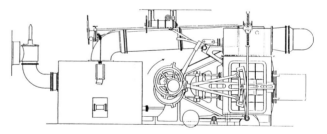

6.4 Penn screw engine installation of HMS Warrior

provided with metallic packing rings rather than the more common hemp-packed glands which were found in engines for commercial service. Hemp-packed glands required frequent attention otherwise excessive steam leakage occurred, but metallic packing was more expensive and hence not used in engines for commercial service. These Penn engines used superheated steam and experience had shown that hemp packing caused damage to piston rods when water droplets were absent. The tubular box boilers were made from iron although brass was used for the tubes. As the ship was intended to operate under sail alone at certain times a lifting screw was fitted together with two telescopic funnels and steam waste pipes; these waste pipes came from the dead-weight safety valves.[17]

Messrs. Penn built similar engines for *Black Prince*,

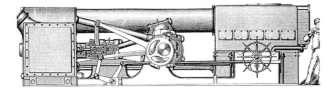

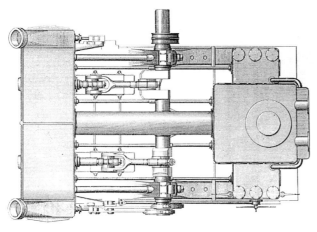

6.5 Penn horizontal two-cylinder screw engine as developed in 1862

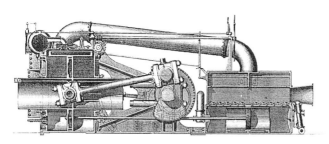

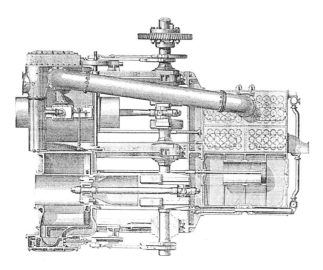

6.6 Section through Penn horizontal screw engine

sister ship of *Warrior*, and for *Achilles* (1864), a subsequent development of these ironclads. Larger engines with a longer stroke went into *Minotaur* (1865), the longer stroke being possible because of the increased beam of the ship, this twin-cylinder installation developing 6,949ihp at 62.5rpm from steam at a pressure of 25psi. Machinery installed in *Minotaur* weighed 1,009 tons or 6.44ihp/ton while that of *Warrior* weighed 898 tons giving 6.09ihp per ton. A reduction in the space the machinery occupied and an increase in specific power were as important to naval authorities as they were to commercial operators; naval ships carried larger crews than merchant steamers while the fighting capabilities of any ship depended upon the storage space available for projectiles and propellants. Although Penn trunk engines were well built and effective there were engineers who did not like the design for a number of reasons. Trunks were difficult to keep steam-tight in service and they presented additional surface to the atmosphere through which heat was lost, thereby reducing efficiency. The larger diameter and higher mass piston resulted in increased cylinder friction wear; all horizontal engines exhibited greater frictional wear in the cylinders owing to the fact that the weight of their pistons acted on the cylinder rather than on the crosshead as in a vertical engine.[18]

Because the connecting rod was attached direct to the piston in a trunk piston engine there was an additional downward force on it when the crank was above the crankshaft centre; this added to cylinder wear problems. The return double piston rod engine, sometimes referred to as a return connecting rod engine, had a crosshead upon which connecting rod thrusts acted, but it also allowed for the use of long connecting rods and thus these thrusts were lower in magnitude. To achieve this the cylinder crosshead was positioned on the opposite side of the crankshaft to the cylinder and two piston rods were needed to connect the piston to the crosshead, one above and one below the crankshaft. The connecting rod returned towards the cylinder in order to attach the crosshead to its crank. Maudslay, Sons & Field developed this type of engine and, in addition to the usual crosshead, provided a support and guide for the extended piston rod at the opposite end of the cylinder; this arrangement was designed to minimise cylinder wear. A two-cylinder jet-condensing engine of this type was fitted in HMS *Agincourt*, a sister to *Minotaur* thus allowing for direct comparison; the engine had a connecting rod 11ft 3in long compared with 8ft for the trunk engine fitted in *Warrior*. From a steam pressure of 25psi her 101in bore by 4ft 6in stroke cylinders developed 6,860ihp when running trials in 1865; this represented 6.7ihp/ton for the 1,022-ton machinery installation of *Agincourt*.[19]

Robert Napier & Sons developed a return connecting rod engine which showed a degree of originality and ingenuity. Attached to the crosshead of each cylinder was a

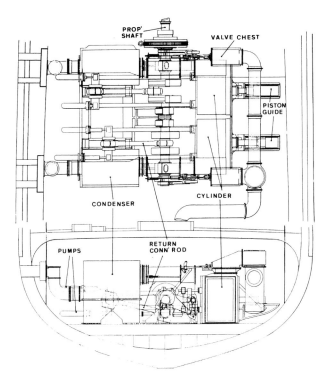

6.7 Maudslay horizontal return crank connecting rod engine as fitted in HMS Agincourt *(1865)*

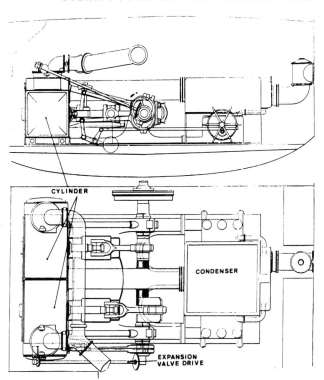

6.9 Humphry & Tennant engine fitted in HMS Prince Albert *(1864)*

trunk piston which operated in a cylinder located in the jet condenser; this was a single-acting, air pump for the condenser. An extension to the piston ran through a gland at the opposite end of the brass-lined cylinder, the whole trunk piston arrangement acting to support the crosshead. The engine would appear to have had the same problems of reactionary forces at the trunk as in Penn's engine but this time at the air pump rather than the engine cylinder. In 1863 Napiers provided a two-cylinder engine of the type, 84in bore by 4ft stroke, for HMS *Hector* and during trials

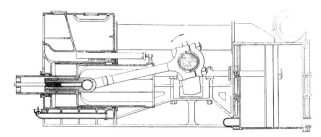

6.8 Napier horizontal trunk engine supplied in 1863 for HMS Hector

the following year it developed 3,256ihp at 59rpm. Steam at a pressure of 22psi came from six rectangular tubular boilers, furnaces and casings being made from iron and the tubes being of brass. In full working order the machinery weighed 768 tons, giving a rather poor rating of 4.24ihp/ton.[20]

The horizontal direct-acting engines of Humphry & Tennant had short connecting rods and thus reactionary forces at the crosshead and crankshaft were high but this resulted in a simpler engine design which found favour among naval engineers. Engines of the type were constructed for many ships during the 1860s and the large one fitted in HMS *Prince Albert* during 1864 was typical. Cylinder slide valves were actuated by means of cam-operated link gear in a manner similar to that of most engines of the period. Also in common with most other engines an expansion valve was fitted in the steam supply line to each cylinder but, as was again generally the case, these valves were subsequently removed, operating experience showing them to be unnecessary and a source of trouble. Humphry's engine had expansion valves actuated by means of a shaft driven by the crankshaft through bevel gears. Two air pumps, one for each cylinder, were positioned below the crankshaft and worked direct from the main pistons; jet condensers were located on the other side of the engine from the crankshaft. From two 72in bore by 3ft stroke cylinders the engine fitted in *Prince Albert* developed 2,130ihp with steam at 24psi. The total weight of the machinery was 361 tons, giving a specific output of 5.9hp per ton, better than the Napier engines but worse than the Maudslay and Penn installations.[21]

A larger, two-cylinder Humphry's engine, 76in bore by 4ft 6in stroke, was fitted in the cruiser *Raleigh* (1874) and this developed some 6,000ihp. The engine was an improvement on the earlier design as it employed surface condensers and used superheated steam, with a pressure of 32psi and superheat temperature of 310°F. Water was circulated through the condenser by independent centrifugal pumps and the engine starting gear was steam-driven although manual operation was possible in an emergency.[22]

Surface condensing had been reintroduced to naval vessels during the 1860s and one of the earliest large installations was provided by Maudslay, Sons & Field with the three-cylinder return crank engine fitted in HMS *Lord Warden* during 1866. The basic arrangement of the engine

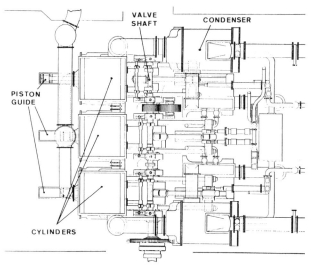

6.10 *Maudslay surface-condensing horizontal engine as installed in HMS* Lord Warden *of 1866*

was similar to the type fitted in *Agincourt*, the three cylinders being arranged alongside each other with cranks at 120°; slide valves were on top of the cylinders rather than alongside. The usual eccentrics were dispensed with and a small crankshaft was used to actuate the valves, this crankshaft being driven from the main one by a gear wheel train. Two surface condensers were positioned on the other side of the crankshaft, these having copper tubes through which exhaust steam passed while cooling water circulated around the tubes. In order to provide for an effective seal, both ends of each tube had a screwed gland packed with cotton. Cylinders, 92.25in bore by 4ft 6in stroke, were entirely steam jacketed and metallic packing was used for the piston-rod glands, the steam supply being superheated. Piston rods were extended through glands in their top cylinder covers and were supported by a slide and guide arrangement; this arrangement reduced the force between the piston and the lower part of the cylinder liner. Steam at a pressure of 25psi was generated by eight box-type tubular boilers which employed a system of induced draught; this consisted of four steam blast pipes at the base of each of the two telescopic

funnels, the arrangement being similar to that employed for steam locomotives. During trials in 1866 the engines developed a maximum 6,706ihp, giving a specific output of 6.65ihp/ton on the total machinery weight of 1,009 tons.[23]

Throughout the 1860s and the 1870s there were many improvements in marine engines, not only in terms of design but also in material quality and manufacturing techniques. The demand for a reduction in weight brought about a demand for higher-strength materials, while the requirement for increased reliability dictated that such materials be of consistent quality. Improvements in machine tools and working techniques led to changes in

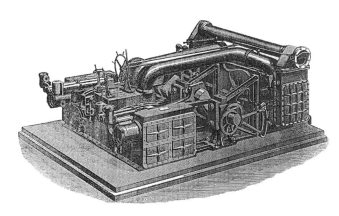

6.11 *Horizontal return crank engine designed by Ravenhill & Salkeld during 1862*

design and improvements in quality and the demand for better economy saw more use of steam jacketing, surface condensers and the introduction of compounding. An increase in boiler pressure was possible through improvements in design, such as the cylindrical boiler and the availability of mild steel plates of consistent high quality.[24] Changes in marine engineering did not happen by accident, they came about through competition and the demand for improvements by shipowners and the Admiralty was the largest steamship owner in Britain; what the Admiralty wanted shipbuilders and marine engine builder competed to give and improvement was a natural consequence.

Naval engineering in other countries followed a similar pattern to that in Britain with many governments ordering their ships from British yards, assured of quality and state-of-the-art products. As an example, in the mid-1860s Robert Napier secured orders for a 1,330-ton armoured turret ship from Denmark, a 2,284-ton turret ship and 1,427-ton monitor from Holland, and three 6,400-ton ironclad frigates from Turkey.[25] France, and later Germany, were military competitors of Britain and to have their naval vessels constructed in Britain would have been unthinkable although both countries turned to British builders for merchant ships. Machinery designed in both countries followed similar patterns to that constructed in Britain for naval purposes, early screw engines being of the horizontal type. In 1847 the French iron dispatch vessel *Biche* was given a two-cylinder, return-crank, horizontal engine built by Mazeline of Le Havre; the design was rather novel and a similar one was used in Britain by Miller, Ravenhill & Co. The engine's two cylinders were positioned back-to-back at the centre of the engine room and drove two crankshafts which then drove the screw shaft through a system of gearing with a 2:1 speed increase ratio. This 120ihp engine was short compared with other two-cylinder, horizontal designs of the period but it suffered severe vibration and in 1852 was replaced by one of the direct-acting type. At the same time *Biche* was given the first Belleville water-tube boiler, but this proved troublesome and was replaced with an ordinary tubular boiler a few years later.[26]

America had little need for an extensive navy during the first half of the nineteenth century but from about 1850 there was a growing realisation that a naval presence was essential in its coastal waters at least. Steam power came through the influence of John Ericsson with the screw frigate *Princeton* illustrating where the future of naval power lay. Six large screw frigates of the 'Merrimack' class were ordered in 1854 and these had two-cylinder horizontal

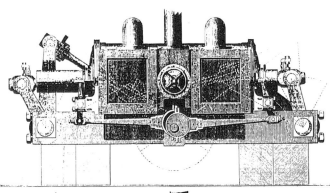

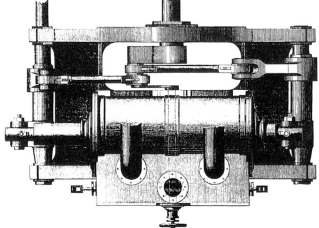

6.12 Ericsson-type, two-cylinder horizontal screw engine as fitted in Monitor *(1862)*

engines. Although the machinery was no more advanced than anything built in Europe, the construction of these ships indicated a growing confidence in America's ability to compete in naval matters, particularly around her own coasts. The Civil War damaged the confidence and cohesion of the nation and retarded progress in many areas, including marine engineering. Although conflicts generally result in increased military budgets the money is usually spent on production rather than development and this would appear to have been the case in the American Civil War. Naval ships were constructed but power plants advanced little from earlier home-built units; the Union forces generally had control of ship and engine building facilities and the Confederacy was forced to purchase ships in Europe. With the coming of peace the rebuilding of the nation and the fleet could commence.

Princeton is generally considered to be the first screw steamer with its machinery completely below the waterline and the horizontal arrangement was later followed for most naval screw installations. In America, Ericsson's design of screw engine subsequently developed into a general type which was used for *Monitor* (1862) and similar vessels. The Ericsson design was modified by a number of builders including Mazeline for installation in *Biche* and Miller & Ravenhill for use in HMS *Amphion*. The Ericsson vibrating-lever engine generally consisted of two trunk cylinders placed back-to-back at the engine room centre, each piston rod connecting with a crank on a vibrating or oscillating shaft; the motion of each piston caused its shaft to rock back and forwards. Also on the shaft but slightly aft of the cylinder was a second but longer crank with a connecting rod which attached to a crankpin on the crankshaft placed on the ship's centre line; connecting rods from both cylinders were attached to the single crankpin. The motion of the pistons caused their separate vibrating shafts to oscillate and they in turn produced rotation at the crankshaft through their connecting rods. Cylinder slide valves were actuated by eccentrics driven by the main crankshafts and the jet condenser was attached direct to the cylinders. The engine fitted in *Princeton* operated in a similar manner 'except that pistons vibrated to and fro like a door moving on its hinges'; such an arrangement would have avoided the need for trunk pistons but it is difficult to imagine how the engine operated effectively.[27]

In the immediate post Civil War period a number of wooden sloops were constructed, wood being favoured because of its availability, return connecting rod engines being used. The design was produced under the supervision of B. F. Isherwood, Chief of the Bureau of Shipping of the US Navy, and followed the arrangement of similar engines built in Britain. The two-cylinder engine, 60in bore by 3ft stroke, built for *Hassalo* in 1866 was of the surface-condensing type, steam passing through the tubes and

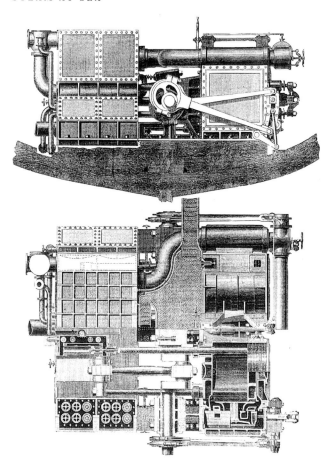

6.13 *Two-cylinder horizontal surface condensing engine installed in the US Navy wooden sloop* Hassalo *(1866)*

cooling water around them. Air pumps and condenser sea-water circulating pumps were located below the condenser and driven from the piston crossheads; the aftermost cylinder crosshead operated the single bilge pump while the forward cylinder crosshead drove the feed pump. Eccentrics for the valve gear, one set for each cylinder, were driven by the crankshaft, the valve operating rods entering the cylinder through the outboard covers.[28]

In general, the horizontal engine intended for screw propulsion of warships was one of the types previously discussed, no matter where it was built. Details differed depending upon the builder, but the basic arrangement remained the same until vertical engines found favour. As steam pressures increased compounding became established, as it had for merchant ships, the economy of such operation being apparent to most but the additional complexity militated against compounding as far as some were concerned. The first British naval vessel fitted with compound machinery was the wooden frigate *Constance* which had an Elder's-built engine. In 1865 she was raced against the sister ships *Arethusa* and *Octavia* between Plymouth and Madeira. All the ships ran out of coal before reaching Madeira but *Constance* went further and her specific coal consumption was less than that of her sisters.

During the late 1860s a number of corvettes were constructed with compound engines from several builders and a series of comparative trials took place; G. B. Rennie fitted two-cylinder return connecting rod, surface condensing, compound engines in *Spartan* and *Briton* to non-identical designs. The engine fitted in *Spartan* was designed by E. E. Allen and had cylinders containing double pistons

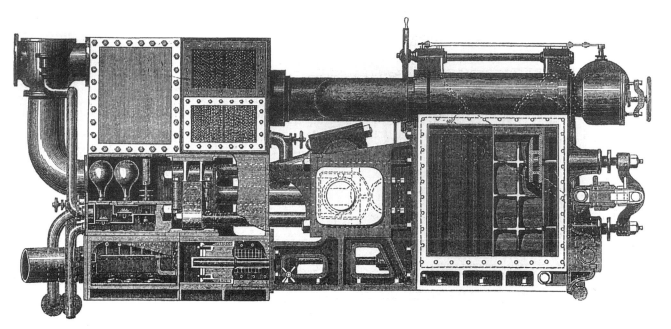

6.14 *Section through the engine fitted in USS* Hassalo

6.15 Iron screw warship of 1870: HMS Sultan

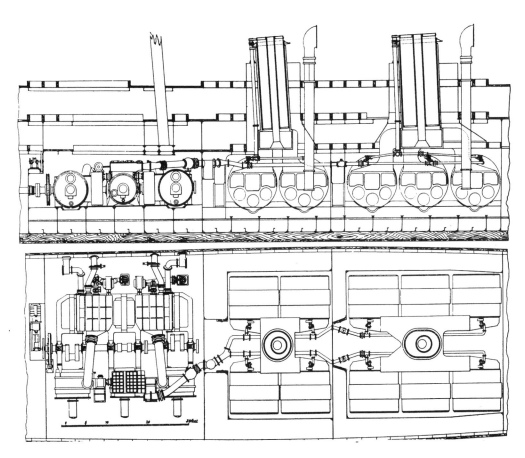

6.16 Engine room arrangement of HMS Boadicea *with three-cylinder horizontal compound engine*

separated by a trunk which produced an annular space between the pistons; a metallic gland contacted the trunk thus forming two high-pressure cylinders between the two low-pressure cylinders. In effect, each cylinder contained two tandem compound cylinders.[29] *Briton* had more conventional cylinders, the engine having 57in bore HP and 100in bore LP cylinders with a stroke of 2ft 9in. When supplied with steam at 60psi the engine developed 2,100ihp and during a full-power test returned coal consumption figures of 1.515lbs/ihp.[30]

The machinery of *Spartan* was unreliable but that of *Briton* was considered very effective. In 1872 the Committee on Designs reported and strongly recommended the adoption of the compound engine for future construction.[31] Although not everybody was in favour, particularly because of the increased machinery complexity, the general move was towards compounding both for naval and merchant service and, inevitably, the coal pile had the final say. Higher steam pressures ensured that compounding was a success but such pressure increases were only obtainable through better quality materials, improved design and enhanced standards of construction.

Most designers produced compound engines based upon earlier horizontal, simple engines, usually by replacing one of the cylinders with a larger low-pressure cylinder, but some designers developed three-crank compound engines by dividing the LP. During 1875 three-cylinder, compound engines were built by Rennie for the unarmoured corvettes *Boadicea* and *Bacchante*, these being of that company's

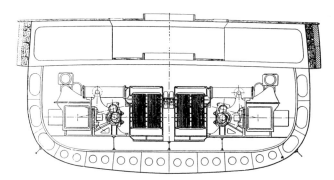

6.17 Section through the engine room of HMS Devastation *(1872)*

standard return connecting rod design. The 74in HP cylinder had 92in diameter LP cylinders on either side, all cylinders being steam jacketed with their pistons supported at their free ends by adjustable sliding blocks. Unlike other engines of the type, the cranks were not arranged 120° apart, the LP cranks were opposite each other and the HP crank at 90° to them. There were two surface condensers placed between the crosshead guides on the port side, circulating sea water being supplied by two centrifugal

pumps independently driven; bilge, feed and air pumps were driven by the main engine. Steam at a pressure of 70psi was supplied by ten cylindrical tubular boilers arranged in two boiler rooms. The engines were efficient giving a specific coal consumption of about 2lbs/ihp/hr under normal circumstances and as low as 1.8lbs/ihp/hr during trials.[32]

The slightly smaller, three-cylinder return connecting rod compound engine built by Ravenhill, Eastons & Co. for HMS *Rover* at about the same time had its cranks at 120°, the designer believing that this arrangement produced a more even turning moment. Surface condensers had steam passing through the tubes as was common to many designs

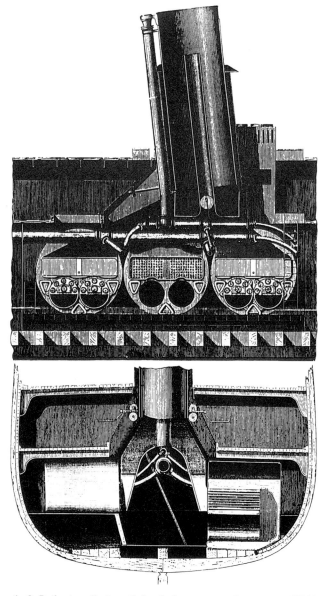

6.18 Boiler installation of the single-screw, wooden corvette HMS Tenedos *built during the late 1860s*

at the time, and steam at a pressure of 70psi was supplied by a cylindrical boiler with brass tubes instead of the more usual iron. During trials the engine developed 4,960ihp from her 72in and 88in bore cylinders.[33]

As in mercantile practice, the compound engine was an important advance but in terms of naval power the introduction of the mastless battleship HMS *Devastation* in 1872 was probably more significant and was a step which other maritime powers had to follow. *Devastation* was not the first mastless ship in the British fleet but she was the first battleship to rely only on the power of her engines; an absence of sailing rig reduced air resistance thereby giving the ship greater speed, it reduced the complement necessary to man the ship and it allowed for a central battery of guns. Machinery had to be reliable but the Admiralty had always insisted upon quality and reliability before cost, and experience had shown that by the 1870s machinery could generally be relied upon. There was, however, always a risk of failure but the provision of two engine systems, driving twin screws, reduced the risk of complete immobilisation and *Devastation* was given a twin-screw propulsion system. Two-cylinder Penn trunk engines were chosen and, although compounding was an established fact at that time, simple expansion was employed in order to reduce the complexity of the plant. The use of trunk engines allowed them to be positioned alongside each other thereby keeping the engine room length reasonable; twin-screw installations for narrower beam ships often had engines positioned one in front of the other. Cylinders were close to the ship's sides with their surface condensers at the centre of the engine room, these having the configuration which became standard of steam surrounding the tubes and cooling water passing through them.

The diameter of the steam-jacketed cylinders was 88in and that of the trunk 36.5in, giving an effective 80in cylinder; the stroke was 3ft 3in. Essentially the design was the same as earlier Penn trunk engines. Eight cylindrical boilers supplied steam at a pressure of 30psi, relatively low for the time but adequate with the use of simple expansion, the steam being superheated. There were two boiler rooms and the chimneys were telescopic with shell-proof gratings at the bottom. A range of auxiliary steam-powered systems was installed, including pumps, ash hoists, capstans and ventilation fans while telegraphs were fitted to allow for communication between the bridge and engine room. Each engine was designed to develop 3,250ihp but during trials the total maximum power reached was 6,638ihp. For a machinery weight of 985 tons at the design power, the specific output was 6.6ihp/ton.[34]

Throughout the 1870s and into the 1880s the mastless ship, often with twin-screw and compound engines, became an established part of the world's fleets and with the introduction of steel higher powers and improved armour

became possible. High-powered horizontal engines occupied considerable engine room space, particularly when placed one in front of the other, and it became obvious that the vertical engine presented the only solution to the problem of high power and limited space. In 1878 HMS *Inflexible* was given two Elders'-built, vertical, three-cylinder compound engines developing a total of 8,483ihp with steam at 60psi, and from then onwards most British naval ships had vertical engines fitted.[35] The availability of steel for armour plating allowed the engine room to be protected and there was not such a great need for the machinery to be completely below the water line. There was still a need to keep the height of naval engines as low as possible and vertical engines for warships tended to be lower than their mercantile counterparts, reduced height being possible through the use of shorter piston strokes and shorter connecting rods.

Apart from the height restriction, mercantile and naval engineering practices followed similar lines until the end of the nineteenth century, with higher steam pressures and triple-expansion machinery being the next development. The introduction of high-speed torpedo boats and torpedo boat destroyers resulted in a demand for high-power, compact machinery and in that naval practice diverted from that of the commercial fleets. Water-tube boilers were a feature of naval steamers long before they were accepted for merchant ships.

References

1 *The Engineer*, vol. 65, 20 Apr. 1888, p. 321; letter from Maudslay, Sons & Field concerning early engines.

2 *Marine Engineer & Motorship Builder*, Aug. 1932, vol 55, pp. 286–7.

3 *The Engineer*, vol. 66, 27 July 1888, p. 74.

4 A. E. M. Laing, 'Introduction of Paddle Frigates to the Royal Navy', *Mariner's Mirror*, vol. 66, 1980, pp. 333–6.

5 E. C. Smith, 'The Centenary of Naval Engineering', *Trans. Newcomen Society*, vol. 2, 1921–2, pp. 109–13.

6 A. E. M. Laing, 'Paddle Frigates', pp. 332–4 makes mention of early paddle frigates with copper boilers specified.

7 The flue boilers of *Great Western* were replaced in 1843 after 5.5 years of service; D. Griffiths, *Brunel's Great Western*, Patrick Stephens, Wellingborough, 1985, p. 82.

8 E. C. Smith, *A Short History of Marine Engineering*, Cambridge University Press, 1937, p. 128.

9 Ibid., p. 68.

10 *Marine Engineer & Motorship Builder*, vol. 55, Mar. 1932, pp. 112–3.

11 P. M. Rippon, *Evolution of Engineering in the Royal Navy*, vol. 1, Spellmount, Tunbridge Wells, 1988, p. 37.

12 *Marine Engineer & Motorship Builder*, vol. 49, June 1926, pp. 232–3.

13 *The Engineer*, vol. 65, 4 May 1888, p. 356.

14 *Marine Engineer & Motorship Builder*, vol. 48, Oct. 1925, p. 375.

15 The story behind the development of a steam-powered Navy is covered in: A. Lambert, *Battleships in Transition*, Conway, London, 1984; D. K. Brown, *Before the Ironclad*, Conway, 1990; and *Steam, Steel and Shellfire*, Conway, 1992.

16 Sir Henry Oram, '50 Years Changes in British Warship Machinery', *Trans. I.N.A.*, vol. 53, 1911, p. 111.

17 Ibid., pp. 96–8.

18 *The Engineer*, vol. 65, 4 May 1888, p. 356.

19 Ibid., vol. 65, 18 May 1888, p. 398.

20 Ibid., vol. 65, 8 June 1888, p. 460.

21 Ibid., vol. 66, 6 July 1888, pp. 2–4.

22 *Marine Engineer & Motorship Builder*, vol. 53, June 1930, p. 238.

23 *The Engineer*, vol. 66, 30 Nov. 1888, p. 446.

24 H. Oram, '50 years of Changes', pp. 99–101.

25 H. B. Peebles, *Warshipbuilding on the Clyde*, John Donald, Edinburgh, 1987, p. 13.

26 *Marine Engineer & Motorship Builder*, vol. 49, May 1926, pp. 186–7.

27 *Engineering*, vol. 1, 22 June 1866, pp. 13–14.

28 Ibid., vol. 2, 21 Sept. 1866, pp. 216–20.

29 E. E. Allen, 'The Double Expansion Engines in HMS *Spartan*', *Trans. I.N.A.*, vol. 9, 1868, pp. 79–85.

30 G. B. Rennie, 'Improved Compound Engines of HMS *Briton*', Ibid., vol. 12, 1871, pp. 1–13.

31 *Report of the Committee on Designs for Ships of War*, HMSO, London, 1972.

32 W. H. Maws, *Recent Practice in Marine Engineering*, Engineering, London, 1883, pp. 237–41.

33 J. R. Ravenhill, 'The three-throw Crank Engines of HMS *Rover*', *Trans. I.N.A.*, vol. 17, 1876, pp. 212–21.

34 W. H. Maws, *Recent Practice in Marine Engineering*, pp. 26–7.

35 H. Oram, '50 years of Changes', Table I.

7
Auxiliary Steam Plant at Sea

Steam power was originally intended for the propulsion of ships but it eventually became useful for other purposes when the necessary equipment was fitted. Small steam engines could be employed to drive any number of machines but there had to be a need for the application of power and suitable machinery had to be devised. Steam replaced human labour in many places where the work required was beyond the capacity of one man and it replaced propulsion-engine-driven devices when it became necessary to do the work of that device, usually a pump, at times when the engine was not working. Necessity ensured that steam power would be applied to auxiliary machinery aboard ship and success prompted new auxiliary applications.

Early engines had to provide power to drive condenser air pumps as a minimum but bilge and ballast pumps were also normally driven by the propulsion engine. In most side-lever engines an assortment of pumps would be driven by shafts connected to those levers; it was a simple and convenient arrangement. In port hand pumps generally sufficed for boiler feed and bilge duties but as ships increased in size manual pumping became both time consuming and difficult. Pumps were the first items of auxiliary plant fitted aboard ships and they generally went unmentioned in reports as they would be employed only when the main engine was not working. Feed pumps and bilge pumps to be used in port required a steam supply but it was considered wasteful to fire a main boiler for that purpose and so steamers were provided with auxiliary or donkey 'boilers' for supplying the 'donkey' engines which powered the pumps. During the 1840s a number of steam-driven, single-cylinder, reciprocating pumps were put on the market including one patented by H. R. Worthington in 1841. An Admiralty specification of 1845 for the machinery of a paddle steamer included the provision of a small donkey engine-driven pump for boiler feed.[1]

Bilge pumping presented many problems as bilge pipes and pump valves could easily become blocked with ashes and with low-pressure boilers there was insufficient pressure in the boiler to blow down the boiler to the sea; blowing down to the engine room became common, a bilge pump then being used to pump the bilges overboard. Jet condensers had a pipe arrangement which allowed water to be drawn into the condenser from the bilge (the bilge injection), thus ensuring that serious leakage into the bilge could be dealt with by the largest pump on the ship (the air pump). Even in recent times the largest bilge suction pipe to the large bilge or ballast pump was referred to as the bilge

injection, this terminology being used long after jet condensers had ceased to be used. If the propulsion engine was out of action this system could not be employed and it became important during the early 1850s to fit separate steam engine-driven pumps capable of working the bilges.

Steering Gear

As ships increased in size the power to drive them also increased but larger ships became increasingly difficult to steer and in heavy seas many men were needed to attend to the wheel; HMS *Warrior* required as many as twelve men to handle her steering in anything other than light seas. A number of individuals proposed schemes for steam-driven steering gear but most early ideas proved to be unworkable. In 1859 the American Frederick Elsworth Sickells obtained

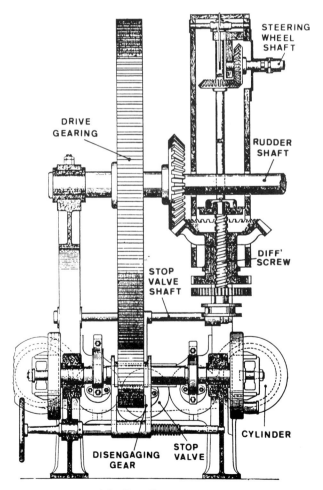

7.1 Steering gear of the Great Eastern

a British patent for a steam-powered steering gear which consisted of two inclined cylinders driving a crankshaft to which was attached a pinion engaging with a toothed wheel on the steering wheel shaft. Whenever the helmsman required the assistance of steam he had only to open the steam valves to the engine.[2] In effect, the steam engine replaced manual power for turning a conventional steering wheel which still employed ropes for moving the tiller. The system was unsuccessful and it was not until 1867 that a practical device was demonstrated by John Macfarlane Gray aboard *Great Eastern*.

Any useful steering gear had to be capable of operation under remote control and Gray's equipment did that as well as fulfilling other requirements set by the owners of *Great Eastern*. These included the capability of moving the rudder at a greater speed than manual force could, the rudder to be held by the steam engine alone and so not require a brake, simplicity of construction, and the capability of the steam engine being used for driving a windlass. An important feature of Gray's apparatus, and all other subsequent steering systems, was that of the hunting gear which allowed manual actuation of the steam engine through the steering wheel, the engine then cancelling this when the rudder had turned through the required angle. The steering gear had a pair of 10in bore by 12in stroke steam cylinders with their cranks at 90°, each cylinder having its own set of valves and, in addition to these, there was a stop valve which directed steam and exhaust; the stop valve was controlled by a differential screw through a bell-crank lever system and

allowed the direction of rotation to be reversed. Movement of the rudder was by means of a rope-operated tiller, these ropes being wrapped around winding drums rotated by the rudder shaft; for manual operation this shaft was turned by means of a large wheel. Steam operation of the rudder shaft was through spur gearing, the engine crankshaft gear being engaged with the rudder shaft gear although the drive could be disengaged to allow the steam engine to drive a windlass.

A wheel on the bridge of the ship was connected with the differential screw through a system of tubular shafting 410ft long, the backlash in the shafting due to the number of universal couplings being about one-eighth of a turn. Rotation of the steering wheel on the bridge caused the differential screw to rotate and that moved a block which caused the bell-crank lever system to open the steam stop valve and start the engine in the required direction. As the engine turned the rudder shaft a bevel gear connected to that shaft moved the block in the opposite direction thus cancelling the movement brought about by the steering wheel; that engine-induced movement caused the steam stop valve to close when the rudder shaft had rotated sufficiently to turn the rudder by the required amount. The steering gear proved to be successful and similar units fitted in HMS *Northumberland* and HMS *Monarch* at the same time also demonstrated the effectiveness of the design.[3]

Other steering-gear systems were devised in the late 1860s and a hydraulic system invented by Captain Inglefield was constructed for a trial in HMS *Achilles* during 1869. Inglefield's gear had two hydraulic cylinders which

7.2 *1,984-grt China coast steamer* Shansi *(1898) showing donkey boiler uptake just aft of the main funnel (John Swire & Son)*

connected with the tiller arm and the movement of these cylinders caused the rudder to turn in much the same manner as the electrohydraulic steering gear systems employed in the twentieth century. A pump provided hydraulic pressure for the cylinders, but that pump was driven by a reciprocating hydraulic motor rather than a steam engine. The pressure for driving the hydraulic motor was that of the sea outside the ship and Inglefield used water pressure to drive a motor which then provided water at a higher pressure to actuate the hydraulic rams. This motor was essentially a differential pressure unit with sea pressure acting on a 36in diameter piston which then acted on a smaller piston producing an output pressure of 600psi; sea water discharged from the motor to the bilge or a separate tank from where it was pumped overboard. The argument behind the use of sea pressure was that steam might not always be available, such as when a vessel operated under sail alone; however, a pump was needed to pump the water overboard after it had worked the hydraulic motor.[4] The trial does not appear to

7.3 Rogers & Co. steam steering engine to Simey's patent (c. 1880)

have been a success and many shipowners decided that the fitting of an auxiliary or donkey boiler was a reasonable way to provide steam when the main boilers were not operating. Steam from that boiler could be used for driving the many steam donkeys, or donkey engines, which were put aboard ship for various duties during the 1870s and later years.

Steam-steering gear became standard equipment for larger and some smaller ships after about 1870 with many designs being produced. They all had two features in common: a steam engine which turned the rudder stock and a form of hunting gear which cancelled the steam supply to the engine when the rudder had turned by the desired

amount. At the Naval and Submarine Exhibition in 1882 many arrangements of steering gear were displayed and most had at least one seagoing installation, the ingenuity of the designs illustrated the depth of marine engineering skill which existed during the latter half of the nineteenth century, not just in Britain but in Europe and America too.[5] An

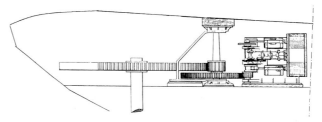

7.4 Steam steering gear fitted in the Atlantic liners Majestic *and* Teutonic *(1890)*

expanding marine industry stemming from the growth in steamship operation encouraged inventiveness in many spheres of which steering gear design was but one; it was, however, an important one. The steering gear fitted in the White Star liner *Teutonic* (1890) was of conventional form with two stationary steam engines driving the rudder stock

7.5 Steering gear fitted in the Cunard liner Campania *(1893)*

through a system of gearing; either engine or both could be employed for steering.[6] The Cunard liners *Campania* and *Lucania* of 1893 had steam steering gear manufactured by Brown Bothers of Edinburgh who became world leaders in the design and manufacture of steering gears during the twentieth century. The arrangement used in these ships employed a steam engine attached to an arm which in turn was connected to the tiller; a toothed wheel was rotated by the steam engine through a system of gearing and that wheel engaged with teeth on a rigid quadrant fitted in the ship. As the engine rotated the gear wheel caused the engine block and tiller arm to turn, thus moving the rudder. Although the system appeared complex it was forced upon the designer through the limited space available in the steering compartment and the fact that the Admiralty stipulated that the entire steering system should be below water line as the ships were built as auxiliary cruisers with government financial assistance.[7]

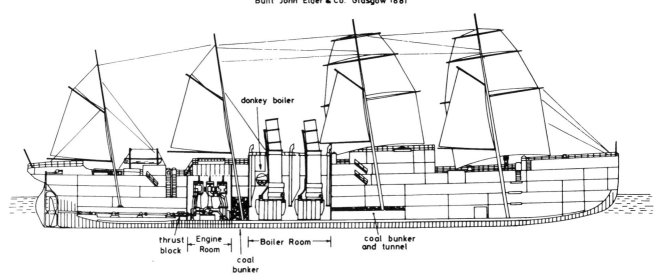

NORDDEUTSCHER LLOYD
"ELBE"
Built John Elder & Co. Glasgow 1881

donkey boiler

thrust | Engine | ← Boiler Room → | coal bunker
block | Room | | and tunnel
coal
bunker

7.6 Section through the German liner Elbe *(1881) showing location of donkey boiler*

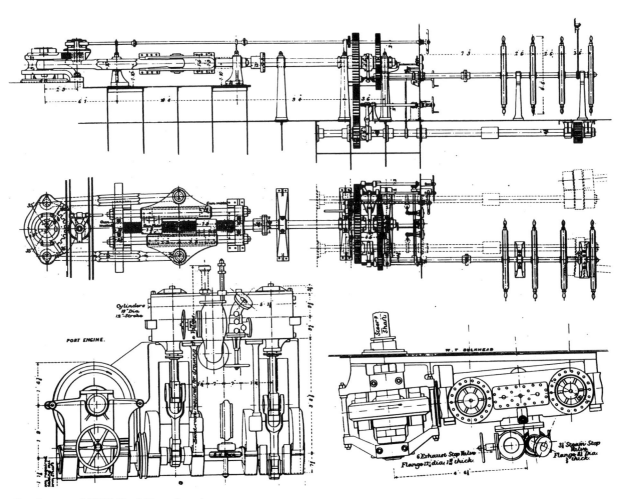

7.7 Steering gear of HMS Good Hope *(1902)*

Deck Machinery

Donkey boilers were not just for powering the steering gear, they could also be used for driving any auxiliary steam engine, and from the early 1860s steam-driven winches and windlasses became common aboard merchant ships. The ratchet-operated windlass had been developed in order to reduce the number of men required for lifting an anchor or other similar duties but the application of steam to such a device did not find favour until a supply could be guaranteed at all times, and that came about with the introduction of the donkey boiler. Fitting winch drums to the ends of the anchor cable-lifting shaft produced a combination machine which could be made to operate as a winch or windlass simply by moving a dog-clutch device. Application of a steam-engine drive to turn the shaft through a system of reduction gearing was a logical step once the basic mechanical structure was in place. By the 1860s a number of such systems had been devised and patented, most having the winch drum and anchor-cable lifter on the same shaft, as was the case with the Graveley patent winch. This had a two-cylinder horizontal steam engine driving two shafts through reduction gearing, there being winch drum, cable lifter, dog clutches and brakes on each of the shafts.[8]

The steering gear fitted in *Great Eastern* had to have a facility allowing it to be converted into a winch and during the 1860s steam-driven winches became popular. Not only did they allow for easier handling of sails but, with the provision of derricks, the ship could load and discharge its own cargo thus reducing the need for manual handling. This increased the speed of cargo work and also allowed heavier and larger items to be loaded or discharged; the time a ship needed to spend in port could be reduced but the means for dealing with large or heavy items of cargo gave the ship an advantage over its competitors. In designing a ship for the winch operation of cargo other factors had to be considered, including the simplification of the rigging so that derricks could operate effectively and increasing the size of hatches

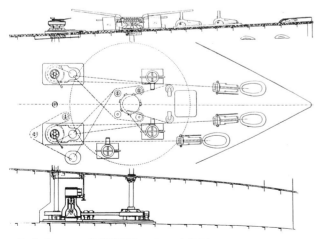

7.8 Anchor gear of HMS Victorious *(1896)*

so that large items could enter the holds. Technological advance did not rely just on the introduction of a new technology. Over the years a number of patent winches were developed but they all had two winch drums which could be driven independently or together. The drums and their associated single-cylinder, reversible steam engines were positioned at each end of a common frame, clutches allowing independent or combined operation of the winch drums. Taylor & Co. of Birkenhead introduced a steam winch in 1856 and the basic design remained popular until well into the twentieth century. HMS *Warrior* was provided with a Taylor winch but this also included a cable lifter and a two-cylinder sea-water pump, clutches allowing any or all devices, including winch drums, to be engaged as required.[9] In order to keep deck spaces free for working, particularly aboard naval ships, the steam plant would often be located below deck; the capstan, windlass and winch were driven by means of vertical shafts projecting through the deck. Deck cranes were also developed in the 1870s, the Guion liner *Arizona* having one on the fore-deck for lifting the anchor on board after it had been raised.[10]

Electricity

Electricity aboard ship was probably the most significant single advance since the introduction of steam as it provided safe and relatively efficient illumination in the darkest part of the vessel and later allowed electric motors to drive many devices without the need to lay on a steam supply. Electric cables were easier to install than steam and exhaust pipes. Lighting by electricity found early favour as it enabled dim, dirty and unsafe oil lamps or candles to be replaced. Gas lighting worked ashore and in 1872 a pair of White Star liners *Adriatic* and *Celtic*, were fitted with open flame, gas-lighting systems, the gas being generated by heating oil in a coal-fired retort. The unit could generate sufficient gas for 300 lights but it proved unsuccessful owing to the number of pipe leaks which developed as the ships moved in a seaway.[11] Electric lighting was the only way forward but installations were expensive and only applicable to the higher class passenger ships during those early years, although some simple electricity generating plants had been installed on warships during the 1870s to provide power for searchlights.[12]

Electric lighting could be justified for passenger ships on the grounds that it reduced the need for the cleaning of accommodation and so allowed a ship to spend more of its time engaged upon profitable voyaging. During the 1870s and the 1880s there were no standards with respect to incandescent lamps or electric cables and early installations suffered many problems through failures. Cable insulation had to cope with an aggressive damp environment while lamps were prone to failure for many reasons including vibration. Much experimental work was undertaken by the

7.9 Steam-engine-driven electrical generator fitted in the Atlantic liner Arizona *during the 1880s*

7.11 Electrical generating equipment for lighting aboard HMS Terrible *(1897)*

suppliers of such items and progress was so fast that many of the early shipboard systems were obsolete within a few years.[13] That progress ensured that electrical installations became standard practice for most passenger ships by the mid-1880s while larger naval vessels of all countries benefited from the use of electrical power. Although the lighting of passenger spaces was the initial objective it is interesting to relate that boiler and engine rooms also formed part of the electric light systems aboard ships with the first such installations. Safety and efficiency depended upon firemen being able to supply coal to furnaces and tend fires effectively while engineers need to monitor boilers and propulsion engines. Skylights allowed some daylight into

the machinery spaces but at night the only illumination came from oil lamps and the glow from the furnaces when doors were opened. Electric lighting provided valuable illumination both night and day.

One of the first merchant ships fitted with electric lighting was the Inman liner *City of Berlin* which had an experimental system installed during 1879. This proved to be so successful that two years later the new liner *City of Rome* was provided with a more extensive system of 100 lamps in the saloon and a further 150 distributed among the other public rooms and cabins; six 300-candle-power arc lamps provided illumination in the machinery spaces and even steerage passenger spaces had ten incandescent lamps.[14]

7.10 Electrical generating plant of the White Star liner Teutonic *(1890)*

When *City of Berlin* was withdrawn for re-engining in 1887 she was given a completely new electrical system with lighting throughout the vessel. Steam engines, simple or compound, provided the motive power for driving the dynamos with the final drive being by means of belts in order to obtain the necessary speed increase. The supply voltage increased little from the 100 volts employed on the early steamers and by the turn of the century 110 volts was rarely exceeded.

The use of electricity did increase dramatically aboard passenger ships, particularly as the advantage of that form of power became evident. Cunard's *Campania* and *Lucania* of 1893 had 100-volt, direct-current systems, supplied by four dynamos each directly driven by two-cylinder, compound steam engines. The ships had lighting systems equivalent to 22,000 candle power, requiring 135 horsepower for generation but, apart from the electric bell communications installation, a searchlight and a motor in the barber's shop the electrical installation was dedicated to illumination.[15] By 1900 the 110-volt electrical installation aboard the German liner *Deutschland* was able to meet a greater lighting demand and also supply power to twenty-five motors, eight electric stoves, two water heaters, two egg boilers, seventy small ventilating fans, and 375 curling iron sockets. The electric motors were used for boiler forced-draught fans, bunker-ventilation fans, as well as hoists for mails and provisions; the ease of control and simplification of installation compared with steam engines gave electric motors the advantage in such cases. Power was supplied by three 77-kW and two 44-kW dynamos and the electrical circuits were designed so that each main area of use had its own main switches.[16]

Companies operating passenger ships could not afford to fall behind the competition and each new liner saw improvements and a greater use of electrical power, but the situation was similar with respect to naval ships as no nation could afford for its ships to be less efficiently armed and operated than those of a potential enemy. Electrical power was a form of armament, even if used only for lighting, and the effective operation of a warship could be improved if its complex system of passageways was adequately illuminated. The battleship *Prince George* (1896) was electrically lit throughout, there being 930 incandescent lamps, 310 of fifty candle power and the remainder of sixteen which illuminated working and living spaces; in addition to these six searchlights were fitted. Electrical power was supplied by three dynamos and twenty-nine miles of cable were used in the ship; a battery back-up system of lighting was also fitted to provide light should the main system fail.[17]

Although reciprocating steam engines were the initial means of driving dynamos the turbine found favour as its high operating speed was suitable for direct drive at constant speed. Probably the first seagoing turbo-generators were installed in the liner *City of Berlin* during its 1887 refit and were popular with the engineers as they required no attention.[18] Turbo-generators were developed for land application on a large scale but they did find favour for shipboard use and soon after the turn of the century many large units were being built for use in passenger ships and naval vessels.

Refrigeration

The first refrigeration systems were put aboard ships at about the same time that electricity was installed, and, although the application was less extensive, its impact on commercial and naval ships was no less significant. Today the idea of any ship setting out on a voyage of more than a few days without refrigerated food storage would not be entertained by regulating authorities and healthy living at sea owes much to the introduction of refrigeration. The ice house was an early means of storing perishable foods aboard ship and one of the first such installations was put aboard *Great Western* during the 1840s. This box structure contained about seven tons of ice and could keep foods in good condition for about two weeks.[19] Ashore large ice houses were used for keeping food fresh throughout the year or for as long as the ice remained, and on the East Coast of America they were particularly popular as extremely cold winters allowed large quantities of ice to be collected.

Obviously the problem with such natural refrigeration was the impossibility of predicting whether or not the ice would last through the summer and during the 1860s a number of engineers occupied their time with mechanical systems of refrigeration. Most ideas proved to be impracticable but others possessed potential and were developed so that by the early 1870s it was possible to reduce the temperature of a chamber by purely mechanical means. European markets for overseas-produced meat did exist but the means of ensuring that the meat reached port in a marketable condition did not. However, in 1874 a consignment of American meat was successfully transported to Europe packed in ice and salt. Further consignments followed but the use of ice limited the quantities and made any venture something of a gamble if there were delays on passage. Mechanical refrigeration systems offered the solution and in 1876 the French steamer *Le Frigorifique* was fitted with a Tellier refrigeration plant and shipped frozen meant from Argentina. The venture was not particularly successful owing to problems with the refrigeration plant, but two years later a similar plant was installed in the *Paraguay* which on its first voyage successfully carried 5,500 carcasses of frozen beef from Argentina to Le Havre.[20]

Refrigeration systems varied but they all basically involved the compressing of a gas, cooling it and then expanding it to produce a reduction in temperature; the gas used varied as did the way in which the temperature reduction in the hold space was brought about. Some installations used ammonia, some carbon dioxide, while others even used air. If air was the refrigerant it would be compressed, cooled and then expanded in order to reduce its temperature before being blown through the hold; this was the operating principle of the Bell–Coleman system. If a different gas was used the expanded gas would be employed to cool brine which would then be circulated through pipes in the hold space, or air would be blown over the cold pipes through which the expanding gas or brine was circulating. In any system it was necessary to provide steam-engine-driven compressors together with steam-engine-driven pumps or fans; refrigeration relied upon steam power.

One of the pioneering refrigerated steamers was *Strathleven* although she completed only one voyage carrying frozen cargo from Melbourne to London, arriving at the latter port in February 1880 after a voyage of nine weeks. Her forty-ton cargo of beef, mutton, lamb and butter was kept frozen by a Bell-Coleman plant which worked effectively throughout the voyage. Although the refrigeration plant was removed from the ship at the end of the voyage the potential had been recognised and a number of ships on the Australian run were given refrigeration plants. Later in 1880 *Protos* brought 4,600 carcasses of lamb and mutton, together with 100 tons of butter from Australia while the following year the Orient Line steamers *Cuzco*, *Orient* and *Garonne* were fitted with Haslam cold air refrigeration systems.[21]

Refrigeration became an accepted part of marine transportation provided that sufficient cargo was available to justify the installation of the equipment and certain routes did offer this. Meat and butter were the main commodities shipped under refrigeration and areas such as Australia, New Zealand, Argentina and the USA could offer large quantities for the dining tables of Europe. Obviously refrigerated cargo was available one way only and holds had to be designed so that they could also accommodate general cargo without the risk of damaging parts of the refrigeration system. Freight rates on the north Atlantic during the final two decades of the nineteenth century were low because of the number of ships operating and for many passenger liners it was hardly worth lifting general cargo. Refrigerated cargo was different and the higher speed of the express liners offered a considerable advantage in that trade with the result than a number of these liners were fitted with refrigerating machinery for cargo spaces as well as provision rooms. A typical installation was that of the White Star ships *Majestic* and *Teutonic* (1889) which were given two meat holds of 40,000ft³ total capacity. Each had its own Linde refrigeration plant employing ammonia as the refrigerant; circulating air was blown over cold coils through which the compressed and cooled ammonia expanded. The

installation also allowed for the cooling of the provision rooms via the forward air circulating system.[22] So successful and profitable were these two ships that in 1892 White Star took the older *Britannic* and *Germanic* out of service for the fitting of refrigerated spaces. In order to simplify the installation in the existing holds an indirect carbon dioxide refrigeration system was chosen, the gas being used to cool brine which was circulated through pipes laid in the hold. Carbon dioxide was used rather than ammonia as the latter caused corrosion of the copper from which the brine pipes were made.[23]

By far the most widespread use of refrigeration at sea during the nineteenth century was in cooling provision rooms as a replacement for the ice house. One of the first such installations went into the Cunard liner *Servia* (1881) which had a Bell-Coleman dry-air system built by Laidlaw & Sons of Glasgow; competition dictated that other ships had to be similarly equipped. Larger warships also received such plants for keeping provisions fresh, but in some cases it was necessary to ensure that ammunition magazines were kept cool and in the tropics refrigeration offered the only solution. Bell-Coleman dry-air systems were installed long after the more efficient ammonia and carbon dioxide systems found general acceptance in the commercial world. Ammonia was not used aboard warships owing to the possible effects on crew members should a shell cause fracture of the pipework while carbon dioxide required high pressures and there was a reluctance to allow these because of the risk of explosion of the gas storage cylinders. The battleship *Sans Pareil* initially had a Bell–Coleman system fitted for magazine cooling but in 1897 this was replaced by a carbon dioxide installation.[24]

Ventilation

As passenger ships and warships grew in size the problem of adequately ventilating interior living spaces increased as natural air draught could not be relied upon to produce the necessary number of air changes needed to ensure passenger and crew comfort. Some form of forced air circulation was required and that was most readily obtained by the use of fans, but an extensive system of ducting had to installed throughout the accommodation. Forced air circulation began to appear during the 1870s and as ships increased in size so the complexity of the installation increased. Dividing passenger and crew spaces into sections allowed the load on the ventilation fans to be kept to a reasonable level and also allowed the amount of ducting to be restricted. For ships trading in tropical areas forced ventilation of all spaces was essential for comfort and safety as temperatures could rise to dangerous levels; even with forced ventilation the opening of ports in the ship's side and the fitting of air scoops in the open port was the most satisfactory means of cooling a cabin. On colder runs, such as the north

Atlantic, forced ventilation was still essential as the opening of ports could be dangerous owing to the ever present rough seas. Even with all ports open ventilation of the interior public rooms could not be guaranteed.

The 9,984-gross ton *Teutonic* and *Majestic* could carry 1,490 passengers together with a crew running into many hundreds and these ships had to be provided with extensive ventilation systems, but air supply to the boilers was on an even larger scale although the amount of trunking was less. Forced draught for boilers will be covered in a later chapter but the forced-draught fans need to be mentioned here as they come under the topic of auxiliary equipment. Each

7.12 Steam-driven, forced draught fan installed in Teutonic *(1890)*

double fan, of which there were fourteen on each ship, could supply 16,000ft³ of air per minute to the boilers via the air heaters, the air being drawn from the engine and boiler rooms thus encouraging natural air circulation in these spaces via ventilators fitted in the upper deck. Fans used for accommodation ventilation were of a similar type although capacities were less.[25]

Warship ventilation was similar but tended to be more extensive for large vessels because of the need to isolate sections of the ship during battle. The British battleship *Prince George* had twelve steam-driven ventilating fans and eight forced-draught fans,[26] their locations being such as to ensure air supply to the required regions with a minimum of trunking and the avoidance of any trunking through watertight bulkheads. Forced-draught and ventilation systems have changed little down to the present day except for the introduction of air conditioning in ventilation systems and the near abandonment of forced draught through the demise of steam propulsion. Some ships early in the twentieth century used electric motors for driving fans on the grounds that control was easier and the provision of cables was less of a problem than steam and exhaust pipes; the systems, however, remained fundamentally the same.

Pumps

With early marine installations it was usual to work all necessary pumps by lever from the main engine thus reducing the amount of plant which had to be installed. When the engine was not operating hand pumps were generally sufficient to cope with bilge, boiler feed and fire pumping duties, but as ships became larger it was impracticable to work in such a manner and separate steam-driven pumps would be installed for certain duties. The basic problem with any steam-driven pump was that it needed a steam supply and that was available only when the main engine operated, but if the main engine was working it could be used for driving pumps through suitable levers. The installation of deck machinery, with the consequent need for donkey boilers, prompted the fitting of separate pumps for emergency work and duty while the ship was in port. Having independent pumps had its advantages, not least being the fact that the entire output of the engine could be devoted to propulsion but with the reintroduction of the surface condenser the need for an independently-driven sea-water circulating pump became apparent.

With a jet-condensing engine cooling water from the sea was no problem as it needed only to be sprayed into the condenser, but the surface-condensing engine required cooling water to be forced through the condenser and out again. Such a cooling flow would not be available until the engine was running and that would result in the condensers being flooded with steam thus causing difficulty in starting. Early sea-water circulating pumps were of the reciprocating type but with development of the centrifugal type of pump during the 1850s the way was open for a more practical

7.14 Twin steam engines driving a single centrifugal pump as built by W.H. Allen in 1882

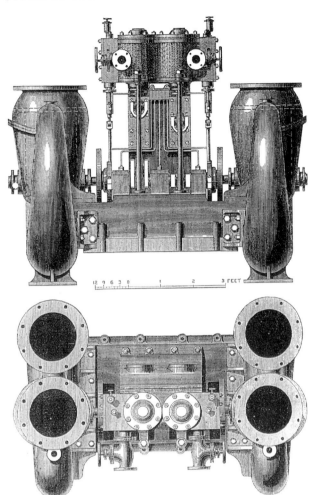

7.13 Steam-driven centrifugal pump; Cunard liner Gallia *(1879)*

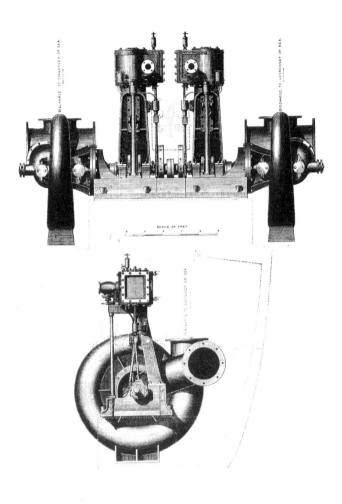

7.15 Double steam-driven centrifugal pumps; Cunard liner Servia *(1882)*

circulating pump; this type could handle large volumes of water at low pressures much more efficiently than a reciprocating pump. By the 1880 such pumps had become common and Cunard Line's *Gallia* of 1879 had two centrifugal pumps manufactured by J. & H. Gwynnes.[27] Larger engines had a larger condenser circulating water and the size of centrifugal pumps increased accordingly. The twin-screw *Teutonic* of 1890 had centrifugal pumps supplied by Messrs. Tangyes of Birmingham, these having 5ft diameter impellers which were rotated at about 90rpm by two compound steam engines. Each circulating pump had a suction pipe connection to the bilge (the bilge injection).[28]

Reciprocating pumps still sufficed for most ships as the flow rates required for many duties were not nearly so high as for condenser circulation. The reciprocating pump could deliver against high-pressure heads and was also self priming, a great advantage for many duties. Grouping pumps together, as in the case of main-engine-driven units, reduced the engine room space taken by the pumps and in many situations allowed for cross connections which enabled any

pump to do the duty of others. The owners of the German liner *Normannia* adopted this grouped arrangement for its auxiliary pumps, using a single three-cylinder compound engine to drive air, bilge and feed pumps; there were two such units as well as a pair of independently-driven centrifugal circulating pumps.[29]

Probably the longest-surviving independent, steam-driven pump was that used for supplying water to the boiler, namely the feed pump. Among the first types of separate pump fitted aboard steam ships, they will be fitted so long as boilers are used at sea. Although most large steam plants employ turbine-driven pumps and the electric drive has found favour for small installations, the reciprocating pump may still be found in a form that has changed little during a century of application. During the mid-nineteenth century many types of feed pump were devised, using an assortment of steam and water cylinder combinations, but the aim was simplicity, reliability and ease of operation, in order that the pump might fulfil its duties with minimum attention. The single-cylinder, direct-acting arrangement offered

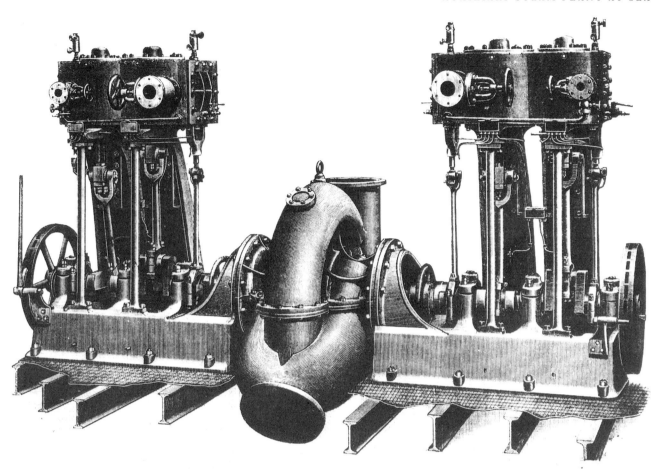

7.16 Tangye's centrifugal pumps with 5ft diameter impeller; fitted in Teutonic *(1890)*

the best solution as there would be no rotating parts and thus no need for a crankshaft, bearings or flywheel; but the problem was how to control the steam supply to the cylinder. With a crankshaft eccentric operation of valves offered the solution while with two cylinders a system of linkages between the piston and valve rods could be used, but getting a single cylinder to regulate its own steam and exhaust was a problem.

In the final two decades of the nineteenth century G. & J. Weir of Cathcart, Glasgow, established a reputation for high-quality, marine auxiliary machinery, but the real triumph of the company was its direct-acting feed pump. Pumps were arranged in pairs but each was independent with a double-acting steam cylinder positioned above a double-acting pump which it operated by a single rod. The valve mechanism was a classic piece of Scottish engineering ingenuity comprising two parts which worked independently. A shuttle in the valve casing contained ports for steam and exhaust and this would be moved from side-to-side by the action of steam; a ported slide valve with its face in contact with the flat surface of the shuttle was moved vertically by a lever connected to the pump rod. By a clever arrange-

ment of ports the pump controlled its own steam and exhaust and all the fireman tending the boiler had to do was regulate the steam supply in order to control the rate of feed to the boiler. This type of pump was still being installed in small steamers and for the auxiliary steam plant of motor ships well into the 1960s.

As the nineteenth century progressed a wide array of other auxiliary equipments were developed for shipboard use, some of these were to assist in the operation of the engine room while others were intended for the comfort of passengers and crew or to increase the fighting qualities of the ship. Distillation equipment was of considerable benefit to all who went to sea as it allowed the production of fresh water from sea water, for human consumption and as feed for the boilers. Simple distillation units had been devised early in the nineteenth century but it was not until the re-introduction of surface condensers and the use of fresh-water feed that they became a necessity. The increasing size of passenger liners resulted in higher demand for fresh water and a consequent need to 'make' the water on board rather than rely upon the chance of obtaining it in some foreign port. Increasing knowledge concerning boiler

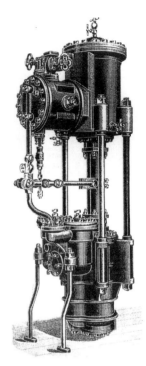

7.17 *Auxiliary engine driven pumps as employed in the German liner* Normannia *(1890); a three-cylinder engine driving air, feed and bilge pumps*

7.19 *Weir feed pumps installed in* HMS Powerful *(1896)*

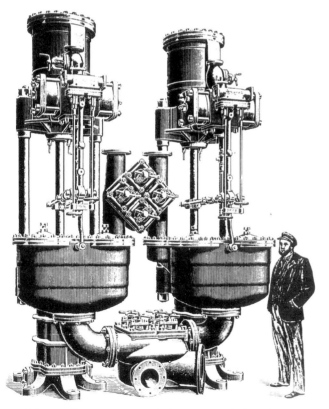

7.18 *Twin Weir reciprocating feed pumps installed in* Campania *(1893)*

corrosion and the effects of oxygen resulted in the development of de-aerators which also doubled as feed-water heaters. Both distillers and de-aerators required an abundant supply of steam for their operation.

Coal-fired boilers produced considerable quantities of ash which had to be disposed of overboard and in early steamers this required sacks of this waste to be man-handled to the deck and then tipped overboard, a time consuming and exhausting exercise. Over the years an assortment of ash-disposal units were developed, some comprising hoists to lift the ash to deck level while others were of the hydraulic type which used high-pressure water jets to force the ash overboard from a hopper located in the boiler room.

Naval ships not only had need for these systems but they also required devices to allow for the easier operation of guns. Steam pipes through the upper deck spaces of a warship could be dangerous should they become damaged in battle, while sparks from electrical machinery might ignite munitions. Hydraulic power offered the solution and thus was used extensively in naval vessels of many nations for rotating turrets, elevating guns and moving munitions. Water was generally the hydraulic fluid because of its plentiful supply, a number of steam-driven pumps being used to raise and maintain pressure with spring or air load reservoirs being employed to minimise pressure fluctuations in the system. While hydraulic pipes could still be damaged in battle the consequences were not so dangerous as with steam, pressurised water not being expansive.

All auxiliary plant had one thing in common: it was steam-driven and so the boiler demand increased. As much of it had to operate in port, auxiliary boilers increased in size and these required constant attention in terms of their fires and water supply. Increasing use of auxiliary equipment required more manpower aboard ship and a number of specialists were needed to cope with the new technologies. Electrical engineers were carried on the large liners and warships to deal with problems in the electrical systems while refrigeration engineers were need to deal with the specialised plants aboard ships operating in the frozen meat trades.

While most large shipbuilders constructed their own boilers and main propulsion engines they were generally ill-equipped in terms of design teams or manufacturing facilities to deal with the construction of the more specialised auxiliary machinery. Whole new industries developed for the designing and constructing of auxiliary plant for marine use and these tended to be concentrated around the major shipbuilding areas. Electrical, refrigerating and hydraulic machinery had applications ashore and specialist industries developed to support these technologies, but the size of the marine industry was such that specialist marine branches were developed. Because of the size of its shipbuilding and marine engineering industries during the nineteenth century many of the large auxiliary machinery producers were centred in Britain, particularly in Scotland. Weirs had an enviable reputation for steam auxiliary equipment while Hasties and Brown Brothers took large shares of the steering gear market. As the new century dawned most ships, even basic cargo vessels, had an extensive array of auxiliary plant and over the coming years that developed even further so that auxiliary machinery became as demanding on the engineer as the ship propulsion system had been.

References

1 E.C.Smith, *A Short History of Marine Engineering*, Cambridge University Press, 1937, pp. 204–7.

2 R. Mallet, *Scientific Record of the International Exhibition of 1862*, Longman Green, London, 1862. pp. 196–7.

3 J. M. Gray, 'Steam Steering Apparatus fitted in the *Great Eastern* and HM ships *Northumberland* and *Monarch*', *Trans. I.N.A.*, vol. 10, 1869, pp. 101–18.

4 Capt. E. A. Inglefield, 'Hydraulic Steering Gear as being fitted to HMS *Achilles*', *Trans. I.N.A.*, vol. 10, 1869, pp. 92–100.

5 *The Engineer*, vol. 53, 21 Apr. 1882, pp. 281–2.

6 Ibid., vol. 70, 19 Dec. 1890, p. 517.

7 *Engineering, Campania & Lucania* Special Supplement, 21 Apr. 1893, p. 27.

8 *The Engineer*, vol. 23, 18 Jan. 1867, p. 65.

9 Ibid., vol. 23, 8 Feb. 1867, p. 121.

10 *Engineering*, 3 Sep. 1880, pp. 196–7.

11 *The Engineer*, vol. 36, 11 Oct. 1872, p. 248.

12 E. C. Smith, *Short History of Marine Engineering*, pp. 228–9.

13 E. W. Beckingsale, 'The Electric Light on Board Ship', *Shipping World*, July 1884, pp. 78–80; Aug. 1884, pp. 112–6.

14 *Engineering*, 5 Aug. 1881, p. 144.

15 Ibid., 21 Apr. 1893, pp. 23–9.

16 Ibid., 7 Dec. 1900, p. 724.

17 Ibid., vol. 82, 18 Dec. 1896, p. 620.

18 J. F. Clarke, *Charles Parsons – an Almost Unknown Great Man*, Newcastle-upon-Tyne Polytechnic, 1984, p. 60.

19 D. Griffiths, *Brunel's Great Western*, Patrick Stephens, Wellingborough, 1985, p. 63.

20 A. R. T. Woods, 'A Short History of Refrigeration', *Trans. I.Mar.E.*, vol. 43, 1931, p. 402.

21 *Marine Engineer & Motorship Builder*, vol. 53, Mar. 1930, p. 109.

22 *Engineering*, 19 Dec. 1890, pp. 722–3; *Engineer*, vol. 70, 19 Dec. 1890, pp. 502–3.

23 *Engineering*, 8 July 1892, p. 58.

24 E. C. Smith, *Short History of Marine Engineering*, p. 234.

25 *The Engineer*, vol. 70, 19 Dec. 1890, p. 498.

26 Ibid., vol. 82, 18 Dec. 1896, p. 625.

27 *Engineering*, 19 Sep. 1879, p. 222.

28 *The Engineer*, vol. 70, 19 Dec. 1890, p. 499.

29 *Engineering*, 12 Sep. 1890, p. 321.

8
Triple-Expansion Engines and High-Pressure Boilers

The development of triple-expansion, or triple compound, engines was as inevitable as the introduction of compounding itself; all it required was an increase in boiler pressure to make the concept into a working machine. However, higher boiler pressure was the problem and failure of designers to deliver boilers which could reliably generate steam at pressures above 100psi delayed the introduction of an effective triple-expansion engine. Water-tube boilers were considered to be the solution to higher pressures and rapid steam generation and they ultimately were, but boiler design and materials did not keep pace with the ideas and several badly designed boilers put back the cause of high pressure and triple expansion. The failed water-tube boilers for the Guion liners *Montana* and *Dakota* have already been considered but there were more including the unit designed and constructed for the first seagoing, triple-expansion-engined ship *Propontis*.

This 2,000-ton cargo steamer was built in 1874 by John Elder & Co. for the Liverpool owner W.H. Dixon who, like

8.1 Kirk-designed, triple-expansion engine installed in Propontis

other owners, wanted high efficiency and low coal consumption. It would appear that the owner was convinced that high-pressure steam was the answer and he decided to install water-tube boilers of the Rowan & Horton type, these working at a pressure of 150psi. In order to make use of such a pressure, Elder's engine designer, Dr A. C. Kirk, devised a three-cylinder, triple-expansion engine with the high-, intermediate-and low-pressure cylinder bores, respectively of 23in, 41in and 62in; the common stroke being 3ft 6in.[1] The engine worked satisfactorily while the boilers functioned, a specific coal consumption of 1.54lbs/ihp/hr being recorded during one ten-hour run; unfortunately, the boilers were unsatisfactory, two out of the four exploding at sea with disastrous consequences. Despite a number of repairs and a reduction in pressure they could not be made to work well or safely and had to be replaced by Scotch boilers working at 90psi. By 1886 a further set of boilers had been installed and the 160psi pressure obtained from these showed how effective the engines of *Propontis* actually were.[2]

Just before *Propontis* entered service the small steamer *Sexta*, constructed by Grays of Hartlepool, was fitted with a three-crank, triple-expansion engine built by the Ouseburn Engine Works of Newcastle to the design of A. C. Franklin; this 100ihp engine, 11in + 17in + 24in bore by 1ft 6in stroke, consumed coal at the rate of 1.3lbs/ihp/hr during sea trials and 1.518lbs/ihp/hr during normal service with steam at a pressure of 120psi.[3] Although some small vessels were given experimental triple-expansion engines no other large seagoing vessel received such machinery until 1881. Kirk continued development work on triple-expansion engines but he knew that owners would take some convincing following the expensive problems with *Propontis*. However, he was well aware that the use of steel and improved furnace design allowed higher pressures to be developed in the Scotch-type cylindrical boiler, hence there was no need to adopt complex and difficult water-tube designs. In 1881 the shipowner George Thomson & Co. entrusted Robert Napier & Sons, for whom Kirk then worked, with the construction of a 2,000-ton ship for its Australian trade and Kirk pressed the case for his triple-expansion engine. The owners agreed to fit the engine and the result was *Aberdeen*, the first successful, seagoing, triple-expansion-engined steamer.

The design of the engine was basically the same as that

fitted in *Propontis* although the cylinders were larger, 30in + 45in + 70in by 4ft 6in stroke, while steam at 125psi was supplied by two double-ended, steel Scotch boilers, each with six Fox corrugated furnaces. During a six-hour run while developing 1,800ihp coal consumption averaged 1.28lbs/ihp/hr, which was exceptional for the period. The high-pressure cylinder was not fitted with a steam jacket but the others were; steam was not superheated but a Weir's feed heater was installed and the entire steam system worked to the satisfaction of builder and owner. The boilers were more substantial than others of the type, employing additional staying in order to comply with recommendations of the classification society, Lloyd's Register of Shipping.[4]

Successful operation of *Aberdeen* encouraged other owners to adopt triple-expansion engines, but, as in the case of compounding, there was no rush and some were content to

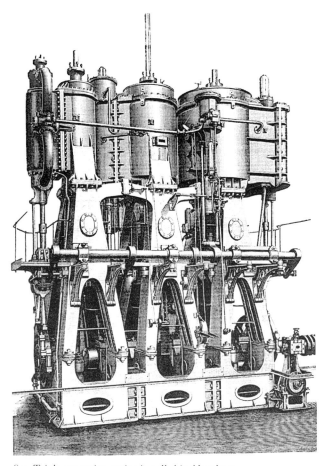

8.2 Triple-expansion engine installed in Aberdeen

wait and see how the situation developed. The reputation Kirk established saw further orders come to Napiers and in 1883 they fitted identical triple-expansion engines in the cargo steamers *Oaxaca* and *Tamaulipas*, the steam pressure being 135psi. As the benefits of three-stage steam expansion became evident and owners expressed an interest, other

designs of engine emerged but they generally followed the three-cylinder, triple-crank arrangement devised by Kirk. However, there were variations to suit the ideas of individual designers and builders. Apart from the fact that steam was expanded in three cylinders, engines still had lever-driven pumps and eccentrically operated valves, but many designers fitted piston valves to the high-pressure cylinders because the high steam pressure acting on the back of a slide valve would have resulted in considerable wear. In some cases the intermediate pressure (IP) cylinder was also provided with a piston valve. Metallic packing, used with superheated steam, was applied to most HP cylinder piston and valve rods even though superheating had been abandoned.[5]

The basic three-crank arrangement was adopted by most designers, particularly for general cargo boat engines, because of its relative simplicity in construction and accessibility for maintenance, however, there was some dispute as to how the cylinders should be disposed. For some the HP, IP and LP arrangement was the most acceptable while others had the LP leading but in some cases the HP was positioned between the other two as it was thought that heat could then be conserved. The length occupied by three cylinders in line was considered to be the greatest disadvantage of the three-crank, triple-expansion engine and some measures were taken to reduce it in order to increase the cargo carrying capacity. Fitting valve gear at the rear of the engine allowed cylinder centres to be positioned closer together, as in the three-crank compound engines. Placing cylinders in tandem was another obvious solution but it added to the complexity of the design; however, the steam yacht *Isa* built in 1876 had such an engine built by Douglas & Grant of Kirkcaldy to the design of Alex Taylor. Her 10in diameter HP cylinder was positioned above the 16in IP while the 28in LP occupied its own crank. Similar engines were built by Earles of Hull and by Wallsend Slipway but it was almost impossible to get the two-crank engine to run smoothly and the three-crank arrangement was preferred even though it required a longer engine room.[6]

Dennys of Dumbarton made use of the two-crank arrangement in its early triple-expansion engines, there being two LP cylinders positioned below the HP and the IP in tandem form. The first of the type was installed in the 5,026-gross ton Shaw, Savill & Albion steamer *Arawa* during 1884 and it developed 4,741ihp during trials from a steam pressure of 160psi; the cylinders were 37in HP, 61in IP and two 71in LP with a stroke of 5ft.[7] The engine had been designed by Walter Brock, a partner in the firm, and during the discussion of a paper at the Institution of Naval Architects in 1885 William Denny defended the arrangement of cylinders claiming that it was superior to the two-crank design with only three cylinders while the design allowed for easy conversion of existing compound engines

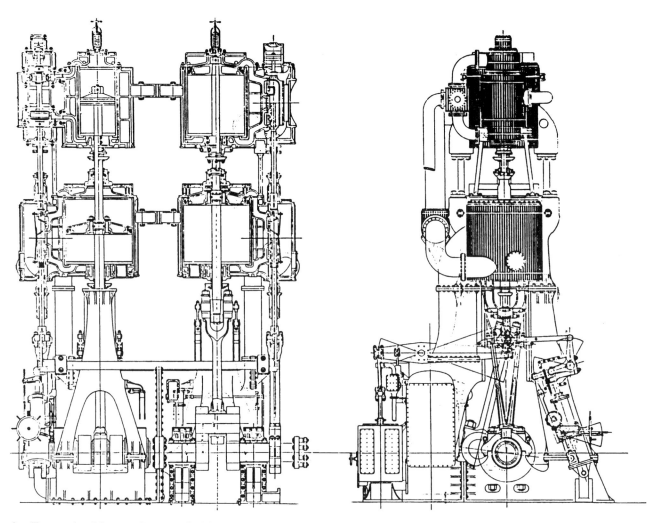

8.3 *Two-crank, triple-expansion engine built by Denny for the steamer* Arawa

8.4 *Palmers' triple-expansion engine installed in* Flamboro

8.5 *View of the engine fitted in* Flamboro *showing engine driven pumps*

to triple-expansion form. He also added his view that the four-cylinder, two-crank, quadruple-expansion engine would supersede the triple-expansion type.[8] The company was actually well on the way to constructing a quadruple expansion engine and later that year fitted one in the 5,197-gross ton British India steamer *Jumna*. This engine had 30in + 42in + 60in + 84in cylinders with a 5ft stroke, HP being positioned above the IP(1) on the forward crank and IP(2) above the LP on the after crank. From steam at a pressure of 160psi the engine developed 3,150ihp during trials.

Alternative configurations for triple-expansion engines were produced for smaller ships including a twin-screw tandem design of 1885 by Rankin & Blackmore of Greenock in which there were two HP cylinders, one above the IP and the other above the LP, each tandem pair of cylinders driving a screw shaft.[9]

As steam pressures increased triple-expansion machinery became more effective and the reduction in coal consumption was enough to convince some owners that the expense of re-engining would be recovered in service. In some cases existing compound engines were modified to triple expansion by replacing the cylinders and fitting additional valve gear and steam pipes. Under the guidance of Robert Wyllie, Richardsons of Hartlepool developed such a conversion system and successfully applied it to a number of steamers. One company, with a mail contract, was so

impressed with the operation of its four converted ships and the consequent reduction in coal consumption that it decided upon the conversion of all of its vessels to triple-expansion form.[10] For large ships complete re-engining was generally adopted, this being the approach taken by the owners of a number of large passenger liners and cross-Channel ferries.

In 1888 the Inman Line took its 5,491-gross ton *City of Berlin* (1875) out of service in order that Laird Brothers of Birkenhead might replace its twin-cylinder compound engine with one of triple-expansion form. The contract stipulated that the new machinery should occupy no more space than the old and this was achieved, the 41in + 65in +101in by 5ft 6in stroke cylinders developing 5,500ihp, some 20 per cent greater than the original machinery. The boiler pressure was 150psi, double that of the original installation, although the new boilers occupied less space than the old thereby increasing cargo space and allowing for more cabins. Coal consumption was reduced significantly, the improvement in consumption and the reduction in space occupied being due to the adoption of Howden's system of forced draught for the boilers.[11] Lairds undertook a number of such contracts; the re-engining of the Holyhead paddle steamers *Violet* and *Lily* with triple-expansion machinery has been discussed in Chapter 2.

Economics dictated whether a ship would be converted

8.6 Triple-expansion engine built by the Central Marine Engine Works of West Hartlepool during 1886

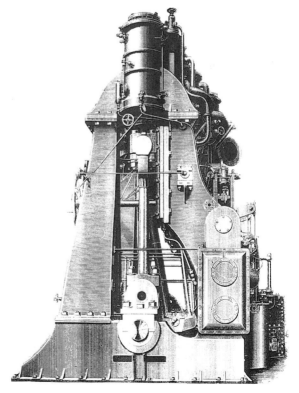

8.7 End view of triple-expansion engine built by the Central Marine Engine Works showing condenser and pumps

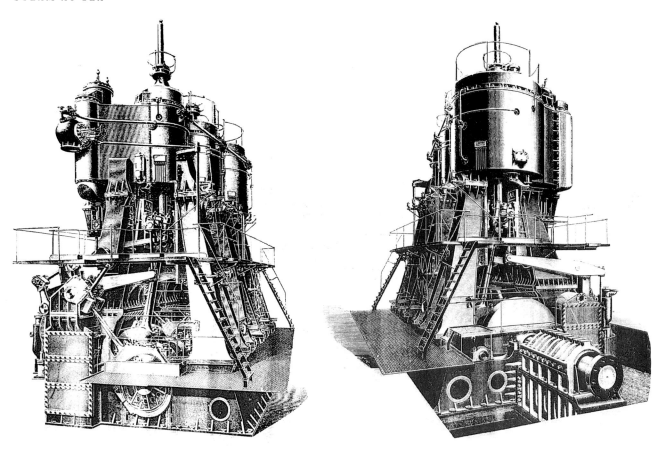

8.8 *Fairfield-built, triple-expansion engine fitted in the Orient liner* Ormuz

8.9 Ormuz *engine viewed from the thrust block end*

and even some older passenger tonnage was deemed fit for such treatment. In 1896 the White Star liner *Germanic* was fitted with a three-crank, triple-expansion engine as replacement for her original 4,900ihp Maudslay four-cylinder, tandem engine of 1874. The new engine, 35.5in + 58.5in + 96in by 5ft 9in stroke, developed 5,700ihp, steam at a pressure of 175psi (60psi originally) being supplied by new Scotch boilers.[12]

Expansion in trade dictated that larger and faster ships would be needed and it was on the north Atlantic that the largest and most powerful engines appeared, but Britain no longer had the ocean to herself. France, Germany and America were keen to make their presence felt for political as well as economic reasons and the final decade of the nineteenth century saw some of the largest and most powerful steam reciprocating engines ever constructed. Large engines were not simply bigger versions of existing machines; they required careful design and manufacturing techniques had to be developed in order to cast and bore the large diameter cylinders and to fabricate the crankshafts. Solid forged crankshafts were replaced by crankshafts made from separate pins and webs shrunk together during the

1880s, but care in the design was required in order to ensure that the shrinkage fits were sufficiently strong to transmit the power developed by the engine. The balancing of rotating and reciprocating parts in order to minimise vibration was another matter and many a fine ship was plagued with serious vibration problems thereby limiting its ability to attract passengers.[13] Vibration induced by the engine could only be solved by balancing the engine and a number of different systems for doing this were developed, the most commonly applied being the Yarrow-Schlick-Tweedy system which required the use of four cranks set at particular angular positions. For a quadruple-expansion engine the four cylinders were arranged in a particular order but with triple-expansion machinery it was usual to divide the LP stage between two cylinders. Even then there was no guarantee that vibration would not be a problem and it was only with the ship in service that the real situation could be assessed.

With larger and more powerful machinery the classification societies were particularly keen to ensure that no failures occurred and strict rules were developed concerning the dimensions of parts, particularly crank-

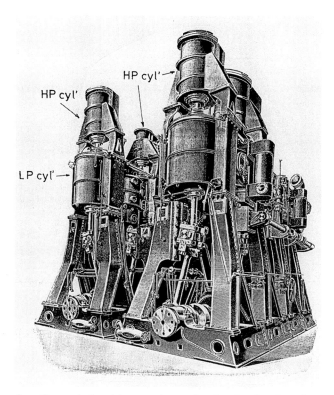

8.10 Cramp built triple-expansion engine for the American liner St Paul *(1895)*

shafts. Classification societies in Britain, France, Germany and America ensured that the highest standards were maintained and the practice has continued ever since.

In 1895 William Cramp & Sons of Philadelphia built 8,oooihp quadruple-expansion engines for the twin screw liners *St. Paul* and *St. Louis*, the first time four stages of expansion were used to drive a large liner. Cylinder dimensions, 28.5in (2) + 55in + 77in + 77in by 5ft stroke, were not particularly large but the engines had unusual cylinder groupings, pairs of tandem HP and LP cylinders being positioned on the forward cranks with the two IP stages on the other two cranks. Scotch boilers employing Howden forced draught supplied steam at 200psi which was high compared with European standards.[14]

It was, however, in the quartet of large German liners constructed around the turn of the century that the steam reciprocating engine may be said to have reached its zenith. Not only was this machinery large, powerful and impressive, it illustrated the advances made in German marine engineering during little more than a decade and put the world on notice about the emergence of an industrial giant. The 14,350-gross ton *Kaiser Wilhelm der Grosse* of 1897 was built and engined by the Vulcan Works at Stettin, her twin triple-expansion engines being balanced on the Yarrow-Schlick-Tweedy system. With steam at a pressure of 175psi her twin 1,320mm +2,280mm + 2,450mm (2) by 1,750mm

stroke engines could develop 30,oooihp.[15] *Deutschland*, built in 1900, had two six-cylinder quadruple-expansion engines with HP cylinders mounted above LP cylinders occupying the centre cranks on the crankshaft (see illustrations overleaf). Each engine could develop 16,500ihp but severe vibration was experienced in service even though the engines were balanced; the problem appears to have been that the structure of the ship had a natural frequency close to that generated at the operating speed and the only solution was to re-engine the vessel with lower powered engines. Such problems were not confined to large passenger ships but they were less noticeable aboard cargo ships, at least the cargo did not complain about the vibration. Shipbuilding and marine engineering had become precise sciences which were interlinked. High-powered engines, increased operating speeds and steel hulls resulted in problems which were not experienced with the wooden-hulled paddle vessel.

Kronprinz Wilhelm (1903) had two six-cylinder, quadruple-expansion engines similar to those of *Deutschland* although her dimensions, and hence power, were slightly less. At 40,oooihp the twin-screw machinery of *Kronprinzessin Cecilie* (1907) was probably the ultimate in terms of steam reciprocating, merchant-ship propulsion, but it was by then outdated as the steam turbine had shown the way for the future. In fact, she had four engines, two on each shaft, with watertight bulkheads separating each engine from the others. The engines on each shaft were effectively independent units as they could be controlled separately and had their own independent support systems; the arrangement was similar to that needed for a warship likely to suffer damage but with a need to maintain power. Each three-crank, quadruple-expansion engine had four cylinders, the 950mm HP being above the 1,250mm first IP on the centre cranks with the 1,900mm second IP being on the forward crank and the 2,850mm LP on the aftermost crank. Steam at a pressure of 225psi was supplied by twelve double-ended Scotch boilers located in four boiler rooms, the pipe work being so arranged that any engine could be supplied with steam from any of them.[16] German ship and marine engine building had made great progress but that progress was not just for mercantile purposes.

Although it might seem that quadruple expansion was only for high-powered engines that was not the case. The idea behind steam expansion in stages was to limit the degree of expansion in any cylinder in order to avoid low cylinder temperatures which resulted in steam condensation on the cylinder walls. Quadruple expansion allowed for that but resulted in a more complex and costly engine compared with triple expansion; it was all a matter of savings compared with the initial and the operating costs. As with triple expansion, there were many proposals for such engines long before they became practicable proposition

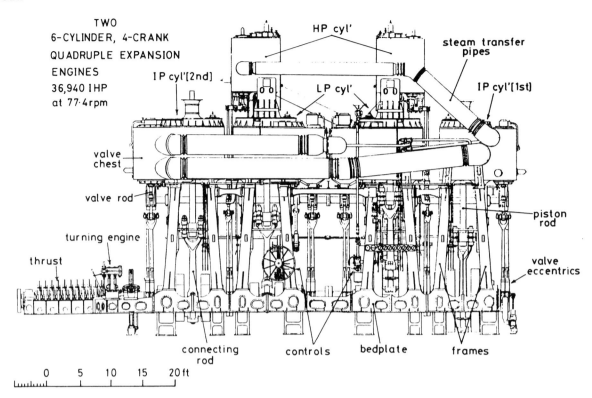

TWO
6-CYLINDER, 4-CRANK
QUADRUPLE EXPANSION
ENGINES
36,940 IHP
at 77·4rpm

HP cyl'

steam transfer pipes

IP cyl'[2nd]

LP cyl'

IP cyl'[1st]

valve chest

valve rod

piston rod

turning engine

thrust

valve eccentrics

connecting rod

controls

bedplate

frames

0   5   10   15   20 ft

8.11 Layout drawing of the triple-expansion engine fitted in the German express liner Deutschland

8.12 Photograph of the two engines for Deutschland *in the erecting shop*

but, as already mentioned, Dennys of Dumbarton were among the first to fit such machinery with the 1886 installation in *Jumna*. The company fitted quadruple-expansion engines in ships from then onwards, depending upon the requirements of the owner; but one of the most interesting installations came in 1894 with the 4,065-gross ton Russian passenger/cargo steamer *Queen Olga*. This vessel was given a combined triple- and quadruple-expansion engine, the engine operating as a triple-expansion under normal circumstances, but when higher economy was needed steam at the 170psi boiler pressure would be directed first to a smaller primary HP cylinder positioned above the main HP cylinder. Cylinder dimensions were 28.25in + 47.5in + 76in by 4ft 6in stroke, but the bore of the primary HP cylinder is unknown.[17]

An interesting quadruple-expansion engine was developed by Fleming & Ferguson of Paisley in 1890 for the steam yacht *Imogen*. This had four cylinders, 17in + 25in + 34in + 50in by 2ft 9in stroke, arranged in groups of two, each pair driving a crank through a triangular shaped connecting rod. With steam at a pressure of 160psi some 1,070ihp could be developed from what was a compact and accessible engine, ideally suited to the yacht market.[18] Engineers of the day were imaginative and resourceful in meeting the needs of their clients; competition for orders was intense and the good firms needed to offer more to attract interest.

Lubrication

All steam engines require some form of lubrication for cylinders and bearings in order to reduce frictional wear and so prolong efficient operation. Although lubrication was applied to early marine engines, and changes came about with reciprocating machinery during the twentieth century, it is opportune to discuss the matter in this chapter as it has been during this period that a scientific approach was adopted to the development of lubricants for cylinders and bearings. Early engines had bearings lubricated by animal fats and cylinders were largely left alone as the water droplets contained within the low-pressure steam provided an adequate lubricant film. As engines became larger and higher steam pressures were employed the problems increased in terms of cylinder and bearing lubrication; the development of metallic piston rings to replace hemp packing to seal pistons in the cylinders improved performance but increased problems with respect to cylinder wear unless an effective lubricant film was present on the cylinder wall. Higher engine loads presented problems at bearings and the supply

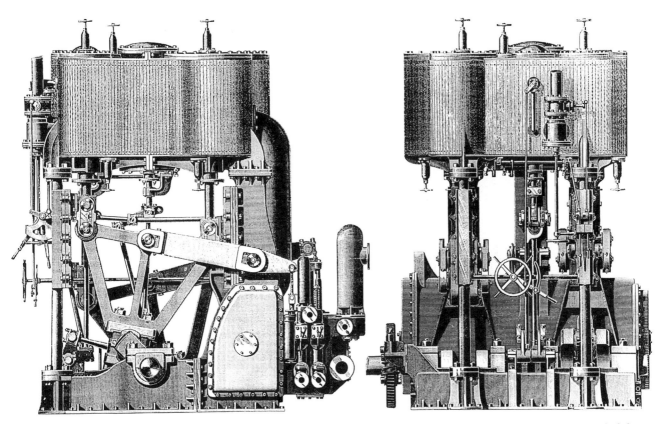

8.13 Four-cylinder, quadruple-expansion engine built by Fleming & Ferguson; the lever-drive arrangement allowed output on a single shaft from a compact design

of lubricant to ensure that surfaces were kept apart was essential to prolonged operation. Overheating of bearings was a constant problem and the only way of detecting this was for the duty engineer to go around the engine feeling each bearing in turn in order to assess its temperature. Bottom end bearings had to be touched as the engine rotated and a misjudged swing of the hand could result in serious injury. Oil pots would be replenished or lubricant would be expertly directed from a can on to the bearing or guide by the engineer as he negotiated a perilous path between moving linkages. As one observer of such events aboard Clyde steamers of the 1850s commented, 'We hardly knew whether to admire more their skill or their bravery'.[19]

Early lubricants for cylinders and bearings were animal oils, essentially fats heated to temperatures of about 140°F; tallow from several animals was a commonly used lubricant in its natural state or when heated to become tallow oil. A number of vegetable-based oils were also developed including castor oil, olive oil and rape oil, usually known as colza oil. In a steam-engine cylinder the lubricant is required to seal the piston rings against the cylinder wall and also to reduce friction. Pots of tallow would be situated on the tops of cylinders to ensure that the lubricant remained in liquid form and it would be applied intermittently through grease cups in the cylinder covers. While the method may appear crude it did work but the use of tallow caused problems since when exposed to steam it decomposed to produce fatty acids and glycerine which resulted in serious cylinder corrosion; steam passages and surface condensers became choked with metallic soaps and other products of the decomposing tallow.[20] Fortunately the chemical industry was able to provide an answer which was generally effective at the time.

An important part of that solution to the problem came through development of the American mineral oil industry which commenced with the discovery of oil in Pennsylvania during 1859. Distillation of mineral oil produced lubricants with known viscosities but with properties inferior to fixed oils made from animal and vegetable products. Extensive experimentation resulted in the development of compound oils which were combinations of mineral oils with vegetable

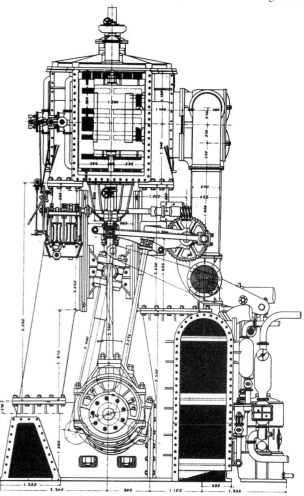

8.14 *Triple-expansion engine constructed by Fairfields for the liner* Normannia

8.15 *Italian-built, triple-expansion engine (G. Ansaldo & Co.) for steamers* Sirio *and* Perseo

and/or animal oils to give the desired properties. This work took time but by the late 1880s satisfactory results were being achieved. However, conditions in engine cylinders differed from high to low pressure, particularly with respect to temperature, and a good cylinder oil had to have the correct viscosity to suit the cylinder temperature. Ideally a number of different grades of oil had to be carried, one for each cylinder, and if steam was superheated a very high quality oil was needed in order to ensure that carbon deposit formation was kept low.[21] Compound oils reacted less with steam and any impurities they might contain than did mineral oils, but they were more difficult to remove from the exhaust steam and so presented problems in the condenser. Engineers had to develop many items of plant, including filters and strainers, to remove oily products from exhaust steam and condensate leaving the condenser in order to prevent those products entering the boiler where they could cause priming and other troubles.

Bearing lubrication, although less of a problem in terms of lubricant decomposition, was still important to engine performance and effective lubrication was needed to ensure a long operating life between overhauls. Most bearings were lubricated via a wick which drew oil from a pot situated on top of the bearing and this arrangement sufficed until rotational speeds and bearing loads increased towards the end of

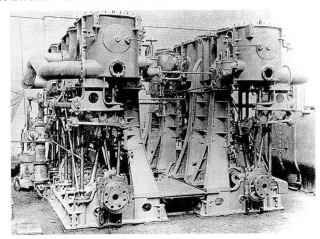

8.17 Denny-built, triple-expansion engines for the cross Channel ferry Arundel

the nineteenth century. The filling of oil pots was an essential part of engine monitoring routine, as was the making and fitting of wicks to ensure that the correct oil flow rate to the bearing was achieved. For bearings without oil pots and for crosshead guides, a well-directed shot of oil from a can was the only way of ensuring that the correct quantity reached the required location. Mineral oils were initially not liked for bearing duties because of their low viscosity if

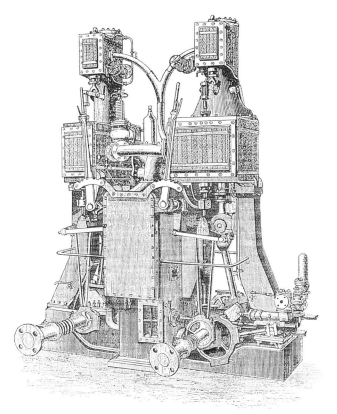

8.16 Tandem triple-expansion engine as installed in the twin-screw vessel Arabian; *the ship had overlapping propellers*

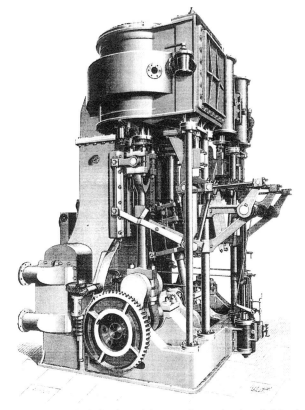

8.18 Blackwood & Gordon triple-expansion engine installed in the steamer Vauban *(1890)*

highly refined or impurity levels if not sufficiently refined. Artificially thickened vegetable oils were used from the 1870s and remained common until enclosed-crankcase, forced-lubrication engines were introduced allowing for the use of mineral oils.[22] In later years mineral oils of improved viscosity became available for open-crankcase steam engines.

Over the years the oil industry has worked closely with the marine industry to develop products which met the ever increasing demands of the marine steam engine.

Steam for Triple and Quadruple Expansion

The key to the success of the triple- and quadruple-expansion engines was higher steam pressure and that depended upon improvements in steel quality and boiler design. The introduction of steel and the development of Fox corrugated furnaces have been mentioned in Chapter 5 but further improvements in steel quality and growing experience in its use allowed boiler designers to adopt increasingly higher pressures. Classification societies such as Lloyd's Register of Shipping and regulatory bodies such as the Board of Trade insisted upon the highest standards of design and construction in order to minimise the risk of explosion, boilers generally being hydraulically tested to twice the working pressure. Higher pressures meant thicker plates in order to comply with strict rules but that resulted in an increase in boiler weight. British naval ships and those of other countries faced no such restrictions and boilers built for the Royal Navy up to 1891 used plates some 18 per cent thinner than those for merchant ship boilers while at the same time test pressures were only 90psi above working pressures. Many engineers of the day considered that some relaxation in boiler rules would allow for a reduction in the weight of mercantile boilers or enable higher

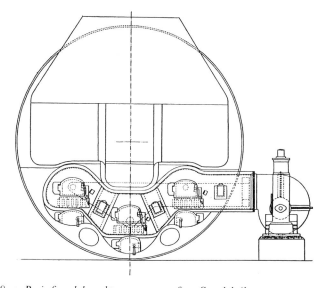

8.19 *Basic forced draught arrangements for a Scotch boiler*

pressures to be achieved without any weight increase.[23]

Scotch boilers were standard steam generators in merchant service during the triple-expansion era, but the demand for steam resulted in large diameter boilers which occupied valuable cargo and passenger space. Increasing boiler output was not simply a case of the firemen increasing the rate at which coal could be fed to the furnaces, more air was also needed. Ideas such as steam blast up the funnel had been tried but the waste of valuable steam and water soon curtailed that practice. However, forcing the air into the boiler by means of a fan offered a more practicable alternative. Others considered that the inducing of a draught by means of a fan in the boiler uptake, thereby drawing combustion gases through the boiler, was a better solution but during the latter years of the nineteenth century forced draught rather than induced draught proved the most popular for marine use. Naval authorities, after conducting many experiments, adopted the closed stokehold arrangement where the entire stokehold was pressurised, while for mercantile practice the closed ashpit form of forced draught found greater favour.[24]

Forced Draught

Forced draught was not new, in the early days of steam at sea a vessel called *Corsair* had been fitted with a primitive system while the steam blast up the funnel projected for *Great Western* was mentioned in Chapter 2. An American Atlantic steamer *United States* (1848) had a forced draught arrangement fitted to her flue-type boilers, the air blast being supplied by a fan when the furnace doors were closed.[25] Advocates of forced draught claimed, with justification, that boiler steam output could be increased by 30 to 40 per cent while allowing for the burning of inferior quality coal. The latter point was of considerable importance to many shipowners as coal costs overseas were high, fuel having to be taken to bunker stations by sailing vessels or steam colliers. The use of inferior quality local coal could reduce operating costs. Forced draught encouraged higher furnace temperatures and that allowed for complete combustion of lower grade coal, but the higher combustion gas temperatures also improved heat transfer and that allowed boiler dimensions to be reduced for a desired steam-generating rate. A reduction in boiler size, even allowing for the space occupied by forced draught fans and air heaters, enabled more cargo to be carried. Most forced draught systems incorporated a combustion-air heater arrangement, the air being heated by uptake funnel gases before entering the furnace, thereby minimising the risk of thermal shock in the furnace and reducing the cooling effect of the air on the furnace gases.[26]

Although there were a number of closed ashpit forced draught systems, that developed by James Howden was by far the most widely used, both in Britain and overseas, for

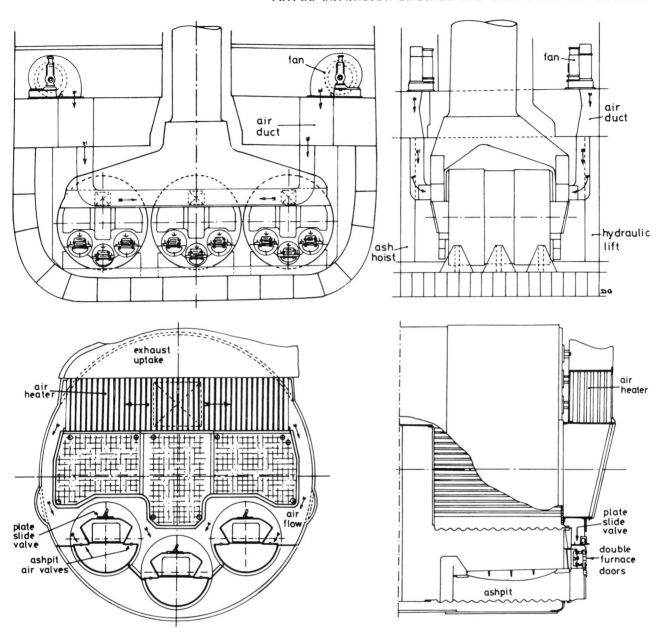

8.20 Howden forced draught system as fitted to Scotch boilers

commercial steamers. Howden's first forced-draught system, tested in 1862, made use of a steam-driven fan to supply air to the boiler furnaces below the grate, but results were disappointing as it proved difficult to introduce the correct amount of air for the depth of coal in the grate. Lessons from the trials indicated to Howden that air needed to be supplied both above and below the grate and over the next twenty years he developed a new arrangement which also allowed for the heating of the air before it entered the furnaces. In addition to the tubular heater through which the air passed, combustion air was also directed over the front of the boiler thereby limiting heat

losses to radiation. This improved boiler efficiency and kept the boiler room cool. The air heater, positioned at the front of the boiler above the smokebox, consisted of a number of tubes through which the hot gases passed on their way to the funnel, air from the fan flowing across the tubes on its way to the furnaces. Each furnace had its own air supply system which could be controlled by the fireman and a special arrangement of valves automatically cut off the air supply when the furnace doors were opened for firing. The fireman could regulate the quantities of air directed above and below the grate and so maintain optimum combustion without the risk of smoke. Despite the fact that Howden demonstrated that his system worked on a small land boiler during 1882, many engineers in the marine industry were sceptical about his claims and refused to accept that reduced coal consumption could be achieved while at the same time the steam output could be maintained from a smaller boiler plant.[27]

In 1884 Howden installed a forced-draught system to the new Scotch boiler fitted in the 1,723-gross ton iron steamer *New York City* and in trials over a period of eighteen months the claims of the designer were vindicated. The new steam plant was smaller than the original but it still allowed for a reduction in specific coal consumption while generating steam at a higher rate.[28] Although many were still sceptical about the merits of forced draught others were convinced sufficiently by the results to adopt the concept. It still took some years, however, before forced draught became established. Probably one of the most convincing demonstrations of its effectiveness came about through an accident aboard the large Atlantic liner *City of Paris* (1889) when fatigue failure of the propeller shaft resulted in the engine destroying itself by overspeed. The ship, and its

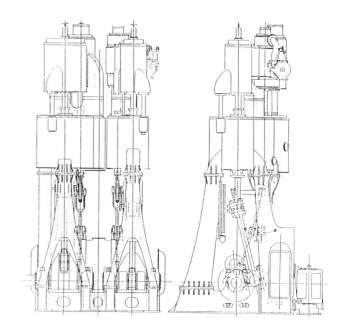

8.21 Denny two-crank quadruple-expansion engine design

8.22 Top of engine room aboard the Cunard liner Campania *showing the cylinder arrangements and the engine room centreline bulkhead*

sister *City of New York* (1888), had been constructed with forced draught on the closed stokehold principle but this had, obviously, proved unsatisfactory. The new Howden forced-draught system allowed for a reduction in the size of the grates although the same boilers were retained and it also avoided the need for engineers, firemen and coal trimmers to pass through airlocks when entering or leaving the stokehold thus avoiding delay.[29] Many ships with closed stokehold systems of forced draught suffered from the problem of coal dust blowing out of the bunker covers when bunkers were located in the boiler spaces; this resulted in a dirty ship and was a particular problem for passenger vessels.[30] It is probably for this reason as much as any other that *City of New York* was converted to the closed ashpit system.

Despite the advantages of forced draught, not all ships were so equipped. Much depended upon the type and size of ship, the nature of its operations and the quality of the coal it could expect to find at bunker stations. Where

quality was poor, or at best variable, forced draught was often employed even in cargo steamers and some tramps as the ability of forced draught to burn such fuel effectively had been established. The reduction in boiler size was another positive aspect of forced draught which found favour with cargo ship owners as it allowed more freight to be carried, but aboard passenger ships these factors were not nearly so important as a reliable and abundant steam supply. It was claimed that Howden forced draught reduced the coal consumption of the Atlantic liners *Teutonic* and *Majestic* (1890) by as much as ten tons per day; they normally consumed 320 tons per day.[31] The contemporary Cunard liners *Campania* and *Lucania* had open stokeholds, the builders Fairfields and the owners preferring that arrangement.[32] The difference can only be put down to personal preference as the ships were of similar size and power and they operated on the same route, thus lifting the same types of coal. Cunard as a company did not appear to have a

8.23 Five-cylinder, quadruple-expansion engine built in 1901 by the Central Marine Engine Works for the Inchdune *and* Inchmore

preference either way but to have left the decision to the builders as *Saxonia* and *Ivernia* of 1900 both had Howden forced-draught systems;[33] indeed most shipowners, whether of tramps or liners, took the advice of shipbuilders and installed whatever propulsion plant was recommended.

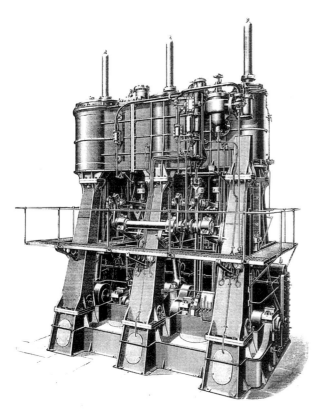

8.24 Typical in-line triple-expansion engine constructed at the end of the nineteenth century; built in West Hartlepool and fitted in the steamer Baria *(1890)*

Superheating

As the nineteenth century drew to a close superheating made a return, again as a means of reducing condensation in cylinders resulting from the reduced temperatures caused by expansion. Superheating apparatus differed from earlier types, generally being of the tubular form located within the gas path. In the cylindrical Scotch-type boiler 'U' tube-shaped, superheating elements were placed in the flue tubes but in the water-tube boilers which became common for warships during the latter years of the nineteenth century superheater elements were positioned in the boiler uptakes. Higher steam pressures resulted in higher saturation steam temperatures and so with the addition of superheat the final steam temperature was considerably in excess of anything previously obtained. (Steam generated at a pressure of 160psi would be at a temperature of 370°F, its saturation temperature, but the addition of 100° of superheat would raise the final temperature to 470°.) During the

1890s superheated steam temperatures of 550°F were not unusual and, although they resulted in improved operating efficiencies, there were problems related to lubrication in the HP cylinder. Improvements in steel quality and manufacturing techniques allowed boilers to operate under such extreme conditions and the oil companies played their part in developing lubricants which could cope with high temperatures. It took some time for the use of superheating to re-establish itself and it was only with the introduction of turbines and water-tube boilers that very high superheat temperatures became an established part of marine engineering life. Even into the twentieth century steam reciprocating plant rarely operated with steam temperatures above about 600°F owing to the problems involved at the HP stage. Under such conditions, however, reductions in coal consumption of about 15 per cent could be expected and this was a worthwhile saving if the ship was at sea for long periods; for ships on short runs the cost of superheating equipment and the necessary additional costs in terms of the engine were not justified as they could not be recovered through a reduction in coal consumption.[34]

Boiler Corrosion

As has already been mentioned, boiler corrosion was a major problem for marine engineers and the situation deteriorated with the use of steel for boiler construction. In the upper parts corrosion was generally due to the effects of tallow and other greasy substances which decomposed to form fatty acids as they did in engine cylinders. The use of mineral and compound oils reduced the problem, as did the introduction of effective grease separators in the condensate lines. Another problem was caused by oxygen dissolved in the water since this resulted in pitting oxidation at the water level, such pitting seriously weakening the boiler. The use of feed heaters and de-aerators helped to lower the level of dissolved oxygen in feed water but in any open-feed system where water was in contact with the atmosphere levels of dissolved oxygen were always liable to be high. The problem still exists today and frequent testing of feed water is necessary to ensure that dissolved oxygen levels are not likely to be a problem. All water tends to become acidic after a period of time and that results in corrosion; the solution is to introduce some alkaline salt such as caustic soda to maintain the water in a slightly alkaline state. Evaporation of water caused the formation of scale on heated surfaces and over a period of time that could seriously impair heat transfer resulting in local overheating and subsequent failure. Engineers were well aware of the problem with salt-water feed and frequent blowing down was resorted to in order to minimise scale formation. With fresh-water feed scale formation was less of a risk, but over a period of time levels could reach problem proportions especially if poor quality or contaminated feed were used. By the 1880s most causes

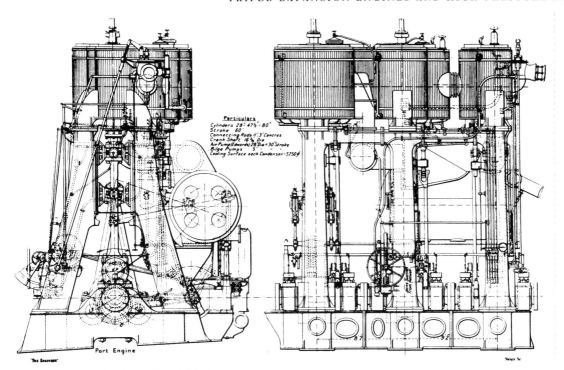

8.25 *Triple-expansion engine fitted in the liner* Adriatic

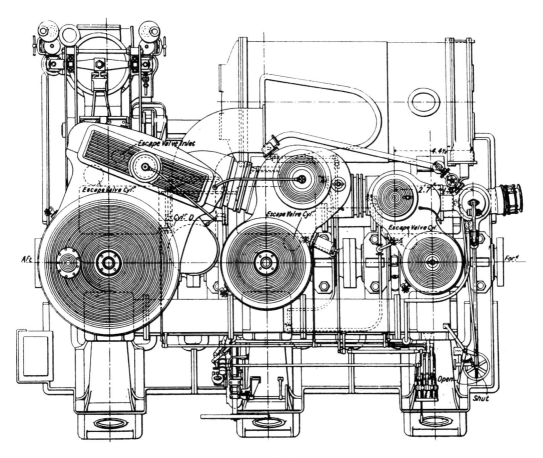

8.26 *Plan view of the large Harland & Wolff engine constructed for* Adriatic

of boiler corrosion had been recognised[35] and chemical treatments for boiler water became available soon afterwards. Management of boilers in terms of testing water and supplying feed treatment increased the workload of the engineer but effective treatment allowed for a reduction in subsequent maintenance and promoted safer operation; the engineer had to add the role of chemist to his other skills.

Boiler Fuel

Throughout the nineteenth century coal was the main fuel for boilers but wood still found favour aboard some American river steamers simply because it was readily obtainable. Coal, however, was still king as far as oceanic shipping was concerned and steamers required large 'black gangs' to man-handle it between bunkers and stokehold and to feed the voracious furnaces. In order to reduce labour requirements a number of land installations had adopted the mechanical stoking of boilers with some success, but such arrangements did not find favour with steamship operators. Scotch boiler furnaces were extremely difficult to stoke in

any other way than by hand, but water-tube boilers had wider grates and it was boilers of this type that lent themselves to mechanical stoking. By the turn of the century a number of American lake steamers had been so equipped and trials on board one fitted with a chain-type stoker indicated that satisfactory performance could be obtained while saving money through a reduction in the size of the crew.[36]

Although coal held an unassailable position as the fuel for marine operations there was a move towards the use of oil for burning under boilers, particularly in ships which transported that commodity in bulk. Oil had been burned under boilers aboard ships operating on the Caspian Sea and the River Volga since about 1870[37] and in the late 1860s the Admiralty had donated a boiler, formerly in HMS *Oberon*, in order that extensive trials might be undertaken on the burning of fuel oil.[38] Although the trials were successful as far as they went, little progress was made simply because coal was more plentiful and steps were then being made to set up a network of coal-bunker stations. By the 1890s little had changed because that network of coal depots

8.27 Quadruple-expansion engine built by Wallsend Slipway for the liner Ivernia *(1901)*

still existed but the benefits of fuel oil over coal were beginning to be appreciated by people in the military. The
British, the German and the Italian Admiralties actively
pursued the use of oil for powering warships but the construction of oil-bunker stations beside those supplying coal
held back development.[39] It was only when the military authorities went over to oil that adequate worldwide facilities
existed and merchant ships could obtained their necessary
fuel, even then it took many years to oust coal from its dominant position and at the outbreak of World War II over 40
per cent of the world's merchant ships were still coal powered, and generally driven by triple-expansion engines.

Oil-fired boilers of the pre-World War I period were
generally the same as coal-fired boilers but with oil-burning
equipment fitted in addition to the usual coal-burning
grate; the fear that a shortage of oil would prevent a ship
from operating appears to have been ever present. The oil
tanker *Bulysses* was constructed by Armstrong, Whitworth
on the Tyne in 1900 and her four-furnace Scotch boilers
were fitted with oil-burning equipment, the fuel oil being

the same as the crude oil she carried. This ship used steam
as a means of atomising the oil and it worked effectively
during trials.[40] Other systems were also being developed including pressure atomisation of oil which tended to be the
system preferred in later years. It was, however, the shortage of bunker stations which delayed the widespread introduction of fuel oil, but even when these were available the
British coal industry fought hard to retain its markets
against the use of oil and particularly the diesel engine.[41]

Steam Pipes

Higher boiler pressures produced a natural anxiety about
explosions but it was not the boiler itself which gave most
cause for concern but the pipes through which steam passed
on its way to the engine. Few failures resulted from the
pipes being made too thin but failures did result from poor
design of the pipe system itself. Of sixty-eight pipe failures
reported between 1885 and 1898 fourteen were due to water
hammer caused by inadequate draining of condensation
from the pipes while thirty-eight resulted from insufficient

8.28 *Taikoo Dockyard (Hong Kong) erecting shop at the end of the nineteenth century showing triple-expansion machinery under construction*
(John Swire & Son)

8.29 China Navigation steamer Changsha *(1886) built by Scotts of Greenock and fitted with a triple-expansion engine, 25in + 40in + 62in, by 4ft stroke (John Swire & Son)*

provision for expansion and contraction. Only in a few cases was failure attributable to poor workmanship or faulty materials. In Britain the Boiler Explosions Acts of 1882 and 1890 allowed for public inquiries into such failures with the result that design improvements were made. Initially high-quality steam pipes were constructed from copper but as temperatures and pressures increased steel became the accepted material.[42] The pipe procedure was slow but it generally had the effect of enhancing standards of construction which were subsequently tried by even higher steam pressures.

Postscript

The triple-expansion engine was at the heart of shipping development during the final two decades of the nineteenth century and for the first two of the twentieth. Even then it played a major role in marine matters for years to come and many tramp steamers, particularly for British owners, were fitted with such engines during the 1940s and the 1950s. There were sound economic reasons for that and the triple-expansion engine had certain capabilities which could not be matched by the turbine or the diesel engine, the ability to make use of plentiful coal being but one. Over the years improvements were made and new features added, such as exhaust turbines, but at the end of its seagoing development the triple-expansion engine could still easily be recognised as the brother of that which had developed in the 1880s.

Evolution may be a slow process but the steam reciprocating engine for driving the marine screw propeller reached its final form as the three-cylinder, triple-expansion engine in about forty years; after that there were only modifications.

References

1 *Marine Engineer & Motorship Builder*, June 1929, pp. 204–5.

2 J. F. Flannery, 'On Water-Tube Boilers', *Trans. I.N.A.*, 1876, pp. 266–9; W. Parker, 'On the Progress and Development of Marine Engineering', *Trans. I.N.A.*, 1886, p. 127.

3 A. Taylor, 'On Triple Expansion Engines', *Trans. N.E.C. I.E.S.*, vol. 1, 1884–5, p. 118; see also a contribution by A. Blechynden to Parker's paper 'Progress and Development of Marine Engineering', p. 144.

4 A. C. Kirk, 'On the Triple Expansive Engines of the SS *Aberdeen*', *Trans. I.N.A.* 1882, pp. 33–7.

5 *Marine Engineer & Motorship Builder*, June 1929, p. 205.

6 *Shipping World*, 1 Nov. 1887, p. 212; *Marine Engineer & Motorship Builder*, June 1929, p. 204.

7 D. J. Lyon, *The Denny List* Part I, National Maritime Museum, Greenwich, 1975, p. 233.

8 A. E. Seaton, 'Some Further Experience with Triple Compound Engines', *Trans. I.N.A.*, 1885, p. 150.

9 *Marine Engineer & Motorship Builder*, 1 Nov. 1929, p. 214.

10 Comment by W. Parker during discussion of the paper by R. Wyllie, 'On Triple-Expansion Marine Engines', *Proc. I.Mech.E.*, 1896, p. 502.

11 *The Engineer*, vol. 53, 3 Feb. 1888, p. 95.

12 Ibid., vol. 82, 17 July 1896. pp. 52–4.

13 *Campania* and *Lucania* both suffered from vibration at certain engine speeds and the German liner *Deutschland* (1900) had to be re-engined because of the problem. D. Griffiths, *Power of the Great Liners*, Patrick Stephens, Sparkford, 1990, pp. 76, 85.

14 *Engineering*, 21 June 1895, pp. 800–801; *Marine Engineer*, 1 Mar. 1896, pp. 479–80.

15 *Engineering*, 11 Mar. 1897, p. 300; 10 June 1898, pp. 721–2.

16 Ibid., 12 Sep. 1907, p. 339–40.

17 D. J. Lyon, *The Denny List* Part II, National Maritime Museum, Greenwich, 1975, p. 366.

18 *The Engineer*, vol. 70, 3 Oct. 1890, pp. 272–3.

19 J. V. Wilson, 'The History and Practice of Lubrication in Marine Engines', *Trans. I.Mar.E.*, vol. 22, 1910–11, p. 514.

20 R. F. Thomas, 'The Evolution of Lubrication for Marine Propulsion Systems', *Trans., I.Mar.E.*, vol. 101, 1989, pp. 72–4.

21 J. V. Wilson, 'History of Lubrication', pp. 518–19; R.F. Thomas, 'Evolution of Lubrication', pp. 74–5.

22 J. V. Wilson, 'History of Lubrication', pp. 520–21; R. F. Thomas, 'Evolution of Lubrication', p. 76.

23 A. Blechynden, 'A Review of Marine Engineering during the Past Decade', *Proc. I.Mech.E.*, 1891, pp. 310–13.

24 *Marine Engineer & Motorship Builder*, June 1929, p. 228.

25 Comment by W. F. Smith during discussion of Blechynden's paper 'Review of Marine Engineering', p. 360.

26 A. Blechynden, 'Review of Marine Engineering', pp. 308–10.

27 J. Howden, 'On Combustion of Fuel in Furnaces of Steam Boilers by Natural Draught and by Supply of Air under Pressure', *Trans. I.N.A.*, 1884, pp. 129–52: many speakers taking part in the discussion expressed doubts about the effectiveness of the system and Howden's claims for it.

28 *Shipping World*, July 1886, pp. 64–7.

29 *Engineering*, 8 May 1891, pp. 559–60.

30 *Shipping World*, June 1886, p. 38.

31 *Engineering*, 12 Dec. 1890, p. 489.

32 Ibid., 21 Apr. 1893, p. 483.

33 Ibid., 5 Oct. 1900, p. 436.

34 A. F. White, 'Marine Engines and Superheated Steam', *Trans. I.Mar.E.*, vol. 21, 1909–10, pp. 442–5; also H. Gray, 'Use of Superheaters and Superheated Steam in Mercantile Steamers', *Trans., I.N.A.*, vol. 55, 1914, pp. 127– 9.

35 J. H. Hallet, 'Corrosion in Marine Boilers', *Marine Engineer*, Nov./Dec. 1884, pp. 213–5, 227–9.

36 J. McKechnie, 'Review of Marine Engineering during the Last Ten Years', *Proc. I.Mech.E.*, 1891. p. 616.

37 *Engineering*, vol. 73, 28 March 1902. p. 407.

38 J. H. Selwyn, 'On the Progress of Liquid Fuel', *Trans. I.N.A.*, vol. 10, 1869, pp. 32–46.

39 *Engineering*, vol. 73, 28 Mar. 1902. p. 407.

40 Ibid., vol. 70, 28 Dec. 1900, pp. 823, 832.

41 D. Griffiths, 'Britain and the Diesel Engine', *Mariner's Mirror*, vol. 81, no. 2, Aug. 1995, pp.313–29.

42 J. T. Milton, 'Steam Pipes', *Trans. I.N.A.*, vol. 41, 1899, pp. 93–7.

9
Naval Engineering in the Late Nineteenth Century

Naval authorities throughout the world reacted to changing technology with great rapidity; they had little option if they were to have the power to compete with potential enemies. The arms race has long been a fact of military planning and the latter years of the nineteenth century were as demanding as any other period, only the destructive force of the weaponry was subject to constant change. The fighting capabilities of battleships increased during those years along with their size and power but the new seaborne weapon was the torpedo and its delivery system the torpedo boat. Although spar torpedoes had existed for a number of years, it was the introduction of the propelled Whitehead torpedo in the 1870s which marked an escalation in the arms race. Space precludes discussion of this significant item of military hardware[1], but the delivery system, the torpedo boat, and its countermeasure, the torpedo boat destroyer are of interest particularly with regard to their power plants. In order to deliver torpedoes at the heart of an enemy fleet the torpedo boat had to be fast and that required high powered machinery which was also small and light enough to fit in the narrow confines of the torpedo boat hull. Torpedo boat destroyers, which were subsequently referred to more briefly as destroyers, were developed almost concurrently and they had to be as fast as the torpedo boats themselves; both classes of vessel required machinery which had not previously been constructed for use at sea, its size and power being important.

Other naval ships were subject to improvements in terms of propulsive plant but the driving force for radical change lay with these new vessels. Larger ships of the early 1880s still could make do with horizontal engines as the need to position propulsive machinery below the waterline still existed. However, as the tonnage of such ships increased the draught also increased making it possible to turn to the more reliable vertical engine. Experience with merchant ships had shown that vertical engines were more economical to operate and suffered less cylinder wear because the pistons acted vertically and did not press constantly on one side of the cylinder. Vertical engines were also more accessible for maintenance and more readily balanced than horizontal engines, while for twin-screw ships they occupied less fore and aft space since they could be placed beside each other. Development of increasingly effective armour plating also allowed machinery to rise somewhat above the waterline since it could be protected by a belt of armour around

the hull or machinery spaces. The idea was still to keep machinery below the waterline and by the mid-1880s vertical engines completely below the waterline were being installed in large warships. One of the first such was the Italian cruiser *Piemonte*, laid down at Armstrong's Elswick yard in 1887.[2]

Space aboard warships was at a premium and the need to generate steam from as small a boiler installation as possible had been apparent for many years. Forced draught on the closed stokehold system allowed boilers to be forced at high rates, but the use of the closed stokehold made the forced-draught arrangement independent of the boilers it served, apart from the fact that steam was used to drive the fans. The Howden and other closed ashpit systems of forced draught required air trunking and heaters to be fitted around the boiler, but the closed stokehold system allowed boilers to be free-standing although there was a need for air-locks to allow access to the stokehold. Warships required watertight subdivisions to afford protection in battle and such arrangements would not have presented too much of an inconvenience; bunkers were generally arranged around the boiler room as that afforded additional protection. The need for high steam-generation rates and the relative freedom in design that the closed stokehold allowed made naval vessels more suitable for water-tube boilers than their commercial counterparts.

Improvements in boiler design allowed for higher steam pressures with the consequent capacity for increased cylinder expansion. The natural step was to triple-expansion in order to avoid the problems of cylinder condensation and that factor applied to all steam engines, naval, merchant or land-based. In effect, the boiler was the driving force behind engine change as increasing steam pressure brought about a move to compounding and then triple or quadruple expansion. Construction of these engines came as a consequence of increased steam pressure and it would be more accurate to discuss boilers before engines, but it seems more logical here to deal with the power system first rather than the boiler which supported the engine. Although the basic concept of the triple-expansion, reciprocating engine supplied with steam from coal-fired boilers working under forced draught was the same for naval and merchant steamers, the developmental pathways of machinery design had diverged. Improved materials and design concepts could be applied to any steam engine or boiler but the requirements of the world's navies and their merchant fleets differed and an engine or boiler designed for one was not necessarily applicable to the other. It would be many years before these paths converged again through the widespread adoption of geared turbines and oil-fired, water-tube boilers and even that would be on a limited scale.

Warship Engines

Torpedo boats constructed by Thornycroft & Co. during the early 1880s were given vertical compound engines with features such as steam jacketing, surface condensers and lever-driven pumps, which were common to engines being employed for commercial ships. In many important respects, however, the design differed considerably from mercantile engines as it needed to be small, light and of low height but capable of developing high power. Cylinder bores were 12.75in and 20.875in but the stroke was only 1ft in order to keep the height limited while the engine operated at a much higher speed, 440rpm, in order to produce an output of over 450ihp. Cylinders, cast together as a single unit, were supported upon eight vertical columns, instead of the usual 'A'-frames while bracing was used to add rigidity. A centrifugal pump was employed to supply cooling water to the surface condenser but the boats were also provided with a steam-engine-driven air compressor to supply air for the torpedoes and also for the impulse tube used to discharge them from the boat.[3]

Although these engines were small, because of the size of the vessels in which they were installed, they had many features which were common to other reciprocating warship engines developed during subsequent years. Reducing the length of the connecting rod allowed for a reduction in engine height but the use of a shorter stroke had a much greater influence on total height as it not only allowed for shorter cylinders it also produced a reduction in crank throw which meant that the distance between the shaft axis and the bottom of the bedplate was less. The consequence of a shorter stroke was less power developed and the only way of increasing engine power without larger-diameter cylinders was to run the engine at higher speed. Naval engines tended to operate at much higher speeds than their commercial counterparts and that required designers to take extra care in ensuring the correct balance of rotating and reciprocating parts; an additional problem relating to higher operating speeds was the increased piston speed which required greater attention to cylinder lubrication. Higher piston speeds also resulted in higher inertial forces in the piston and connecting rods when the piston changed direction at the top and bottom of its stroke; these forces put an increased loading on the bearings. In order to minimise this problem most naval engines had lighter pistons than commercial engines of a similar size and power. High operating speeds, particularly at levels used in torpedo boats

and destroyers, created difficulties outside the hull as cavitation and other propeller problems were experienced. Aspects of ship operation concerning propellers and hull design are beyond the scope of this book but it has to be realised that the machinery was only one part of a ship, albeit an important one, but a part which could not be treated in isolation from the ship itself.

The use of vertical bars to support cylinders was also a common feature as was the fitting of bracing to give engine rigidity. The engine builders had their own approaches to the weight problem and no standard design evolved for engines of any nation during this period.

Most of the restrictions which applied to machinery for small boats also applied to large engines of the period but designs differed depending upon the builder. The 1881-built, twin-screw ironclads, HMS *Nelson* and *Northumberland* were similar in design but their engines differed, J. Elder & Co. supplying machinery for *Nelson* and John Penn for *Northumberland*. In inviting tenders the Admiralty called for machinery capable of developing 6,000ihp from as low a weight as possible and both ships were given surface condensing compound engines. The Penn engines had three cylinders of the same bore, the centre being HP and the two outer LP, the engines working as compounds during normal operations. However, when maximum power was required full-pressure steam could be directed to all cylinders allowing the engines to work as a three-cylinder simples. The weight of machinery and boiler, in full steaming condition, was 1,113 tons.

Elder's machinery weighed only 998 tons and, as the oval boilers were practically identical in both ships, the difference in weight was attributable to the much lighter engines which were designed by A.C. Kirk. Kirk's machinery could only work compounded, the steam-jacketed cylinders being 60in and 104in bore with a 3ft 6in stroke. When rotating at 82rpm with a steam pressure of 60psi the engines could develop a total of 6,624ihp. Cylinders were supported on four wrought-iron columns, the rear pair also carrying the guides, while bracing held cylinders together in each engine and also connected the engines together.[4]

This type of machinery was typical for warships of the period and the design changed little over the next decade apart from the introduction of triple-expansion which, as in the case of commercial steamers, was not immediately applied across national fleets. Increased boiler pressure allowed for the use of triple-expansion but naval ships were not faced with the same economic constraints as merchant steamers. However, any reduction in coal consumption was worth having if it reduced the bunker and boiler space needed while also allowing for a reduction in the number of coal trimmers and stokers; such gains had to be paid for in increased complexity, greater weight and longer engines. As with commercial operators, much debate ensued concerning triple expansion, but by 1885 the ability to generate steam safely at pressures of 130psi and above put the issue beyond doubt. With but a few exceptions propulsion engines in new British naval vessels would all be triple-expansion.[5]

During the 1880s some British cruisers were still being constructed with horizontal engines. *Severn*, *Mersey*, *Thames* and *Forth* of 1885-6 had twin, horizontal, two-cylinder compound engines which developed about 4,500ihp with steam at 110psi; the first-class cruiser *Australia* and her six near sisters of 1887-8 had twin, horizontal, triple-expansion engines which developed about 5,800ihp with steam at 135psi. These were among the first large triple-expansion engines in the British fleet, having been adopted mainly as a result of a suggestion made by A.C. Kirk.[6] The Naval Defence Act of 1889 called for the construction of seventy warships in order to modernise the fleet and that allowed for a move to vertical triple-expansion engines for all ships. The heavy cruisers *Blake* and *Blenheim* were the first vessels produced under this Act to enter service. *Blenheim* was launched from the yard of the Thames Ironworks in July 1890, her twin engines and those of her sister being constructed by Humphrys, Tennant & Co. These triple-expansion engines, 36in +52in + 80in bore by 4ft stroke, could develop a total of 15,000ihp when turning at 95rpm, the steam pressure being 155psi. There were effectively four engines, two on each shaft, each engine being in its own watertight compartment, thus reducing the risk of the ship being disabled in battle. Cutting out one of the engines on each shaft allowed the ship to proceed more economically at a slower speed.[7]

Many of the large ships built under the 1889 Act were cruisers and, though their builders, sizes and classes differed, they had one thing in common, the vertical triple-expansion engine. Many were fitted with water-tube boilers

but a number of the second-class cruisers still made use of cylindrical boilers. Medium and light cruisers, in British designation second- and third-class cruisers, were ordered in large numbers from the Royal Dockyards and commercial shipbuilders and they were matched by similar vessels built by other European nations. 'Apollo'-class medium cruisers began to appear in 1891 with HMS *Sybille* being a typical example. Constructed by Robert Stephenson at Hebburn she had machinery built by Hawthorn Leslie of Newcastle, this consisting of a pair of triple-expansion engines, 33.5in + 49in + 74in by 3ft 3in stroke, which were designed to develop a maximum 9,000ihp from steam at 145psi. That steam was supplied by three double- and two single-ended cylindrical boilers operating under closed stokehold forced draught. Engine cylinders were supported by columns at the front but cast frames were employed at the rear in order to provide mounting points for the guide bars. Cylinder tops projected above the waterline and were protected by a casing formed of armour plating 5in thick.[8]

'Pearl'-class medium cruisers were somewhat smaller and less powerful, *Pearl* and *Philomel* being typical examples built at the naval yards in Pembroke and Devonport, respectively, with engines supplied by Earle's Shipbuilding Co. of Hull to a design prepared by A.E. Seaton, general manager and a director of Earle's. The contract called for twin-screw machinery which would develop 4,500ihp under natural draught and 7,500ihp with forced draught, although these ships developed some 7,800ihp with forced draught during trials.[9] In order to ensure lightness, steel was used for most engine parts, including columns, frames, pistons and cylinders while extensive bracing was employed to minimise vibration. The rear support columns carried guide bars and were of a special shape to give the maximum base support and structural stiffness. Cylinders, 20.5in + 45in + 68in by 2ft 9in stroke, were supplied with steam at a

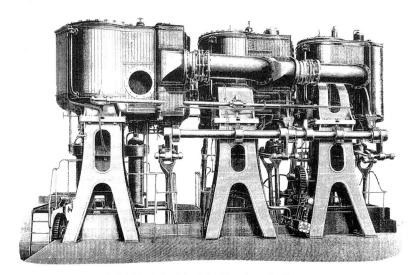

9.1 *Engine for HMS* Sybille *(1891) built by Hawthorn Leslie*

9.2 *Front view of engine fitted in HMS* Sybille

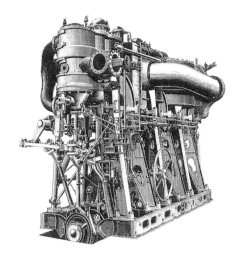

9.3 Earle-built engine for the medium cruiser HMS Pearl *(1891) showing the column supports*

9.4 Front view of one of the engines fitted in HMS Pearl

pressure of 155psi from four double-ended cylindrical boilers; boilers were located in two boiler rooms while each engine was in its own watertight compartment. Cylindrical condensers, made from cast naval brass, were positioned at the after end of the engines and the air pumps were driven by levers from the LP crosshead; separate centrifugal pumps supplied condenser circulating water.[10] These ships indicate the general situation with respect to British warships of the period in that their construction was either at a naval dockyard or with a private builder to a very rigid design while engines were invariably ordered from outside with much of the detailed work being left to the designer, only aspects such as power, weight and dimensions were rigidly specified.

Heavy cruisers required more powerful engines and the 360ft, 7,350-ton displacement 'Edgar'-class of 1891 required some 12,000ihp to be developed under forced draught or 7,500 under natural draught. Ships of this class were built at Royal Dockyards and at a number of commercial yards on the Thames, Clyde, Tyne and Humber, bunker space having to be provided to enable the ships to steam 10,000 miles at 10 knots or 2,800 miles at 18 knots. The Earle-built engines for a member of the class, *Royal Arthur*, developed some 12,851ihp from her 40in + 59in + 88in bore by 4ft 3in stroke cylinders while working under forced draught; steam at a pressure of 155psi came from four double-ended and one single-ended cylindrical boilers.[11]

Probably the most impressive, although not the most successful, of the heavy cruisers were *Terrible* and *Powerful* which entered service during the mid-1890s. The Navy Estimates of 1893–4 made provision for two heavy cruisers which were to be the largest, fastest and most powerful of the type built to that time and tenders were invited for their construction. The construction of *Terrible* was put in the

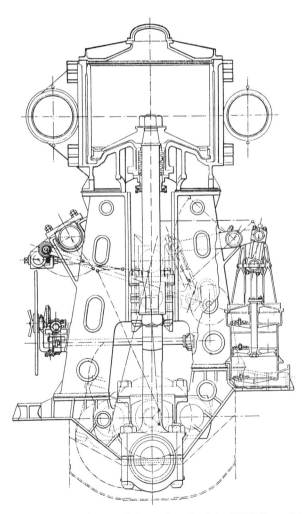

9.5 Section through one of the engines fitted in HMS Powerful *(1895)*

9.6 J. & G. Thomson-built, triple-expansion engine for HMS Terrible *(1895)*

hands of J. & G. Thomson of Glasgow and that of *Powerful* was entrusted to the Naval Construction and Armaments Company, Barrow-in-Furness, formerly the Barrow Shipbuilding Company. These 14,200-ton ships were the first in the British fleet to be given Belleville water-tube boilers and both had twin, four-cylinder, triple-expansion engines. Apart from minor differences which resulted from the ideas of the builders, the machinery fitted in both ships was identical with cylinders 45in + 70in + 76in (2) bore by 4ft stroke; high-pressure cylinders were positioned forward and these had piston valves while the IP and LP cylinders were given flat slide valves. Steel was used extensively in the construction of the engines. When working at the design speed of 112rpm each engine could develop 12,500ihp from steam supplied at a pressure of 210psi; the boiler pressure was actually 260psi but a reducing valve reduced steam supply to the engine to the lower value.

It was that steam pressure which made the difference in terms of the power-to-weight ratio compared with other cruiser engines of the period, about 11.25ihp/ton on design output power compared with 10.5ihp/ton for the 'Edgar' class. There were forty-eight Belleville boilers arranged in four watertight compartments and an extensive array of auxiliary plant including electrical generators and air compressors for the torpedoes.[12] In engineering terms these

vessels showed what could be accomplished with money and the expertise of established shipyards. Their singular lack of success in military terms was due to the fact that they were constructed to counter a perceived Russian threat which never materialised and they were then too large to be used

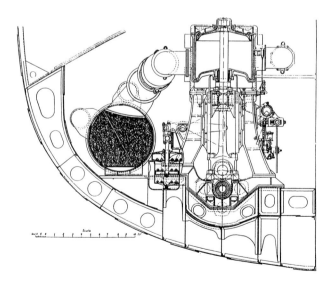

9.7 Section through engine room of HMS Terrible *showing engine installation*

9.8 Penn-built, triple-expansion engine fitted in HMS Magnificent *(1895)*

against commerce raiders; their Belleville boilers also proved troublesome and expensive to operate.[13]

Engines for battleships built under the 1889 Defence Act proposals were not that much different from heavy cruiser engines, the essential differences resulting from the preferences of the builders. The 14,900-ton displacement HMS *Magnificent* (1895) was built at Chatham and fitted with two triple-expansion engines built by Penn, these being capable of developing 12,000ihp under forced draught. As with other naval engines of the period, steel was used extensively in their construction, including cast steel for the rear columns and forged steel for the front cylinder supports. The forged steel crankshaft, made in three sections bolted together, was hollow in order to reduce weight, the cranks being 120° apart. Cylinder dimensions of 40in + 59in + 88in by 4ft 3in stroke were identical to those of the engines fitted in the cruiser *Royal Arthur*. The steam pressure of 155psi was lower than that used in the *Terrible* and the *Powerful* but the boilers were of the cylindrical type rather than of water-tube type. Interestingly, they were fitted with a system of induced draught, fans being placed in the boiler uptakes, rather than forced draught, this being the first large installation of induced draught in the British fleet.[14]

In the same class of battleship was *Prince George* (1896) which, consequently, had the same propulsive plant

9.9 Engine fitted in HMS Magnificent *showing combined system of cylinder support*

123

9.10 Humphry & Tennant triple-expansion engine constructed for the battleship Prince George *(1896)*

requirement but her engines came from Humphrys, Tennant & Co. although they were identical in size and power to those constructed by Penn. Requirements for condenser cooling water were met by four centrifugal pumps, each capable of pumping 1,200 tons of water per hour; in an emergency these pumps could be used for removing water from any compartment in the ship. The main difference in terms of machinery compared with *Magnificent* was in the steam-generating plant, and then only in the fact that forced draught was employed for the eight single-ended cylindrical boilers rather than induced draught. So extensive was the power requirement of this class of battleship that eighty-six sets of engines were provided for various duties including air compressors, capstans, winches, dynamos and hydraulic pumping.[15]

By contrast torpedo boats and destroyers had fewer auxiliary engines but they required considerable power to ensure high speed; machinery occupied most of the hull space

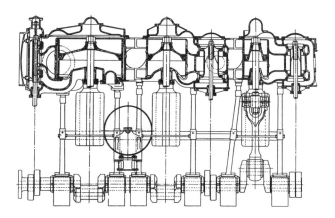

9.11 Arrangement of cylinders of the triple-expansion engine fitted in HMS Psyche

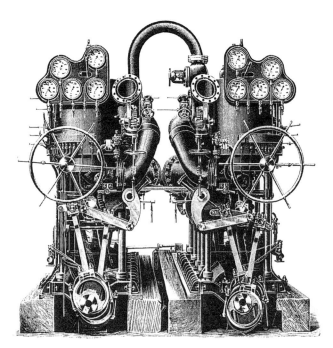

9.12 End view of a J. & G. Thomson-built, triple-expansion engines for a torpedo boat (c. 1890) (see 9.13 for side view)

leaving little room for anything else. In the twenty years between 1880 and the end of the century a great many such vessels were built in Britain and many other countries with the demand for higher speeds being an ever-present problem. Reciprocating engines were the only form of motive power until turbines were tried in 1898 and the demands placed on the designers of such machinery increased with each successive order. In Britain many orders went to commercial shipyards and a number of these, particularly Yarrow of Poplar and Thornycroft of Chiswick, appeared to specialise in these ships producing them not just for the home market but for other countries too.

In 1895 Thornycrofts built the destroyer *Ardent* and fitted her with two four-cylinder, triple-expansion engines, 19in + 27in + 27in (2) by 1ft 4in stroke, running at 170rpm and developing a total of 4,500ihp, sufficient to drive this 201ft-long vessel at 28 knots. Steam at 215psi was supplied by three Thornycroft water-tube boilers. In describing this ship the journal *Engineering* congratulated the builder and commented, 'By their production they have distinctly advanced the science of marine construction and marine engineering; a thing which the torpedo boat builders have constantly done since these wonderful craft were first introduced'.[16] The same year J. & G. Thomson offered the destroyer *Surly*, fitting her with two three-cylinder, triple-expansion engines, 18.125in + 26.625in + 40.125in by 1ft 6in stroke, which developed a total of 4,200ihp at 400rpm from steam at 185psi. The three members of this class were of similar size to *Ardent* and her sisters and could

9.13 Side view of Thomson-built torpedo boat engine

achieve almost the same speed from slightly less powerful engines. Steam came from four Normand water-tube boilers.[17] It is interesting to compare the engine designs from the two builders as in total length they were both about the same; a lower mass piston would have been more suitable for the higher operating speed of 400rpm, but it was the Thornycroft engine which employed two LP stages while the higher speed Thomson engines had single, large-diameter LP pistons. Illustrations of the engine shows balance weights on the LP and IP crank webs indicating that steps were taken to achieve balance.

Torpedo boats of the period were somewhat smaller than the destroyers but they needed powerful machinery to achieve high speeds. Yarrows built many torpedo boats and destroyers for the British Navy and those of other countries, *Viper* of 1896 for the Austrian Navy being typical of the yard's products. In order to drive this 140ft-long boat at 27 knots engines developing some 2,000ihp were required. The builder also constructed the reciprocating engines and provided the water-tube boilers which worked at a pressure of 175psi.[18] Both Yarrows and Thornycrofts had enviable reputations for these small, high-speed craft but their water-tube boilers also went into much larger vessels. As a builder of large warships for the world's navies at this time Armstrong, Whitworth of Elswick probably had few equals, orders being directed to the yard from Japan, Italy, Argentina, Turkey, Brazil and many other countries, including Britain. Although Armstrong guns and armour were specialities, some machinery was also constructed at the yard, but propulsion plant generally went to outside

contractors such as Humphrys, Tennant & Co. thus ensuring that British engines went into warships of other countries. The basic type remained much the same as that produced by other British engine builders, three- or four-cylinder, triple-expansion with low height; in some cases the engines projected above the waterline and these were protected by an armoured belt.[19]

Japan was a good customer for British-built warships in the late nineteenth century, with a number of other yards receiving orders for ships both small and large. Between 1894 and 1899 six battleships were constructed in Britain for Japan and all were fitted with triple-expansion engines. Humphrys and Tennant supplied machinery for four of these ships while machinery for *Asahi* and *Mikasa* was constructed by the builders, Thomsons of Clydebank and Vickers of Barrow, respectively; Vickers had by this time taken control of the shipyard at Barrow. *Mikasa* was typical of the final trio built in 1899, her two 31in + 50in + 82in by 4ft stroke engines developing 15,000ihp and with steam being supplied by twenty-five Belleville boilers. The engines were also typical of the design used for large warships of the period having cylinders supported on machined forged steel columns at the front and cast steel columns at the rear. The total weight of the machinery was 1,355 tons, giving a specific output of 11ihp/ton.[20] The Japanese Navy also came to Britain for smaller warships including destroyers. *Shirakumo*, delivered in 1902, was a twin-screw Thornycroft product with the company's four-cylinder, triple-expansion engines; this installation was larger and more powerful (22in + 29.5in + 31in [2] by 1ft 7in stroke

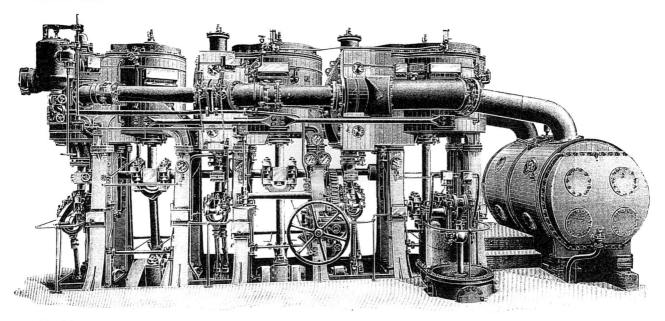

9.14 Maudslay engines constructed for the Russian ironclad Admiral Oushakoff *(1895)*

and developing a total of 7,650ihp from the two engines) than that fitted in *Ardent* during 1895.[21]

Russia had warships built in a number of countries and she also constructed her own and for these often came to Britain for machinery. In 1895 Maudslay, Sons & Field supplied two three-cylinder, triple-expansion engines for the 330ft-long ironclad *Admiral Oushakoff*, one of the last major orders the company completed before it went out of business. The ship was built by the Baltic Shipbuilding and Engineering Company at St. Petersburg and Maudslays supplied the engines complete with pipework and condensers. Cylinders, 31in + 46in + 68in by 2ft 9in stroke, were cast separately and each was supported on two sets of cast iron legs, the only connection between the cylinders appearing to have been through the steam pipes.[22]

France and Germany built all their own warships during the final years of the century but they also constructed vessels for the navies of other nations, Germany in particular becoming a world power both in terms of its fleet and warship-building facilities. Machinery was much the same in type and form as that supplied by British builders, there was no reason for it to be otherwise as the steam reciprocating engine had effectively been perfected in the triple-expansion form. Competition ensured that only the best survived.

America developed her late-nineteenth-century steam-powered navy somewhat in isolation from the European powers but she had to have an effective fleet in order to ensure success in the war with the Spanish. The American coastline had to be defended even if there was no overseas territory to defend and in 1883 Congress authorised a construction programme which would modernise the fleet.

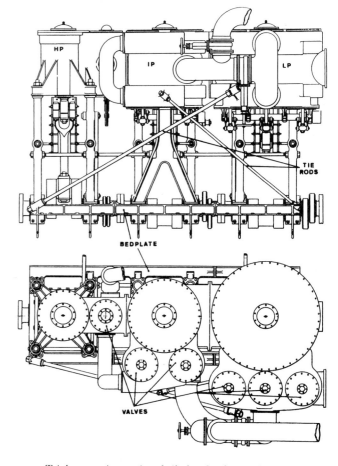

9.15 Triple-expansion engines built by the Quintard Ironworks of New York for the American cruiser Maine *(1890)*

The twin screw cruiser *Maine* was built as part of that fleet renewal programme and she was given triple-expansion engines by N. F. Palmer & Co. of the Quintard Ironworks, New York. These 4,000ihp engines followed a similar pattern to that employed elsewhere, hard, cast-iron liners being used for each cylinder with a jacket of steam surrounding the liners. HP and LP cylinders were supported on hollow, cast-steel columns while the IP cylinder rested upon straight columns in the front and inverted 'V' columns at the back; bracing added necessary rigidity. The crankshaft was made in three interchangeable parts, interchangeability being used extensively in the construction of the engines. All valves were of the piston type and were of the same size, 22in diameter; the HP cylinder having a single valve, the IP two and the LP three. Cylinder dimension were 35.5in + 57in + 88in by 3ft stroke with the total height from the bottom of the bedplate being only 14ft.[23]

Although triple-expansion engines were normally employed for warships of the period, two twin-screw battleships being constructed at Philadelphia during 1891 had 34.5 + 48in + 75in by 3ft 8in stroke cylinders,[24] and the cruiser *Charleston*, delivered by Union Ironworks of San Francisco in 1889, was given two compound engines. The use of steam at a pressure of only 90psi would account for the use of compound engines but it is difficult to understand why such a low pressure was employed. Her engines, designed by Hawthorn, Leslie, were inclined outwards at 7.5°, each having a 44in diameter steam jacketed HP cylinder and an 85in diameter LP cylinder. Engines were placed in separate watertight compartments, one in front of the other, with the starboard propeller beings driven by the forward engine.[25]

The cruisers *Columbia* and *Minneapolis*, built by Cramp & Sons of Philadelphia, marked a departure from normal propulsion as they were given three screws. Each engine was placed in its own watertight compartment, that containing the centre shaft engine being aft of those containing the port and starboard engines. The triple-expansion engines were of standard design with 42in + 59in + 92in by 3ft 6in stroke cylinder; all valves were of the piston type, there being one for the HP, two for the IP and four for the LP cylinders. Each cylinder was supported on an inverted cast steel 'Y'-frame at the back and two 8in diameter, forged hollow steel columns at the front.[26] American practice in terms of engine design followed that of the major European marine engine builders, but more modern manufacturing practices were adopted including the use of standard parts as far as possible, an extreme of standardisation being to make use of a number of identical engines. The 9,270-ton cruiser *Brooklyn* had four triple-expansion engines, two on each shaft and all in separate watertight compartments. This feature had also been adopted for the cruiser *New York*, forward engines on each shaft being capable of

disconnection to allow for more economic cruising operation.[27]

Warship engines varied little in design from their merchant counterparts or from country to country but it was in the steam-generating plant that major differences could be observed.

Warship Boilers

Naval ships tended to use the same type of boiler as merchant vessels as there was generally no alternative. Such a situation presented no real problems until the introduction of torpedo boats and destroyers, their narrower hulls and restricted space limiting the size of the boiler installation. As these vessels required high power in order to operate at high speed it was necessary to provide a steam-generation system which could meet the demand. Cylindrical boilers of sufficiently high output were too large for the hull space available and many builders made use of locomotive-type boilers for these small ships. Although such installations were satisfactory they were limited and other steam-generation solutions had to be found.

The idea of a water-tube boiler goes back to the infancy of steam propulsion but it was not until the introduction of the Belleville boiler in France during the 1850s that a successful design was produced. Development of the boiler over the following thirty years resulted in its adoption for French naval and commercial ships but the Royal Navy was interested enough to send one of its engineer officers on a fact-finding trip aboard a French mail steamer fitted with Belleville boilers. His report to a departmental committee on boilers was favourable and the committee recommended that the Belleville boiler be tried in a warship.[28] In 1892 the gunboat *Sharpshooter* had her unsatisfactory locomotive-type boilers replaced by eight Belleville boilers working at 245psi and trials conducted in 1894 showed the new boilers to be economic, reliable and capable of maintaining a high steaming rate.[29]

Without waiting for the results of trials with *Sharpshooter*, the Admiralty selected Belleville boilers for the cruisers *Powerful* and *Terrible*, but the choice was, apparently, the right one as trials with these ships in 1896 showed that the steam-generating plant was more efficient and easier to fire than an equivalent cylindrical boiler installation.[30] So successful were these trials that other installations were authorised and water-tube boilers became the normal steam-generating plant for British warships with the Belleville boiler being the standard unit for battleships and cruisers; other types of water-tube boilers, often to the design of the builder, were fitted in torpedo boats and destroyers as will be discussed later. Unfortunately, the good Belleville boiler trial results did not continue into normal service and failures began to appear with regularity as operating hours increased. Ships became unreliable due to the

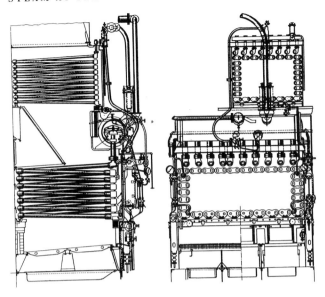

9.16 Arrangement of a Belleville boiler

failure of boiler tubes and a committee of enquiry was appointed under Admiral Sir Compton Domville to look into the use of these boilers in general. The interim report of 1901 reported favourably on the use of such boilers for warships but made a number of unfavourable comments with respect to the Belleville boiler. In reporting the outcome of the investigation *Engineering* commented, '...the Belleville boiler will doubtless cease to appear in future ships of the British Navy'.[31]

The Belleville boiler consisted of a number of inclined straight tubes connecting with cast iron junctions at their ends, the whole arrangement forming a nest of tubes over which combustion gases from the furnace below passed. The upper tubes passed to a cylindrical steam drum which was provided with baffles in order to prevent priming. Later boilers, including almost all those fitted in British warships, had an economiser, for heating boiler-feed water, located above the steam-generating tubes, this being a similar arrangement to the steam-generating section. Boilers were provided with automatic feed-water control.[32] The catalogue of Belleville boiler problems included defective water circulation, trouble with the automatic-feed control, false water-level readings and higher than expected maintenance costs, but they were not the hopeless cases made out by many and with attention could be made to function effectively. The final report of the Domville committee was issued in 1904 and confirmed its initial findings, however, Domville himself added a covering letter and this cast doubt on many of the unfavourable comments made about the Belleville boilers. He considered that earlier boilers of the type were badly made, as his recent experience with them showed that they were effective steam generators.[33] It is possible that the early boilers were indeed badly made, but

there is also the possibility of antipathy towards a foreign design, particularly one emanating from France; a number of other water-tube boilers became available during the 1890s and some, but not all, were British.

The Yarrow boiler was introduced in 1891 and used extensively in the torpedo boats and destroyers built by that firm and in later years it was employed in larger vessels. The boiler consisted essentially of an upper steam drum with two banks of tubes extending downwards and outwards in the form of an inverted 'V'. At their lower ends the tubes connected with water drums while the grate was located between these drums and the combustion gases passed upwards through the tubes. One of the first boilers of the type was fitted in a gunboat built by Yarrow for the Argentinian Navy, being designed to work at pressures up to 170psi.[34] Over the years improvements were made and higher pressures achieved but the basic design remained much the same although in the twentieth century the lower water drums were made cylindrical; larger boilers generally had two firing doors whereas smaller boilers could manage with one. In 1896 two boilers of the type were fitted in the Yarrow-built Austrian torpedo boat *Viper* and others were constructed for three Dutch cruisers being built in Holland.

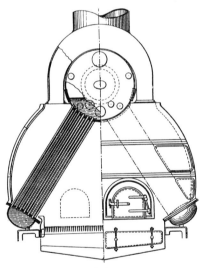

9.17 Yarrow water-tube boiler design

Tubes were expanded into the steam drum and into the tube plates which formed part of the lower water drums, if tubes failed they could be simply plugged and the boiler fired up again to resume service. Plugging meant that the lower part of the water drum had to be removed to gain access to the tube plate and an engineer had to enter the steam drum, obviously with the boiler cooled down, but plugging was easier than fitting a new tube and the steaming of the boiler did not suffer unduly provided that not too many tubes were plugged. Dutch cruisers had eight Yarrow boilers and two Scotch boilers, the latter, being more efficient to operate,

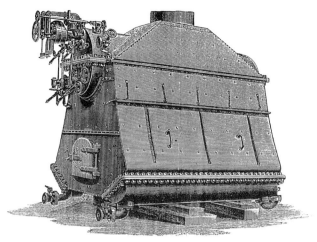

9.18 *Modified design for Yarrow water-tube boiler*

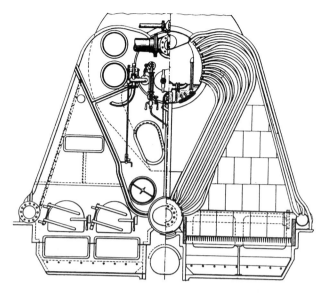

9.20 *Thornycroft water-tube boiler installed in the destroyer* Daring

were used for cruising while the water-tube boilers had a more rapid steam-generation rate which could be used when high speed was required.[35] This arrangement was employed for a number of large warships of many nations before the advent of oil firing.

Thornycrofts offered the biggest challenge to Yarrows in terms of small craft and also with respect to water-tube boilers. A two-drum boiler was developed, the curved tubes connecting the large steam drum with a single water drum located at the bottom centre of the boiler and two smaller drums positioned at grate level but located outside of the grate; tubes joining the steam drum to the outer water drums effectively formed walls around the boiler combustion chamber. Three boilers of this type were installed in the destroyer *Daring* which ran trials in 1896 and the type

central grate was located between the two water drums with combustion gases passing upwards through a number of rows of water tubes.[37] The first of these boilers was successfully tried in the torpedo gunboat *Speedy* during 1891 and was subsequently used for a number of both small and large vessels built in Britain and overseas.

Several other water-tube boilers were developed including the Normand type which was similar to the Yarrow and Thornycroft three-drum boilers. Thomsons of Clydebank took a licence to built this boiler and fitted it in a number of its destroyers including HMS *Surly* in 1895.[38]

American naval authorities experimented with different types of water tube-boiler including the Yarrow, the Belleville, the Normand and the Thornycroft three-drum type, but a favourite was the Babcock & Wilcox marine boiler, which was based on that company's tried and tested land boiler. A number of such boilers had been installed in power stations and several used automatic stokers, the basic difference between the land and the marine version being that the marine boiler was smaller. The boiler consisted

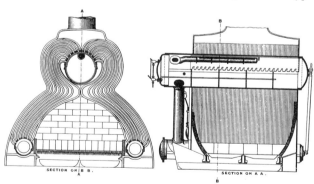

9.19 *Thornycroft water-tube boiler designed for the torpedo gunboat* Speedy *(1891)*

subsequently became known by the name of that vessel.[36] Thornycrofts had earlier developed a three-drum, water-tube boiler, the upper steam drum connecting with two water drums by means of curved tubes of a rather elaborate shape. The outermost of these tubes also surrounded the combustion chamber and formed an effective water wall. A

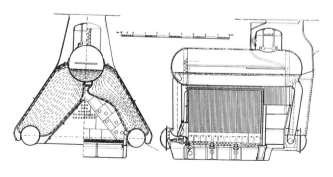

9.21 *Normand boiler licensed by J. & G. Thomson*

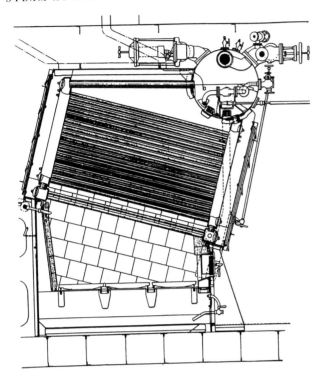

9.22 Babcock & Wilcox header-type water-tube boiler as fitted in the torpedo gunboat Sheldrake *(1899)*

essentially of a large steam drum connecting with inclined headers at the front and back of the boiler, a nest of inclined tubes, positioned above the grate, joining these headers. The first British vessel to be fitted with Babcock & Wilcox boilers was the torpedo gunboat *Sheldrake* in 1889, the results being satisfactory;[39] improved versions of the boiler went into other ships and by the turn of the century the Babcock & Wilcox boiler was well established with naval authorities on both sides of the Atlantic.[40]

Despite the apparent problems the British experienced with the Belleville boiler it still proved popular with other navies and many were installed after the turn of the century. Boilers of the type installed in many British ships performed well and certain of the problems experienced initially could be attributable to poor construction and operation.[41] Despite this no new boilers of the type were fitted in British naval ships but a good water-tube boiler was still sought by the Admiralty; of the six cruisers ordered in 1902 two were to have Yarrow boilers, two Niclausse boilers, one Durr boilers and one Babcock & Wilcox boilers.[42] This choice resulted from recommendations of the Admiralty boiler committee in its interim reports:[43] '... the Committee have had under consideration four types of large straight tube boilers which have been tried in war vessels, and are now being adopted on an extended scale in foreign navies. These are; (a) the Babcock & Wilcox boiler; (b) the

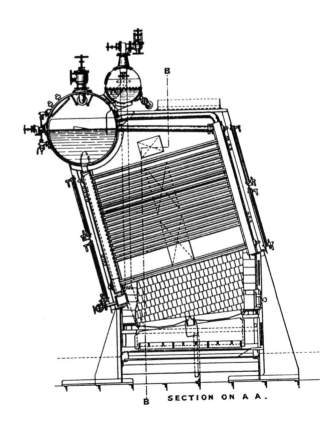

9.23 Arrangement of Babcock & Wilcox header type boiler

Niclausse boiler; (c) the Durr boiler; (d) the Yarrow large tube boiler. (a) and (b) have also been tried in our own navy with satisfactory results. ... the Committee suggests that some or all of these types be taken.'

Many more different water-tube boilers were available, some produced by boiler manufacturers and others by shipyards, and at the turn of the century they all competed for orders, mainly naval. It took another twenty years before the Babcock & Wilcox boiler and the Yarrow boiler established themselves as the market leaders, a lead they retained for the next fifty years.

References

1 The development of torpedoes is discussed in A. Lambert (ed.), *Steam, Steel and Shellfire*, Conway, London, 1992, Ch. 8.

2 P. Watts, 'Elswick Cruisers', *Trans. I.N.A.*, vol. 41, 1899, p. 288.

3 *Engineering*, vol. 30, 24 Sept. 1880. pp. 243–5.

4 Ibid., vol. 29, 9 Aug. 1880, pp. 279–80.

5 H. J. Oram, '50 Years' Changes in British Warship Machinery', *Trans. I.N.A.*, vol. 53, 1911, p. 99.

6 A. J. Durston, 'The Machinery of Warships', *Proc. I.C.E.*, vol. 119, Pt. 1, 1894–5, pp. 17–19.

7 *The Engineer*, vol. 70, 11 July 1890, pp. 28–9; A.J. Durston, 'Machinery of Warships', p. 19.

8 *The Engineer*, vol. 71, 2 Jan. 1891, p. 8; 20 Feb. 1891, p. 145.

9 Ibid., vol. 71, 5 June 1891, p. 440.

10 Ibid., vol. 71, 12 June 1891, pp. 464–8.

11 Ibid., vol. 71, 20 Feb. 1891, pp, 139–40; A.J. Durston, 'Machinery of Warships', pp. 34–5.

12 *Engineering*, vol. 59, 7 June 1895, pp. 725–7; 28 June 1895, pp. 822–3: *Engineer*, vol. 82, 2 Oct. 1896, p. 337.

13 A. Lambert (ed.) *Steam, Steel and Shellfire*, Conway, 1992, Ch 7.

14 *Engineering*, vol. 59, 12 Apr. 1895, pp. 485–6.

15 *The Engineer*, vol. 82, 18 Dec. 1896, pp. 618–28.

16 *Engineering*, vol. 59, 12 Apr. 1895, p. 485.

17 Ibid., vol. 60, 22 Nov. 1895, pp. 630–2.

18 *The Engineer*, vol. 81, 3 Apr. 1896, pp. 343–5.

19 P. Watts, 'Elswick Cruisers', pp. 288–93, 303–7.

20 *Engineering*, vol. 73, 7 Feb. 1902, pp. 180–2.

21 Ibid., vol. 73, 7 Mar. 1902, p. 310.

22 Ibid, vol. 59, 25 Jan. 1895, p. 116.

23 *The Engineer*, vol. 69, 25 Apr. 1890, p. 340.

24 Ibid., vol. 71, 22 May 1891, p. 404.

25 Ibid., vol. 71, 22 May 1891, p. 405.

26 *Engineering*, vol. 60, 15 Nov. 1895, pp. 600–1.

27 H.M. Neuhaus, 'Fifty Years of Naval Engineering in Retrospect', Part 1, *Journal of the American Society of Naval Engineers*, vol. 50, no. 1, Feb. 1838, pp. 20–1.

28 Sir W. H. White, I.C.E. Presidential Address, *Proc. I.C.E*, vol. 155, 1903–4, p. 53.

29 A. J. Durston, 'The Machinery of Warships', pp. 28–9.

30 *The Engineer*, vol. 82, 2 Oct. 1896, p. 337.

31 *Engineering*, vol. 71, 15 Mar. 1901, pp. 341–2.

32 P.M. Rippon, *Evolution of Engineering in the Royal Navy*, Spellmount, Tunbridge Wells, 1988, vol. 1, pp. 72–3.

33 Engineer Rear Admiral Scott Hill 'The Battle of the Boilers', *Journal of Naval Engineering*, July 1955, p. 26–33.

34 *The Engineer*, vol. 71, 16 Jan. 1891, p. 43.

35 *The Engineer*, vol. 81, 3 Apr. 1896, pp. 343–5.

36 J. T. Milton, 'Water-Tube Boilers for Marine Engines', *Proc. I.C.E.*, vol. 137, part 3, 1898–9, pp. 195–6.

37 Ibid., p. 195.

38 *Engineering*, vol. 60, 22 Nov. 1895, pp. 629–31.

39 Ibid., vol. 71, 21 June 1901, p. 800.

40 H. M. Neuhaus, 'Fifty Years of Naval Engineering', pp. 22–3.

41 F. J. Kean, 'A Review of the Belleville Boiler', *Trans. I.Mar.E.*, vol. 18, 1906, pp. 19–28.

42 *Engineering*, vol. 73, 23 May 1902, p. 689.

43 Ibid., vol. 71, 15 Mar. 1901, p. 335.

10
Engineers at Sea

Putting machinery in a ship presented problems not only in terms of the machinery itself but also because people were needed to attend it and ensure that it operated correctly. These people would operate in an alien environment as they were not seafarers in the traditional sense, their job took them to sea but working with the sea and dealing with its ways was a job for the mariner not a mechanic or fireman. Engine-room staff had to learn to cope with life at sea as well as deal with the machinery and it took a special kind of person to do that. Over the years many able engineers found that they could not handle life at sea and, despite their mechanical talents, were forced to return to shore employment.

In both the merchant and the naval service engine-room staff were looked upon as outsiders for many years and the view that oil and water did not mix, which was established when the first engines were put aboard ship, remained entrenched in the British Navy and the merchant service. The first attempts to remove these divisions were taken by the Royal Navy in the late nineteenth century with the Selborne scheme[1] instituted by Fisher, then Second Sea Lord, but these were strenuously resisted by people who were firmly entrenched in the past and living on tradition. The British merchant service kept its deck and engine departments firmly apart until the advent of dual-training schemes in the 1980s but the British merchant service engineer officer enjoyed a better status than his naval counterpart.

Mercantile Engineers

During the early years of the nineteenth century powered ships operated on river or short sea services and it was necessary for engine-room personnel only to be able to keep the machinery operating and undertake rudimentary repairs. The fact that the ship did not venture far from land ensured that help was generally available to undertake major repairs at one of the ports around the coast. Personnel would consist of senior engineers, assistant engineers, coal trimmers and firemen. Engineers were required to tend the machinery, ensure that it was operating satisfactorily, undertake repairs, start, stop and reverse the engines when arriving or leaving port, and supervise the firing of boilers. The chief or first engineer would also be responsible for reporting to the owners on the state of the machinery under his control, ensuring that he had sufficient coal for a passage as well as the hiring and dismissing of other personnel. During the early years of steam at sea engineers were obtained from wherever the shipowner could get them and there was no recognised system for assessing the suitability of any individual for the position he was to hold. In many cases the owner left it to the engine builder to arrange for the employment of suitable engineering staff, at least the initial complement for the ship. No training schemes existed for potential seagoing engineers let alone firemen or coal trimmers.

Good shipowners recognised the need for competent people to tend their expensive engines and understood that the safety of the ship could well depend upon the ability of the engine room staff to keep the machinery working. With a new ship the advice of the engine builder would often be sought and that was certainly the case with Brunel's *Great Western* when she entered service in 1838. Her owners left the engine builders, Maudslay, Sons & Field, to nominate the engine-room personnel and the chief engineer George Pearne was their choice, probably as a result of his having been employed by that company. It is obvious that he was concerned at having responsibility for such powerful machinery far from land as is indicated by an unfinished note he wrote upon the ship's first arrival at New York; '...you are aware of the mental depression I experienced from having the engines...'; the note was not finished because Pearne was fatally scalded when he was called to the engine room in the middle of writing it.[2] The engine-room log book for that outward journey indicates some of the problems faced by engineers aboard the early ocean-going vessels, not just in terms of machinery defects but also the problems encountered in dealing with drunken and recalcitrant firemen.[3] These problems were still being faced by marine engineers over a century later.

Firemen and coal trimmers were, of necessity, tough individuals who had to be kept under control by the engineer in charge of the watch. The number of engineers, firemen and trimmers on any watch would vary with the size of the ship but there would always be one senior engineer who had general control in the machinery spaces for the duration of the watch. Watches were usually four hours long, midnight to 4.00 am, 4.00 am to 8.00 am and 8.00 am to noon, with similar periods between noon and midnight. Not all firemen and coal trimmers were drunkards but many were hard drinkers, their interest in alcohol being heightened by the hard and hot nature of their work. Aboard many ships during the nineteenth century and into the next the sale of alcohol to crew members was prohibited, but bottles of alcoholic beverages could readily be smuggled aboard and consumed during off-duty periods in the early days of the voyage. The task of preventing crew members returning to the ship with alcoholic drinks fell to the night-duty deck officer, who was generally the most junior. Discretion would generally allow a muscular fireman, much the worse for drink, to return aboard with whatever liquor he carried while the young duty officer went unharmed. In preserving his dignity the deck officer put problems in the path of the engineer who then had to deal with the drunken fireman at sea. When the ship was at sea and the drink was finished life in the engine room returned to normal but times in port were always a problem as donkey boilers had to be kept under steam in order to ensure that winches and other auxiliary plant would operate. With firemen the worse for drink it fell to the engineers to take their turns on the shovel in order to see that steam was maintained.

Fights between drunken firemen were not uncommon and it was left to the engineer to sort them out, or at least attempt to minimise the damage individuals inflicted upon each other since injured firemen did no work and that influenced engine room efficiency. More than one engineer was injured in attempting to sort out a dispute, 'In one fight, in a north Atlantic liner, the senior engineer concerned had a complete finger bitten off.' That engineer was a friend of the renowned Harland & Wolff engineer C.C. Pounder.[4] Many engineers themselves would also enjoy a drink but they had the responsibility of ensuring that the ship was operational and the firemen did not.

For many years there was a degree of antagonism between the deck and the engine department and in the early years of steam this was attributable to the fact that by their scarcity the experienced marine engineer was a much sought after commodity. An incident aboard one of the early Royal Mail steamers in the West Indies during the 1850s illustrates this situation. While the steamers *Tweed* and *Medway* were in Bermuda together engineers from both ships held a party aboard *Medway* and refused to end it when told to do so by the duty deck officer; he called the dockyard guard to end it by coercion and was severely reprimanded by the shipowner and transferred to another ship because the engineers from the *Tweed* complained that they were forced to spend the night in the guardroom. The deck officer related the tale in his autobiography,[5] bitterly commenting that the blame was put on him '...as engineers in those days were more scarce than they are now.' Throughout the nineteenth century good engineers were always scarce, and they are today, but then that scarcity carried a premium and wages were good compared with what could be commanded ashore and in comparison with others aboard ship. During 1846 the chief engineer aboard *Great Western* received £5.00 per week, the second engineer £15.25 per month and the third engineer £13.25 per month, while the mate received £14.00 per month. Monthly wages of firemen amounted to £4.00 and seamen received £3.50 or £3.00 depending upon experience.[6] By 1890 the average

10.1 Engineers on duty in the engine room of a large liner with reciprocating machinery

annual pay of a chief engineer aboard ships of 2,000 tons and over was £233.25, while that for a second engineer was £166.00 and for a third engineer £120.50. For large liners a chief engineer could receive from £300 to £450 depending upon the ship. Average pay for firemen was £56.75 to £66.00.[7]

By 1890 the British steam-powered merchant fleet was very large and offered employment to thousands of engineers, firemen and coal trimmers, but there does not appear to have been a shortage of people willing to spend time away from their families in working conditions which can only be described as hostile. Keeping a steamer's boiler fired was hard, hot and dirty work and keeping the boilers and engines in an efficient operating state was equally demanding. Work was hot and often dangerous, many engineers suffering injury through coming into contact with operating machinery or being scalded while repairing some part of the steam plant. Leaking boiler tubes had to be repaired quickly otherwise precious water would be lost and serious damage could occur. Leakage was often due to tubes becoming loose at the tube plate and re-expanding the tubes was the solution, however, this had to be done while the boiler remained under steam since shutting down a boiler and then letting it cool was both inefficient and resulted in delay to the ship. In the case of Scotch boilers the fires would be drawn in the furnaces where leaking tubes were located,

10.2 Engine room of the liner Teutonic *illustrating the size of the machinery*

wooden boards inserted into the grates for the engineers to crawl on; they would then take turns going into the furnace to spend about 30 seconds expanding leaking tubes. The boiler remained under full steam as this was taking place. In order to reduce the risk of being burned the engineers would wear a number of boiler suits and thick gloves; furnace doors would be shut while an engineer was in the boiler in order to avoid draughts of hot air which would make the 30 seconds even more unbearable than it was. Many engineers even into the 1950s were faced with such a task if tubes leaked and over the years several were severely scalded through such leaks getting worse while the engineers were in the furnace. Life at sea was not a cruise for the engineers and they certainly earned their money.

Throughout the nineteenth century, and in fact up to the 1960s when the engineer-cadet training scheme became firmly established, seagoing engineers aboard British vessels continued to be drawn from the ranks of those who had gained their engineering experience in shipyards and engineering establishments ashore. The experience of British engineers varied considerably and there were no defined rules regarding the standards of training needed for seagoing engineers. In order to ensure that ships were manned to a reasonable standard rules were introduced in 1862 in the form of an amendment to the Merchant Shipping Act. Seagoing engineers were required to obtain certificates of competency and all ships had to carry certificated engineers, the number depending upon the power of the ship's machinery. Two grades were available, first class and second class, with an extra first class certificate being available to those engineers who wished to demonstrate a superior level of knowledge. Certificates of competency were granted to engineers who passed the necessary written and oral examinations; for a limited period a certificate of service was available to those who had extensive seagoing experience in the appropriate rank. Before sitting for a certificate the engineer needed to have spent a minimum number of months at sea as a watchkeeping engineer but he also had to have received training to an approved standard before setting out on his seafaring career. The fee for the examinations was set at £1.00.[8]

The introduction of certificates of competency gave engineers in the British mercantile fleet a status they had not previously enjoyed and it put them in the same position as deck officers. Standards of training still varied widely and the Institute of Marine Engineers, established in 1889, became the driving force behind moves to change the rules relating to apprenticeships. The Board of Trade, which controlled the granting of British certificates of competency, had initially insisted upon an apprenticeship lasting a minimum of three years, six months of which had to be spent in a drawing office. As shore apprenticeships throughout Britain lasted a minimum of five years the Institute requested that this term should also be required for potential seagoing engineers as it would ensure that they had completed their apprenticeships. This request was resisted under pressure from influential shipowners who feared that a shortage of engineers would result and eventually a compromise was reached on a four-year apprenticeship with allowance being granted for time spent at a technical college.[9] New regulations were introduced in 1901 and since then they have been frequently amended with respect to the training and examination requirements ensuring that the high standard of the British certificate of competency or 'ticket' is recognised throughout the world.

Seagoing engineers of the nineteenth century were much

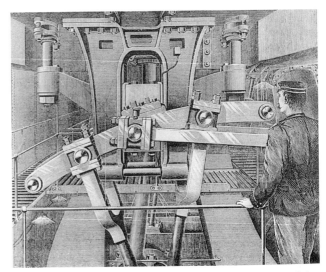

10.3 Valve gear expansion links of a large reciprocating engine being observed by an engineer

10.4 The twin-screw China coast steamer Yochow *(1901) required a large engineroom complement to tend her two 13.5in + 22in + 36.5in by 2ft 6in stroke engines and coal-fired boilers (John Swire & Son)*

on their own when the ship left port and a safe return home was essentially in their hands. Without sails the ship depended upon its engines and the engineers needed to keep them going and repair them if they failed. Over the years many ships have made port through the inventive genius and practical skills of their engineers; crude propellers have been constructed from whatever materials existed on board, fractured shafts have been repaired with only hand drills and files, pistons have been replaced, bearings have been repaired and journals bedded in as the ship rolled furiously in a gale. The list is endless but that is what the engineers were on their ships for, to ensure that the ship, its cargo, passengers and crew reached port safely. In addition to these manual tasks the marine engineer had to be a chemist in order to handle the problems of boiler-water treatment and he also needed to have the ability to estimate coal quantities with some degree of accuracy. Being able to assess how much coal had been taken during bunkering ensured that the owner was not overcharged, but knowing how much to take was also important in order to ensure that the ship could reach port. Bunker spaces were not regular shapes, and to assess the coal remaining at any time could be difficult, an incorrect assessment of the remaining coal resulting in the need for a ship to divert from its route in order to pick up supplies. During a passage to New York in 1873 the White Star liner *Atlantic* was forced to head for Halifax, Nova Scotia in order to obtain additional coal as gales had prolonged the passage and the chief engineer was not happy that sufficient coal remained to complete the voyage. The result was a tragedy as the ship went aground on the coast of Nova Scotia with the loss of 562 lives.[10] During that

10.5 An engineer at the controls of one of the engines fitted in the Atlantic liner Campania; *a typical scene at the end of the nineteenth century*

passage *Atlantic* also suffered a bunker fire and the engine-room staff spent much of their time dealing with the problem. Bunker fires were not uncommon as coal would often spontaneously combust; the situation was serious as it resulted in a waste of coal and could, in extreme cases, result in the fire spreading. More often, however, it was just an inconvenience which had to be controlled and that usually meant digging to the seat of the fire and spraying water on to it until the fire was extinguished.

Although the issuing of certificates gained them the status their work deserved, few engineers during the nineteenth century wore any form of uniform other than a boiler suit. The work was hard, hot and dirty and a uniform would have been a wasteful luxury; only senior engineers aboard passenger ships had the time to wear a uniform and being seen in public was part of their job. The founding of the Institute of Marine Engineers established seagoing engineers, and their shore counterparts, as professionals through the publication of their transactions and papers and by ensuring that standards of education and training were maintained and enhanced; it has been performing that role ever since.

10.6 Middle platform of one of the engines aboard Campania

Naval Engineers

The role of the naval engineer was identical to that of his mercantile counterpart: he had to keep the machinery working whenever it was required. However, naval operations differed from those of the commercial fleet and engineers were looked upon as being necessary but not as important as the fighting men; engineers were very much second-class citizens aboard British warships for almost the entire nineteenth century. Tradition in the Royal Navy was hard to change and engineers did not fit in with the usual class of man recruited to the fighting forces; they were looked upon as crude and not at all like the gentlemen who normally joined the Senior Service. That was certainly true but it took many years before engineers were made to feel welcome and an accepted part of the service; engineers aboard a fighting ship could die just as readily as anyone else but they were still not accepted as full members of a ship's establishment, they were auxiliary seamen. Only the chief engineer was accepted as a wardroom officer and allowed to mess with lieutenants, paymasters and surgeons, the remainder of the engineers were kept separate and had their own mess and living spaces combined.

Over the years there was much comment in the press concerning the treatment of engineers in the Navy but inertia at the Admiralty and prejudice on the part of those serving aboard ship prevented any real remedial action.[11]

The first steam engineers in the Navy were treated as petty officers although no rank was assigned to them, but by an Order in Council in 1837 three grades of engineer were established ranking with, but after, the gunners, boatswains and carpenters who were warrant officers. First-class engineers received £9.60 per month, second-class engineers £6.80 and third-class engineers £4.90; considerably less than engineers aboard *Great Western* were getting at the same time. Within a year rates were increased to £12, £8 and £5, respectively, as engineers were leaving to take up positions aboard merchant steamers. A further Order in Council during 1847 changed the situation somewhat by establishing seven grades of engineer officer and increasing wages to levels which could compete with those offered by merchant shipowners.[12]

At the end of the Crimean War in 1856 it became difficult to find sufficient qualified engineers to man the fleet to a satisfactory level and in 1859 the Inspector of Machinery (George Murdoch) went on a recruitment drive around the shipyards of northern Britain where he succeeded in recruiting 103 apprentices. Poor publicity regarding the status of engineers in the Royal Navy and levels of pay which were inferior to what could be expected in the merchant service still resulted in a shortage of good engineers to serve the fleet; many of the Murdoch recruits were of poor quality and fewer than half were still in the service by 1870. There was a need for an improvement in manpower, status and training, and steps were taken to ensure that dockyard apprentices were given a better education and to recruit young men of quality. In 1864 the Royal School of Naval Architecture and Marine Engineering was opened in South Kensington to offer a more scientific training to naval engineers, and the year before boys receiving training in the Royal Dockyards became known as engineer students and became eligible to compete for places at the new school. Education in the sciences formed an essential part of the training of young men entering the Navy but the management of men was also an essential for a good officer aboard ship.

With the general adoption of steam-powered warships the attitude of the 'sailors' had to change and by time the mastless HMS *Devastation* appeared in 1871 the essential role of the engineer could no longer be ignored. In 1868 a major change took place in the manning arrangements aboard warships when the new class of rating to be known as Engine Room Artificer (ERA) was created. This divided the engineering branch into professional and mechanical sections with the engineers supervising the work done by the ERAs and ensuring the safe and efficient operation of the ship with respect to all of its machinery. Engineers were

trained in the service, spending much of their time at college before being posted to their first ship; as with the deck and fighting sections of the service young people were recruited and received their training at the expense of the service. There were, however, still complaints regarding the treatment and status of the engineer with respect to their fellow officers and it was difficult to attract sufficient young men to the engineering branch. Even at the end of the nineteenth century engineers still felt themselves badly treated compared with other branches, for the reasons that:[13]

1 Engineers were classed as a civil branch and had no executive control over their departments and hence had no power to award punishments;

2 Promotion prospects were not as good for engineers as for executive officers;

3 The Engineering Branch was not represented on the Admiralty Board; and

4 Engine-room complements were generally too small for effective operation of the ship at all times.

These points and others were brought before the First Lord, Earl Selborne, in 1901 but met with little sympathy and it was obvious that those in power at the Admiralty were averse to any change in the condition and status of the

10.7 Starting platform aboard the battleship Prince George *(1896)*

10.8 Upper engine platform aboard Prince George

10.9 One of China Navigation Company's vessels being coaled by hand from a barge. Such coaling was a long job despite the number of individuals involved. Note the wind scoops extending from the accommodatioin ports, the only effective ventilation available aboard many vessels. (John Swire & Sons)

engineering branch.[14] The attitude was parochial as major changes were taking place in the engineering industry and the British fleet would have to embrace such changes or be left behind by their French and German rivals. Britain's navy was built upon tradition and still attempted to live on it to the detriment of skills without which it could neither function nor fight. Engineers were totally unrepresented on the Admiralty Committee which sat during 1900–01 to investigate their grievances and this contrasts sharply with the US Navy Personnel Board, established in 1897, which consisted of seven executive officers and four engineer officers.[15] The appointment of John Fisher as First Sea Lord in 1904 heralded a new era in British sea power and also a change for the engineering branch. Unfortunately many of Fisher's innovative ideas did not find approval among the more traditional and with his departure many were reversed. Eventually, however, the importance of the engineering branch was recognised and British naval engineers received the status they deserved. The story of the fight for recognition is recorded in *Up Funnel, Down Screw!* [16]

Engineers worldwide have performed their duty in the engine rooms of ships large and small, commercial and naval, that duty sometimes being undertaken at considerable risk to their well-being. Naval engineers of all countries were in the same danger as executive and fighting officers aboard their ships even if their workplace was surrounded by a belt of armour. For safety all watertight compartments of a fighting ship would be secured when in battle and engineers down below stood little chance of surviving if the ship sank. They did their duty and understood the risks. Merchant ships during a conflict had little protection and their engineers were equally as vulnerable, perhaps more so as they had no protective armour belt. Even in peacetime the job had its dangers as a grounding or collision would necessitate engineers being present in the engine room to keep pumps working and ensure that electricity for lighting and other purposes would be available for as long as possible. When *Titanic* sank all the engineers were lost with her; they kept pumps and lights working for as long as possible and sacrificed their lives doing their duty.

References

1   R. Hough, *First Sea Lord*, Severn House, London, 1969, pp. 151–6.

2   D. Griffiths, *Brunel's Great Western*, Patrick Stephens, Wellingborough, 1985, pp. 30, 40.

3   C. Claxton, *Logs of the First Voyage of the Steamship Great Western*, Great Western Steamship Co., Bristol, 1838.

4   C. C. Pounder, 'Human Problems in Marine Engineering', *Trans. I.Mar.E.*, 1959, p. 99.

5   R. Woolward, *Nigh on Sixty Years at Sea*, Digby, London, 1895, pp. 88–90.

6   D. Griffiths, *Brunel's Great Western*, pp. 138–9.

7   *The Engineer*, vol. 71, 13 Feb. 1891, pp. 121–2.

8   W. H. Thorn, *Reed's Engineers Handbook*, Thomas Reed, Sunderland, 1866, pp. 1–6: *Engineer*, vol. 71, 13 Feb. 1891, pp. 121–2.

9   *Engineering*, vol. 71, 24 May 1901, p. 677.

10 C. H. Milsom, *The Coal Was there for Burning*, Marine Media Management, London, 1975.

11 *Marine Engineer* various months in 1882 contain articles and letters; *Engineer*, 10 No. 1922, vol. 70. pp. 181, 533–4, 538–9, vol. 71, pp. 5, 193–4.

12 E. C. Smith, 'The Rise of the Engineering Branch of the Royal Navy', *Engineering*, vol. 114, pp. 576–8.

13 D. B. Morrison, 'The British Naval Engineer', *Trans. NECIES*, vol. 16, 1899–1900, pp. 215–6.

14 E. C. Smith, 'Rise of the Engineering Branch', p. 578.

15 D. B. Morrison, 'The Engineering Crisis in the Navy', *Trans, IESSS*, vol. 44, 1901–2. p. 104.

16 G. Penn, *Up Funnel, Down Screw!*, Hollis & Carter, London, 1955.

II
The Steam Turbine

The marine steam turbine was not the overnight sensation many people believe it to have been, it took years of work and experimentation before a practical product could be put before ship operators and shipbuilders. Charles Parsons is generally given the credit for introducing the marine propulsion turbine by virtue of the dramatic run made by *Turbinia* through the assembled British fleet at Spithead in 1897. That high-speed passage was the culmination of many years' work both in terms of steam turbine and ship propulsion. Turbo-generating sets had been developed in the 1880s and by 1887 Parsons could claim to have sold sets developing a total of 1,280 horse power, two-thirds of the generating sets being for installation in ships.[1] Parsons was aware of the potential for the steam turbine but he was not alone as others had also been working on the idea most notably the Swedish engineer Gustaf de Laval. The work of both men was of considerable importance to the development of marine engineering. The history of the turbine is complex and space limitations preclude more than a brief glance at the early years which included many blind alleys and frustrating failures before either man produced a working machine.

Before continuing the narrative it is important to discuss the basic elements of the turbine. Turbines may be axial or radial; in the axial turbine steam enters at one end and passes axially through the casing before leaving at the other, whereas in the radial turbine steam enters the casing at the shaft and passes radially outwards. In both cases steam acts on the blades of the turbine as it moves either axially or radially. The shape and the arrangement of the blades were dictated by the type of the turbine which could be either impulse or reaction. In the impulse turbine steam is expanded through nozzles where its pressure is reduced and its velocity increased. The high velocity steam then impacts on the blades fitted to the turbine disc where they give up some of their energy; the effect is similar to that of water hitting the paddles of a waterwheel. To extract the maximum energy from the steam a number of stages of blading could be used with fixed blades being employed to redirect the steam to the next stage of rotating blades. A reaction turbine operates in a different way as steam is made to expand through sets of blades producing the reaction effect which causes the turbine to rotate. Blades are shaped so that each pair in any stage acts like a nozzle, steam expanding through that nozzle causing a reaction in the same way that water leaving the nozzles of a rotary garden sprinkler causes it to rotate. A large number of stages could be incorporated in any turbine with expansion of the steam taking place at each and fixed guide blades being used to redirect the steam on to the next set of moving blades.

Parsons and de Laval experimented with different turbine arrangements, de Laval having a reaction unit running in 1883 while a year later Parsons had his compound reaction turbine working; he also established a factory for producing these at powers up to 20kW. From then on de Laval concentrated on impulse turbines and in 1892 established the Swedish de Laval Steam Turbine Company; the same year a geared 11kW propulsion turbine, incorporating an astern turbine, was built. De Laval's company produced geared single-stage impulse turbines which were generally used for electrical generation but as early as 1889 de Laval had built impulse turbines with two rows of moving blades separated by a set of fixed guide blades. The concept of a double impulse turbine was not patented by de Laval but in 1895 the American Charles Curtis saw its advantages and took out a patent on it. With the higher steam pressures and temperatures which were to come about in later years the multiple-row Curtis arrangement proved much more advantageous than the single impulse wheel of de Laval and the former became firmly established while the de Laval turbine disappeared.

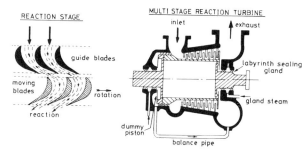

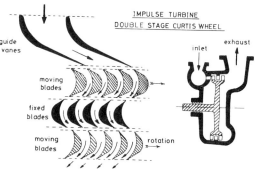

11.1 Diagram showing arrangements of reaction and impulse turbine systems

Parsons concentrated on reaction turbines and established the Parsons Marine Steam Turbine Company in 1894, the same year commencing trials with *Turbinia* fitted with a radial turbine on a single shaft. During the next three years many alternative arrangements were tried before he arrived at the triple shaft system using axial reaction turbines. The HP turbine drove the starboard shaft, the IP the port and the LP the centre, the centre shaft also having a separate astern turbine. Steam turbines are not directly reversible and so a separate astern turbine must also be fitted, this operating in condenser vacuum during normal operation thus offering little loss of power. With full power (2,000hp) and a propeller shaft speed of 2,000rpm *Turbinia* managed 34.5 knots during her dash through the fleet. Each shaft had three screws but there were problems of cavitation which were never overcome. Parsons quickly became aware of the problems involved with high propeller speeds and carried out numerous tests in a cavitation tank. In spite these troubles, however, *Turbinia* demonstrated the high power to size/weight ratio of the steam turbine and everybody took notice.[2]

Despite the fact that Parsons had somewhat embarrassed the fleet at Spithead the Admiralty became aware of the steam turbine's potential and immediately set in motion moves to test this new form of propulsion. In 1899 the Parsons Marine Steam Turbine Company received an order for construction of the 370-ton displacement *Viper*, the ship itself being built by Hawthorn, Leslie. The contract called for a guaranteed speed of 31 knots but a maximum speed of 36.5 knots was achieved during trials, satisfying even the most sceptical observer at the Admiralty. Parsons provided a quadruple screw arrangement with HP turbines driving the outer shafts and LP units the inner shafts; astern turbines were connected to the inner shafts only. Each turbine could develop 2,500 shaft horse power (shp) at 1,200rpm from steam at a pressure of 175psi and although this gave a maximum speed above expectation the cruising performance was poor. Concurrent with the construction of *Viper* Armstrong, Whitworth & Co. laid down a slightly larger turbine-driven destroyer named *Cobra*, the Parsons turbine installation being similar to that of *Viper*'s. Construction was speculative but the trials performance, where a mean speed of 34.6 knots over a three-hour period was attained, encouraged the Admiralty to purchase the vessel. Unfortunately both ships were lost during 1901, *Viper* due to a grounding and *Cobra* due to structural weakness, but the steam turbine had proved its worth for fast naval ships. In an attempt to improve the slow-speed cruising economy of the turbine destroyer Parsons constructed *Velox* similar in design to *Viper* with an almost identical steam plant save for the fact that a 150ihp triple-expansion steam reciprocating engine was connected to each of the LP shafts by means of a clutch coupling. For high-speed running the turbines

alone operated but when the vessel was cruising steam was supplied to the reciprocating engines which then exhausted to the turbine plant. After initial teething troubles had been overcome the ship was purchased by the Admiralty which also ordered a similar vessel *Eden*, with cruising turbines instead of reciprocating engines. This 550-ton destroyer had triple screws, the single HP turbine driving the centre shaft and the two LPs the outer shafts; cruising turbines were connected to the outer shafts. Comparative trials between *Velox*, *Eden* and other similar destroyers with reciprocating machinery demonstrated the superiority of the turbine for high speeds and confirmed the necessity of cruising turbines for economy at lower speeds.[3]

Despite the fact that the turbine had indicated its superiority for developing high powers from low weight and machines of small size while having inherent balance, there was still a call for the reciprocating engine in naval circles, but the naval application of this type of engine was drawing to a close. In 1902 the Fairfield-built armoured cruiser *Good Hope* was given twin, four-crank, triple-expansion engines balanced on the Yarrow-Schlick-Tweedy system. Low pressure cylinders (82.5in) were fitted at each end of the crankshaft with the 43.5in HP on the forward centre crank and the 71in IP on the other crank; pistons had a stroke of 4ft. With steam at a pressure of 278psi these engines could develop some 31,000ihp, the boilers burning coal at the rate of 1.92lbs/ihp/hr. There were 43 Belleville boilers in four stokeholds and the machinery occupied a length of 247ft 6in, half the total length of the ship.[4]

Among the last large ships in the British Navy to be fitted with reciprocating engines was the cruiser HMS *Defence*, built at the Pembroke Dockyard in 1908; her twin 13,500ihp, four-crank, triple-expansion engines, 74.625in (2) + 65.5in + 40.625in by 4ft stroke, came from Scotts of Greenock. They were of conventional form with piston valves for HP and IP cylinders and flat valves for the LP; Stephenson link motion actuated the valves, a steam cylinder being used for reversing the motion. Contrary to the usual practice of the time steam flowed through the condenser tubes with sea water circulating around them in each of the two condensers. Steam came from twenty-four Yarrow boilers constructed by the engine builder, the boilers working under closed stokehold forced draught.[5] In naval terms, however, the reciprocating engine had had its day and the new era belonged to the turbine despite its many disadvantages: a direct-drive turbine was less efficient than a reciprocating engine and there were still problems of propeller cavitation owing to the high rotational speed. Following trials with the Parsons turbine-driven cruiser *Amethyst* and investigations into astern power and manoeuvring, a decision was made in 1905 to equip the battleship *Dreadnought* with turbines and the new age of marine propulsion had truly dawned.

Commercial operators could also see the advantages of the turbine and some adopted the drive with the same enthusiasm as the naval authorities although the reasoning was, perhaps, less clear cut. Obviously turbine drive did not suit all merchant ships because of its lower fuel efficiency and the tendency for propellers to suffer cavitation damage, but it did have a place in the propulsion of the faster and more powerful passenger ships. In such ships the saving in engine room space compared with reciprocating machinery could be significant, while the avoidance of vibration was important to passenger comfort. Dennys of Dumbarton took an early interest in turbine propulsion and during 1901 put into service the first commercially successful turbine-driven passenger ship, the 250ft long Clyde pleasure steamer *King Edward*. Her machinery, built by Parsons, consisted of one HP turbine driving the centre shaft, fitted with two screws, and two LP turbines on the outer shafts, fitted with single screws.[6] The success of this ship immediately prompted construction of the slightly larger (279ft) excursion steamer *Queen Alexandra*, having a similar but more powerful engine, 4,000shp compared with 3,500shp for *King Edward*; in this case the outer shafts were fitted with two screws.[7] Parsons' machinery for *Queen Alexandra* cost £10,500, an increase of £2,500 compared with the less powerful plant for the earlier ship. Triple-shaft turbines were installed in the South Eastern & Chatham Railway Company's 21-knot, 1,676-gross ton cross-Channel steamer *The Queen*, delivered by Dennys in 1903, the suggestion to fit turbines coming from the builder. Other turbine-driven railway steamers were built by Dennys during the following years indicating both the suitability of this type of vessel for turbine propulsion and the quality of the machinery built by Parsons and its licensees.

11.2 Partly-bladed LP rotor of turbine set for Victorian *at Parsons' works*

In terms of commercial shipping the breakthrough really came when the Allan Line chose turbine propulsion for its new Atlantic liners *Victorian* and *Virginian*. Originally both ships were to have been constructed by Workman, Clark & Co. of Belfast with reciprocating engines but after construction commenced the owner was persuaded to fit turbines. That change of mind caused a delay with the result that the order for building *Virginian* went to Alexander Stephen & Co. of Glasgow. Both of these 10,700-gross ton ships were identical with turbines provided by the Parsons Marine Steam Turbine Company, some 12,000shp being needed to propel them at 17.5 knots. A triple-shaft arrangement was chosen, there being a single screw on each with the HP turbine driving the centre shaft and the LP units turning the outer shafts; astern turbines were connected to the outer shafts only. In total 1.5 million blades were fitted to the turbines in each ship, half being rotating blades and the remainder fixed guide blades. Each LP turbine weighed

11.3 Victorian *after re-engining and renaming as* Marlock *(Canadian Pacific)*

11.4 Sets of turbines for Mauretania; *astern turbine, LP ahead turbine and HP ahead turbine*

100 tons and the HP unit weighed 60 tons, the total weight of the plant being much less than for reciprocating engine installation of equivalent power, while the turbines

occupied less space and offered less risk of vibration.[8] *Virginian* entered service in April 1905 and *Victorian* a month later; both ships were re-engined with geared turbines during the 1920s and *Virginian* survived until 1955 when, as *Homeland*, she was broken up in Italy.

Although it is generally believed that *Virginian* was the first ocean-going turbine-driven merchant ship, this is not the case as that honour goes to the 2,448-gross ton *Loongana* built by Dennys for the Union Steamship Company's service between Australia and Tasmania. This ship, also fitted with Parsons turbines on three shafts, started her long voyage from the Clyde in August 1904.[9]

The construction of *Lusitania* and *Mauretania* provided the real test for the marine steam turbine and it took considerable courage for the Cunard board to adopt what was effectively a new form of engine on such a large scale. Built with the aid of government money by way of a £2.6 million loan and an annual running subsidy of £150,000[10] the ships were to be larger and faster than any other passenger vessels at sea. John Brown & Co., formerly J. & G. Thomson,

11.5 Complete ring of LP stator blading for Mauretania

received the order for *Lusitania* and Swan, Hunter & Wigham, Richardson of Wallsend was awarded the contract for the sister ship, later to be known as *Mauretania*. Tank tests showed that to achieve the desired service speed of 23.5 knots these 31,500-gross ton ships would need machinery capable of sustaining 68,000shp and in 1903 Cunard appointed a commission of leading engineers to investigate the ideal form of propulsion. A detailed investigation of different propulsion systems was undertaken and tests were carried out on board turbine-driven steamers, but the decision of the commission to propose adoption of steam turbine machinery was an act of faith. The commission reported in 1904 but in December 1903, when tendering for the construction of a sister to the 19,500-gross ton *Caronia*, John Brown proposed the use of turbines instead of reciprocating engines and early in 1904 the company was awarded the contract for the turbine-driven *Carmania*.

The 21,000shp needed to drive *Carmania* had never before been produced by a marine turbine and a three-shaft system was again adopted with the HP turbine on the centre shaft and LP plus astern turbines on the outer shafts. The engine rooms of *Caronia* and *Carmania* were the same length but the turbines were lower than the reciprocating engines thus giving a much roomier appearance. In order to gain experience John Brown constructed an experimental, three-screw turbine set developing 1,800shp, thus putting the Clydeside concern ahead of its many rivals in terms of marine turbine technology. *Carmania*'s turbine plant weighed 5 per cent less than the reciprocating engines of her sister, there was less ship vibration and during trials she maintained a higher speed by about 1 knot.[11] Although such information might indicate that turbines were superior in every way to a reciprocating installation that was not the case in service as after eight years on the Atlantic the coal consumption of *Carmania* was greater than that of her reciprocating-engined sister and Cunard's naval architect Leonard Peskett concluded that service results did not warrant the adoption of direct-drive turbines in ships of that type and speed.[12] Indeed, for the intermediate class ships Cunard returned to reciprocating engines, constructing *Franconia* (1911) and *Laconia* (1912) with two 6,000 brake horse power (bhp), four-crank, quadruple-expansion engines, 33in + 47in + 67in + 95in by 5ft stroke, built by the Wallsend Slipway & Engineering Company.[13]

It has been claimed that operating experience with *Carmania* prompted the fitting of turbine machinery in *Lusitania* and *Mauretania* but that was certainly not the case as Cunard made the decision to adopt turbines in 1904, following the engineering commission's recommendation, and *Carmania* did not enter service until 1905. It was not just Cunard which leapt into the dark with that decision as the engine builders John Brown and Wallsend Slipway were also innovating with turbine machinery of unprecedented

11.6 Bottom half of LP turbine casing, Mauretania

proportions. In order to transmit the necessary power a quadruple-screw arrangement had to be installed, each shaft being directly connected to a turbine, the outer shafts being driven by HP units while the inner shafts were connected to the LP and astern turbines; at normal full speed each ahead turbine would develop 18,250shp at a speed of 190rpm. During manoeuvring, only the LP turbines were used, steam being directed to these via a throttling valve, steam was directed to the HP turbine only when shaft revolutions exceeded half speed.

The machinery installed in both ships was the same in general arrangement but constructional details differed to suit the ideas of the turbine builders, particularly with respect to the blades. For *Lusitania* the bronze blade material was drawn through dies in order to produce the desired section shape with sections being cut to the required length for each blade. Blades were individually caulked into slots cut in the rotor drums, distance pieces providing the necessary spacing between them. For longer blades, as used in the LP turbine, rows of shrouding connected adjacent blades at three points thereby introducing stiffness to them. Similar fitting arrangements applied to the fixed blades in the casing. Wallsend Slipway adopted a different method of construction and initially formed blades into segments which were subsequently inserted into the rotors and casings. This method offered the same security of fixing and strength as individual blade fitting but it enabled the task of fitting to be done more rapidly. Both ships had 8ft diameter HP rotor drums with blade lengths varying between 2.5in and 12in; LP rotor drums were 11ft 8in diameter and blades varied in length from 8in at the entry side to 22in at the exhaust end of the turbine. The gradual increase in blade length was required as steam expanded and increased its volume as it passed through successive rows of blades. Steam at a pressure of 195psi was supplied by twenty-three double-ended and three single-ended Scotch boilers. Turbine casings were

11.7 Mauretania *under power (Harry Weston Collection)*

castings and neither engine builder had the facilities for casting such large items; those for *Lusitania* came from Thomas Firth & Sons of Sheffield and casings for the turbines fitted in *Mauretania* were cast by Fullerton, Hodgart & Barclay of Paisley.[14]

Upon entry into service in 1907 both ships performed to expectation and in their turn captured the Blue Riband for the fastest Atlantic crossing, *Mauretania* proving to be slightly the quicker achieving a crossing at an average speed of 25.89 knots during 1909. Coal consumption was prodigious at between 900 and 1,000 tons per day at full speed but both ships proved the effectiveness of turbines for high power in fast ships and also showed the quality of British marine engineering as the installations far exceeded the power of any other marine turbine plant constructed up to that time. In ten years engine powers had increased from 2,000shp in *Turbinia* to 73,000shp in the giant Cunarders; it was a giant leap forward which was not to be repeated in the marine industry.

Although mercantile steam turbine installations during the first decade of the twentieth century were confined to passenger ships, almost exclusively British, the naval use of turbines during that period was much more widespread. Admiral Fisher held strong views in favour of large and fast ships for which the turbine was admirably suited and the 'Swift' class of 37-knot, 2,400-ton destroyers was ordered requiring 35,000shp to be developed. The building of the battleship *Dreadnought* proved, however, to be the turning point both in terms of naval power and marine engineering. Her quadruple-screw arrangement had HP ahead and astern turbines on the outer shafts and LP ahead and astern turbines on the inner; cruising turbines were fitted to the inner shafts. The fitting of turbines is claimed to have reduced the displacement by 1,000 tons and saved approx-

imately £100,000 on the cost of the ship.[15] Maximum ahead power of 23,000shp could be developed, double that of the plant installed in the cruiser *Amethyst*. This quadruple-screw arrangement of Parsons' cross compound turbines (HP + LP on separate shafts) became standard for subsequent large naval ships for a number of years. Output steadily increased with the battle-cruiser *Invincible* (1908) having a 44,000shp plant while that fitted in *Lion* (1912) could develop 70,000shp. A change was, however, coming and the monopoly enjoyed by the Parsons turbine came to an end in 1908 when Brown-Curtis cruising turbines were stipulated for HMS *Bristol*.

In that year John Brown obtained a licence from Curtis for the construction of impulse turbines and the Brown design team set to work on the design of a marine impulse turbine, producing the Brown-Curtis impulse wheel which subsequently found extensive use for naval and merchant shipping, generally in combination with Parsons' reaction turbines. Brown-Curtis turbines were more compact than the Parsons type, they also had fewer stages and could operate with a good efficiency. With the design it was possible to simplify the engine-room layout and achieve high power from a twin-shaft arrangement which would have needed triple or quadruple shafts for Parsons' turbines. The system installed aboard *Bristol* achieved the required speed with only two shafts and a much simplified valve and piping system; in addition economy was good at full power and cruising speed. For the 40,000shp ships of the 'Arethusa' class the five vessels fitted with Parsons' turbines required a four-shaft arrangement while the three which had Brown-Curtis turbines required only two shafts.[16]

Parsons countered the Brown-Curtis turbine by developing an impulse-reaction arrangement which was essentially a hybrid incorporating the two types of turbine. This design had high-pressure steam admission over only part of the inlet to the impulse blading which was placed before the reaction stages; this was known as partial admission and it allowed for improved efficiency from the impulse effect. By the time the steam reached the reaction stages there was full 360° steam supply to the rotating blades. The Parsons partial-admission impulse-reaction turbine showed an improvement in efficiency of about 7 per cent compared with the full admission reaction type.

In America turbines did not break into the marine field until 1905 when the US Navy ordered three identical light cruisers, *Chester*, *Salem* and *Birmingham*, fitting them with Parsons turbines, Curtis turbines and triple-expansion engines respectively. American requirements differed slightly from those of Britain or her European neighbours as the US Navy needed a greater cruising range and so economy was of considerable importance. At lower speed the reciprocating machinery proved superior in terms of economy although the turbine-driven vessels proved to be better at

higher speeds. The results of these trials were not particularly positive as far as turbine machinery was concerned
and there was no general move towards that form of power;
as in Europe, the approach was cautious. Further turbine
installations were tried and in 1907 similar comparative trials were authorised with four battleships *Delaware*, *North
Dakota*, *Utah* and *Florida*, the first having reciprocating
engines, the second Curtis turbines and the other two
Parsons turbines. With these larger but slower ships conditions were not as favourable for the turbine as with the
cruisers and coal consumption figures at cruising speed
showed the turbines to be extremely uneconomic. It was not
until 1911 that any further large turbine-driven vessels were
ordered. The introduction of geared cruising turbines
dramatically improved fuel consumption in the battleships
Oklahoma and *Nevada* and the adoption of turbo-electric
drives for the battleship *New Mexico* in 1914 showed
equally encouraging results. Destroyers with their need for
high speed offered greater potential for turbines and many
were constructed with direct-drive Parsons and Curtis
turbines in the years between 1907 and 1915.[17]

French licences for Parsons turbines were taken by
Forges et Chantiers de la Méditerranée in 1906 and by
Chantiers et Ateliers de St. Nazaire-Penhoet and the
Ateliers et Chantiers de la Loire a little later. Developments
followed similar lines to those of Britain and America and in
1908 France's first turbine-driven passenger ship, the
Compagnie Generale Transatlantique's *Charles-Roux* left
St. Nazaire. The same year the first turbine-driven French
capital ship, *Voltaire*, was built by Forges et Chantiers de la
Méditerranée.[18] In 1910 Chantiers de l'Atlantique of St.
Nazaire conceived the triple-expansion turbine system with
HP, IP and two LP turbines driving separate shafts in a
quadruple-screw installation. The first such system went
into the 23,650-gross-ton Atlantic liner *France*, completed
in 1912; LP turbines powered the inner shafts with the HP
connected to the port outboard shaft and the IP to the starboard outboard, outboard shafts also having astern turbines.
Ahead power of 45,000shp could normally be developed
with steam at a pressure of 200psi, a relatively low pressure
to require the use of triple-expansion turbines, but the installation was economic producing coal consumption
figures of 1.3lbs/shp/hr which was better than the express
Cunarders managed.[19]

Similar triple-expansion, direct-drive turbines were
adopted for Cunard's *Aquitania* (1914) and for the German
trio of Atlantic liners planned by Albert Ballin for the
Hamburg American Line: *Imperator* (subsequently
Cunard's *Berengaria*), *Vaterland* (subsequently the
American-owned *Leviathan*) and *Bismarck* (to become the
White Star Line's *Majestic*) were giants of over 52,000 gross
tons and required machinery of 65,000shp to push them
through the water at 23 knots. There was nothing unusual

about the triple-expansion Parsons turbine installations of
these ships except that they were larger and more powerful
than those fitted in the French-built ship. *Vaterland* and
Bismarck were larger than their sister and *Aquitania*, with
machinery capable of developing 100,000shp.[20] German
shipyards quickly developed the technology to construct
high-powered turbines and these went into naval vessels as
well as larger liners. AEG acquired a Curtis licence in 1906
and Parsons machinery was also constructed by other
builders such as Vulcan and Blohm & Voss. As with other
countries, there was a certain degree of uncertainty about
the effectiveness of turbine propulsion and in a number of
cases vessels of the same class were given different forms of
propulsion in order to obtain comparative data. This was
the case with the light cruisers *Dresden* and *Emden* delivered
in 1908, the former having two sets of Parsons direct-drive
turbines and her more famous sister had two three-cylinder,
triple-expansion engines. By 1910 all larger ships were
being given turbine machinery.

Despite their high power to size and weight ratio,
turbines were not suitable for the propulsion of slower ships
which comprised the majority of those at sea during the
early years of the twentieth century, and subsequently too
for that matter. Reciprocating engines were still much more
economic in terms of fuel consumption and that was the
major expense as far as the merchant-ship owner was concerned. The turbine could allow steam to expand down to
very low pressures thereby recovering more energy from it
but there was a limit to how low the steam pressure could be
allowed to fall in a reciprocating engine owing to the size of
the LP piston needed and the difficulty encountered in
keeping slide valves against the valve face; although the
latter could be overcome to some extent by using piston
valves. The solution was to combine both system and

*11.8 Four-cylinder, triple-expansion engines built by Scotts in 1908
for HMS* Defence

11.9 Engines fitted in Defence *were among the last reciprocating machines used to power a large British warship*

11.10 Reciprocating engines for the Cunard liner Franconia; *reciprocating machinery was superior to direct drive turbines for inter-mediate liners in the years before the outbreak of the First World War*

11.11 Reciprocating engined Franconia *(1911) (Harry Weston Collection)*

effectively expand exhaust steam from the reciprocating engine in a separate turbine; early installations of this type used the turbine to drive a separate shaft but later variants employed gearing to supply the turbine power to the single-engine crankshaft and that arrangement was still being used in the 1950s.

The first installation of this type went into the New Zealand Shipping Company's 10,630-gross ton *Otaki*, delivered by Dennys during 1908. This steamer was to have been fitted with twin triple-expansion reciprocating engines like her sisters *Orari* and *Opawa* but the owner was persuaded by the builder to try the combination machinery and did so on condition that Dennys would guarantee the performance and that the cargo space would not be less than that of her sisters. All ships had the same steam-generating installation, consisting of five single-ended Scotch boilers operating under Howden forced draught with steam supplied at 200psi. *Otaki* had three propeller shafts, the outer

two being driven by reciprocating engines and the inner one powered by the turbine; in order to make up for the reduction in cargo space because of the third propeller shaft, the length of the ship had to be increased by 4ft 6in. Reciprocating engines aboard the two normally powered ships were 24.5in + 41.25in + 69in by 4ft stroke, while those fitted in *Otaki* had cylinders 24.5in + 39in + 58in by 3ft 3in stroke. The total output power for all three ships was nominally the same giving a speed of 15 knots. The combination machinery proved to be more expensive at £46,612 whereas that fitted in each of the other ships cost just over £39,000. Unfortunately, there are no fuel consumption figures available by which the two types of installation may be compared but the same company had identical machinery fitted in the 1910 Denny-built *Rotorua*.[21]

Combination steam machinery is generally associated with the White Star Atlantic liners built by Harland & Wolff, particularly the three *Olympic*-class ships and most

11.12 Kristianafjord *(1913), an intermediate-sized liner built by Cammel Laird with twin quadruple-expansion engines (Harry Weston Collection)*

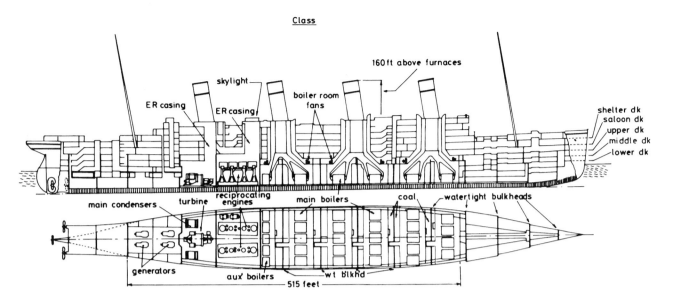

11.13 Arrangement of hybrid reciprocating and turbine machinery in the Olympic-*class liners*

notably *Titanic*. The first Belfast-built ship with this type of machinery was *Laurentic* (1909), the outer shafts being driven by four-crank, triple-expansion engines, the centre shaft being powered by a directly-coupled, low-pressure turbine built by John Brown, as Harlands had no turbine expertise at that time. A sister ship *Megantic* had a conventional machinery installation consisting of two four-cylinder, triple-expansion engines developing the same power. For the same steam and coal consumption the combination machinery showed a 20 per cent increase in power from a lower weight compared with the twin-screw reciprocating plant.[22] For the same power, the coal consumption of *Laurentic* was about 12 to 15 per cent less than that of her sister.

The *Olympic*-class ships had similar machinery but on a much more massive scale, the total output being of the order of 55,000hp. Combination machinery had advantages when it was compared with both straight reciprocating engines and direct-drive turbines, in that steam could be expanded down to a much lower pressure in the turbine while the reciprocating engines could be directly reversed. Compared with the similarly sized Cunard liner *Aquitania* the specific coal consumption was not so good in *Olympic*, 1.4lb/shp/hr against 1.38lb/shp/hr, but it was better than in the high-speed *Lusitania* and her sister which averaged 1.43lb/shp/hr.[23]

Harlands built a number of ships with this type of machinery, the last of the type going into the second White Star *Laurentic*, built in 1927 to replace the first of that name which was a war casualty. Interestingly this ship was also given boilers which had provision for coal firing although the use of oil was by then standard practice aboard Atlantic liners; the ship never operated under coal firing. The adoption of such an installation at that time is difficult to understand as advances in marine engineering had allowed for much more effective propulsion systems using geared turbines, although gearing itself presented problems as the quality of gear cutting was extremely variable.

During the early years of the twentieth century it was acknowledged that the major disadvantage of the turbine was its high rotational speed in order to obtain maximum efficiency. However, for maximum propeller efficiency the shaft rotational speed had to be relatively low, particularly for slower cargo ships. Parsons recognised this problem very quickly and he also realised that the real gains in terms of turbine sales were to be achieved if such machinery were installed in cargo vessels. A system of speed reduction through gearing was needed, but the idea was much easier to express than to deliver as extremely accurate cutting of gears would be needed and there were few machines available to undertake that sort of work. Geared turbines were not new, Gustaf de Laval having developed such an arrangement in 1893, but geared systems for the propulsion of ocean-going ships would have to transmit much greater power while maintaining alignment despite the rolling and pitching of the ship and the reaction from the thrust of the propeller. The solution was not going to be easy and there were many problems along the way to it.

During the latter years of the nineteenth century Parsons was sceptical about gearing and he had every right to be because the quality of gear cutting was not good. However, as an engineer he realised that gearing offered the only prospect for the more widespread adoption of the steam turbine for marine propulsion. At this stage it must

11.14 Geared turbine system for the liner Antonia *built in the early 1920s*

be emphasised that Parsons was not the only engineer engaged upon the development of geared turbines, work was going on in Sweden, Germany and America, but Parsons directed his work specifically towards marine systems. Following several years of experimental work he developed a geared system which he considered would work and, in 1909, in order to demonstrate that the turbine propulsion of slow cargo ships was feasible he purchased the 4,350-displacement-ton steamer *Vespasian*. Her triple-expansion engine was removed and replaced by a geared cross compound turbine system, HP and LP turbines being positioned alongside each other. The gearing reduced the speed from 1,700rpm at the turbines to 74rpm at the propeller shaft. At this speed the turbines developed 1,100shp driving the ship at 11 knots, compared with a speed of 9.5 knots with her original machinery; steam pressure remained at 145psi. Steam consumption was also less and the turbine installation proved itself to be successful.

The gearing for *Vespasian* had been bought from the specialist gear manufacturer, the Power Plant Company, but Parsons experienced severe noise problems with his own gearing. There were a number of reasons for this but the main problem lay with the large pitch errors which resulted when the main wheels and pinions were cut with the equipment which existed at that time. After much work he succeeded in developing his own gear-cutting system, known as the creep method, which spread pitch errors over all the teeth and that minimised noise. Other people, including the Americans John MacAlpine and George Westinghouse, were engaged upon similar work at the same time and produced their own solutions shortly after Parsons. The subject of gearing is complex and beyond the scope of this book but the work of these pioneers enabled more efficient steam tur-

bine installations to be developed and greatly extended the application of the turbine in terms of ship propulsion.[24]

In order to even out loading on gear teeth, helical gearing was developed, this system having teeth cut at an angle to the axis of the wheels and pinions. Thus a number of teeth on the pinions and wheel were in contact at any one time. With such an arrangement there would be an axial force between the pinion and the wheel resulting in axial displacement. To overcome this problem double helical gearing was used, the helix angles on each part of the mating pinions and wheel being angled in opposite directions. Initially single-reduction gearing was used but to allow for greater speed reductions without the need for large main gear wheels, known as bull wheels, double reduction gearing was developed. However, gear-cutting problems prevented its early widespread adoption. The first use of geared turbines in British naval vessels was in the destroyers *Badger*

11.15 Typical design of double helical marine gearing

11.16 Empress of Australia *(1913) (formerly* Tirpitz*), a twin-screw ship fitted with turbines and Fottinger fluid clutches*

and *Beaver*, ordered during 1911. Only the HP turbines were geared, the LP being directly connected to their propeller shafts. The destroyers *Leonidas* and *Lucifer*, ordered a year later, were given fully-geared 25,000shp Parsons cross compound turbines, forty other similar ships having direct-drive turbines. At about the same time the cruisers *Calliope* and *Calypso* were given 40,000shp geared installation with the same type of turbine. By the time these ships were in service World War I had begun. Experience showed the geared turbine to be more effective and economical than the direct-drive type; however, the shortage of gear-cutting equipment and the demands of wartime construction forced the Admiralty to accept many ships with direct-drive turbines until the emergency eased.

Gearing had its problems of which gear cutting difficulties and the need to fit an astern turbine were but two. The German engineer Dr H. Fottinger had the idea of avoiding mechanical gearing altogether by employing hydraulic transmission. He believed that such a system would be lighter, more self-contained and cheaper than a geared installation and at the same time allow for a reversal of direction. Fottinger accepted that hydraulic transmission was less efficient than gearing but he believed that this disadvantage would be outweighed by the advantages. In basic terms the steam turbine was used to drive an impeller unit which delivered hydraulic fluid (water) at high velocity to a turbine wheel attached to the shaft thus rotating the shaft. The desired speed reduction was achieved by correctly designing the hydraulic impeller and turbine units, particularly with respect to size. For reversal the hydraulic fluid was directed to an astern impeller and turbine unit attached to the same input and output shafts, this turbine having its vanes angled for rotation in the reverse direction. Each impeller/turbine

set was referred to as a 'transformer' and the first pair of these were demonstrated in a tug appropriately named *Fottinger Transformer*, during 1909.

Several systems were installed in German destroyers during the war and a set was fitted in the passenger vessel *Königin Luise,* but the largest installation was that of the 21,833-gross ton liner *Tirpitz* (1914), which after the war became Canadian Pacific's *Empress of Australia* in 1921. Each main turbine, of impulse-reaction form with two Curtis impulse wheels before the Parsons reaction stages, developed 7,250shp at 800rpm and the transformer on each shaft produced a speed reduction of 5 to 1 giving a normal propeller shaft speed of 160rpm. The fuel consumption of 205 tons per day for this size of vessel travelling at 16.5 knots was not considered to be satisfactory and in 1926 a set of geared Parsons reaction turbines was fitted together with Scotch boilers to replace the troublesome water-tube boilers. The re-engined vessel was able to steam at 19 knots with a daily fuel consumption of 150 tons.[25]

The other alternative turbine drive was through the use of electricity with the high speed turbine driving an electrical generator and the propeller shaft being driven by an electric motor. The idea was not new but practical application had to await development of suitable electrical equipment of sufficient size to deal with the power needing to be transmitted. Some of the first electric drives actually went into small craft powered by internal combustion engines, electricity being employed in order to achieve reversing of the propeller from the unidirectional engine. In 1913 Swan, Hunter & Wigham, Richardson produced the diesel-electric vessel *Tynemount* for work on the Great Lakes but there appears to have been little interest in combining steam and electricity for ship propulsion. In America the situation was somewhat different with W. L. R. Emmet of the General Electric Company being a strong advocate. In 1905 he proposed the idea of turbo-electric machinery to the US Navy. In 1911 he received approval to fit such an installation in the large, 20,000-ton, collier *Jupiter*, a sister ship of the *Neptune* which had been fitted with an experimental Westinghouse geared turbine during 1910. *Jupiter* had a single-impulse turbine driving a three-phase alternator at 2,000rpm, propulsion being through two propeller shafts, each driven by its own 2,600kW induction motor at a speed of 110rpm. Speed control was by adjustment of the steam supply to the main turbine and reversal was achieved by means of suitable change-over switches to reverse the motor poles. At low speeds and during manoeuvring the speed control of the motors was by means of rheostats in the motor armature circuits. After World War I *Jupiter* was rebuilt as the aircraft carrier *Langley*.

Performance of the turbo-electric machinery fitted in *Jupiter* proved to be satisfactory and encouraged the use of this type of machinery in many US Navy ships built during the following twenty years; some of these will be discussed in subsequent chapters. Turbo-electric drives had advantages over geared installations although their transmission efficiency was lower. Such advantages included the following factors: reversing was achieved by electrical switching thus an astern turbine was not required; as there was no need for gearing the problems associated with gear cutting and gearbox noise were eliminated; propulsion motors could be fitted at the stern of the ship thus avoiding the need for long propeller shafts and saving on the cargo space occupied by shaft tunnels. During the 1920s turbo-electric systems similar to that fitted in *Jupiter* were looked upon with favour for merchant and naval ships but before then that a different turbo-electric system had proved popular with some Scandinavian shipowners.

In 1913 the Swedish Svenska Turbinfabriks AB Ljungstrom (STAL) was formed to exploit the contra-rotating steam turbine, developed by the brothers Birger and Fredrik Ljungstrom, this turbine having no fixed blades but two sets of rotating blades. The turbine was of the radial type with steam passing outwards from the axis of the rotors through successive sets of blades, alternate rows of blades being attached to different turbine wheels which rotated in opposite directions. The Ljungstrom turbine was more compact, used fewer blades and was more efficient than conventional axial turbines, but centrifugal forces were high, thus limiting the size and maximum rotational speeds. Because the rotors turned in opposite directions the turbine could effectively be connected only to electrical generators; in fact two generators, one for each rotor. Such equipment was popular with shore establishments but in 1914 an order was received for a 730kW installation for the Swedish cargo ship *Mjolner*.[26] Between 1918 and 1920 a number of other ships were fitted with similar equipment and a mechanical drive was also developed in the early 1920s and tried, without success, in three steamers. In 1918 the 6,400-deadweight ton British steamer *Wulsty Castle*, built by J. Blumer & Co. of Sunderland, was given a 1,120kW installation manufactured by the Brush Electrical Company to the design of the British Ljungstrom Marine Turbine Company,[27] but the installation proved to be unsatisfactory. The ship was purchased by the shipbuilder William Beardmore of Dalmuir on the Clyde during 1920, Beardmores believing that the unsatisfactory performance resulted from neglect shown by the engineers in charge rather than any inherent fault in the plant. However, the machinery still proved to be unsatisfactory and in 1925 *Wulsty Castle* was re-engined with two Beardmore-Tosi double-acting diesel engines connected through Vulcan hydraulic clutches of the same type as developed by Fottinger.[28]

Only an outline of the steam turbine has been given in this chapter, the technicalities being complex. Other features of turbines apart from the blades included forced lubricated bearings and seals at the ends of the shafts, the good performance of these being essential for effective turbine operation. For the high speeds involved correctly lubricated bearings were essential and seals were needed to prevent high-pressure steam escape or the leakage of air into the turbine and the condenser at the low-pressure stages. Mechanical-type seals could not be employed and special labyrinth seals were developed which had no contact between the fixed and the rotating parts. Effective lubrication of gearing was needed to ensure that no damage occurred at the teeth and lubricant manufacturers worked with turbine designers to ensure that the correct products were developed, as they had done in the case of reciprocating engines.

Although the Parsons and the de Laval/Brown-Curtis turbine have been covered here there were other designs which found marine application, notable the German Zoelly impulse turbine and the French Rateau design. The last type was, however, used to a much lesser extent.

The steam turbine was one of the major developments in terms of marine propulsion but its impact was less than it might have been because of the almost concurrent development of the internal combustion engine. During the 1920s the diesel engine had developed to such an extent that it took much of the business which the turbine might have expected, the problems with gearing not helping the turbine's cause. In the end only the high-powered passenger ship market remained the preserve of the steam turbine as far as merchant shipping was concerned, the more economical diesel attracting the interest of the shipowner with his need to keep costs under control. Naval shipping was a different matter as economy was less of a concern than other factors such as high power to size/weight ratio and this distorted the economic case for the turbine. Despite its significance, the turbine was not a major player in terms of commercial shipping and there were never more than 1,500 turbine-driven merchant in service at any one time.[29]

References

1 J. F. Clarke, *Charles Partous: An Almost Unknown Great Man*, Newcastle upon Tyne Polytechnic, 1984, p. 56.

2 The development of the marine steam turbine is extensively covered in I. Jung, *The Marine Turbine, Part I 1897–1927*, National Maritime Museum, Greenwich, 1982.

3 R. W. Skelton, 'Progress in Marine Engineering', *Proc. I.Mech.E.*, 1930, p. 32; also I. Jung, *The Marine Turbine, Part I*, pp. 22–3, 46–7.

4 *Engineering*, vol. 73, 28 Feb. 1902, pp. 286–8.

5 Ibid., vol. 86, 18 Dec. 1908, p. 835.

6 D. J. Lyon, *The Denny List, Part II*, National Maritime Museum, Greenwich, 1975, p. 477.

7 Ibid., p. 488.

8 *Marine Engineer*, 1 Oct. 1904, pp. 252–5; 1 Jan. 1905, p. 423; 1 May 1905, pp. 58–9.

9 D. J. Lyons, *The Denny List, Part II*, p. 516.

10 M. Warren (ed.), *Lusitania*, Patrick Stephens, Wellingborough, 1986, p.13.

11 *Marine Engineer*, 1 Aug. 1904, pp. 172–8; 1 Dec. 1905, pp. 341–3.

12 L. Peskett, 'Design of Steamships from an Owner's Point of View', *Trans. INA*, 3 Apr. 1914, p. 177.

13 *Shipbuilder*, vol. 10, 1915, pp. 189–99; vol. 11, 1916, pp. 126–38.

14 M. Warren, *Lusitania*; M. Warren, *Mauretania*, Patrick Stephens, Wellingborough, 1987; L. Peskett, 'Design of Steamships'.

15 E. C. Smith, *A Short History of Marine Engineering*, Cambridge University Press, 1937, p. 284.

16 I. Jung, *The Marine Turbine, Part I*, pp. 56–8.

17 C. W. Dyson, 'The Development of Machinery in the US Navy During the Past Ten Years', *Journal American Society of Naval Engineers*, vol. 29, May 1917, pp. 196–237.

18 *Marine Engineer & Motorship Builder*, June 1929, p. 247–8.

19 *Shipbuilder*, vol. 7, 1912, pp. 11–6.

20 *The Engineer*, vol. 117, 22 May 1914, p. 572; *Shipbuilder*, vol. 9, p. 91.

21 D. J. Lyon, *The Denny List, Part III*, 1975, pp. 545, 550, 577, 610.

22 C. C. Pounder, 'Human Problems in Marine Engineering', *Trans. I.Mar.E.*, 1959, p. 93.

23 D. Griffiths, *Power of the Great Liners*, Patrick Stephens, Sparkford, 1990, p. 105.

24 Gearing is discussed more fully in I. Jung, *The Marine Turbine, Part I*, and S.F. Dorey 'Sir Charles Parsons and Mechanical Gearing', *Trans. I.Mar.E.*, 1942.

25 *Marine Engineer & Motorship Builder*, Aug. 1927, pp. 293–7.

26 I. Jung, *The Marine Turbine, Part I*, pp. 94–106.

27 *The Engineer*, vol. 125, 17 May 1918, pp. 423–8.

28 I. Johnson, *Beardmore Built*, Clydebank District Libraries, 1993, p. 116.

29 I. Jung, *The Marine Turbine, Part I*, p. 129.

12
Coal, Oil and the War

The burning of coal under marine boilers remained the standard means of generating steam in merchant ships throughout the First World War and for many years beyond it. Much of the output from Britain's mines went into exports or the bunkering of ships and it was a trade which the mine owners guarded jealously, other nations and other fuels posed a threat which had to be defeated. Before the outbreak of the war the bulk of world trade was carried in steamships powered by coal and most of the world's navies relied upon coal. But there was another fuel, oil, which offered many advantages. Coal was the dominant fuel for so long because of the extensive bunkering facilities which had been developed. An owner knew that he could lift the required coal at practically any port in the world, although quality was something which could not be guaranteed and poor quality coal presented many problems for the fireman and often prevented a ship from making its required speed. The disposal of ash was almost as time consuming as the bringing of coal to the boilers. It was, however, that ready availability which endeared coal to the shipowner and through that continued use boiler development remained firmly wedded to the burning of solid fuel.

In theory, steam generation was independent of the type

12.1 Stokehold of the coal-fired liner France *(1912) (Harry Weston Collection)*

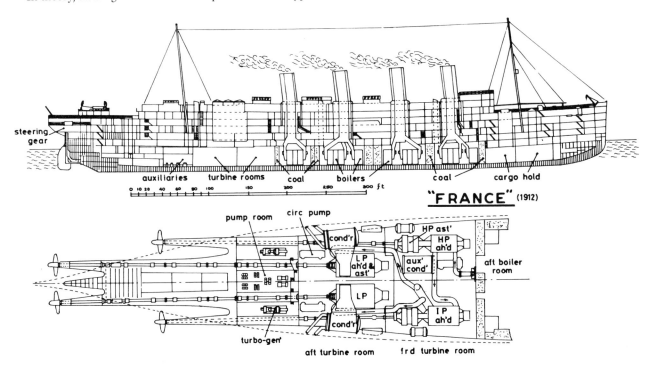

12.2 Sectional drawing of the liner France *and her engine room layout*

of fuel being burned as it was the hot combustion gases which transferred their heat to the water through the furnace and tubes, or tubes alone in a water-tube boiler. Poor quality coal or inattention on the part of the fireman in maintaining his fires could result in a shortage of steam and loss of power. Even a good fireman had trouble maintaining steam when clinker formed on the furnace firebars and many laborious hours had to be spent removing the slag from between the bars in order to ensure an adequate air flow to the furnace. Large lumps of coal had to be broken before they could be burned and fine coal was almost impossible to keep on the grate; neither the firemen nor the engineers had any control over the coal which was delivered, they had to make the best of it. The situation was much the same for fighting ships as for merchant ships except that the merchant ship could generally plan its voyage so that sufficient bunkers could be lifted, but for a warship the voyage might be prolonged through the action of an enemy. Bunkering at sea was a possibility but it was not undertaken lightly as coal had to be manhandled, a time consuming and dangerous operation.

For the warship liquid fuel offered many advantages over solid fuel, not the least being its ease of bunkering and storage. Fuel oil could be pumped between ships or from a shore storage facility to the tanks of a ship with the need for fewer people and in less time than an equivalent amount of coal could be transferred. As mentioned earlier, the burning of liquid fuel had been first tried by the Royal Navy during the late 1860s but the experiment was short lived due to the problems associated with its combustion in existing marine boilers, but primarily because the fleet and the entire marine world was then geared to the burning of coal. Towards the end of the century interest was renewed because of the increasing availability of fuel oil and a number of systems were developed for the burning of oil. Russia was to the fore in the early use of oil for marine boilers and in 1898 installed a combined coal- and oil-firing system in the battleship *General Admiral Apraxim*, half of the boilers being oil fired and the remainder burning coal.[1] That year the French submarine *Narval* was constructed, this vessel having an electric-motor drive for running submerged and a steam engine which provided power on the surface and for recharging the electrical accumulators.[2] The Royal Navy was not unaware of the military implications of oil firing and in 1902 a research team was established at Haslar to investigate the use of oil and report on its potential for naval ships. Extensive use was made of the oil-burning equipment made available by the Wallsend Slipway and the destroyer *Surly* was converted to oil firing as part of the investigation. In America similar work was undertaken with the battleship *South Carolina* being constructed in 1905 with a capability for burning coal or oil. In 1907 the US Navy decided to construct two 'Dreadnought'-type battleships, *Delaware*

and *North Dakota*, with turbines driven by superheated steam, the boilers being capable of coal or oil firing. A detailed investigation was conducted into the best form of oil burner and a mechanical pressure system was adopted since that was more compatible with the forced-draught blowers required by the coal-burning installation. Boiler furnaces could be oil or coal fired, fire bars being removed and furnace fronts changed when converting from coal to oil. Problems were encountered owing to the inexperience of firemen in dealing with oil-burning equipment and a serious fire on the *North Dakota* resulted when a gauge glass on a fuel tank burst.[3] Despite these problems the US Navy persevered and oil firing by the use of the pressure atomisation of oil became established.

Other navies, such as the Royal Navy, examined the possibility of burning oil but they all reacted rather slowly. Despite the success of the installations in the destroyers *Surly* and *Spiteful* many at the Admiralty were not convinced of the advantages oil firing could give the fleet, believing that the assured supply of British coal was to be preferred to having to rely upon imported oil. Sir John Fisher, as First Sea Lord in 1904, had ordered a number of oil-fired destroyers but by 1909 those doubts about oil supplies had surfaced and the compromise solution of combined oil and coal firing was employed.[4] Fisher remained a firm advocate of oil firing but he left office in 1910 and could only offer advice not make policy. However, in 1912 the First Lord of the Admiralty Winston Churchill invited him to become a member of the Royal Commission on Fuel Oil. The Admiralty had been steadily turning towards the use of oil since about 1903 and the 1914 report of the Royal Commission gave weight to it as it came down firmly on the side of the oil firing of naval boilers. The major implication of that change to oil was reliance upon outside resources and steps had to be taken in order to guarantee fuel for the fleet. Acquisition of a 51 per cent shareholding in the Anglo-Persian Oil Company by the British Government ensured that the Navy's new oil-fired ships would have their fuel throughout World War I but that was only the beginning as oil-fuel depots had to be established beside coal bunker stations.

The advantages of oil were not lost on other nations and in the pre-war days there was a gradual move towards liquid fuel but, as in Britain, there was an understandable reluctance to rely upon imported fuel when local coal was available in substantial quantities. America had its own oil and in 1914 a decision was made to adopt oil firing for all future warships. National requirements ensured that oil bunker stations were made available at many ports and refinery capacity increased in order to meet the new demands, but merchant shipping could not take advantage of these changes and had to wait for the end of the war before oil was available in sufficient quantity and at enough ports to make

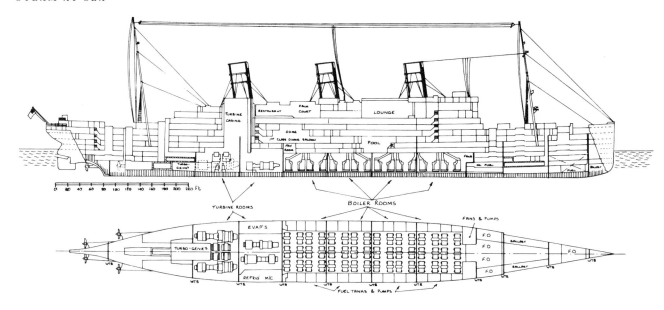

12.3 Imperator-*class ship* Majestic *fitted with water-tube boilers which were coal-fired in the two earlier members of the class*

oil firing in commercial ships a realistic option. In general, most boilers could be easily modified for burning oil, in fact, many water-tube boilers operated more effectively on oil than they did on coal. Experience with the water-tube boilers fitted in the German express liners *Imperator* and *Vaterland* showed that large grates were extremely difficult to manage and keep clear of clinker and fly ash tended to build up between the tubes leading to overheating; to maintain an even fire over the grate was almost impossible. When the boilers were converted to oil firing these problems diminished.[5]

Conversion of boilers from coal to oil firing was not a difficult task, fuel pumps, heaters and oil-spray equipment having to be fitted at the boiler together with the associated pipework. The removal of the coal grate and adjustments to the air supply system completed the conversion, but there

was also a need to provide oil storage and not all coal bunker tanks could be readily converted, many ships making use of double-bottom tanks for storage, suitable heating coils having to be installed. After the war a number of large passenger liners were converted to oil firing, but that was as far as it went for merchant shipping. The oil revolution had to wait many more years as far as the steamship was concerned. Coal was still a plentiful commodity and with the coming of peace vast quantities were virtually dumped on the market from mines in the former German territories now occupied by France and Poland; the price of coal fell but so did the price of bunker oil as there was less of a demand from the military, that reduction in demand also making more available for merchant ships. Although the large liners received much publicity and consumed vast quantities of oil, *Mauretania* burning 620 tons per day compared

12.4 Stokehold of the Mauretania *after conversion to oil firing*

12.5 Boiler cleaning aboard the liner Belgenland; *the cleaning of Scotch boilers was still a dirty job even with oil firing*

with 1,000 tons of coal,[6] the small cargo ships had a much greater share of trade and they tended to remain coal fired. From about the mid-1920s until the outbreak of World War II the percentage of the world's merchant ships burning oil under boilers remained about the same but the percentage burning coal fell steadily due to the inroads made by the diesel engine.

Although this book is devoted to the story of steam power at sea it is important to relate that throughout the 1920s and the 1930s the diesel engine found increasing favour with many shipowners because it was more economic to operate; only in Britain was there a reluctance to accept this method of propulsion and that was due to the strong coal interests. Scandinavia shipowners turned almost exclusively to the diesel engine but many of Britain's shipowners and shipbuilders remained firmly wedded to a technology which was effectively obsolete as far as the slow-speed cargo ship was concerned. Only in terms of the large express liner could steam be classed as more economic than diesel during the late 1930s.[7] Steam, however, was not finished and the rearguard action was long and interesting.

Boilers developed during and after the First World War were equally at home with coal and oil firing; essentially only the furnace region was altered to suit the type of fuel being burned. Generally water-tube boilers were favoured by naval authorities because of their small size and ability to raise steam more quickly than the Scotch-type boiler. Although a number of designs were available, the Yarrow type proved popular with the Admiralty and with many European countries. In America the Babcock & Wilcox boiler was favoured, this also finding application in British ships and those of other European powers. Superheating re-appeared with the turbine and most water-tube boilers of the period also had superheaters, usually in the form of a tube nest placed in the combustion gas flow either between the steam-generating tubes or at the boiler-gas outlet. During the war Royal Navy ships experienced problems with leakage at the 'D'-shaped water drums of Yarrow-type boilers, known as 'wrapperitis', this being overcome by the use of cylindrical water drums and the development of the three-drum Admiralty boiler.[8]

From large battleships to small destroyers the turbine reigned supreme for driving warships and even found its way into submarines. Steam-driven submarines had been introduced towards the end of the nineteenth century the Turkish *Abdulhamid* and *Abdulmecid*, which ran trials in 1887, each having a single steam reciprocating engine and single coal-fired cylindrical boiler. Both were completely unsuccessful.[9] The French *Narval* had steam-turbine propulsion for use on the surface and this proved to be fairly successful in that a number of similar vessels were constructed, but the internal combustion engine proved itself to be much more acceptable for use in the confined space of

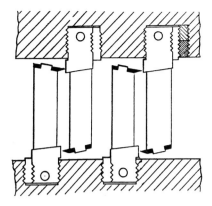

12.6
Arrangement of turbine blading end tightening

a submarine. Gasoline engines were not, however, ideal because of the risk of fire and explosion, but with the advent of the diesel (or heavy oil) engine that risk was reduced considerably. By about 1910 the diesel engine had become the accepted means of driving submarines on the surface and for recharging batteries, but its power to size ratio was relatively low and that restricted the maximum speed on the surface. A number of people in the Admiralty considered that submarines should form part of surface battle fleets and thus they needed to maintain high surface speeds in order to keep up with the fleet. However, the diesel engines of the period were not sufficiently powerful to allow for surface speeds much above 15 knots without seriously encroaching upon the living and working space within the submarine.

Scotts of Greenock had obtained a licence for the use of the Italian Laurenti submarine hull design and just before the outbreak of World War I proposed the construction of a steam-powered fleet submarine using this design. The result was *Swordfish* which had two geared, compound, impulse-reaction turbines of Parsons design driving twin screws and generators for charging batteries; the total output of the turbines was about 4,000shp and astern turbines were incorporated in each of the LP casings. A single Yarrow water-tube boiler supplied steam at a pressure of 250psi and 100°F superheat. The submarine was large by the standards of the day, 231ft long and 1,470-tons submerged displacement and could maintain 18 knots on the surface and 10 knots submerged. *Swordfish* was not a success and after a number of trials was converted into a surface patrol vessel.[10]

While *Swordfish* was still at the construction stage the fleet submarine enthusiasts at the Admiralty continued to push their views and in 1913 an earlier design for a steam-powered submarine produced by Sir Eustace Tennyson-d'Eyncourt, Director of Naval Construction, was resurrected. After further discussion, the First Sea Lord Sir John Fisher agreed to the construction of four steam-powered fleet submarines and the infamous 'K' class was born. The story of these submarines has been told in detail elsewhere[11]

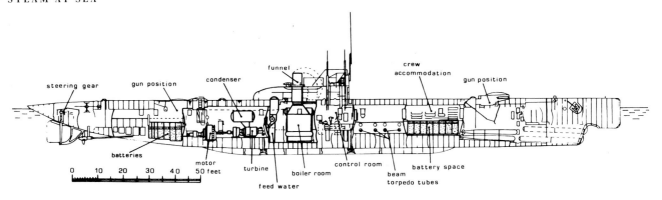

12.7 *Sectional drawing of the steam-driven submarine* Swordfish

12.8 *Steam submarine* Swordfish *(Harry Weston Collection)*

and need not be repeated here save for some details of the machinery and its problems. Orders for the construction of the 2,600-ton submerged displacement 'K'-class boats went to HM Dockyards at Portsmouth and Devonport, Vickers, Fairfields, Scotts, Armstrongs and Beardmore, all seventeen boats being launched during 1916 and 1917. They were powered by two geared steam turbines with a total output of 10,500shp, steam being supplied at 235psi by two Yarrow-type water-tube boilers. An auxiliary diesel engine of 800hp was employed to charge the batteries thus enabling the steam plant to be used for surface propulsion.

Like *Swordfish*, the 'K' boats were a disaster, problems being experienced with almost all aspects of the design, particularly the sealing arrangements for the twin funnels and air inlets. The time taken to shut down the steam plant in order to allow the boats to submerge was greater than had been anticipated thus losing the craft much of their effectiveness. Although the boilers were enclosed in their own watertight compartments these became unbearably hot following a dive and caused considerable inconvenience to the crew. The hull shape and the high speed of the vessels produced an alarming propensity for nose diving to the bottom when submerging and *K13* foundered during trials in

1917 for that reason with the loss of many lives. At the time there was no alternative to a steam-turbine plant in terms of the high power to size ratio required for propelling these submarines, but the problems encountered with respect to the boiler, the sealing of funnels and the air vents, certainly militated against a successful conclusion of the experiment. These were not the only problems which prevented the design from being a success, but as far as the propulsion plant was concerned they were significant. The turbines operated satisfactorily and were ideal in that they developed high power from a relatively small unit but it was the steam-generating plant with its requirement for air and a need to expel the combustion gases which presented major problems. Some fifty years later the turbine proved itself to be an excellent drive unit in the nuclear submarine where the air breathing boiler was not required.

Throughout the First World War the needs of the military were paramount but progress could be made in terms of machinery developments in order to maintain reliability and improve performance, both of which served the purpose of defeating the enemy. Steam turbines and water-tube boilers were firmly established for propelling warships of all nationalities with gearing being generally employed by

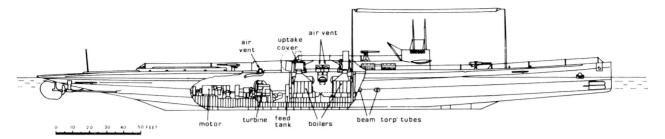

12.9 Sectional drawing of the steam driven 'K'-class submarines

European countries, although the electric drive found favour for some American ships. British surface warships were generally given single reduction geared turbines, Parsons and Brown-Curtis types being chosen to suit the particular needs of the vessels concerned. Although most large cruisers had been given Parsons turbines up to the early years of the war, the compact Brown-Curtis design was attractive because of the high power which could be developed using a relatively small machinery space and in 1916 this type of turbine was stipulated for the battle-cruiser *Hood*. Four 38,000shp geared sets were chosen in order to give this 41,000-displacement-ton ship a maximum speed of 32 knots; astern and cruising turbines were also fitted, the cruising turbines being connected to the output shaft by means of claw couplings. The high-pressure turbines had two Curtis double-wheels followed by eight single impulse wheels, while the LP turbine consisted of eight ahead wheels and two Curtis triple wheels for running astern; all blades were made from phosphor-bronze. The HP turbine rotated at 1,500rpm and the LP at 1,100rpm, both rather low for impulse turbines indicating a probable low operating efficiency. Because of the high powers of the turbine sets the gearing was massive, the bull wheel being of 12ft diameter with a peripheral speed of 132ft/sec. Outer shaft turbines were in an engine room placed forward of the inner shaft sets, these having separate engine rooms of their own. Twenty-four Yarrow boilers supplied steam at a pressure of 230psi, no superheating equipment being fitted.[12]

Despite the fact that a war was taking place, competition between engine designers and builders was intense, orders from the warring governments being lucrative. Impulse turbines had fewer blade rows than reaction turbines and they could accommodate larger clearances between the fixed and the rotating parts, steam leakage not being so critical. To overcome steam leakage the gap through which steam could escape had to be reduced and in British practice this was generally achieved by 'end tightening'. In simple terms blades were given shrouds at their tips, the clearance between the shroud and the next blade being very fine. This required turbine axial clearances to be kept small and adjustable axial thrust bearings were required. Such improvements meant that reaction blading was more efficient,

particularly when geared, and to meet increasing competition from the combined impulse-reaction geared turbines, the designers of impulse turbines moved to higher speeds and thinner, lighter blade discs. This resulted in problems during the war when a number of impulse turbine discs failed through fatigue brought on by vibration, the series of incidents between 1917 and 1922 being known as the 'Great Disc Flutter'. The trouble was so serious that the American General Electric Company was forced to spend a considerable sum in its solution while the Brown-Curtis turbine eventually ceased to be produced. Gearing problems also contributed to Brown-Curtis turbine failures.

German shipbuilding was affected by the war perhaps to a greater extent than that of Britain and machinery installed in warships had to reflect the prevailing conditions. Before the outbreak of the war the steam turbine had become the usual means of propulsion, generally Parsons- or Curtis-type turbines, but the Zoelly impulse-reaction turbine, constructed by Escher Wyss of Zurich, was also stipulated for a few destroyers and torpedo boats. Although German industry was capable of cutting effective gears for marine turbines the facilities were insufficient to meet demand and up to the middle of the war all torpedo craft had direct drive turbines except for *V.46* which was fitted with an experimental Fottinger transformer. The destroyer *B.97*, ordered from Blohm & Voss in Hamburg during 1914, had twin-screw direct-drive turbines developing 40,800shp. The most powerful German destroyers of the period were, however, *V.116* and *S.113*, these being capable of developing 56,000shp. From about 1916 geared turbines were fitted to some destroyers and all larger ships had geared installations. In 1914 eighty-four torpedo boats were on order or under construction, oil firing being stipulated in all cases; however, the cutting off of oil supplies from Galicia and Romania presented problems and the water-tube boilers had to be modified in order to burn coal. Boilers in other ships were modified in order to burn tar oil and the fuel problem had a serious impact on the design and construction of ships during the first year of the war.[13]

In America the Curtis turbine found considerable favour but because of its relatively high speed direct drive was not liked. Direct-drive turbines were installed in some ships, as were geared installations, but following the unqualified success of the machinery fitted in the collier *Jupiter*, a decision was taken in 1914 to fit the battleship *New Mexico* with a turbo-electric propulsion system. The sister ships *Idaho* and *Mississippi* had geared Parsons and Curtis turbines, respectively; all the ships had nine Babcock & Wilcox water-tube boilers. *New Mexico* had two turbo-generators and four propeller shafts, each with its own drive motor, the total power available being 27,500shp compared with 32,000shp for the sister ships.[14] The operational performance of the ship was satisfactory and encouraged the general adoption of electric drive for subsequent large naval ships. The electric drive was not as economical as a geared installation but there were advantages as far as the US Navy was concerned and these outweighed the higher fuel consumption. As propulsion motors were located in the after region of the ship it was possible to provide for better subdivision into watertight compartments. Experience had shown, at least to the satisfaction of the US Navy engineers, that the electric drive was more reliable than a geared installation; this was almost certainly due to the fact that American electrical practice was more advanced than that of Britain and other European countries, whereas marine-gear-cutting experience was less. After the war the battleship *Tennessee* was laid down with similar equipment to that fitted in *New Mexico* although the more powerful turbo-electric 'North Carolina'-class battleships were scrapped as part of the naval agreements reached at the Washington Conference. The 42,300-displacement-ton 'North Carolina'-class ships would have had a propulsive capability of 60,000shp. Although electric propulsion was considered preferable for the post-war larger ships, geared turbines remained the first choice of drive for smaller vessels including destroyers. American engineers did not like the British practice of locating condensers below the turbines and giving the shaft a large rake angle and the arrangement adopted by the US Navy tended to produce longer engine rooms.[15]

At the outbreak of the First World War the majority of British merchant ships were propelled by triple-expansion reciprocating engines, the steam turbine being adopted only for the larger express passenger liners. Although most shipbuilders constructed their own engines, those that did not relying on the specialist engine builders such as the North Eastern Marine Engineering Company, there was little difference in the designs offered by most companies. The three-cylinder, triple-expansion engine for cargo ship propulsion with its engine-operated pumps had evolved into that form over many years and until the type disappeared there would be little change. In effect the three-cylinder, marine triple-expansion engine was a standard design, only the size and power differing much in order to suit the ship in which it was to be installed.

In the first two years of the war Britain lost 1,600,000 tons of merchant shipping through enemy action and a major shipbuilding programme was required in order to ensure that the country survived. Up until 1916 the ordering of ships was much as it had been in pre-war days with the shipping companies dealing with shipyards on an individual basis for a ship or ships to a particular design as dictated by the owner or offered by the yard. Even then merchant ship construction still tended to be on a 'one-off' basis to meet specific orders and the requirements of warship construction also had to be met. The establishment of a Shipping Ministry under the direction of the Shipping Controller in November 1916 allowed for a more systematic requisition of shipping and construction to meet losses.[16] The ordering of 100 standard cargo ships initiated the new policy and shortly afterwards ten classes of standard cargo vessel were designated, these being of several sizes and for several types of cargo, including frozen meat. Prefabrication was to be used in the construction of these ships and certain yards were to specialise in particular types. They all were to be propelled by triple-expansion reciprocating engines with steam supplied by Scotch boilers, boilers and engines being standard for a number of ship types.[17] Sir George Carter of Cammell Laird, when discussing the prospects for diesel-engine development, commented to a representative of the Fullagar Engine Company in January 1917, 'the policy adopted [by the Shipping Controller] was to build as many ships as we can with the cheapest and commonest engines'.[18]

The steam reciprocating engine was relatively easy to construct, presented few problems in terms of maintenance and was reliable, making it the clear choice for such standard ships. In fact, it was the only choice as, at the time, most engine works were equipped for building such engines and they were certainly well known to all marine engineers. Standard design ships constructed in America and Canada during the war were also fitted with reciprocating engines for the same reason. The same arguments applied to the use of Scotch boilers, that type being well known to marine engineers, easy to maintain and operate, relatively simple to construct and capable of operating with coal or oil firing.

Turbine construction during the war went mainly to naval ships but with the coming of peace naval construction practically ceased and there were plenty of standard cargo vessels available for carrying post-war freight, a shipbuilding slump having followed the armistice. Only in the area of passenger ship construction was there any real progress and much of the engineering of these ships went to the geared steam turbine. Canadian Pacific's 21,517-gross ton trans-Pacific liner *Empress of Canada*, which entered service in 1922, is typical of the period. Her propulsion plant consisted of two sets of Brown-Curtis turbines employing double reduction gearing, each set consisting of four separate

12.10 *Starting platform of the turbine-driven liner* Empress of Canada *(1922) looking aft*

12.11 *Starboard turbine and gear set aboard* Empress of Canada *(1922)*

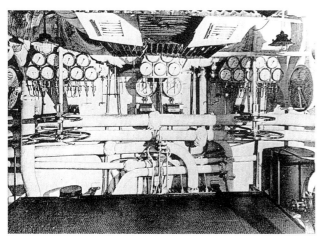

12.12 Empress of Canada; *starting platform looking forward*

turbines in series. HP and LP turbines drove one gear pinion while the two IP turbines drove the second pinion, each transmitting 6,100shp at 2,000rpm. Astern turbines, fitted in the after part of each turbine casing, could develop two-thirds of the ahead power. This turbine arrangement was chosen in order to produce a more compact design than would otherwise have been possible had just two or three stages of expansion been used. The double reduction gearing reduced rotational speed to 111rpm at the propeller. Steam was supplied at a pressure of 215psi by eight double-ended and four single-ended Scotch boilers working on Howden forced draught with oil firing.[19] There were obviously problems with the double reduction, Brown-Curtis turbines as in 1928 the ship was taken out of service for re-engining. Single reduction Parsons reaction turbines were fitted, the pinions of the HP, IP and LP units driving a single bull wheel. At the same time the opportunity was taken to fit superheating apparatus to the Scotch boilers, this feature by then being standard practice for turbine installations.[20]

Double reduction gearing had been introduced during the war, the first installation being in the steamer *Pacific* constructed by the Union Iron Works of San Francisco during 1915 with machinery by the General Electric Company.

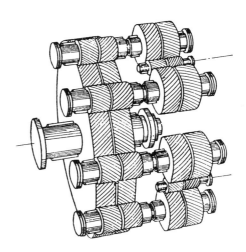

12.13 *Diagrammatic arrangement of double helical gearing*

The first British-built vessel to be given double reduction gearing was the Federal Steam Navigation Company's 9,770-gross ton *Somerset*, built in 1918. Her 4,500shp installation turned the single propeller at 85rpm and the gearing remained in service until 1933 when it was reconditioned.[21] Double reduction gearing had a number of advantages over single reduction not least among these being the fact that the turbine could be allowed to operate at higher speed thereby allowing for increased efficiency and a reduction in size. The size of the main gear wheel could be

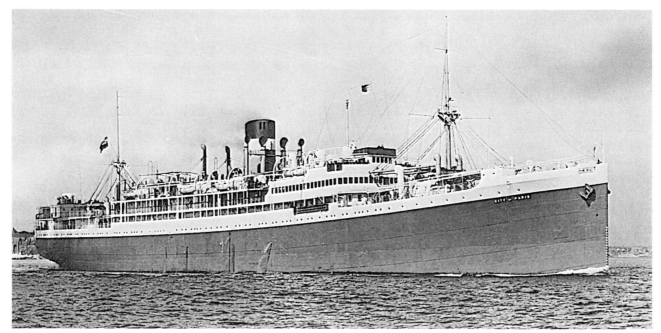

12.14 Single screw, 10,902-grt liner City of Paris *(1922) fitted with double reduction geared turbines driven by steam at 225psi supplied by five oil-fired Scotch boilers (Ellerman Lines)*

reduced and the diameter of the pinions could be increased thus minimising the risk of pinion flexure. Accuracy of gear cutting was even more important for double reduction than it had been with single reduction as any minor errors on the first reduction would be result in further troubles at the second reduction. Although many installations were trouble free, serious noise and wear problems were experienced in a number of cases. Experience showed that accuracy of cutting was essential, but not all manufacturers had equipment of the necessary accuracy and the service problems that resulted turned many shipowners away from double reduction and back to single reduction.

The water-tube boiler consolidated its presence in terms of the warship, but for merchant ships the cylindrical Scotch boiler remained the means of steam generation although a number of owners opted for water-tube boilers. As has already been mentioned, there were problems with the coal firing of water-tube boilers owing to their relatively large grate areas and a fire of even thickness was essential for efficient operation. Even when oil firing was adopted during the early 1920s owners remained with the Scotch boiler because of its reliability and ease of operation but also because it was less sensitive to feed-water impurities than the water-tube boiler. Scale formation in the tubes of a water-tube boiler resulted in poor heat transfer and overheating and scale could not be avoided if make-up feed water from a shore supply was taken on board. The use of distilled water was not a common practice and any leakage at the condenser would result in sea water entering the feed system which could have major implications on the operation of water-tube boilers whereas the Scotch boiler would suffer little damage. Corrosion was a problem with impure and it was also more serious in the water-tube boiler than in the cylindrical type.

Boiler corrosion was a major problem for all marine boilers, although the nature of corrosion was by now better understood than it had been in the late nineteenth century. Acidity of boiler water resulted in corrosion but there were many forms of corrosion including those caused by dissolved gases. The presence of dissolved oxygen and carbon dioxide in boiler water was known to increase corrosion, and the introduction of the Weir closed-feed system during the First World War did much to minimise the problem. This system kept the feed water in a totally enclosed circuit between the condenser and the boiler thus preventing contact with the atmosphere and hence preventing the water from absorbing its gases. The use of a heater in the system improved the efficiency of the steam plant as it increased the temperature of the feed water and so more of the heating effect of the boiler went into generating steam rather than heating water. The idea of a feed heater was not new, Field's refrigerator fitted in Brunel's *Great Western* being one of the earliest applications, but its incorporation in a closed-feed system had other advantages as the heater liberated dissolved gases from the make-up feed water drawn from storage tanks. Five torpedo boats, *Strenuous*, *Seawolf*, *Tourmaline*, *Tyrian* and *Venomous*, were given Weir's closed-feed system and successful operation in these ships encouraged its adoption throughout the fleet in later years.[22]

Manpower availability remained a problem for naval and commercial ship operators and during wartime or periods of high shore employment it was difficult to attract engineers, firemen and coal trimmers. A coal-burning ship required a small army of engine-room hands to tend the boilers alone, the number, obviously depending upon the size of the ship. Fuel cost money but so did manpower and an owner would need to assess carefully whether to adopt the oil firing of boilers or retain coal firing; the availability of fuel supplies along the intended route also had to be taken into account. For large liners on the short Atlantic route the adoption of oil firing made sense as adequate supplies of oil could be obtained at terminal ports in Europe and America and oil offered the potential for major reductions in manning levels and hence crew costs. As a coal burner *Mauretania* required an engine room complement of 366, including 192 firemen and 120 coal trimmers, but following the conversion to oil burning only 79 men were employed in the engine department.[23] For the cargo ship, particularly the tramp, with its need for a single fireman and coal trimmer per watch there was less potential for savings.

An installation could not be judged upon its technical superiority or operating efficiency alone, many other factors influenced the adoption of a particular form of machinery installation, including the preference of the owner. The tramping cargo ship with triple-expansion engine and coal-fired Scotch boilers remained very much part of the British merchant fleet until the outbreak of World War II. British yards specialised in such ships and there was a plentiful supply of coal to power them.

References

1 N. Swindells, 'Oil Fuel and Ship's Propulsion', Mari-Tech 86 Conference, Vancouver, 1986, p. 2.

2 A. Preston, *Submarines*, Bison, London, 1982, p. 19.

3 C. W. Dyson, 'The Development of Machinery in the US Navy During the Past Ten Years', *Journal American Society of Naval Engineers*, vol. 29, May 1917, pp. 205–6, 215–16.

4 P. M. Rippon, *Evolution of Engineering in the Royal Navy*, vol. I, Spellmount, Tunbridge Wells, 1988, p. 178.

5 D. Griffiths, *Power of the Great Liners*, Patrick Stephens, Sparkford, 1990, p. 121.

6 Swindells, 'Oil Fuel and Ship's Propulsion', p. 3.

7 D. Griffiths, 'Britain and the Diesel Engine' *Mariner's Mirror*, vol. 81, Aug. 1995, pp. 313–29.

8 P. M. Rippon, *Evolution of Engineering in the Royal Navy*, vol. I, p. 147.

9 B. Langensiepen and A. Guleryuz, *The Ottoman Steam Navy 1828–1923*, Conway, London, 1995, p. 160.

10 Scotts of Greenock, *Two Hundred and Fifty Years of Shipbuilding*, 1961, pp. 95–106.

11 Don Everitt, *The K Boats*, Harrap, London, 1963.

12 I. Jung, *The Marine Turbine, part 1, 1897–1927*, National Maritime Museum, Greenwich, 1981, *pp. 63–7*.

13 'German Destroyer Building During the War', *Engineering*, vol. 114, 4 Aug. 1922, pp. 135–9.

14 C. W. Dyson, 'Development of Machinery in the US Navy', p. 236; also *Jane's Fighting Ships of WWI*, Studio Editions, 1990, p. 133.

15 S. V. Goodall, 'American Warship Practice', *Engineering*, vol. 113, March 1922, pp. 320–3, 371–3.

16 Details of the effects of war on the shipping and shipbuilding industries are beyond the scope of this book but a detailed account of events in the two World Wars is given in M. Doughty, *Merchant Shipping and War*, Royal Historical Society, London, 1982.

17 P. N. Thomas, *British Ocean Tramps*, vol. 1, Waine Research, Wolverhampton, 1992, pp. 54–60.

18 Letter from Sir George Carter dated 31 Jan. 1917, file 017/0006/000, Cammell Laird Archives, Birkenhead Town Hall.

19 *Engineering*, vol. 114, Sep. 1922, pp. 317–20, 385–8.

20 J. Johnson, 'The Propulsion of Ships by Modern Steam Machinery', *Trans. I.N.A.*, vol 21, 1929, p. 44.

21 S. F. Dorey, 'Sir Charles Parsons and Mechanical Gearing', *Shipbuilding & Shipping Record*, 24 Sep. 1942, p. 299.

22 P. M. Rippon, *Evolution of Engineering in the Royal Navy*, vol. I, pp. 144–7

23 N. Swindells, 'Oil Fuel and Ships Propulsion', p. 3.

13
Marine Engineering between the Wars

The years between the two World Wars saw considerable changes in marine engineering, but it was not a period which produced any new concepts in terms of steam plant. Turbines and reciprocating engines competed with each other while steam still came mainly from Scotch boilers with the water-tube type finding favour for naval tonnage; oil firing failed to oust coal from the seas but there were improvements in machinery design and performance in order to maintain competition against the common enemy, the diesel engine. The twenty years between the wars saw diesel-engine propulsion establish itself for merchant ship tonnage although express passenger liners and the majority of warships continued to be driven by steam. Such was the progress of the marine diesel engine that, in 1924, the renowned naval architect Sir Westcott Abell felt confident enough to say, 'the disappearance of the steam engine from overseas trade is largely a matter of time.'[1] The diesel engine was adopted widely for new cargo vessels built by many European countries, although British owners and builders tended to adhere to the steam engine and coal-fired boilers. America constructed few merchant ships between the wars because of the large number of vessels remaining from the First World War emergency building programme. In the years between 1922 and 1937 only two dry cargo ships, a few tankers and twenty-nine passenger-cargo vessels were built with money provided under the 1928 Mercantile Marine Act. There was, however, action in American shipyards as a re-engining programme was instituted, the purpose being to fit more economical diesel engines to many of the surplus ships in order to make them more efficient. The programme failed and American merchant shipping underwent a severe recession until the US Maritime Commission instigated a ten-year building programme in 1937.

Warship construction in the United States suffered as a result of the Washington Disarmament Conference, with new building being severely restricted. In one area, however, America was ahead of its maritime rivals and that was in turbo-electric propulsion. Double reduction gearing had been installed in a number of vessels after the end of the First World War and results were good with fewer problems than those experienced with British and other European installations.[2] It was, however, turbo-electric propulsion which found widespread favour for larger vessels, the plants installed in the 33,000-displacement-ton carriers *Saratoga* and *Lexington* attracting worldwide attention. These ships had been planned as battle-cruisers during the war but as a result of agreement at the Washington Conference they were built as America's first carriers, construction of the other three battle-cruisers in the batch being cancelled. Turbo-electric propulsion had been planned from the outset with the work being undertaken by the General Electric Company. Both quadruple-screw ships entered service in 1927, their 180,000shp machinery being the most powerful installed in any ship to that time. The electrical plant consisted of four turbo-alternators rated 35,200kW at 1,755rpm, the turbines being of the thirteen-stage impulse type; electricity was generated at 5,000volts, three phase. Each propeller shaft was driven by two electric motors and turned at 317rpm during the normal full speed of 33 knots. When the speed fell below a certain level only one propulsion motor was used in order to improve operational efficiency; air motors were employed for actuating the switch gear, reversing being accomplished by changing a pair of poles on the drive motors. *Lexington* was fitted with sixteen forced draught Yarrow-type boilers built by the Bethlehem Shipbuilding Corporation with superheating equipment supplied by Babcock & Wilcox; *Saratoga* had sixteen White-Foster boilers. Steam pressure for both ships was 295psi and fuel consumption at full power was estimated at 2,000 tons per day.[3]

In addition to electrical power for propulsion purposes these ships were fitted with six 750kW turbo-generators for supplying general power, there being in excess of 1,000 electric motors on each vessel. *Lexington* made the 2,228-mile voyage from San Diego to Honolulu at an average

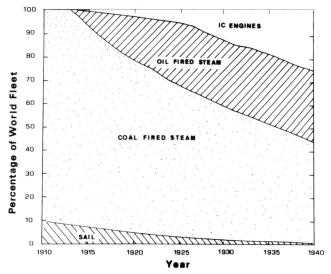

13.1 Changes in methods of ship propulsion during the inter war years

13.2 Turbo-electric passenger liner Queen of Bermuda *built during the 1930s (Furness Withy)*

speed of 30.7 knots and she also achieved a one-hour speed of 34.5 knots, developing 210,000shp,[4] but in 1929 her power was put to more pressing needs when she was employed as a floating power station for the city of Tacoma. An unprecedented drought in the northwestern USA that year resulted in low levels in the hydroelectric reservoir and the Navy Department ordered *Lexington* to be used to supply power to the city, the city agreeing to pay the Navy at the rate of 0.25 cents per kWhr for the connected load and 1 cent per kWhr for electricity actually received. During the period mid-December 1929 to mid-January 1930 some 4,250,960kWhrs were supplied for which $78,509 were paid; as the fuel bill amounted to $18,627 there was a healthy surplus to pay for repairs and the running of the ship.[5]

Turbo-electric propulsion was not confined to American warships, a number of merchant shipowners finding the idea acceptable; the first British installation was the twin-screw, 19,700gross ton P&O liner *Viceroy of India*, built by Alexander Stephen & Co. of Linthouse in 1929. The machinery installation followed the general arrangement for turbo-electric ships, with two turbo-alternator sets supplying power to two propulsion motors, one on each shaft. The design output of the three-phase alternators was 9,000kW and 2,720volts at 2,690rpm; maximum speed rating was 6,536kW and 3,150 volts at 3,110rpm. Each synchronous

motor had a speed of 109rpm under these maximum turbine speed conditions. All electric gear came from British Thomson-Houston at Rugby, as did the eighteen-stage Curtis impulse turbines, which closely followed the land turbines developed by that company. Bled steam was taken from the turbines at a number of points to supply the three-stage feed heaters. At reduced power one of the turbo-alternators could be used for driving both propulsion motors; at motor speeds below 20 per cent of maximum the propulsion units operated as induction motors and above they operated as synchronous motors. Six oil-fired, Yarrow water-tube boilers supplied superheated steam at 375psi and 700°F, Howden forced draught on the open stokehold system being used. A Weir closed-feed system was used for all boilers, a low-pressure evaporator being used to distil water for make-up boiler feed.[6]

In the early 1930s Furness Withy & Co. ordered two 22,500-gross ton luxury liners *Monarch of Bermuda* and *Queen of Bermuda* for the New York to Bermuda service, the latter being constructed as a replacement for the slightly smaller diesel-engine-driven *Bermuda* which was lost through fire in 1931. Turbo-electric propulsion was chosen for the new ships as it was considered to offer more advantages than geared turbines in terms of manoeuvrability and absence of noise or vibration; the former factor was considered important due to the fact that the ships would spend so

13.3 Turbo-electric fruit-carrying vessel Sinaloa *(1932) (formerly* Veragua*) built by Bethlehem S.B. Corp.*

little time actually at sea between ports and the latter in order to minimise the inconvenience to passengers. At the time of their construction British builders were experiencing little or no trouble with geared drives but it would appear that the owner was being ultra cautious. A quadruple-screw arrangement was chosen although the 19,000shp needed to drive the ships at 19 knots could easily have been obtained on two shafts; the shallow draught needed to enable the ships to enter the harbour at Hamilton, Bermuda limited propeller size and must have been influential in the choice of quadruple screws.

Power came from two 7,500kW GEC – Fraser & Chalmers turbo-alternators, these generating power at 50 hertz and 3,000 volts when turning at 3,000rpm. The turbines were of the impulse type and were designed to operate with steam at a pressure of 350psi and temperature of 650°F. Synchronous motors turned the propellers at a maximum 150rpm, taking power direct from the main switchboard; switch gear allowed any motor to be powered by either or both turbo-alternators, speed variation being accomplished by changing the speed of the turbo-alternator(s). The arrangement of motors and alternators gave maximum flexibility in terms of propulsion and enabled all propellers to be driven from one alternator, a major advantage over geared-turbine installations. Eight Babcock & Wilcox water-tube boilers, in two boiler rooms, supplied

steam for propulsion and all hotel services. The boilers operated under closed stokehold forced draught, tubular air heaters being fitted in the flue uptakes.[7]

Similar considerations regarding vibration and noise influenced the owners of the French liner *Normandie*, laid down in 1931, in their choice of machinery. At that time French builders had little experience in cutting marine gearing successfully and no installation of the size planned had been constructed; the choice of turbo-electric propulsion was probably the only option as to have built machinery for such a prestigious ship elsewhere would have had an adverse effect on national pride. The American carriers had demonstrated that high powers could be obtained with turbo-electric units and to drive this ship of 80,000 gross tons at 29 knots required at least 130,000shp. The French turbine company Alsthom was chosen to build the turbines and these were of the Zoelly impulse type with HP and LP stages driving the output shaft, condensers being positioned below the LP turbines. Each of the four turbo-generator sets developed 30,000kW at 5,500 volts and 81 hertz when rotating at 2,430rpm. Alsthom also made the synchronous propulsion motors which allowed for a speed reduction of 10:1, speed regulation being by varying the speed of the turbo-alternators and hence the electrical supply frequency. Superheated team was supplied at a pressure of 390psi and temperature of 660°F by twenty-nine Penhoet three-drum

13.7 The largest turbo-electric liner built, the French Normandie *(1931) (Harry Weston Collection)*

water-tube boilers, a design similar to the Yarrow type. The saving in boiler weight achieved by the use of high-pressure steam compensated for the greater weight of the turbo-

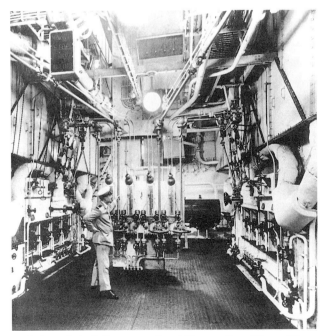

13.8 One of the boiler rooms aboard Normandie *(Harry Weston Collection)*

electric propulsion system. Closed stokehold forced draught was applied to the main boilers and the four auxiliary Scotch boilers. These auxiliary boilers supplied steam to the turbine jackets and to the feed heaters but they also acted to purify the make-up feed water. Raw feed could contain scale-forming salts which would cause problems for the water-tube boilers but the Scotch boilers were not so sensitive and so raw make-up feed was always directed to these boilers, condensed steam supplied by them passing into the main boiler system.[8]

This dual-boiler system had been successfully used by the Penhoet company aboard the same owner's 28,100-gross ton geared-turbine steamer *Champlain* which entered service in 1932. Credit for developing the system, however, should go to Canadian Pacific's engineering superintendent John Johnson who introduced the concept with the 'Duchess'-class vessels in 1928. These 20,000-gross ton geared-turbine vessels were very efficient for their day returning specific fuel consumptions of 0.57lbs/shp/hr for propulsion and 0.625lbs/shp/hr for all purposes. The Cunarder *Aquitania* of 1914 burned 1.12lbs/shp/hr after being converted to oil firing while the German express liners *Bremen* and *Europa* burned 0.735lbs/shp/hr for all purposes and the *Queen Mary* consumed 0.56lbs/shp/hr for propulsion alone; these ships were faster and larger than the 'Duchess'-class vessels making true comparisons somewhat

13.4 Comparisons of engineroom arrangements for Canadian Pacific 'Duchess'-class ships and Cunard 'Scythia'-class vessels

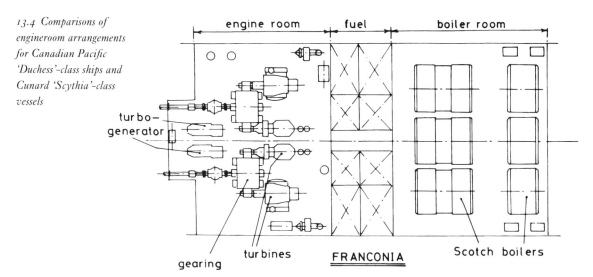

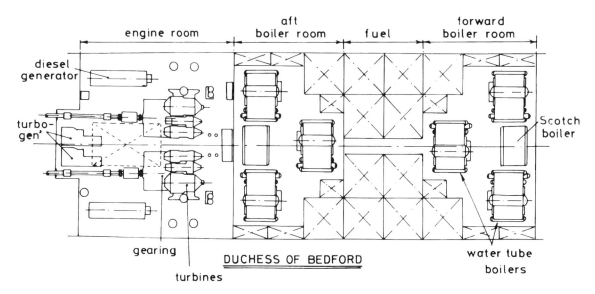

unrealistic but the advanced nature of Johnson's 1928 plant may be appreciated when it is compared with that of the same company's 1956-built 27,000-ton *Empress of Britain* which consumed 0.537lbs/shp/hr for all purposes and the 1958-built Union Castle liner *Pendennis Castle* which burned 0.573lbs/shp/hr.[9]

These figures would suggest that the steam turbine installation had reached something close to its maximum operating efficiency by 1930 and that there was little scope for real further improvement. Diesel engines of the period had specific fuel consumptions in the region of 0.4lbs/shp/hr although they burned higher quality, and hence more expensive, oil. The competition was there, however, and when the reliability of the diesel engine improved it made serious inroads into the market share of the steam engine, whether turbine or reciprocating, for cargo ship and small- to medium-sized passenger ships.

The four 'Duchess'-class vessels had two sets of single-reduction Parsons turbines, there being three separate turbines, HP, IP and LP, in each set. Astern turbines were located in the IP and LP casings, the total astern power being 13,000shp compared with 20,000shp for ahead running; gearing reduced the 2,000rpm turbine speed to 120 at the propeller shaft. Essentially the turbine installations differed little from others of the period except that they took steam at a higher temperature and pressure than was normal in commercial practice. Johnson was an advocate of high-pressure steam believing that it was the only way in which the turbine could ultimately compete with the diesel engine and he designed the plant to operate at 370psi and 686°F, representing a higher degree of superheat than had been previously used for merchant ships. Although high pressure and temperature conditions required the use of better quality, and hence more expensive, materials they did

13.5 Duchess of Bedford *(1928) (Canadian Pacific)*

allow for smaller and less heavy plant than other similar ships. The specific weight of the 'Duchess'-class machinery was 0.126 tons/shp while that of *Empress of Canada* built eight years earlier was 0.17 tons/shp. Steam came from six Yarrow three-drum boilers and two single-ended Scotch boilers which worked at a pressure of 200psi. The Scotch boilers provided steam for heating and auxiliary purposes

but they also supplied steam to the IP turbines thereby introducing make-up feed to the high-pressure steam system. The water-tube boilers used only distilled water feed and thus any scale from the make-up feed was deposited in the Scotch and not the Yarrow boilers. Johnson made full use of feed heating and air heating so that the boilers operated to maximum efficiency and high-pressure steam was used only

13.6 Cunard's intermediate turbine liner Scythia *at Liverpool*

13.10 Empress of Britain *(1930); the first large liner fitted with a Johnson water-tube boiler (Canadian Pacific)*

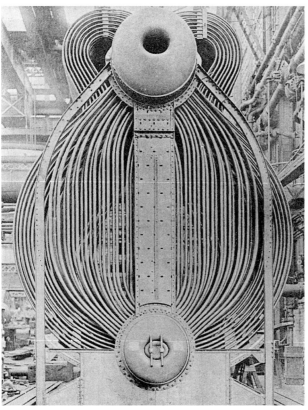

13.9 Tube arrangements of a Johnson water-tube boiler

for the main engines, turbo-generators and turbo-feed pumps in order to minimise the risk of contamination.[10] These ships had steam plants designed as integrated systems rather than a collection of items, which was normally the case, and it was only through such system design that the efficiency of steam plant could be improved.

Johnson was an imaginative engineer and had a number of boiler designs to his credit. His design for a water-tube boiler was first employed in the 42,348-gross ton *Empress of Britain* of 1930. Eight Yarrow boilers supplied steam at 425psi and 725°F, further emphasising his belief in high-pressure steam, but in addition a single Johnson boiler was also fitted. This consisted of two drums, a lower water drum and an upper steam drum, connected by curved tubes which allowed for a combustion chamber between the tubes and the two drums. The design provided for a greater heating surface than any boiler of equivalent dimensions but it also weighed less, 166 tons in operating condition compared with 244 tons for the ship's Yarrow boilers which had a lower output.[11] Johnson boilers were subsequently installed in the Royal Mail liners *Alcantara* and *Asturias* when they were re-engined in the mid-1930s and boilers of the same type, then known as Babcock-Johnson boilers, were also fitted in the liner *Andes* and the re-engined *Arundel Castle* and *Windsor Castle* during the late 1930s.[12]

Johnson's other boiler was a combined water-tube and

13.11 Forward turbine room aboard Empress of Britain *(Canadian Pacific)*

fire-tube type and was marketed as the Howden-Johnson boiler, the first of the type appearing in 1935. The boiler was similar to the Scotch boiler in that it was cylindrical with three furnaces. However, combustion gases from the furnaces passed to a single chamber, at the rear of the boiler, before returning through fire tubes to the smokebox located at the front. The rear chamber contained water-tubes, and superheater tubes and because the usual combustion chambers of the Scotch boilers were absent there was less need for stays and the boiler could operate at a higher pressure. The first boilers of the type were fitted in the Booth liner *Crispin*[13].

A similar design of boiler, the Prudhon-Capus, had been constructed in the 1920s, twelve double-ended and eight single-ended models being fitted in the French liner *Ile de France*. The furnaces directed hot gases to a combined combustion chamber at the rear of the boiler where they heated water contained in tubes joining water drums at the bottom with steam drums at the top, these drums connecting with

the cylindrical shell of the boiler. The principle was the same as the Howden-Johnson boiler except that in the latter curved tubes were employed thus avoiding the need for drums. Double-ended boilers were effectively single-ended units placed back-to-back. It was claimed that this type of boiler was 10 per cent more efficient than a conventional Scotch boiler and at the same time allowed for a higher evaporation rate.[14] Prudhon-Capus and Howden-Johnson boilers could be arranged to burn coal or oil, depending upon the desire of the owner, giving them an advantage over water-tube types; the burning of coal in conventional water-tube boilers with their large grates never being entirely satisfactory. The higher efficiency and evaporation rate gave these units an advantage when compared with Scotch boilers in that the size of the boiler room and the weight of boilers could be reduced. Both types of boiler failed to make an impact despite these advantages, the disadvantages of the hybrid arrangement being greater than the advantages.

Ile de France appears to have been a liner constructed

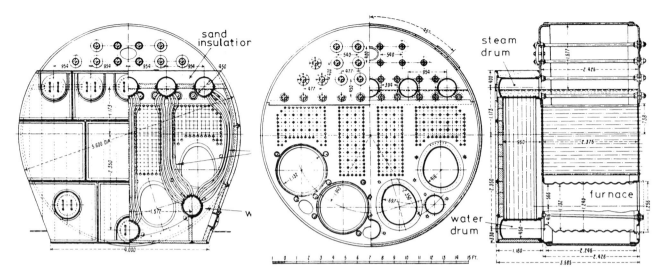

13.12 Prudhon-Capus boiler as fitted in Ile de France

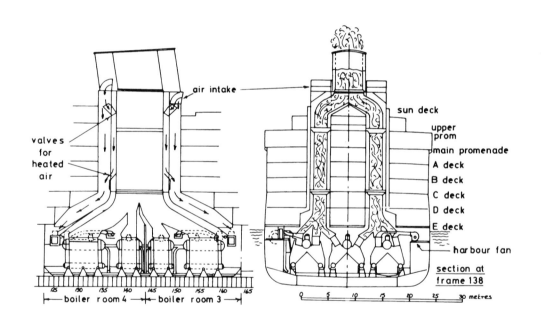

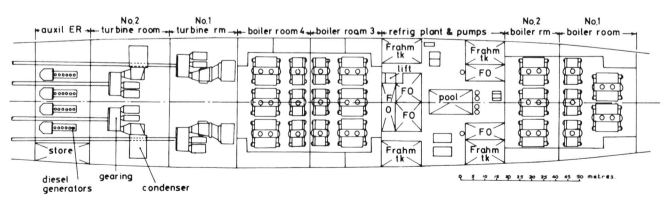

13.13 Machinery layout of the liner Bremen

after her time as far as the machinery was concerned for she was fitted with four sets of direct-drive Parsons turbines, each set developing 13,000shp. At the time of building during the mid-1920s it is difficult to imagine why direct-drive turbines were employed as the geared turbine had become firmly established in marine practice. The installation was similar to that adopted for the liner *Paris* which entered service in 1921 but which had been laid down during 1913, the war having delayed her construction. During the 1920s few French ships were fitted with geared turbines, apart from those constructed abroad, and it is likely that trouble was being experienced in cutting gears in French shipyards. The retrograde, but understandable, decision to fit direct-drive turbines avoided the risk of gearing problems or the indignity of having machinery for a prestige vessel built abroad.

For most large passenger liners geared turbines were the obvious choice during the 1920s and the 1930s as the system offered reliability, compactness and a general freedom from vibration. Scandinavian owners tended to adopt diesel propulsion and many of the liners built for companies in the Kylsant empire such as Royal Mail Line, Union Castle and White Star were fitted with Burmeister and Wain diesel engines constructed by Harland & Wolff. Although the diesel

had a better fuel consumption and was becoming increasingly more reliable most British owners stayed with the turbine for driving passenger liners and for the large express liner there was little option due to the power to weight/size ratio of the turbine.

North German Lloyd's express Atlantic liners *Bremen* and *Europa* were fine examples of the shipbuilder's craft and the 135,000shp needed to drive these 51,660-ton ships at 28.5 knots could only realistically be provided by steam turbines. Both ships employed a quadruple-screw arrangement but the machinery design differed, *Bremen* having her installation designed by Deschimag, the ship being built by A.G. Weser, while Blohm & Voss, builders of *Europa*, also constructed the turbines for it. Deschimag used single-reduction geared turbines arranged in three stages; the HP stage having a single Curtis wheel followed by Parsons reaction blading with the IP and LP stages being of the reaction type. A 10:1 gearing reduction produced a propeller speed of 180rpm at normal service speed. A Curtis astern turbine was fitted at the IP stage with an astern reaction turbine at the LP. Blohm & Voss used only two pinions with HP and IP stages in tandem on one pinion and the LP stage driving the other. The HP stage comprised a large Curtis wheel

13.14 Turbine installation fitted in Bremen

13.15 One of Bremen's *geared turbines with casing covers removed*

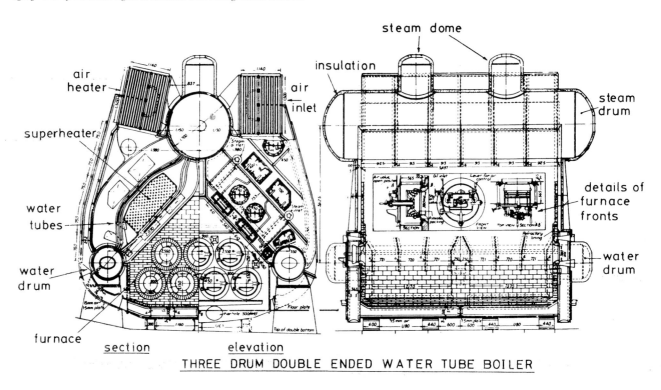

13.16 Water-tube boilers installed in Bremen *and* Europa

followed by reaction blading, both other stages having reaction blading. Pinion speeds were higher than for *Bremen* and the propeller rotated at 218rpm necessitating a different design of propeller. Curtis wheels were employed as astern turbines in the IP and LP casings. Both ships used boilers of the same three-drum design although the size and number differed in each ship as did the method of forced draught, *Bremen* operating on the closed stokehold and her sister on the Howden closed ashpit system with assistance from induced draught. Both ships employed superheated steam, supplied at a pressure of 330psi and a temperature of 700°F.[15] In service there was little to choose between the ships in terms of performance indicating that the same power result could be achieved by a number of different turbine designs.

An effective steam-turbine installation had to consider the turbines, gearing, boilers and feed systems, but all ships differed in their requirements with respect to speed and power and so all installations, of necessity, differed. Turbines extracted the maximum energy from steam because it could be expanded down to a very low pressure, this being achieved by means of the condenser. An effective condenser required a great many tubes in order to achieve a large cooling surface but a vacuum had to be maintained by the provision of an air ejector to remove the gases liberated from the water as it was heated in the boiler. These points could be accounted for by the designer but he had no control over the temperature of the sea water passing through the condenser tubes, and that could vary considerably around the world. A ship operating on the north Atlantic where sea water temperatures were low could achieve a lower condenser vacuum than one operating in the tropics where water temperatures were much higher. While some account could be taken of sea water temperature in arranging the cooling surface area of the condenser, the advantage was always with the ship operating in cold water areas. The operating efficiency of the diesel engine was less sensitive to sea water temperature and motorships could certainly compete more readily with steamers operating on warm water routes than on the north Atlantic.

Naval propulsion remained largely the preserve of the steam turbine, apart from smaller ships and the German 'Pocket' battleships *Deutschland*, *Admiral Graf Spee* and *Admiral Scheer* which were given geared MAN diesel engines driving twin screws through Vulcan fluid clutches.[16] Although the Washington Treaty limited the size of fleets it did not prevent modernisation and in the years to 1935, when major rearmament commenced, most nations took the opportunity of introducing new technology in terms of machinery and armaments. Britain built new ships to replace ageing tonnage and tended to go for the tried and tested machinery in terms of Parsons single-reduction geared turbines. The battleships *Rodney* and

Nelson, delivered in 1927, were fitted with Brown-Curtis impulse turbines which had proved satisfactory in HMS *Hood*, however, it soon became evident that there were problems with the design. Blade failures occurred in both the HP and LP turbines and cracks appeared in blade discs, the problems being similar to those which had plagued the American General Electric Company earlier in the decade. Although General Electric overcame the problems Brown-Curtis did not and the Admiralty excluded the company and its licensees from further contracts; from 1930 only Parsons turbines were fitted in Royal Navy ships.[17]

Following good reports from experience in America and Germany and as a result of tests undertaken by the Parsons company, the Admiralty decided to try high-pressure steam for ship propulsion and in 1930 took delivery of the destroyer *Acheron*. The hull was built by Thornycrofts of Southampton but the machinery came from the Parsons Marine Steam Turbine Company and consisted of two sets of single-reduction Parsons turbines, each set comprising HP, two IP and an LP stage with an astern turbine being located in the LP casing. The HP turbine had an impulse wheel before the reaction blading and the astern turbine comprised impulse wheels. Nozzles directing steam to the HP turbine were specially grouped for economy under low power and cruising conditions; at full power steam was directed to the impulse and reaction blading through separate nozzles, but when cruising steam went only to nozzles at the impulse wheels. Turbines were designed to make use of steam delivered at 500psi and 750°F, all impulse blading being of stainless steel and HP reaction turbine blades of monel metal. Because of the high pressures involved, HP casings had to be strengthened with high tensile strength steel in the bolts joining the casing halves together. Three

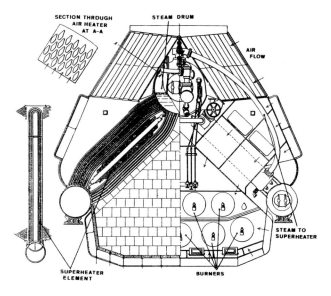

13.17 High-pressure, water-tube boiler as fitted in HMS Acheron

boilers, to a three-drum design developed by Thornycroft in collaboration with the Admiralty, supplied superheated steam, a form of closed ashpit forced draught being employed with air heaters in the flue uptakes. During trials at full power the specific fuel consumption for propulsion alone was 0.608lbs/shp/hr but at cruising speed (60 per cent of full power) it rose to 0.675lbs/shp/hr.[18]

Although the plant fitted in HMS *Acheron* was economical and compact the trials were not successful owing to excessive vibration in the HP turbines. Further research into the use of high-pressure steam was abandoned and the Admiralty reverted to the choice of more normal steam conditions of 400psi and 700°F for subsequent warships.[19] America had more success with high-pressure turbines, particularly during the 1930s, with pressures of 600psi becoming standard for destroyers from 1935 onwards. The need for powerful but compact machinery was greater in destroyers than in the larger cruisers, battleships and carriers where more space was available for machinery and hence high-pressure steam found its initial application in these ships. The mid-1930s saw the introduction of controlled superheat boilers which permitted more precise control of steam conditions. Boilers up until that time had superheater elements placed in the flue gas outlet from the boiler and the gas temperature at that point depended upon a number of factors including the steam generating rate; it could thus not be predetermined for all conditions. Boilers fitted in the 'Somers'-class destroyers had two furnaces separated by a bank of tubes and flue gases from only one of these furnaces passed over the superheater tubes. By regulating the fuel to the furnaces it was possible to control the steam generation rate and the temperature of the steam leaving the superheaters.[20]

In 1931 Samuel Murray Robinson was appointed Engineer-in-Chief and Chief of the Bureau of Engineering in the US Navy and entered office with a number of goals in mind including the introduction of high-pressure steam and the use of high-speed, double reduction-geared turbines in place of electric propulsion.[21] In these he succeeded and it put American naval engineering ahead of that of other nations. Development of stronger heat-resistant materials helped turbine, gearing and boiler designers to produce plant which suited the needs of the Navy in terms of power and size but it took co-operation between industry and the Navy to produce the desired results. Turbines were still of the impulse-reaction type but they were more compact and operated at higher speed owing to the improved steam conditions.

Other navies followed their own ideas but these were generally along the lines adopted by the US Navy although they were a number of years behind. German warship production accelerated during the 1930s and machinery development at least kept pace with that of Britain even

surpassing it at times. In 1929 a project had been started to develop an efficient high-pressure steam plant for marine use and by the mid-1930s high-pressure steam was being stipulated for new destroyers. The cruisers *Gneisenau* and *Scharnhorst*, laid down in 1934, each had twelve Wagner three-drum, water-tube boilers supplying superheated steam at 740psi and 840°F but their turbine plants differed. The former received Deschimag turbines, the HP stage comprising a Curtis wheel and three single Rateau stages driving through double reduction gearing; the IP turbine consisted of a single Rateau stage and seventeen reaction stages while the LP consisted of five single and two double Rateau stages. Astern Curtis wheels were provided as was a cruising turbine connecting via a fluid clutch. *Scharnhorst* had Brown-Boveri impulse reaction turbines driving through single-reduction gearing, the cruising turbine also being connected via a fluid clutch which was common practice in the Kriegsmarine. The 'Bismarck'-class battleships had similar boilers and operated with steam at the same conditions. The three-shaft, geared-turbine installations differed as they were made by different manufacturers, *Bismarck* getting three-stage Blohm & Voss impulse reaction turbines while *Tirpitz* had impulse reaction turbines from Brown-Boveri.[22]

Water-tube boilers developed during the interwar years in order to meet demands for higher pressures and steaming rates. Improvements in efficiency were met by several means such as economisers in the uptakes for heating feed water and air heaters also placed in the uptakes. Both of these features had been introduced many years earlier but the systems used were refined during the 1920s and the 1930s and the use of normally waste heat in the flue gases resulted in improvements in plant efficiency. Although tubular air heaters had been employed with early Howden forced draught systems during the 1880s, the cleaning of heating tubes presented difficulties and introduction of the Ljungstrom air heater in the 1920s went some way to overcoming problems encountered with these heaters. The device essentially consisted of a rotor unit located in a circular casing above the boiler, the rotor containing a large number of corrugated, mild-steel plates. The circular casing was divided in two above and below the rotor, with one half acting as a flue gas uptake and the other half the air supply duct to the boiler furnaces. During boiler operation the rotor turned allowing the steel plates which had been heated by the flue gases to pass into the air stream where they gave up their heat to the combustion air. Rotation of early Ljungstrom heater rotors was brought about by the flue gas acting on a turbine unit but later an electric drive was used. The Ljungstrom air heater proved to be popular as it was compact, virtually self cleaning and offered very little resistance to either air or gas flow.[23]

Although water-tube boilers were to be found on

13.18 Passenger/cargo liner Palestinian Prince *(1936): fitted with a triple- expansion engine (19in + 31in + 55in by 3ft stroke) and two coal-fired Scotch boilers working at a pressure of 220psi (Furness Withy)*

warships and many large passenger liners the majority of merchant ships stayed with the trusted Scotch boiler throughout the 1920s and into the 1930s. The cylindrical boiler was flexible enough to cope with wide variations in demand and rugged enough to handle indifferent water quality and firing; it was also ideal for burning coal which

the majority of steamers during the interwar years still did. The coal firing of boilers was labour intensive as the fuel had to be brought to the boiler, the fire supplied with it and the ash removed; even during the 1920s and the 1930s labour was expensive and shipowners looked for ways of reducing costs while still making use of the relatively

13.19 Manchester Progress *(1938): single-screw steamer driven by a three-stage single reduction turbine supplied with steam by three coal-fired Scotch boilers (Manchester Liners)*

13.20 Stokehold of an oil-fired steamer with Scotch boilers

13.21 Rajula (1926): twin-screw passenger/cargo liner fitted with two four-cylinder triple-expansion engines (22.5in + 37.5in + (2) 46in by 3ft 9in stroke; five oil-fired Scotch boilers supplied steam at a pressure of 215psi (British India Steam Navigation Co)

inexpensive and plentiful coal. Chain grate stokers had been used successfully in shore installations but they proved to be difficult to operate with relatively small marine boilers and some alternative arrangement had to be found. Considerable confidence was put in the burning of pulverised coal as it could be treated in much the same way as fuel oil and was felt to be suitable for use with water-tube and Scotch-type boilers. During the late 1920s a number of systems were developed by specialist boiler makers such as Yarrows and shipyards such as the Todd Shipbuilding Corporation in the USA, as well as a number of specialist companies. [24]

In Britain there was a desire to develop a system which would enable British coal to compete with imported oil while American concern centred around the conserving of stocks of oil and work there was carried out under the Fuel Conservation Section of the US Shipping Board in conjunction with the Navy Department. The Todd equipment was fitted to the three Scotch boilers of the 1918-built, triple-expansion-engined steamer *West Alsek* and early results were promising. Coal from the bunkers was transported to a crusher from where it passed via a screw conveyor to the pulverisers, one for each furnace. Pulverised coal was blown into the boiler using primary air, secondary air being regulated in order to ensure correct combustion. Apart from ensuring that the equipment was functioning all the fireman had to do was regulate the coal and air supply in order to produce the desired steam generating rate.[25]

British systems were similar in that they all included

pulverising equipment on board ship and some means of blowing coal into the furnaces. Yarrows conducted extensive trials before installing a pulverised-coal system in the steamer *Amarapoora*, the furnaces of the Scotch boilers fitted for pulverised coal burning being provided with brick-lined pre-furnaces in order to ensure ready ignition of the coal and avoid flame impingement on the main furnace walls. In 1929 the cargo steamer *Berwindlea* and the tramp steamer *Swiftpool* entered service with powdered-coal firing of their Scotch boilers; that of the former ship was developed by Clark, Chapman & Co. while the latter had an installation provided by The Brand Powdered Fuel System. Although a considerable amount of money was invested in such systems and many hours were spent on their development they did not find lasting favour with shipowners. Much greater skill was needed to regulate powdered-coal firing than was required for normal coal burning, but major problems were experienced with the pulverising plant and that was essential for the operation of the system. If coal could not be pulverised then it could not be burned. In the end pulverised coal was abandoned and coal burners reverted to the manual firing of grates which had been used since the first steamers went to sea.

The coal-fired ship is, for many people, synonymous with the triple-expansion engine and during those years between the wars a major portion of the British merchant fleet was driven by triple-expansion engines supplied with steam from coal-fired boilers. Although many overseas operators turned to diesel engines for driving cargo and tramp ships,

13.22 Shenking *(1931), an oil-fired passenger/cargo turbine steamer built by Scotts of Greenock; the ship was fitted with an ice-breaking bow for use in the coastal waters of northern China (John Swire & Son)*

the British owner tended to stay with the reciprocating engine and engine designers did all they could to ensure that this type of plant was as economical as possible. Expanding exhaust steam from the LP cylinder in a turbine had been used for a number of liners built by Harland & Wolff before and during the First World War, however, the turbine powered a third propeller shaft and such an arrangement was unsuitable for single-screw cargo ships. The solution was to employ an exhaust turbine but to connect it in some way to the main shaft from the reciprocating engine and during the interwar years a number of designs were developed, some more successful than others.

The Parsons Marine Turbine Company developed a design which was typical of many, the geared exhaust turbine connecting with the propeller shaft via flexible couplings incorporating friction plates, as in an automobile clutch. Double reduction gearing was used, the final reduction being to a main wheel attached to the propeller shaft. In order to minimise damage to the turbine blades through the impingement of water droplets a vortex-type steam dryer and separator was located in the steam line to the turbine; this device caused the exhaust steam to swirl around as it passed through a chamber, the water droplets being thrown outwards and the steam passing to the turbine inlet pipe positioned in the centre. A changeover valve was located at the exhaust outlet from the reciprocating LP cylinder and allowed steam to be directed to the condenser when the ship was manoeuvring, the turbine not being capable of running astern. The turbine outlet was always connected to the condenser. One of the earliest installations of this type went into the steamer *Kingswood* during 1931, this vessel having a 1,750ihp triple-expansion engine, the total power being raised to 2,100ihp, without any increase in steam consumption, when the exhaust turbine was operational.[26]

Other similar systems were developed, including one by Brown-Boveri, but it was the Bauer-Wach arrangement which tended to be most popular with installations being made as late as the 1950s. The concept, first introduced in 1927, was devised by Gustave Bauer and found immediate popularity with British and European engine builders so much so that in the three years from its first application systems had been installed in sixty-three ships. The basic arrangement of turbine, gearing, steam dryer and changeover valve was similar to that described for the Parsons installation but the Bauer-Wach system made use of a Vulcan Fottinger hydraulic clutch between the two sets of gearing. The hydraulic clutch absorbed torsional vibration and allowed for a smooth coupling and decoupling of the turbine. Although the system was developed with the vertical reciprocating engine in mind, it could be applied to any steam reciprocating engine and a unit was incorporated in the propulsion plant for the Rhine paddle tug *Toulon* with its two-cylinder diagonal engine. The Booth liner *Boniface* of

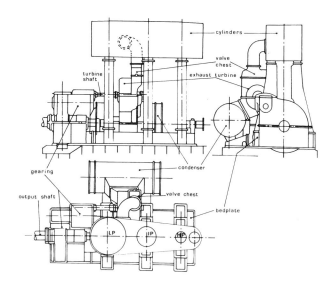

13.23 Bauer-Wach exhaust turbine system

1928 was given a Bauer-Wach system and showed reductions of 24.4 per cent in steam consumption compared with a sister ship without the exhaust turbine. The two-year old Anchor Liner *Britannia* had her superheated steam, quadruple-expansion engine retro-fitted with a Bauer-Wach turbine in 1928 and showed reductions of 20 per cent on fuel consumption; during trials the specific fuel consumption was 1.04lbs/ihp/hr without the turbine and 0.832lbs/ihp/hr with the turbine operational.[27]

Some considered the gearing and clutch to be weak areas of such arrangements and Metropolitan-Vickers developed a turbo-electric auxiliary drive to avoid these systems. The turbine took exhaust steam from the LP cylinder of the reciprocating engine via a changeover valve and vortex separator as did the other systems but the turbine drove a generator and had no direct connection with the propeller shaft. Power developed by the generator was supplied to a direct-current electric motor mounted on the propeller shaft, the turbine drive to the generator being via single-reduction helical gearing. The first such system was installed in the Ellerman passenger-cargo liner *City of Hongkong* (built by Earle's of Hull in 1924) by Workman Clark of Belfast during 1929. This ship had a quadruple-expansion engine which developed 4,000ihp at 80rpm, the turbo-electric system being rated at 1,300hp at 83rpm.[28] This ship survived in service as the Italian *Centauro* until 1955 when she was scrapped after running aground in Bermuda.

The Swedish engineering company Gotaverken developed a system similar to the Bauer-Wach but it also devised another arrangement which had no input to the propeller shaft. An exhaust turbine was employed but this drove a compressor, the idea being to improve steam conditions within the reciprocating engine by increasing the pressure of the HP exhaust steam flowing from the IP cylinder. Steam leaving the LP cylinder passed either to the condenser or to a Ljungstrom turbine via the usual changeover valve, the turbine shaft driving a seven-stage centrifugal compressor which increased the steam pressure by about 30psi from 55psi to 85psi depending upon the initial steam conditions. Because there was no input to the propeller shaft the Gotaverken system was considered ideal for retrofitting to existing engines and a number of installations were undertaken, improvements in power of up to 26 per cent being claimed. A number of British engine builders, including David Rowan and Hawthorn Leslie took licences.[29]

A much simpler way of improving steam conditions within the engine was through the adoption of reheat and a number of engine builders developed such systems, but that of the North Eastern Marine Engineering Company (NEM) was certainly the most widely used and the longest lasting in general application. As has already been discussed, the excessive expansion of steam resulted in the formation of water droplets on a cold cylinder wall and that represented a loss of energy which could not be recovered.

13.24 Poppet valve arrangement on HP cylinder of North Eastern Marine reheat engine

By reheating the steam between the engine cylinders a superheated condition could be maintained at all times and so any condensation avoided, thus improving engine efficiency. Steam could be passed to heating elements in the boiler for reheating but that required considerable runs of pipework which could result in loss of heat and in the NEM reheat engine a much simpler arrangement was adopted. Reheat applied only to steam leaving the HP cylinder and this was heated by superheated steam passing between the boiler and the HP cylinder inlet; in effect the heater also acted as a desuperheater for the supply steam to the engine. A tubular heater was fitted at the engine, superheated steam to the HP cylinder passing through the tubes and HP exhaust steam passing around them. Many vessels were fitted with NEM reheat engines, before, during and after World War II and the system was successful in improving the efficiency of the triple-expansion reciprocating engine. The 9,280 dwt ton cargo ship *Lancaster Castle* had such an engine and when developing 1,790ihp burned coal at the rate of 1.02lbs/ihp/hr. Her Scotch boilers generated steam at 220psi and 750°F, the steam temperature at the HP cylinder inlet being reduced to 635°F after reheating the HP exhaust which entered the IP cylinder at a temperature of 560°F. Due to the high temperature of the HP and IP cylinder supply steam it was considered preferable to use poppet-type valves rather than the usual slide or piston valves. These valves were cam operated and in order to simplify the operating mechanism and give easy access to the valves the HP and IP cylinders were positioned at the ends of the engine.[30]

Throughout the interwar years Britain retained its position as the world's premier ship owning and shipbuilding nation as far as merchant shipping was concerned. However, the title rested uneasily as British shipbuilding and marine engine practices fell behind those of more progressive nations. Britain's lead was based upon history and not technological development in terms of new materials or manufacturing methods, even the fuel-efficient diesel engine found more favour overseas. The 1920s and the 1930s probably represented the high-water mark of British marine engine building despite the brief Indian summer it enjoyed in the 1950s and that zenith of achievement was probably reached in two outstanding ships, the Cunarders *Queen Mary* and *Queen Elizabeth*.

In terms of their turbines these ships were practically identical, having four sets of single-reduction, quadruple-expansion Parsons impulse-reaction turbines. The HP stage had an impulse wheel at the inlet in order to shorten the reaction part but all other stages were pure reaction, the LP being of the double-flow type with steam entry at the middle of the casing. For astern running a single-impulse stage was incorporated in the second IP casing with a low pressure impulse stage in the LP casing. HP and IP(1) turbines

13.25 Queen Mary : *note the large boiler room ventilators*

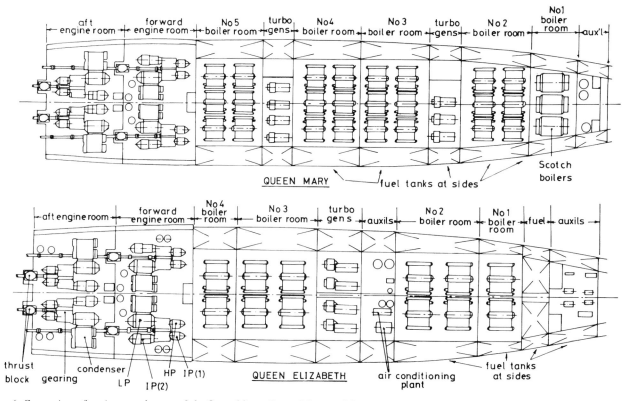

13.26 *Comparison of engine room layouts of the Cunard liners* Queen Mary *and* Queen Elizabeth

13.27 Queen Elizabeth : *boiler room vents located at the base of the funnels*

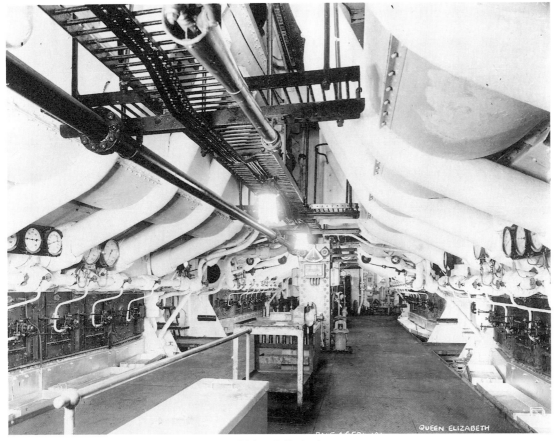

13.28 *No. 2 boiler room aboard* Queen Elizabeth *(Philpot Collection)*

13.29 Queen Elizabeth *after engineroom looking forward and to the port side of the ship (Philpot Collection)*

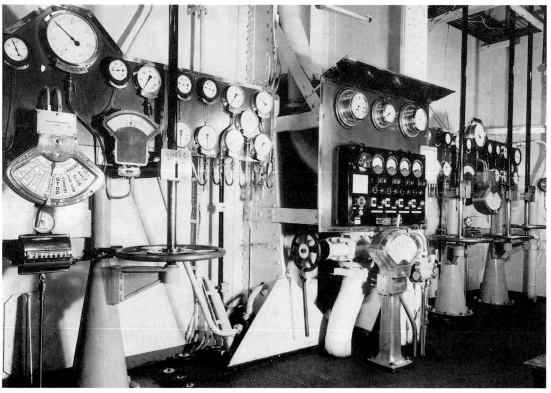

13.30 Queen Elizabeth *after engineroom manoeuvring platform (Philpot Collection)*

were mounted on the opposite side of the gear casings to the LP and IP(2) turbines, giving a more compact arrangement but all turbines had their own pinions. Each turbine set could develop 40,000shp but during the *Queen Mary*'s winter overhaul in 1936–7 supplementary nozzles on the HP turbines were opened enabling each turbine set to develop 45,000shp. While the turbine installations for both ships were similar the steam-generating plants differed reflecting advances in boiler construction during the years which separated their construction. *Queen Mary* had twenty-four Yarrow five-drum, water-tube boilers working at 350psi and 700°, little advance on what had been used for *Bremen* and *Europa*, built seven years earlier. A pressurised stokehold system of forced draught was employed, tubular air heaters increasing the combustion air temperature. Seven 1,300kW turbo-generators supplied the ship's electrical power. The *Queen Elizabeth* was given twelve Yarrow double-flow, five-drum, water-tube boilers and that reduction in the number allowed for a more convenient grouping and the use of only two funnels rather than three as in *Queen Mary*. Steam pressure and temperature remained the same as for the earlier ship.[31]

In terms of engineering plants both ships were massive and certainly a triumph of the engine builder's skill but they marked little advance on the technology of the time, particularly in the case of *Queen Elizabeth*. The choice of geared turbines for *Queen Mary* by the committee appointed by Cunard during 1929 was something of a step in the dark as nothing of the size had been constructed previously but the turbine and boiler technologies were familiar. In view of the cost involved in the construction of both ships and the prestige attached to them as symbols of Britain's shipbuilding and marine engineering industries it is not surprising that tried and trusted technologies were used. The lack of innovation in these ships contrasts sharply with the adoption of the relatively untried turbine for *Lusitania* and *Mauretania* only three decades earlier and the major advances in engineering put into the prestige passenger ships of the nineteenth century.

References

1 Sir Westcott Abell, Presidential Address, Institute of Marine Engineers, *Trans. I.Mar.E.*, vol. 37, 1924–5, p. 780–1.

2 J. L. Booth, 'Double-Reduction Gears of Marine Use: United States Practice', Engineering, vol. 114, 27 Oct. 1922, pp. 516–17.

3 C. S. Gillette, 'History, Description and Acceptance Trials of the USS *Lexington*', *Journal American Society of Naval Engineers*, vol. 40, 1928, pp. 438–95.

4 *Jane's Fighting Ships of WW2*, Studio Editions 1989, p. 268.

5 H. L. White, 'Naval Electrical Power in Commercial Use', *Naval Engineering Journal*, vol. 107, Jan. 1995, pp. 109–10.

6 *Marine Engineer & Motorship Builder*, Apr. 1929, pp. 129–37.

7 Ibid., Feb. 1931, pp. 447–54.

8 *Shipbuilder & Marine Engine Builder*, June 1935, pp. 99–107.

9 T. W. F. Brown, 'A Marine Engineering Review', *Trans. INA*, 1960, Table VI.

10 J. Johnson, 'The Propulsion of Ships by Modern Steam Machinery', *Trans. INA*, 1929, pp. 39–60; *Marine Engineer & Motorship Builder*, July 1928, p. 259.

11 Ibid., May 1932, pp. 377–86.

12 E. C. Smith, *A Short History of Marine Engineering*, Cambridge University Press, 1937, p. 314.

13 *Shipbuilder & Marine Engine Builder*, Jan. 1935, pp. 65–7.

14 *Marine Engineer & Motorship Builder*, July 1927. p. 252.

15 G. Bauer, 'Machinery Installation of the Liner *Bremen*', *Journal American Society of Naval Engineers*, 1930, vol. 42, pp. 684–715; *Shipbuilder*, Apr. 1930, pp.2 67–71; Oct. 1930, pp. 787–97; Dec. 1930, pp. 934–45.

16 M. J. Whitley, *German Capital Ships of WW2*, Arms & Armour Press, London, 1989, p. 21.

17 I. Jung, *The Marine Turbine, Part 2 1928–1980*, National Maritime Museum, Greenwich, 1986, pp. 50–1.

18 *Marine Engineer & Motorship Builder*, July 1931, pp. 247–9.

19 I. Jung, *The Marine Turbine, Part 2*, p. 55; P. M. Rippon, *Evolution of Engineering in the Royal Navy*, vol. I, Spellmount, 1988, p. 116.

20 I. Jung, *The Marine Turbine, Part 2*, pp. 16–17.

21 J. D. Alden, 'The Fathering of the Engineering Duty Corps', *Naval Engineers Journal*, Jan. 1995, pp. 115–17.

22 M. J. Whitley, *German Capital Ships of WW2*, pp. 38–9, 48–9.

23 *Engineering*, vol. 114, 7 July 1922, pp. 24–6; publicity brochure 'Howden Ljungstrom Marine Air Preheater' James Howden & Co. [1930s].

24 *Marine Engineer & Motorship Builder*, Sep. 1929, pp. 357–67.

25 Ibid., Sep. 1929, pp. 260–1.

26 J. W. Sothern, *Verbal Notes and Sketches for Marine Engineers*, Munro, Glasgow, 1936, pp. T174–8.

27 G. Bauer, 'The Bauer-Wach Exhaust Steam Turbine', *Marine Engineer & Motorship Builder*, Dec. 1929, pp. 490–3.

28 Ibid., Dec. 1929, pp. 481–5.

29 Sothern, *Verbal Notes and Sketches*, pp. T141–55.

30 Sothern, ibid., pp. F91–102.

31 *The Engineer*, 15 Jan. 1937, p. 74; 11 June 1937, p. 674; T. Crowe, 'Recent Advances in Mechanical Engineering aboard Ship', *Trans. I.Mech.E.*, June 1948, p. 264.

14
The Demands of World War II and its Aftermath

The outbreak of World War II found Britain as badly prepared in terms of merchant shipping as did the previous world conflict with the result that German submarines almost brought the country to its knees. The bombing of shipyards and the demands of warship construction left little capacity for merchant ship building and those that were built had to be of the basic cargo-carrying type. Propulsion was by diesel engine, steam turbine or steam reciprocating engine depending upon the requirements of the owner and the ability of the builder to construct that type of machinery in war-damaged yards. As early as 1940 the situation had become critical, with losses to submarines exceeding the rate at which vessels could be built since many shipyards were forced to construct warships for convoy protection. The rate of construction was not helped by the slowness of traditional British building practices. The construction of vessels in the USA and Canada offered one means of coun-

tering the effect of the submarines and in December 1940 contracts were signed for sixty tramp ships to be built in American yards with others to be constructed in Canada. So began the saga of the 'Liberty' ship but it is not intended to repeat that here[1] except to mention aspects relating to the propulsion plant.

A British Technical Merchant Shipbuilding Mission, headed by the engineers R. C. Thompson and H. Hunter, went to America and Canada in order to discuss the prospects of building merchant ships in their yards. The mission took with it plans for the ship which was required, and with but minor modifications the British ships produced in America and Canada were to this design with a three-cylinder, steam reciprocating engine and coal-fired Scotch boilers. The Unites States Maritime Commission had been established in 1936 with the purpose of modernising the American merchant fleet and a number of

14.1 'Liberty' ship Jeremiah O'Brien *alongside the cruiser HMS* Belfast *; the 'Liberty' ship is in her as-built condition*

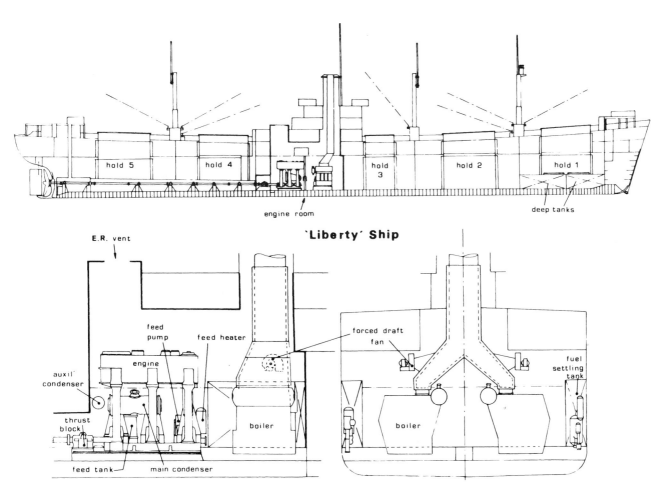

14.2 Sectional drawing of a 'Liberty' ship showing machinery layout

standard designs had been produced, some ships actually having been constructed before the outbreak of war. In 1941, reacting to events in Europe, President Franklin D. Roosevelt decided upon a more ambitious plan of ship construction and the New York firm of naval architects Gibbs and Cox, was given responsibility for developing a new design. The 'Liberty' ship was born but its parentage lay in the British design taken to America by Thompson. Modifications were made to suit the ship for mass construction in new American yards but it was fundamentally the same hull design with the same propulsion plant and auxiliaries. Coal-fired Scotch boilers were not considered suitable for the 'Liberty' ships and these were replaced by oil-burning, water-tube boilers to a design by Babcock & Wilcox. Coal firing had long since ceased to be American practice as the country had considerable oil reserves and construction of Scotch boilers was thought to present difficulties in terms of mass production, hence the choice of the Babcock & Wilcox boiler which could be readily manufactured.[2]

The engine fitted in the 'Liberty' ships was originally de-

veloped in Britain by the North Eastern Marine Engineering Company and was typical of the thousands of three-cylinder, triple-expansion marine engines which had been built over the years; it differed little from similar engines of the type constructed during the nineteenth

14.3 Front of port Babcock & Wilcox boiler fitted in 'Liberty' ships

14.4 *Top of a 'Liberty' ship engine looking from the LP cylinder*

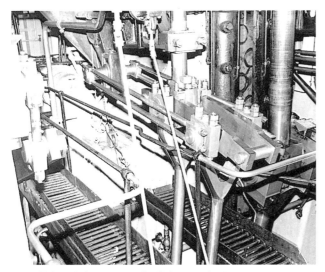

14.5 *'Liberty' ship engine valve linkage mechanism*

14.6 *'Liberty' ship engine crankcase showing main bearings, IP valve eccentric rods, IP connecting rod and crankshaft*

century. The cylinders were supported upon three sets of columns, the rear column of each set acting as a mounting for the crosshead guide bars. Valves were actuated by eccentrically operated link motion, the 24.5in diameter HP cylinder having a piston valve while the IP (37in) and the LP (70in) had slide valves; the piston stroke was 4ft. When working at 76rpm with steam at a pressure of 220psi the engine could develop 2,500ihp. The crankcase was open and all bearings were lubricated by means of oil pots or manually by the skill of the engineer. To the crosshead of the LP cylinder was connected a pair of levers which actuated the pump for removing air from the condenser, together with bilge and ballast pumps. A separate steam-engine-driven pump circulated sea water through the condenser. The engine was an antiquated design but it worked effectively and generally required little attention if constructed and assembled correctly, which was not always the case. The need for a simple, easy to run engine was obvious since

America had no pool of experienced marine engineers, its merchant fleet having been almost non-existent throughout the interwar years.[3]

Boilers for the 'Liberty' ships were to a standard Babcock & Wilcox design of the cross-drum sectional header type. This boiler had a large steam drum at the front of and connecting with slightly inclined boxes or headers at the front and the rear; inclined water tubes connected the front and the rear header. A superheater comprising a series of 'U'-shaped tubes was provided, the superheated steam temperature being 450°F and the pressure 220psi. Each of the two boilers had four fuel-oil burners, forced draught being provided by means of fans located above the boilers. At the normal service speed of 11 knots the daily fuel consumption was 30 tons and in general the boilers performed well in service.[4] The Babcock & Wilcox sectional header boiler remained a standard marine design for many years with but slight

14.7 A 'Liberty' ship in peacetime; the Harrison Line vessel Successor *in 1961*

modifications such as the fitting of economisers and air preheaters in the uptakes.

'Liberty' ships were essentially dry cargo vessels although there were variations to suit particular requirements such as colliers and oil tankers. Even as the first ships were entering service thoughts turned to more modern and faster designs and this gave rise to what became known as the 'Victory' ship. This faster vessel was powered by a 6,000shp cross compound, double reduction geared turbine driving a single screw at 100rpm. The turbine machinery was based upon the design approved for the standard C-2 ships which were part of the pre-war US Maritime

Commission scheme; C-2 class ships were constructed during and after the war. 'Victory' ships had two Babcock & Wilcox sectional header boilers of the same design as that used for the 'Liberty' ships but with a greater capacity, 27,500lbs/hr compared with 24,000lbs/hr. The steam pressure and temperature were higher at 465psi and 750°F respectively.[5]

Another major class of ship produced by American yards during the war period was the T-2 tanker and this was given a different type of propulsion plant from the 'Liberty' and 'Victory' ships. Availability of gear-cutting facilities was a limiting factor in the choice of propulsion plant, the

14.8 American standard design cargo ship of late Second World War vintage American Miller *fitted with compound turbines and double reduction gearing to a single shaft*

14.9 'T2' tanker Caltex Durban at Abadan in 1964

14.10 'T2' tanker Esso Glasgow in Southampton Water during 1962; built as Waukatchic in 1947

14.11 British standard war-design steamer Empire Haven, built at Taikoo Dockyard, Hong Kong in 1941 and fitted with a triple expansion engine 23.5in + 39.5in + 66in by 3ft 9in stroke (John Swire & Son)

availability of turbines and boilers not being restricted by the middle years of the war. American companies had considerable experience in the manufacture of electrical machinery and the turbo-electric drive had given good service in American naval ships despite its greater weight compared with that of the geared drive. The relative ease with which American companies could build the machinery made

turbo-electric propulsion acceptable for the T-2 tankers and the slightly greater weight was not considered to be a problem. These ships, and others to standard American designs, played a significant part in the allied victory and with the coming of peace many were sold for commercial service throughout the world. Many remained in service until the 1970s proving that their design and that of the machinery was more than adequate for the job they had to do. The machinery may not have been a major advance in technological terms but many a marine engineer of the 1940s, 1950s and 1960s learned his trade on these ships.

Although surplus wartime tonnage was available it did not meet the needs of all owners and the rebuilding of shattered merchant fleets, particularly that of Britain, became a priority. The problem was, however, that much of Britain's shipbuilding and marine engineering industry had been devastated by bombing and full production could not be expected for some time. Specialist trades such as gear cutting were seriously restricted and even the construction of the diesel engine was hampered by a shortage of crankshaft forgings.[6] Rather than wait for new tonnage with diesel engines a number of owners accepted ships with steam reciprocating engines and exhaust turbines while others adopted electric drives instead of geared turbines. Canadian Pacific fell into the latter category when, in 1946, it constructed a series of four 9,900-gross ton cargo steamers for its Europe to Canada service. An investigation into the most suitable machinery for fast cargo ships had actually been instigated by the company's superintendent engineer in 1940 with C.A. Parsons and the Parsons Marine Steam Turbine Company being actively involved. As a result of these investigations and in the light of restricted manufacturing facilities available a single-screw, turbo-electric drive was chosen, some 9,000shp being needed to drive the ships at 18 knots.

A single turbo-alternator provided electrical power for propulsion, the turbine operating with reheat of the steam between the high and the low pressure unit which were arranged in tandem on the single shaft. Steam came from a single Johnson boiler at a pressure of 850psi and at 850°F, significantly higher than was normal at that time, the boiler being provided with separate superheater and reheat tube elements constructed by the Superheater Company Ltd. The superheater was fitted within the boiler casing on the port side of the steam drum and the reheat element on the starboard side. In the uptake above the steam drum was a tubular economiser for feed-water heating and a Howden-Ljungstrom air preheater. Steam reheat was known to be advantageous in reducing the risk of water droplet formation and increasing operating efficiency but the problem was one of controlling the reheat temperature and this was achieved by means of a large damper fitted in the uptake above the reheater. No isolating valves were provided on the

14.12 Canadian Pacific turbo-electric cargo ship Beaverlake *(1946) (Canadian Pacific)*

steam side of the reheater but a pipe was provided at the turbine so that in an emergency the reheater might be by-passed. Induced and forced draught fans were fitted in order to give improved control of combustion and flue gas flow.

Exhaust steam from the HP turbine at about 180psi and 580°F was returned to the boiler where its temperature was raised to 850°F before it passed to the LP turbine. The HP

14.13 Engine control station aboard turbo-electric steamer Beaverdell *(Canadian Pacific)*

turbine had a single two-row impulse wheel followed by re-action blading and the LP turbine consisted of all reaction blading. When the turbines were running at their full speed of 3,450rpm three-phase alternating current was generated at 3,000 volts and this was supplied to a sixty-four pole double synchronous motor arranged to develop its full power at 108rpm. At reduced power either half of the motor could be used and at full power both parts were powered; for emergency running either half of the motor could be supplied with current from an emergency alter-nator coupled to one of the three diesel-driven generators which supplied direct current for normal ship services. This feature was needed because only one main boiler had been provided, the small Howden-Johnson auxiliary boiler supplying saturated steam at 100psi for fuel and other heating purposes. Control of the steam supply to the turbine and switching for the motor was carried out at the control panel situated alongside the main alternator.[7]

Canadian Pacific, under Johnson's guidance, was certain-ly innovative in terms of these ships particularly with re-spect to the use of reheat, high-pressure steam and a single boiler. The use of high-pressure and high-temperature steam was made possible by advances in materials tech-nology during the war but its use in a merchant ship so soon afterwards was an act of faith and an indication that there

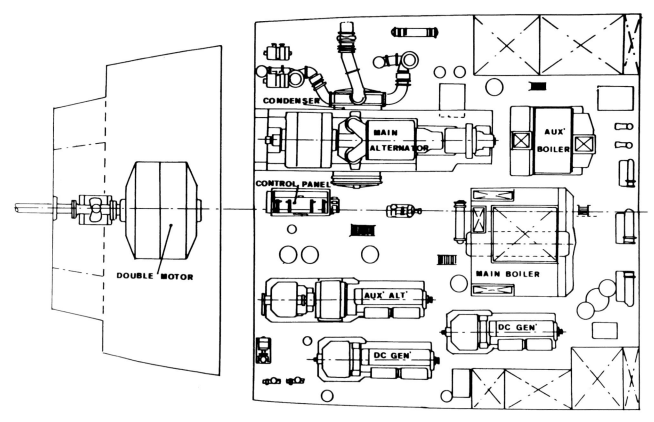

14.14 Engineroom layout of Canadian Pacific 'Beaver'-class turbo-electric ships

were still progressive marine engineers and commercial shipowners. Cunard, on the other hand, was much more cautious when it came to the construction of its cruise ship *Caronia* in 1949. A conventional twin-screw, double-reduction geared turbine arrangement was chosen, each set comprising impulse-reaction HP and reaction IP and LP units driving separate pinions; a system of cross connected pipes allowed any turbine in a set to be bypassed should failure occur although why such a feature should have been considered necessary in a twin-screw design is difficult to imagine. Six Yarrow five-drum, double-flow boilers similar to those fitted in the 'Queens' provided steam at 600psi and 800°. Boilers worked under forced and induced draught, induced draught fans being provided in the uptakes below the dust collectors but above the Ljungstrom air preheaters.[8]

Turbines for *Caronia* were constructed by the shipbuilder John Brown and incorporated some new features including fabrication of the LP casings and the gearbox casings but the IP and HP casings were cast. Such improvements in manufacturing came about during the war but during the 1930s and into the 1940s British turbine design progressed little whereas American turbines advanced considerably and it was realised that a concerted approach to research and development was needed. To that end in 1944 the Parsons and Marine Engineering Turbine Research and Development Association (PAMETRADA) was formed by C.A. Parsons and the Parsons Marine Steam Turbine Company together with a number of licensees and other British turbine manufacturers with the aim of modernising existing designs and to develop new forms of turbine machinery; a research and development facility was established at Wallsend. A brake capable of absorbing 30,000shp, which had been used to test the turbines of *Scharnhorst* and *Bismarck* was located in Germany and installed at Wallsend.[9]

Although the Admiralty had used reaction-type turbines almost exclusively since 1930 it did not commit itself to PAMETRADA except by supporting its establishment and indicating that PAMETRADA turbines might be purchased should they be suitable. For the first of the post-war ships, the 'Daring'-class destroyers planned in 1946 but launched in 1950, three different sets of machinery were chosen; five members of the class received all reaction turbines developed by PAMETRADA and one a hybrid arrangement comprising an HP impulse turbine developed by British Thomson-Houston followed by a Parsons reaction LP turbine. Two ships were given all impulse turbines developed by the English Electric Company and these proved to be the most satisfactory resulting in further cooperation and orders.[10] The English Electric HP turbine

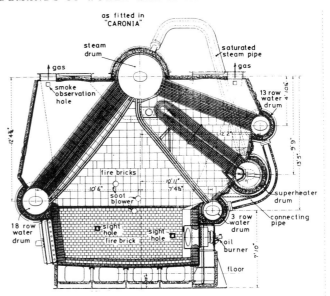

14.16 *Section through Yarrow five-drum water-tube boiler fitted in* Caronia *and the 'Queen' liners*

14.15 *Turbines for Cunard liner* Caronia *(1949)*

had a single Curtis stage and eight impulse stages while the double-flow LP turbine had two sets of six impulse stages, steam entering at the middle of the turbine casing. Not only was the English Electric design more compact than the other 'Daring' turbines, it also had superior performance. Steam conditions specified for these turbines were 600psi and 850°F, the pressure being the same as that used for American destroyers in the mid-1930s.

In order to make use of high turbine speeds with low propeller speeds the Admiralty specified double-reduction gearing but at that time British double-reduction gearing was unreliable resulting in the establishment of another association with the aim of improving it. The Admiralty-Vickers Gear Research Association (AVGRA) included representatives from gear manufacturers and metallurgists as well as engineers from Vickers and the Admiralty. Gear-grinding machines were purchased from Maag of Switzerland and a set of hardened and ground gears was obtained from the company for installation in the 'Daring'-class vessel *Diana*.[11]

The Admiralty never returned to PAMETRADA for turbines although use was made of the testing facilities. In the immediate postwar period there was an awareness of how far British turbine design had fallen behind American practice but during the 1930s the Admiralty had done little to force development, being content to stay with existing designs which operated at relatively low pressure and temperature conditions. Contact with American ships during the war did show the Admiralty what progress was possible and in 1946 it established its own research group in conjunction with Yarrows, the Yarrow Admiralty Research Department (Y-ARD), which looked at many areas of marine engineering, not turbines alone.

With the transfer of old American destroyers to Britain followed by the entry of America into the war British naval engineers could see at first hand the superiority of American turbine practice and the engineering developments which allowed American ships to operate more effectively. Many large British warships suffered from a shortage of fresh water due to the innumerable steam leaks from pipe joints, such leaks also making engine rooms unbearably hot and uncomfortable in tropical regions. Distilled water was essential for boilers and had to be made from sea water by evaporator plant. American ships used much more effective means of jointing pipe flanges and sealing glands such that steam leakage was minimised. On an exchange of duties transfer from HMS *King George V* to the USS *Missouri*, at the end of the war, a senior engineering lieutenant found it difficult to believe that the latter was steam driven.[12] The shortage of vessels to escort convoys was made worse by a regulation concerning boiler cleaning which actually kept ships in port when they could have

14.17 Post-war cargo ship Bahadur *built by Lithgows in 1948 and fitted with a triple-expansion engine having an LP exhaust turbine and double reduction gearing with a hydraulic clutch, steam supplied at 230 psi from Scotch boilers*

been at sea. British warships did not use feed-water treatment in order to minimise scale formation and avoid corrosion; they were opened for interior inspection and cleaning at frequent intervals which, during the early years of the war, was set at twenty-one days' steaming. Even if a boiler had only operated for a few minutes on certain days they still classed as days of steaming; the result was that boilers were opened at a maximum of 504hrs' steaming and the ship was out of action not only for the time spent in port but for the period spent getting back to port or its patrol area. Reluctantly the period was extended to 750hrs during 1941, but the use of boiler-water treatment was prohibited even though its use allowed American ships to steam their boilers for 2,000hrs before being opened and even then the boilers were in better condition than those aboard British ships. The argument against the use of chemical treatment was that it caused boiler priming (the carry-over of water droplets to the turbine) but this had been shown to be incorrect by American practice. An argument in favour of the 750hrs cleaning period was that it allowed crews a period of rest, though obviously not the boiler cleaners. Matters did improve at the end of the war but it took strong action by some marine engineers to force the issue and the experience of working American ships did much to show

14.18 Turbine-driven Blue Funnel liner Pyrrhus *(1949); built by Cammel Laird with a three-stage, double-reduction turbine taking steam from two watertube boilers at 570psi and 540°F*

the way in which British naval ships should be engineered.[13]

American marine engineering progressed rapidly in the 1930s and during the war years but the progress was strictly naval as there was little merchant ship construction during the interwar years. By 1939 steam pressures of 600psi and temperatures up to 850°F were being used and double-reduction gearing was established as the norm for tonnage from destroyers to aircraft carriers. Impulse turbines predominated and General Electric took the lead in developing high-speed turbines which required greater accuracy in terms of gear cutting than had been achieved before. Westinghouse, Allis Chalmers and De Laval also built turbines for American warships during the 1940s but the compact, high-speed General Electric impulse unit found considerable favour for all types of ship. Power requirements were raised as speed, size or both were increased to meet the demands of ever more sophisticated warships; 'Midway'-class carriers of 1945 had four sets of double-reduction, cross compound turbines, each set developing 56,000shp. Effective use of stronger heat-resistant

materials allowed American designers to push their turbines and boilers to higher limits, but the American naval authorities encouraged them to do this despite the number of setbacks that must have occurred. Warships were designed to fight at sea and the US Navy ensured that its builders provided ships which could do so reliably and then it ensured that they were able to operate at sea for long periods by providing necessary refuelling and restoring facilities.

While serving as an engineer officer with the Pacific Fleet aboard the battleship *Duke of York*, Louis Le Bailly, subsequently Vice-Admiral Sir Louis, had the opportunity to visit a number of American vessels and was subsequently asked to provide a report on the problems which plagued British warships in the Pacific. His report was a catalogue of engineering failures which could be attributed to poor design or management, such as not allowing the use of chemical boiler treatment or pipe-flange jointing. American battleships could be ready for sea at 30 minutes notice but British ships needed a minimum of four hours. Le Bailly concluded that the high mobility of American ships, despite the lower standard of the enlisted men, was achieved

14.19 Balancing a turbine rotor at Taikoo Dockyard during the early 1950s (John Swire & Son)

through quality design and the use of technology whereas the mobility of British ships, even though it was poor, was a triumph of the professionalism of officers and men despite outdated and inefficient ship and machinery design.[14]

Before the outbreak of war marine engineering advances were made by Germany and Japan with the former achieving major improvements in terms of steam conditions. Although steam pressures of 1,800psi had been used for some destroyers during the late 1930s the more usual level was a mere 1,045psi with a temperature of 840°F, triple-expansion turbine sets developing some 35,000shp. Deschimag impulse turbine sets were arranged with HP and IP units driving one pinion and the LP unit driving the other. The use of high-pressure steam followed from the practice of German land-turbine builders but the transfer

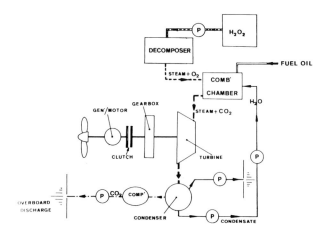

14.20 Diagrammatic arrangement of Walther hydrogen peroxide propulsion system

of technology to the marine environment did not prove to be as straightforward as was expected and many problems were experienced. Compared with American designs German turbine installations were heavier, larger and had a higher specific fuel consumption.[15]

Japanese turbine designers were more conservative but there was a greater interest in battleships and carriers and thus a need for powerful turbine installations. A number of engine works such as Mitsubishi, Ishikawajima and Mitsui took licences for Parsons, Brown-Curtis and Zoelly designs but modified them to suit the needs of the Japanese Navy. The Parsons type was effectively abandoned during the late 1920s and designs based upon the Brown-Curtis impulse turbine perfected. Through the use of heavy turbine discs and relatively low rotational speeds the vibration, or disc flutter, problems experienced by American and British Curtis turbine builders were not encountered. Steam conditions were moderate, even compared with British practice, the battleship *Yamato*, delivered in 1941, employing steam at 350psi and 665°F. Her four 37,500shp turbine sets had

single HP and IP impulse turbines placed at the after end of the gearing and two LP impulse turbines at the forward end; the LP turbines had triple Curtis astern wheels attached. A cruising turbine, rotating at 6,350rpm, was attached to the HP pinion by means of gearing and a clutch. Although turbine design was somewhat behind that of America or even the major European powers, Japanese builders were able to construct some of the most powerful turbine sets of their time.[16]

Boiler development progressed together with that of the turbine, with the demand for higher steam conditions from the turbine builder being met by the boiler designer with the co-operation of the metallurgist. Turbines became the driving force behind all but the smallest warships and the submarine which remained the preserve of the internal combustion engine. The need for air forced the submarine to operate on the surface in order to charge its batteries, unless a snorkel was fitted, and that left the boat vulnerable to attack by aircraft or surface vessels. High speed under water and extended submersed operations were the requirements of the submarine but with combined diesel engine and battery power that could not be achieved. However, the German engineer Professor H. Walter thought that he had the solution.

During the 1930s Walter developed a submarine turbine drive unit which was powered by concentrated hydrogen peroxide, known commercially as High Test Peroxide (HTP). In the Walter engine HTP was supplied at high pressure to a chamber containing a catalyst where it decomposed, with the liberation of heat, into steam and oxygen which then passed to a combustion chamber. Fuel oil was burned with the oxygen forming steam and carbon dioxide with a further rise in temperature; water was also injected into the combustion chamber thus increasing the amount of steam generated. The gases comprising about 83 per cent steam and the remainder carbon dioxide passed to the turbine where power was generated before the steam was converted into water in the condenser. Carbon dioxide was compressed and pumped overboard while the water was passed to the combustion chamber as feed with the excess being pumped overboard. The system was effective as it did not require an air supply and waste products could be discharged. The first submarine designed to use the system, *V.80*, was completed in 1940 and used a 'cold' system without the combustion chamber, the steam generated by catalytic breakdown of the hydrogen peroxide driving a 2,000 hp turbine coupled to a 20:1 reduction gear system. Although the plant worked successfully the trail of oxygen bubbles pumped overboard allowed for easy detection of the submarine.

A 'hot' system with a combustion chamber avoided this problem and construction of U-boats with such equipment was authorised but the war ended before they were ready.

Britain acquired *U-1407*, renaming her HMS *Meteorite*, and, following trials decided to construct two experimental HTP boats in order to determine the effectiveness of their propulsion and to test high-speed submarines. HMS *Explorer* and HMS *Excalibur* did achieve submerged speeds in excess of 25 knots but the HTP plant was not considered suitable for submarine propulsion owing to its unstable nature. HTP is a powerful oxidant which means that it will react with any material which will burn or oxidise such as oil, woollen clothing, rust, most metals and dust. Storage on board, loading or transfer all presented potential hazards and minor explosions did occur on both vessels resulting in their being known as the 'exploders'.[17] The concept was abandoned but the idea of steam-powered submarines with prolonged underwater endurance was not and saw fulfilment in the development of the nuclear submarine.

Wartime requires resources to be concentrated to defeat the enemy making innovation difficult but there was innovation during the war and there were lessons to be learned. Even the 'Liberty' ships were innovative, although their machinery was essentially from a bygone age as the factory-type production of such machinery necessitated the construction of marine engines by companies who had no previous experience in the field. For Britain the war illustrated many things including how far turbine technology had fallen behind American practice. Gradual reconstruction during the late 1940s allowed British shipyards to return to their premier position, but that was short-lived, as was the late flowering of steam power at sea during the 1950s and the 1960s.

References

1 The story of the 'Liberty' ships is given in L. A. Sawyer and W. H. Mitchell, *The Liberty Ships*, David & Charles, Newton Abbot, 1970; I. G. Stewart, *Liberty Ships in Peacetime*, Ian Stewart Marine Publications, Rockingham Beach, Western Australia, 1992; and W. W. Jaffee, *The Last Liberty*, Glencannon Press, Palo Alto, California, 1993.

2 G. E. Weir, 'A Truly Allied Undertaking', *Naval Engineers Journal*, vol. 106, part 3, 1994, pp. 175–83.

3 F. J. Duffy, 'The Liberty Ships', *Marine Propulsion International*, Apr. 1980, pp. 30–35.

4 W. W. Jaffee, *The Last Liberty*, pp. 451–2.

5 W. W. Jaffee, *The Last Victory*, US Merchant Marine Veterans WWII, 1991, p 293.

6 D. Griffiths, 'British Shipping and the Diesel Engine: the Early Years', *Mariner's Mirror*, Aug. 1995, pp. 313–29.

7 *The Engineer*, 15 Mar. 1946, pp. 239–41.

8 *Shipbuilder & Marine Engine Builder*, Apr. 1949, pp. 365–6.

9 Contribution by Cdr E. Tyrrell to D. G. Nicholas, 'Review of the Marine Steam Turbine over the Last 40 Years', *Trans. I.Mar.E.* vol. 102, 1990, p. 99.

10 D. G. Nicholas, 'Review of the Marine Steam Turbine', p. 93.

11 Sir Frank Mason, 'Review of Naval Propulsion Engineering in the Last 10 Years', *Trans. NECIES*, 1957, pp. 53–4.

12 Vice Admiral Sir Louis Le Bailly, *The Man Around the Engine*, Kenneth Mason, London, 1990, p. 132.

13 Ibid., pp. 65–6, 127–34.

14 Ibid., pp. 132–4.

15 I. Jung, *The Marine Turbine Part 2: 1928–1980*, National Maritime Museum, Greenwich, 1986, pp. 80–5.

16 Ibid., pp. 71–9.

17 P. R. Compton-Hall, 'Turbine-Powered Submarines', *Marine Propulsion*, Sep., 1980, pp. 36–41.

15
Post-War Resurgence

The 1950s proved to be something of an Indian summer for the use of steam at sea but throughout that period a rearguard action was being fought against the diesel engine. During the 1950s Britain retained its place as the world's major shipbuilding and ship-owning nation, but it was a position based upon past glories rather than leadership in technology. The reasons for Britain's decline in ship owning and shipbuilding are many and complex and no attempt will be made to analyse them here since this book is concerned about steam machinery and not Britain's place in the maritime world. However, the decline of the British shipbuilding industry also saw the emergence of Japan as a world power in terms of shipbuilding and marine engineering in so far as commercial tonnage was concerned. As the centre for shipbuilding moved from Europe to the East there was also an acceleration in the change from steam to diesel propulsion which was due to the development of large diesel engines capable of burning boiler oil. Until the 1950s most diesel engines had burned more expensive, lighter oils which gave the steam plant an advantage, although the specific fuel consumption of a marine diesel engine was considerably less than for a steam plant, even the most efficient. British ship owners and ship builders still tended to be more favourably disposed towards steam machinery than their European neighbours, but as the 1960s

dawned even the most fervent supporter of steam could not ignore the benefits of the diesel engine and the days of steam at sea were numbered. Steam did, however, have a niche market in terms of the high-powered passenger tonnage and the more specialist ships such as large oil tankers with their requirement for considerable steam heating. Fuel consumption was not the main criterion as far as naval ships were concerned and the high power to weight or size ratio of the steam turbine gave it an advantage over the diesel engine. But it was another internal combustion engine, the gas turbine, which proved to be the main competitor for naval ships. This chapter will look at the years between 1950 and 1970 when steam played its last major roles in the powering of merchant ships, after that it was popular only in naval circles and for a few specialist commercial ships.

Even during the 1950s steam reciprocating engines were still being installed in ships, mainly small vessels although some British tramp ship owners stipulated triple-expansion engines with reheat or exhaust turbines. As late as 1956 Esso took delivery of the 1,965-gross ton, single-screw coastal tankers *Esso Preston* fitted with a 16.5in + 28.5in + 47in by 2ft 6in stroke reciprocating engine which was supplied with superheated steam at 225psi. The same year Hogarths of Ardrossan took delivery of three 5,500-gross ton tramps propelled by reciprocating engines with exhaust turbines

15.1 Coastal tanker Esso Preston *(1956), propelled by a steam reciprocating engine supplied with superheated steam (Esso Petroleum)*

15.2 Typical British-built cargo steamer of the postwar period, Pacific Reliance *(1950) fitted with double reduction HP and IP turbines and single reduction for the LP pinion (Furness Withy)*

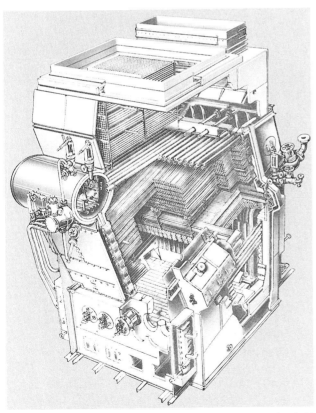

15.3 Babcock & Wilcox header-type boiler of the 1950s (Babcock & Wilcox)

having double-reduction gearing and hydraulic clutches. Two years earlier *Baron Ardrossan* entered service with the same company, this ship having the same sort of machinery but with an NEM reheat system. Although such installations are interesting they were rarities since tramp tonnage was normally, by then, the domain of the diesel engine and all ships built for Hogarths after that time had diesel machinery. Steam-turbine propulsion of passenger ships lasted longer but throughout the 1950s and into the 1960s many tankers and some general cargo ships were still being fitted with turbine machinery. Double-reduction gearing had proved itself to be effective and free from problems by the 1950s with the result that a number of ships were provided with such an arrangement although the form of gearing employed depended upon the turbine size and speed. In certain cases combined single- and double-reduction was used, the faster turbine HP shaft having double-reduction gearing and the slower IP and LP using single reduction. PAMETRADA licensees provided many turbines for ships built in British yards but other turbine builders also entered the market including Associated Electrical Industries (AEI).

Steam pressures for merchant tonnage steadily rose during the 1950s, reaching 800psi in some cases, there being a corresponding increase in steam temperature; pressure and temperature were chosen to maximise performance of the turbine machinery. Although there were other manufacturers, boilers designed by Foster, Wheeler and Babcock &

Wilcox were chosen for the bulk of steam tonnage built in Britain at that time, most large shipbuilders constructing such boilers under licence. The Foster, Wheeler D (Drum) type became almost a standard type from that designer but there were three types of Babcock boiler in common use: the selectable superheat, the integral furnace and the header type, which was based upon a design originally introduced just after the beginning of the twentieth century. Each type provided particular features which served the needs of the turbine designer and, consequently, the ship owner.

The superheat temperature needed to be kept within certain limits in order to maintain operating efficiency and at the same time avoid excessive temperatures which could result in a weakening of the superheater elements and turbine blades. As the heat required for a particular temperature depended upon the mass of steam flowing, which could vary, the simplest method was to fit a separate superheating unit alongside the boiler and such was the case with a number of ships. However, that increased the initial cost and also took additional space in the engine room. In order to meet the requirements of the Navy for steam generation and superheating in a single furnace boiler, Babcocks developed one which was subsequently modified to suit the needs of commercial operation, this became the selectable superheat

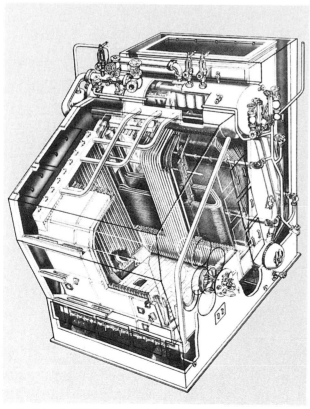

15.6 Babcock & Wilcox integral furnace boiler (Babcock & Wilcox)

boiler. Essentially the boiler was a two-drum unit with bent tubes forming a wall around the furnace; the main bank of steam generating tubes between the upper and the lower drum was divided into two sections by a vertical baffle thus providing two parallel gas flows. The relative amount of gas in each part of the flow could be regulated by means of dampers at the gas outlets from the boiler. The superheater element was entirely contained within one of the gas flows and thus the temperature could be regulated by means of the damper settings. The integral furnace boiler was similar to the selectable superheat boiler except that there was no vertical baffle and the entire gas flow passed over the superheater elements. In order to regulate superheat temperature with such a boiler an attemperator could be incorporated or a desuperheater used.

The standard Babcock header-type boiler found general application throughout the 1950s and into the 1960s having proved its reliability and economy. The design allowed for pressures up to 700psi and temperatures of 850°F, compared with pressures up to 1,000psi and temperatures of 950°F which could be handled by the integral furnace design. Although it required more headroom than most bent-tube boilers of similar capacity, the header-type boiler occupied less floor space making it particularly attractive for cargo ship use.[1]

The use of reheat for turbines found favour during the 1950s when a reheat boiler was developed by Foster, Wheeler, one of the first installations going into the Canadian Pacific liner *Empress of Britain*, delivered by Fairfields during 1956; a similar installation went into the sister ships *Empress of England* (1957) and *Empress of Canada* (1961). The ship was given two Foster, Wheeler two-furnace controlled superheat boilers and a single reheat boiler which, in addition to its normal steam evaporation of 50,000lbs of steam per hour could reheat the entire steam flow from the HP turbine back to the original temperature of 850°F. Each main boiler, operating at 650psi, could normally generate steam at the rate of 73,500lbs per hour with a maximum evaporation of 122,000lbs per hour. Boilers worked under combined forced and induced draught. Control of the reheat side of the boiler was by means of fuel-oil firing, a quick closing valve being fitted in the fuel line to shut off fuel to the burners when the steam pressure in the reheater fell below a predetermined value. Steam for heating and auxiliary purposes was obtained from a steam-to-steam generator with saturated steam from the main boiler drums being circulated through heating coils in the low-pressure steam generator. A Howden-Johnson boiler supplied steam at 200psi for use in port.

Two sets of PAMETRADA turbines generated 27,000shp under normal conditions, tandem HP and IP units being all impulse while the LP was of the reaction double-flow type; for astern running there was an impulse

15.4 8,511-grt P&O cargo steamer Baradine *(built as* Nardana *in 1956); fitted with three-stage, double-reduction geared turbine and Babcock & Wilcox header-type boilers*

15.5 Clan Shaw (1959) 7,698-grt cargo ship fitted with double-reduction geared turbines and two header-type boilers working at 450psi and 750°F (Clan Line)

15.7 Esso Cambridge (1954), 17,524-grt tanker with compound turbines and double reduction gearing; fitted with two Babcock & Wilcox integral furnace boilers working at 850psi and 850°F (Esso Petroleum)

HP turbine in its own casing and exhausting to an impulse LP unit in the ahead LP casing. Double-reduction gearing of the double-helical type was used for both pinions. The system functioned effectively encouraging its use in the two subsequent ships[2] and it was also economic in returning fuel consumption figures for propulsion alone of 0.495lbs/shp/hr, better than most contemporary passenger liners.[3]

Throughout the 1950s steam turbines were installed in a number of British cargo ships but owners from other nations turned towards the diesel engine in increasing numbers and it was not until the advent of the fast container ship during

the 1970s that the turbine became, for a short period of time, the favoured propulsion system for the cargo ship. Oil tankers, particularly the very large crude carriers (VLCC) and subsequently the ultra large crude carrier (ULCC), remained firmly in the court of the steam turbine but the steam propulsion of tankers was more usually a marriage of convenience because of the tanker's need of a steam supply for tank heating and cargo pumps than a choice of the most efficient propulsion system. Certainly single-screw propulsion was favoured for tankers as it offered the most efficient arrangement and until the late 1970s the turbine was the only means of achieving sufficiently high powers on a single shaft

15.8 Tanker British Victory *fitted with two Babcock & Wilcox selectable superheat boilers (British Petroleum)*

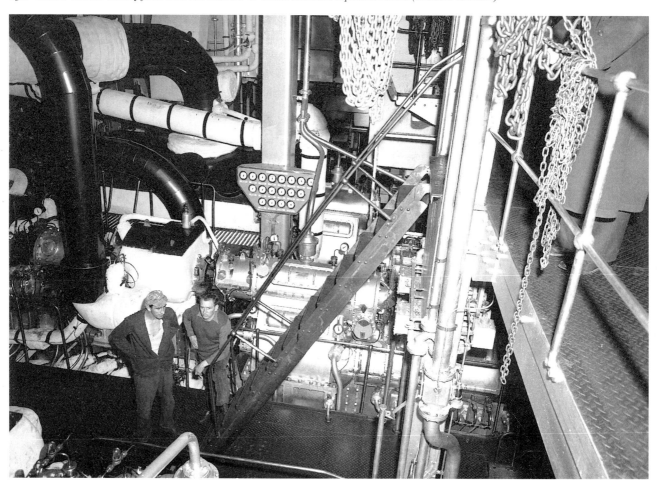

15.10 Turbine room of the liner Empress of Britain; *the vertical pipe on the left is the exhaust steam pipe from the HP turbine to the reheat boiler; the turbine gearbox is behind the ladder (Canadian Pacific)*

15.11 Canadian Pacific liner Empress of Britain *(1956) (Canadian Pacific)*

for the propulsion of tankers in the 250,000-ton category. During the 1960s British shipbuilders found themselves increasingly unable to compete with yards in the Far East and particularly Japan for such ships and thus the orders for turbines ceased and so did the main part of British commercial marine turbine development work when PAMETRADA was closed in the late 1960s.[4]

15.9 Front of Babcock selectable superheat boiler fitted in the liner
Pendennis Castle *built during the late 1950s (Babcock & Wilcox)*

The 1950s and early 1960s were, however, bright for the steam turbine since the diesel engine could not compete for the propulsion of large passenger ships and many of these were constructed during that period. Most notable was the American express liner *United States*, significant not only for its power and speed but because few other merchant ships were built in the USA during the decade following the end of the war. In order to drive this 53,329-gross ton ship at a service speed of up to 35 knots, 240,000shp was required on four shafts representing 4.56shp/ton compared with 2.01shp/ton for the British 'Queens'. Despite the secrecy which surrounded the ship and her power, the machinery was essentially the same as that fitted in the large 'Midway'-class American carriers of the period. Each turbine set consisted of a cross compound, double-reduction set, the HP turning at 5,000rpm and the LP at just over 4,000rpm; the HP had one Curtis wheel and six impulse wheels with some steam being bled off between the HP and the LP turbine for auxiliary purposes. The LP turbine was of the double-flow type incorporating two Curtis wheels followed by impulse wheels, the casing also incorporating astern turbines. Steam at a pressure of 925psi and 1,000°F was supplied by Babcock & Wilcox boilers working under forced draught, the boilers being in two separate rooms. In effect, the machinery was arranged with two turbine, two boiler and two auxiliary machinery rooms with suitable arrangement of pipework allowing any set of turbines, or auxiliary plant to be powered from either or both boiler

15.12 Blue Riband holder United States

rooms. The 'Big U', as the ship was affectionately known, took the Blue Riband during her maiden voyage with a speed of 35.59 knots eastbound and 33.92 westbound but maintained a normal service speed of about 29 knots on a daily fuel consumption of about 740 tons.[5] Spectacular though her steam plant was, her high fuel consumption and competition from large aircraft on the lucrative Atlantic run, together with the effects of labour disputes, saw her withdrawal from service in the late 1960s as commercially uneconomic.

Away from the Atlantic, large aircraft offered less severe competition and many British-built, stream-driven passenger vessels survived into the 1970s and beyond, often as cruise ships rather than on liner routes. Among the most innovative passenger ships of the 1950s was the 20,204-gross ton *Southern Cross*, delivered in 1955 by Harland & Wolff for Shaw Savill's round-the-world service to Australia and New Zealand. This ship had no provision for the carriage of cargo but, more interestingly, her machinery was installed in the after part of the ship thus allowing for large, uninterrupted public rooms. Compound, double-reduction steam turbines were selected to provide the 20,000shp needed to drive the ship on twin screws, HP ahead turbines being of the impulse-reaction type while the LP were all reaction; impulse HP and LP astern turbines were incorporated in the main HP and LP casings. Steam at 500psi and 800°F was supplied by three Yarrow boilers fitted with Melesco-type superheaters. Although the steam plant fitted may not have marked any major advance on contemporary installations the idea of an aft positioning was a novel way of re-

ducing the impact of boiler uptakes on passenger spaces. Boilers were actually located aft of the turbines with the propeller shafts passing below the boiler deck, thus allowing the boilers to be as far aft as was practically possible.[6] A number of earlier Atlantic liners, including *Bremen* and *Europa*, had employed divided uptakes in order to provide for long saloon spaces in the central part of the ship, but there was still the problem of boiler uptakes having to join at some point in order to enter the funnel.

The aft engine arrangement was repeated by Harlands when building the 45,733-gross ton liner *Canberra* for P&O's Australian service. This ship was intended to run in consort with the Orient Line's 41,915-gross ton *Oriana*, the latter company being a wholly-owned subsidiary of P&O. Although of similar size and intended to operate on the same service, these two ships were of completely different design and each was radical in its own way. *Oriana*, delivered in November 1960, was built and engined by Vickers-Armstrong of Barrow, her twin-screw, geared turbine installation being of PAMETRADA design. Each triple-expansion turbine set could develop 32,500shp at a propeller speed of 147rpm during normal operation with a maximum capability of 40,000shp at 157.5rpm; astern power of 21,000shp was available from each set. HP turbines were entirely impulse, consisting of a double-impulse wheel followed by eight single rows of impulse wheels; the all impulse IP turbine consisted of nine single-row wheels while the LP was of the double-flow type with each flow having four impulse stages and six reaction stages. A two-row impulse HP astern wheel was fitted in the IP casing

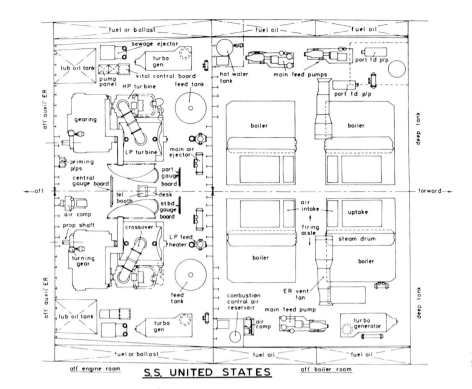

S.S. UNITED STATES

aff engine room   aft' boiler room

15.13 Boiler and engineroom layout of United States

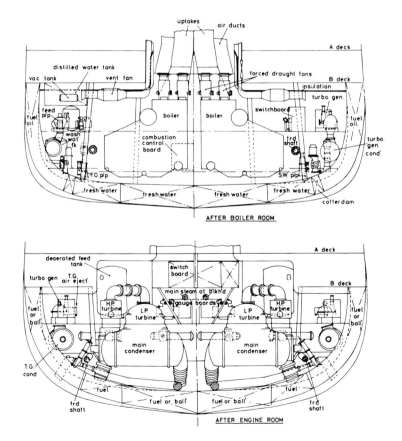

AFTER BOILER ROOM

AFTER ENGINE ROOM

15.14 Section through after engine and boiler rooms aboard United States

15.15 *Engine room of the 37,647-grt liner* Windsor Castle *(1960) showing both sets of turbines and gearing; a typical passenger liner turbine installation of the period*

with a two-row astern LP turbine in the LP casing. At full power HP, IP and LP ahead turbines were designed to run at 4,085rpm, 3,588rpm and 2,918rpm, respectively. Weir's regenerative condensers fitted below each LP turbine had cooling surfaces of 32,000ft² and were capable of maintaining a 28in vacuum with the sea temperature as high as 86°F. That factor was important as the ship would operate in tropical waters and a high condenser vacuum was essential for efficient turbine performance.

Steam at a pressure of 700psi and a temperature of 960°F came from four Foster, Wheeler ESD (external superheat drum)-type boilers working on a balanced draught system using a combination of electrically-driven forced- and induced-draught fans. Air heaters were positioned in the flue uptakes with additional heating of the air being provided by means of attemperators. Attemperators permitted control of the superheat temperature and consisted of coils through which superheated steam passed, the flow of combustion air over the coils regulating the temperature of the steam as it flowed between the first- and the second-stage superheaters. Closed-feed systems were provided and in addition to the feed-heating effect of the regenerative condensers two high-pressure feed heaters were fitted, one of which condensed steam from the evaporators and the other bled steam from the turbine system. The two turbine-driven feed pumps each had a capacity of over 700,000lbs of water per hour against a pressure head of 1,050psi. The distillation plant on the ship

15.16 Turbine driven Orient liner Oriana

15.17 Oriana's *main engine control platform situated below the main turbines (P&O)*

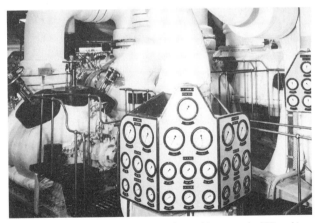

15.18 Oriana's *engine room looking forward between the HP turbines (P&O)*

could produce 650 tons of fresh water per day for boiler feed and domestic purposes. On trials, when developing an overload power of 82,500shp, the ship achieved a speed of 30.6 knots with a specific fuel consumption, for propulsion alone, of 0.46lbs/shp/hr.[7]

For *Canberra* a turbo-electric system of propulsion was chosen, P&O having had previous favourable experience with such plant in *Viceroy of India* (1929), *Strathnaver* (1931) and *Strathaird* (1932). As has already been discussed, turbo-electric propulsion was heavier and tended to have a

higher specific fuel consumption than geared turbine drives but it was considered to be quieter and offered a much greater astern power The electric drive fitted in *Canberra* possessed a further advantage in that her twin propellers could be electrically locked so that they rotated at exactly the same speed thus enabling vibration to be minimised. As any propeller rotates vertical and sideways forces are exerted because the propeller has a number of separate blades rather than being a complete disc, these periodic forces tend to induce vibration particularly when the forces from each

207

15.19 Oriana's engine room; view of port turbine arrangement (P&O)

15.20 Arrangement of burners on Oriana's starboard aft boiler (P&O)

propeller are in step. With an electric drive the propellers could be locked together so that the impulses effectively cancelled each other out and the propulsion motor control system fitted in *Canberra* allowed this to take place. Such an arrangement necessitated the use of synchronous motors and the rotational speed of these depended upon the frequency of the electrical supply which in turn depended upon the rotational speed of the turbines to which the propulsion alternators were directly connected. Speed con-

trol was by regulation of the steam supply to the turbine which adjusted the speed of the turbine and hence the frequency of the electrical supply.[8]

The regulation of motor speed and direction were undertaken at the main console which had twin sets of controls, one for each propulsion motor. Motors were actually double units, there effectively being two separate motors for each shaft and they could be controlled separately or together. Turbines were operated under no load at 25 per cent

15.21 *Turbo-electric powered* Canberra *at Capetown (Geoff Johnson)*

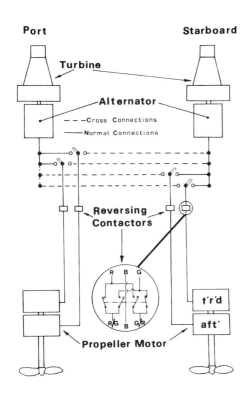

15.22 *Diagram of the electrical connections for* Canberra's *propulsion system*

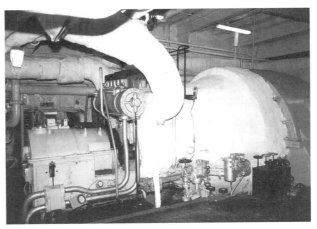

15.24 *Port turbine aboard* Canberra

of normal speed and would be run this way whenever the ship was in port for a short period rather than shut down. This enabled temperatures to be maintained and avoided problems of rotor or casing distortion and also avoided any delay in warming-through the turbine. When starting, the reversing switch on the console would moved to the required position for ahead or astern running thus connecting the motor stator with the alternator stator. The alternator would then be excited in order to produce current and the motor would start as an induction motor; when it reached

15.23 Canberra's *turbine room with control console in the foreground and turbine-driven main alternator in the background*

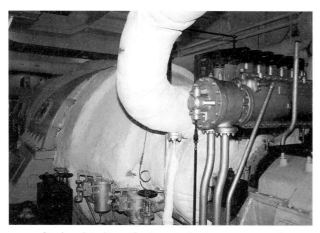

15.25 *Starboard turbine* (Canberra) *showing cam-actuated steam nozzle valves*

synchronous speed (25 per cent of full speed) the motor field would be excited and it would then run as a synchronous motor in step with the alternator. From this point the speed of the motor would be regulated by the speed of the turbine and this was achieved by controlling the steam supply. For reversing, the motor would be stopped, the

reversing switch changed over and the process of excitation repeated with the turbine operating at 25 per cent of full speed. With two alternators and two double motor units a number of combinations were possible in order to produce a propulsive drive:

(a) each alternator could drive its own motor;

(b) one alternator could drive both motors;

(c) with motors synchronised the port alternator could power both forward motors and the starboard alternator could power the after motors; this was the situation in order to avoid vibration.

Each propulsion turbo-alternator set was rated at 32,200kVA generating three-phase alternating current at 51.5 hertz when turning at 3,087rpm; under these conditions electricity would be generated at 6,000 volts. For normal cruising operations the alternators would generate 30,700kVA at 4,670 volts and 40 hertz when turning at 2,400rpm.[9]

The electrical system and turbo-alternators were supplied by Associated Electrical Industries (AEI) of Rugby, a company which had extensive land-based turbine and electrical experience but little background in marine work. AEI had been formed by a merger between the major

15.26 *Boiler room aboard* Canberra

British industrial companies British Thompson Houston, Metropolitan Vickers and English Electric. Eventually through other mergers this became the General Electric Company (UK). The choice of equipment followed the practice adopted in America many years before where shore turbine design had been applied to marine work and it marked a major change for the British marine industry although three Blue Funnel Line ships had been given machinery based upon power-station turbines during 1953.[10] Each of the alternators was driven by a single-cylinder turbine comprising eighteen stages of blading, the steam supply being regulated by means of cam-operated admission valves. A double-impulse wheel was followed by eight stages of impulse blading and a further eight stages of impulse-reaction blading at the low-pressure end of the turbine. Twin governors were fitted, one for regulating speed at 25 per cent full speed during manoeuvring and the other being adjustable between 85 per cent full speed and full speed. In common with land turbines, monitoring equipment was fitted to record the differential expansion between rotor and casing. An extensive series of vibration trials was conducted on the turbines.[11]

The steam supply aboard *Canberra* came from three large Foster, Wheeler ESD type boilers, the pressure being 750psi and the temperature 960°F. Each of these boilers was rated at 175,000lbs per hour and two could normally supply the steam for normal running. In addition, a smaller, 40,000lbs per hour, boiler was available for use in port. Boilers operated on Howden forced draught with fans being driven by steam turbines. Superheat temperature was regulated by means of attemperators, the flow of combustion air over them being controlled by dampers. Boilers were located aft of the turbines and above the propeller shafts thus allowing the twin side-by-side funnels and flue uptakes to be placed as far aft in the ship as possible thereby giving the maximum clear space for public rooms. This arrangement allowed for short main steam pipes, made from chrome-molybdenum steel, connecting boilers and turbines; the short length enabled the pipe runs to be made with the minimum of joints.[12]

The steam propulsion system employed for *Canberra* was radical in that, for the first time in a large British ship, it made use of the best land-turbine practice but it was also effective and, in general, less troublesome than other steam turbine installation of the period. The choice of any propulsion system, particularly a large one for a passenger ship, requires careful consideration of many factors and the incorrect choice may lead to considerable expense in terms of repairs or modifications, high operating costs through excessive fuel consumption, or passenger dissatisfaction from vibration problems. Time leads to improvements and no technology remains the preferred choice for long but the decision to fit AEI turbo-electric propulsion in *Canberra*

would appear to have been a good one. In 1997 the ship continued in service with her original machinery while many younger passenger vessels have retired or been re-engined. One of those re-engined ships was the Cunard liner *Queen Elizabeth 2*, built by John Brown in 1967 and given the PAMETRADA designed turbines, one of the last designs from that organisation before it was closed.

The *QE2* had two sets of double-reduction, cross compound turbines capable of developing 110,000shp for normal service. The HP turbine had a Curtis wheel followed by eleven impulse stages and rotated at 5,207rpm at full speed. The LP turbine was of the double-flow type, each flow comprising two impulse stages and eight reaction stages. Cunard insisted upon two astern turbines for each unit, a single Curtis wheel on the HP pinion and two rows of blading on the LP pinion, although a single astern Curtis wheel followed by a single row of blading would have been capable of developing the required power. Three Foster, Wheeler ESD II boilers, constructed by John Brown, supplied steam at 850psi and 950°F although the choice of materials for boilers and turbines allowed for operating temperatures up to 1,000°F. Each boiler had five fuel burners and the fuel turn-down ratio of 14:1 allowed for wide control of steam generation. Each boiler could normally generate 231,000lbs of steam per hour with a maximum output of 310,000lbs/hr. The method of controlling steam temperature was similar to that employed for the ESD boilers of *Canberra*.[13]

In many respects there was nothing special about the propulsion plant fitted in the *QE2* and to some extent the turbines were rather dated as a result of the decline in British shipbuilding which limited the research funding available to PAMETRADA. While the ship which was to become the *QE2* was at the planning stage the Ministry of Technology advised the Chief Engineer of Cunard to consider a turbine manufacturer from outside the marine industry as it was believed that PAMETRADA might not be in existence by time the ship went to sea. That advice was ignored but it proved correct in terms of the demise of PAMETRADA, to which the Ministry contributed as it refused a request for funding from PAMETRADA in 1967 on the grounds that only a small number of marine steam turbines were then being constructed in Britain. During trials in 1968 serious problems occurred as several rows of rotating blades in the HP turbine failed from vibration, resulting in the ship's entry into service being delayed until May 1969. The trouble was a setback to British maritime pride and resulted in a Parliamentary investigation which concluded that the blades had been designed without due consideration of the vibration caused by vortices from the stationary guide blades. This was a similar problem to that encountered with Curtis impulse turbines during the 1920s and it was evident that the lessons had not been learned. In

15.27, Turbine control platform aboard QE2 *(Martin S. Harrison)*

view of the demise of PAMETRADA and the significance of the ship for Britain the Ministry of Technology paid Metropolitan Vickers to advise on a solution and when the defective turbine blading had been replaced there was no further such trouble.[14]

Although large liners may have been the prestige projects, cargo ships formed by far the greater part of the world's merchant fleet and ships had been increasingly turning to diesel propulsion because of its better fuel consumption. The only other areas available to the steam turbine were the large tankers and fast container ships which became popular during the early 1970s. Diesel engines were not then capable of developing high enough powers, above about 25,000shp, which were needed for single-screw propulsion of large tankers or the twin-screw propulsion of fast container ships, and between 1960 and 1975 the steam turbine dominated this market. Britain was left behind as its yards were not equipped to build these ships and orders went to the Far East and particularly Japan; with the orders for ships went orders for turbines and boilers and thus a number of Japanese companies became dominant in marine turbine development although imported designs such as the

American General Electric and Swedish Stal-Laval also proved popular.

Improvements in turbine design allowed steam plant to compete with the diesel engine in the large tanker market but it was a constant battle. Although higher steam pressures could be accommodated, increasing the steam temperature above about 950°F was a problem as that

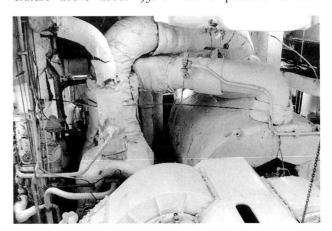

15.28 QE2's *starboard turbine set (Martin S. Harrison)*

15.30 Double helical gearing in opened gearbox (QE2) (Martin S. Harrison)

15.29 One of QE2's double flow LP turbines with upper casing lifted (Martin S. Harrison)

necessitated the use of much more expensive materials for the boiler superheater, steam pipes and the HP turbine. In 1980 Stal-Laval developed a high-pressure, high-temperature turbine plant, designated VAP, with a steam pressure of 1,812psi and a temperature of 1,112°F, but by that time there was little market for such a system. Gearing offered potential for improvements in terms of cost, size and efficiency, and many manufacturers spent considerable sums of money developing systems which could transmit high powers from relatively compact

15.31 Furnace front of Foster, Wheeler boiler fitted in QE2 (Martin S. Harrison)

designs. In conjunction with the British engineering firm W.H. Allen of Bedford, Stal-Laval developed an epicyclic gear system which was more compact than the traditional double-reduction system. Significant improvements in propulsive efficiency with large tankers could be achieved by turning the propeller at the relatively slow speed of 80rpm rather than the more usual 105rpm and steps were taken to achieve this through the use of triple-reduction gearing. Low-pressure turbines generally rotated at lower speeds than the HP unit and so it was possible to derive a hybrid system with double-reduction for the LP pinion and triple reduction for the HP.[15] Reheat fell from favour because of the complication of the plant and the difficulty of control while manoeuvring but during the early 1970s the Japanese builder Kawasaki constructed a number of reheat plants operating at 1,420psi and 970°F, these returning specific fuel consumptions of 0.41lbs/shp/hr.[16] But it was a losing battle and the OPEC oil crisis of 1973 turned the maritime world on its head. Fuel costs became the significant part of ship-operating costs and the higher fuel consumption of the steamship was no longer acceptable. High-powered diesel engines attained specific fuel consumptions as low as 0.27lbs/hp/hr and they were able to achieve this from reliable and relatively simple plant whereas the steam installation had to resort to complex and expensive systems such as triple-reduction gearing and reheat cycles.[17] The steam turbine effectively ceased to be a major power source for commercial shipping from that time although it did continue to have a role for certain specialist ships and naval vessels.

For naval purposes the steam turbine was unchallenged by the diesel engine, except for smaller craft, and development tended to follow similar lines to that of the commercial steam turbine. An exception to that was Britain where, apart from being responsible for the establishment of PAMETRADA, the Admiralty pursued a different course and directed its attention to impulse-type turbines developed in conjunction with Yarrow and English Electric, as mentioned in Chapter 14. The experimental turbines YEAD 1 and YEAD 2 (Yarrow, English Electric Admiralty Designs), based upon the General Electric turbine, were planned during the 1950s but only the first was constructed and proved to be unsuitable for service. The next development was the English Electric Y100 design which came into being following a competition open to all British turbine manufacturers to supply 30,000shp machinery for 2,000-ton anti-submarine frigates. The design became something of a standard for British warships, being first fitted in the 'Whitby' and 'Blackwood' classes of frigate during the early 1950s; modified versions went into subsequent classes of frigate including the 'Leanders' built during the 1960s. The design was simple and one of the briefs was that the plant should be capable of being operated during wartime by

relatively inexperienced crews,[18] although by the time these ships were fully in service peacetime conscription had ended. The ahead section of the single pinion turbine had eight impulse stages and the astern part was a single Curtis wheel. In the Y100 machinery a cruising turbine was fitted but problems with the clutch mechanism resulted in this feature being absent in later versions of the design. Steam conditions were moderate, 450psi and 825°F, but the turbines performed reliably and effectively; maximum efficiency was achieved at 60 per cent power and the turbines had to operate under a poor condenser vacuum of 23in of mercury at full load owing to that fact that a small condenser and exhaust trunking were fitted in order to give a compact design. The design was still being constructed during the 1990s, forty years after its introduction, for the Indian Navy's 'Godavari'-class frigates.[19]

Boilers for Y100 turbine installations were of the Babcock & Wilcox selectable superheat type and boilers in general for British warships followed commercial practice as far as the space limitations in the hull would allow. One of the restrictions was on height and so warship boilers tended not to have the extensive array of uptake economisers and air heaters as could be found in merchant ships. The compact design of the boilers presented problems of cleaning which was exacerbated by deteriorating oil quality during the 1960s and boiler fouling created many operational difficulties. A change to the use of diesel oil reduced the need for cleaning and by the early 1970s all British warships burned this light fuel.[20]

The greatest post-war naval building programme was undertaken by the USA and steam plant was developed in order to improve performance and reliability. Considerable effort went into gearing design which had fallen behind British practice, as developed by the Admiralty-sponsored AVGRA consortium, but, in general, double-reduction gearing was retained while turbines remained essentially of the impulse type. Steam conditions gradually increased during the period 1950 to 1970, as they had done with British and European practice, but the major change which was imposed upon steam plant was the means by which steam was generated. The year 1955 saw the advent of nuclear power at sea in the American submarine *Nautilus* and in the decades to come it was the nuclear reactor which enabled steam to retain its tenuous place in the propulsion of shipping.

Another major innovation in terms of propulsion came by way of the gas turbine which effectively removed steam from the powering of ships. The gas turbine had many advantages over its steam counterpart, not least being its ability to deliver high power almost immediately without the need for a warming-through or steam-generation period. It was compact and well balanced but it was also reliable as designs were based upon proven aircraft engines.

Effectively a jet engine acted as a gas generator with the high temperature, high-velocity gas, which in an aircraft provided the thrust, acting on a further set of turbine blades to produce propulsion power. Gas turbines required better quality fuel (kerosene) than was traditionally burned in boilers but overall fuel costs could be lower for the reasons given earlier. In 1961 the Admiralty decided upon a combined system which would offer the immediate availability and high power of the gas turbine and the relatively low operating cost of the steam turbine in the COSAG system (Combined Steam and Gas Turbine); for high-power running the gas turbine plant would be used but for cruising the steam plant offered greater efficiency. The 'Tribal'-class frigates (1958) and the 'County'-class destroyers (1959) were the first British warships to be designed for such a system with the power requirement of the larger destroyers being in the region of 60,000shp. In the twin-screw 'County'-class each set of machinery consisted of a cross compound steam turbine developing 15,000shp and two gas turbines of 7,500shp each; an astern steam turbine was connected to the LP turbine shaft. The gas turbines were also available for manoeuvring and so were fitted with a reversing gear arrangement which could be connected through hydraulic couplings; all gas and steam turbine shafts went to the same gearbox. Two boilers supplied steam at 700psi and 900°F. The 'Tribal'-class frigates had similar but less powerful installations. The AEI-designed G6 gas turbine was used for both classes, this having been developed specifically for marine propulsion, but for the COSAG system fitted in the single Type 82 destroyer, HMS *Bristol*, ordered in the early 1960s, Olympus aero engines were fitted. The conversion of HMS *Exmouth* to all-gas turbine propulsion showed that warships could operate effectively on gas turbines alone and from the early 1970s all large British surface warships have been so powered.[21]

American and Soviet naval authorities reached similar conclusions as to the effectiveness of gas-turbine propulsion at about the same time as the British and by the 1970s many surface warships were being constructed with gas-turbine machinery.[22] The only place left for steam in the world's fighting fleets was through nuclear power and only the major powers had access to that technology.

Nuclear Power at Sea

The nuclear-powered ship is still a steam ship as the reactor simply acts to generate steam instead of its being raised by a conventional oil- or coal-fired boiler, that steam then being used to drive a conventional steam turbine. Nuclear power requires a controlled nuclear reaction to liberate heat which is then used to generate steam. Nuclear plant is complex in nature but a simple description of the pressurised water reactor used extensively at sea must suffice here. Credit for the introduction of nuclear propulsion must go to Admiral

Hyman G. Rickover of the US Navy for it was through his foresight and efforts that the first nuclear submarine *Nautilus* (SSN 571), was built and proved the effectiveness of the technology. At the end of the war Rickover recognised that the conventional diesel-electric powered submarine had reached the end of its development and even with the use of snorkel devices its underwater capability was limited; the true submarine should be capable of remaining underwater indefinitely in order that it might remain undetected. Only a non-air breathing nuclear power plant could achieve that and Rickover worked hard to convince a sceptical Department of Defense that the nuclear submarine was the way to maintain naval supremacy. Even after permission had been granted in 1948 it took many years before the first submarine was operational as designers and engineers were working at the forefront of technology. The new marine engineers were in a similar position to that of their predecessors at the turn of the eighteenth century, only the technology and the stakes had changed.

In 1948 the US Atomic Energy Commission set in motion research projects which were to lead to the building of *Nautilus* with the Westinghouse Electric Corporation being awarded the contracts for the construction and testing of two reactors. The Mark I was a land-based prototype upon which work commenced in 1949, with the almost identical marine Mark II version following soon after. A pressurised water reactor design was chosen as being the most suitable for marine operations and uranium-235 was the fuel. Reactor operation is complex but in summary it depends upon the controlled fission of uranium-235. This radioactive isotope of the element is present as only 1 per cent of natural uranium and therefore its concentration must be increased by the process known as 'enrichment' before a mass of the metal is capable of supporting fission. The spontaneous breakdown of uranium-235 atoms produce neutrons. The impact of these neutrons on other uranium atoms in the reactor produces yet more neutrons, and

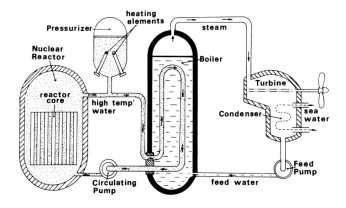

15.32 Diagrammatic arrangement of pressurised water reactor nuclear propulsion system

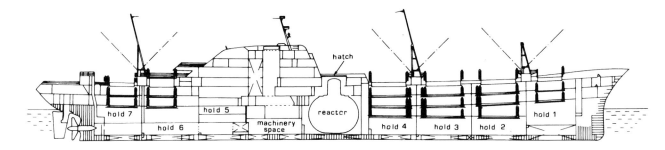

15.33 Sectional drawing of nuclear ship Savannah

so on. This is the essence of a chain reaction and when allowed to continue unchecked is the principle of atomic weapons.

Heat energy is released through fission and this is removed by a coolant. In the pressurised water reactor circulating water, under pressure so that it does not boil, acts to absorb the heat of the fission reaction but the hydrogen in the water also acts as a moderator which slows down the neutrons needed to sustain the chain reaction. This reduction in neutron velocity increases the chance of a neutron encountering a uranium atom thus allowing for further fission and also allows for recovery of heat as the kinetic energy of the neutron is converted to heat.

Regulation of the rate of reaction, and hence of heat production, in a reactor is obtained by raising and lowering control rods made from neutron-absorbing materials such as hafnium. The rods material absorb neutrons thus enabling control to be exercised over the rate of nuclear reaction and hence the amount of heat generated. The process of raising or lowering the rods alters the effective nuclear reaction and is similar to increasing or reducing the fuel supplied to a conventional boiler. Fission of one pound of uranium-235 produces the heat equivalent to the combustion of 2,000 tons of coal. Over time the uranium is converted into other materials which no longer release energy and so the effectiveness of the fuel is reduced. The hot water in the reactor is used as the heat source in a steam generator in order to produce steam to drive a turbine. This was the essence of the system fitted in *Nautilus*.

Nuclear reaction also produces radiation and this must be contained in order to protect personnel. Thus the reactor had to be contained within a shield and any openings in shield, for pipes or cables had to be fitted with glands in order to prevent the leakage of any radioactive airborne particles. By the nature of heat exchange in the steam generator, dry saturated steam, not superheated steam, was produced and this passed to a separator which removed water droplets before the steam was directed to the HP turbine. Water droplets produced in the first stage of the turbine had to be removed before the steam passed to the LP turbine otherwise the impingement of the droplets on

the blades could result in serious damage. Propeller drive was through a system of gearing with a clutch, propulsion motor and thrust block also being fitted to each of the two propeller shafts.[23]

Nautilus, 319ft long and 4,092-tons submerged displacement, was commissioned in September 1955, putting to sea on nuclear power in January 1956. She proved the effectiveness of nuclear submarine propulsion by maintaining submerged high speeds for prolonged periods and making the first submerged passage under the North Pole. In 1957 she was refuelled after steaming more than 62,000 miles and was decommissioned in April 1979 after completing her 2,500th dive and steaming 510,000 miles. *Nautilus* is preserved at Groton, Connecticut,[24] a significant steamship which was torchbearer of the new age of steam at sea and a testament to the foresight and inspiration of Admiral Rickover.

The successful application of nuclear power to submarine propulsion resulted in the belief that it could be made to power surface commercial ships and a number of schemes were proposed, with the Soviet icebreaker *Lenin* and the American passenger-cargo ship *Savannah* being the first. There were advantages in the use of nuclear power for driving an icebreaker since such vessels were not expected to operate in a truly commercial manner; the long periods such a ship could stay on station were advantageous and the additional weight of the nuclear plant was of no disadvantage to a large vessel which relied upon its mass for much of its effect. In a truly commercial vessel the cost of the nuclear plant, the high price of uranium fuel and the space taken by the reactor were all disadvantages, but the number of ports around the world willing to accept nuclear-powered ships proved to be the major restriction on the commercial application of nuclear power at sea.

Construction of the 545ft long, 9,990-dead-weight ton *Savannah* was authorised in 1956, with the vessel being built to the order of the US Maritime Administration and the Atomic Energy Commission by the New York Shipbuilding Corporation. She was launched on 21 July 1959 and ready for sea the following year, but even at the planning stage it was acknowledged that the ship would not

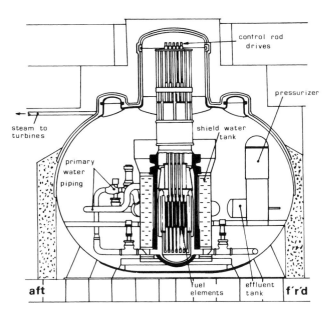

15.34 *Fore and aft section through reactor containment vessel fitted in* Savannah

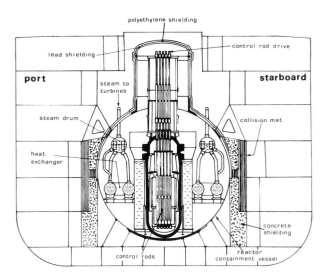

15.35 *Port and Starboard section through* Savannah's *reactor containment vessel*

be economically competitive. Her propulsion plant was designed to develop 22,000shp under normal conditions and comprised a cross compound, double-reduction turbine installation constructed by the De Laval Steam Turbine Company of Trenton, New Jersey. The HP turbine comprised nine stages of single-row impulse wheels and the LP turbine had seven rows of impulse blading; the LP casing also contained the 8,000shp astern turbine which had two impulse wheels, a double-row wheel and a single-row wheel. Because dry saturated steam was supplied to the HP turbine its exhaust contained about 12 per cent water droplets and these had to be removed before the steam could enter the LP stage; a two-stage water separator was fitted in the steam line, the first stage comprising a baffle which directed water droplets to a drain and the second a centrifugal separator in which the rotation of the passing steam caused the droplets to be thrown outwards as the steam passed through the centre of the separator. Apart from the use of steam under such conditions, 465psi and 463°F at normal power, the turbine installation was similar to that supplied by the company for normal ship propulsion.

The nuclear reactor fitted in *Savannah* was similar to that used for *Nautilus* with two heat exchangers for generating steam from the circulating pressurised water. The entire reactor, heat exchangers and associated equipment were housed in a containment vessel made from steel which had a maximum thickness of four inches. The containment vessel was 35ft in diameter by 50ft long, being designed to withstand a pressure of 186psi. long. Some 2,000 tons of concrete and lead were employed for shielding purposes and because of the total weight of the structure it had to be

15.36 *One of* Savannah's *heat exchangers under construction* (Babcock & Wilcox)

located amidships in order to ensure the ship's stability. The primary reactor shield consisted of a lead-lined, water-filled tank and lead, concrete and polyethylene provided for the secondary shielding of the containment vessel. The core contained thirty-two fuel elements each having 164 fuel rods, uranium enrichment being 4.2 per cent for the inner elements and 4.6 per cent for the outer ones; the initial fuel charge was 7,100kg of uranium, 312kg being of uranium-235. Each of the twenty-one control rods could be actuated separately by the combined use of electromechanical and hydraulic force while safety features ensured that the rods would move down into the core in the event of a system failure. A system of latches ensured that the rods would remain in the core should the ship capsize. Water, at a pressure of 1,750psi, was circulated through the reactor core and the heat exchangers, there being two independent, closed-loop circulation systems; the temperature of the water entering the reactor was 494°F and at exit 521°F.[25]

The propulsion system fitted in *Savannah* worked effectively and, within the limitations of the pressurised water reactor, efficiently but the cost of the plant and the restrictions placed upon operation of the ship militated against nuclear propulsion ever being a commercial success. Similar operating problems were experienced by German and Japanese nuclear-powered, experimental ships. Cost and port restrictions were not prime factors so far as the military was concerned and the fact the non-air-breathing reactor could operate for prolonged periods on one fuelling made it ideal for submarines and surface warships. Steam power at sea had had a stay of execution by virtue of nuclear power.

References

1   Babcock & Wilcox, *Babcock Marine Boilers*, Publication No. 1703, c. 1960.

2   *Shipbuilder & Marine Engine-Builder*, June 1957, pp. 384–99; May 1961, pp. 313–24.

3   T. W. F. Brown, 'A Marine Engineering Review – Past, Present and Future', *Trans. RINA*, 1960, Table VI.

4   D. G. Nicholas, 'Review of the Marine Steam Turbine over the Last 40 Years', *Trans. I.Mar.E.*, vol. 102, 1990, p. 85.

5   *Marine Engineering Log*, Nov. 1968, pp. 69–73: *Naval Architect*, Jan. 1987, pp. E11–15: I. Jung, *The Marine Turbine Part 2: 1928–1980*, National Maritime Museum, Greenwich, 1986, pp. 144–7.

6   *Journal of Commerce*, Special Southern Cross supplement, 25 Mar. 1955.

7   *Engineering*, 2 Dec. 1960, pp. 768–9; *The Engineer*, 16 Dec. 1960, pp. 1002–6.

8   *Journal of Commerce*, Special *Canberra* and *Oriana* supplement, 30 June 1961, p. 9.

9   AEI, Publicity Brochure No 3471–72 'SS *Canberra* – Turbo-electric Propulsion', Rugby, 1960.

10   Nicholas 'Review of the Marine Steam Turbine', p. 86.

11   AEI, SS *Canberra*,; T.W. Bunyan *et al*, '*Canberra*', *Trans. I.Mar.E.*, 1962, pp. 317–25.

12   Ibid., pp. 313–15.

13   *Shipping World & Shipbuilder*, Jan. 1969, pp. 112–18

14   Comment by Cdr E. Tyrrell on D. G. Nicholas, 'Review of the Marine Steam Turbine', p. 99.

15   I. Jung, *The Marine Turbine Part 3: 1928–1980*, National Maritime Museum, Greenwich, 1986, pp. 102–30.

16   Ibid., p. 70.

17   D. G. Nicholas, 'Review of the Marine Steam Turbine', pp. 86–7.

18   P. M. Rippon, *Evolution of Engineering in the Royal Navy, Vol. 2*, Inst. of Marine Engineers, 1994, p. 165.

19   D. G. Nicholas, 'Review of the Marine Steam Turbine', pp. 94–5.

20   M. A. Vallis, 'The Evolution of Warship Machinery 1945–1990', *Trans. I.Mar.E.*, vol. 104, 1992, p. 6.

21   Ibid., pp. 6–7.

22   The change to gas turbine propulsion is outlined in I. Jung, *The Marine Turbine, Part 3*, pp. 134–63.

23   *The Engineer*, vol. 199, 27 May 1955, pp. 753–6.

24   Department of Defense, *The United States Naval Nuclear Propulsion Program – June 1994*, 1994, pp. 33–7.

25   *The Engineer*, vol. 208, 4 Sep. 1959, pp. 203–5; 11 Sep. 1959, pp. 242–5; 18 Sep. 1959, pp. 282–5; *Babcock Marine Boilers*, Babcock & Wilcox, Brochure 12,950, 1961.

16
Steam's Finale

The sharp increase in oil prices during the 1970s[1] effectively killed the steam turbine as a major source of power as far as merchant shipping was concerned simply because the diesel engine consumed less fuel per unit of power developed. A long-stroke, slow-speed diesel engine had a specific fuel consumption of 0.352lbs/shp/hr while a conventional steam turbine plant (840psi and 950°F) burned 0.41lbs/shp/hr. The use of reheat cycles reduced the specific fuel consumption of steam plant but at the cost of added complexity and higher capital charges. In 1979 it was calculated that, with fuel costing $160 per tonne, a diesel plant for a 16,000shp installation showed an annual saving of some $240,000 compared with a steam plant of equivalent power and for higher powers the saving was even greater.[2] Since the 1950s large, slow-speed diesel engines had been designed to burn boiler fuel rather than the more expensive diesel oil but they had also become more efficient and reliable. By the 1970s slow-speed diesel engines were capable of developing 25,000shp on a single shaft, thus enabling them to compete in the large bulk-carrier market; effectively steam was ousted from the merchant-ship propulsion market except for a few specific cases and they related to fuel rather than to any advantage the turbine might have had over the diesel engine. However, because there were still uses for the steam turbine at sea development continued and the centre for such work moved to Japan where a number of builders, particularly Mitsubishi, invested heavily in turbine and boiler design. The geared marine steam turbine of the 1980s and the 1990s was a refined piece of technology compared with that introduced by Charles Parsons a century before, being more compact, better balanced and much more efficient.[3]

Although fuel costs were important to naval authorities other factors dictated the choice of propulsion plant for fighting ships, including the space occupied, safety and the time taken to provide full power. In the case of the submarine the advantage of the non-air-breathing nuclear plant over the diesel-electric drive had been proved by the 1970s. By that time British warships were burning lighter oil in boilers rather than the traditional furnace oil. There had been no change to diesel-engine propulsion for large warships simply because of the high power to weight and size ratio of the steam plant when compared with slow- and medium-speed diesel engines. Similar situations applied to all the other major maritime nations but there was a competitor in the form of the gas turbine. This machine is an internal combustion engine and so forms no more part of

the story of steam at sea than does the diesel engine, save for the fact that it has effectively replaced steam as the propulsion plant aboard most of the world's surface warships built since the mid-1980s. Such plant can develop full power immediately from a cold start and occupies much less room than a steam plant since there is no boiler or condenser. High-quality fuel must be used to prevent blade damage but this is not significant compared with the advantages offered by the gas turbine.

Steam-driven surface warships still roam the oceans of the world but these tend to be vessels constructed before the 1980s and probably the most powerful oil-fired, steam-driven warships afloat are the American *Kitty Hawk*-class carriers built between 1955 and 1964. These 56,300-ton vessels have quadruple screws driven by steam plant which generates 280,000shp when driving the ships at 34 knots. At 20 knots the ships carry sufficient fuel for 12,000 miles. By contrast the 81,600-ton 'Nimitz'-class nuclear-powered carriers also develop 280,000shp on four shafts with two nuclear reactors but the reactor cores will last for over twenty years. The first nuclear-powered aircraft carrier, USS *Enterprise* (CVN 65), put to sea in 1961 and was slightly smaller than the 'Nimitz'-class vessels; she could develop the same power but was fitted with eight reactors, the cores of which initially lasted for three years but subsequent cores have a lifetime expectancy in excess of twenty years.[4] As far as surface warships are concerned, the advantage of nuclear propulsion lies in the freedom from the need for frequent refuelling as a nuclear ship can remain at an action station for prolonged periods without risking vulnerable replenishment tankers.

Though nuclear-powered surface ships are large they are relatively few in number, but nuclear plant has had a much greater impact in terms of submarine propulsion owing to the fact that the machinery is quiet in operation. Large, powerful vessels may be constructed and submerged operation may be for long periods, limited by factors other than fuel supply. Since *Nautilus* proved the effectiveness of nuclear propulsion the size and power of nuclear submarines operated by the world's leading military nations has increased dramatically. Alternative reactor arrangements have been tried, including the liquid-sodium-cooled reactor fitted in USS *Seawolf* (SSN 575) during the 1950s, but the pressurised water reactor has proved itself to be the most suitable. American 'Sturgeon'-class boats (4,650-tons submerged displacement) built during the 1960s were given nuclear plants capable of developing 15,000shp while the

16.1 Oil-fired and steam-turbine-powered, the 58,300-ton American carrier Kitty Hawk *(CV-63); 280,000shp on four shafts. (US Navy)*

'Los Angeles' -class of the 1970s has a submerged displacement of 6,927 tons and can develop in excess of 35,000shp. 'Ohio'-class *Trident* ballistic missile submarines have a submerged displacement of 18,700 tons and a classified power potential to match.[5]

The naval employment of steam in the final decade of the twentieth century is essentially associated with a particular fuel, fissionable uranium, and is only employed because that fuel allows for extended operation and, in the case of the submarine, does not require an air supply for power generation. The situation is much the same with respect to merchant ships where the burning of oil is more efficiently undertaken in the diesel engine. During the 1980s a number of very large crude-oil tankers were constructed with steam turbine plant but the demise of that type of ship and the increasing power availability from large diesel engines denied the large oil tanker market to the steam turbine. There are, however, fuels which the marine diesel engine cannot burn effectively but which can be burned under boilers and these include coal and liquefied natural gas (LNG).

Coal is transported around the world in significant quantities making its use as a bunker fuel in large colliers an interesting proposition. However, such coal-carrying ships would have to be dedicated to the trade and most are simply general bulk carriers capable of lifting a variety of cargoes. The availability of bunker fuel at terminal ports is the critical factor and coal-burning ships need not necessarily be dedicated to the carrying of coal as a cargo. During the late 1970s and the early 1980s there was considerable interest in coal as a fuel for merchant ships with developments taking place in the USA, Spain, Italy, Korea and Japan.[6] During 1982 a Spanish shipping company Empresa Nacional Elcano took the step of replacing the after sections of two of its steam-powered tankers with new after units containing diesel engines. The after sections removed from the tankers were fitted to newly constructed bulk-carrier hulls and the

16.2 Bow view of the Kitty Hawk-*class aircraft carrier* John F. Kennedy *(CV-67) (US Navy)*

oil-fired boilers were replaced by coal-fired units. The bulk-carrier hulls incorporated two coal-storage tanks and coal-transportation systems to the engine room.[7] In 1982 the Italian shipbuilder Italcantieri constructed two 75,500-ton coal-fired bulk carriers for the Australian company TNT Bulkships, *TNT Capricornia* and *TNT Carpentaria*. The 19,000shp turbines were constructed by Cantieri Navali Riuniti under licence from General Electric and consisted of one HP and two LP stages with bled steam being taken

for a two-stage feed heater and a deaerator. The ships had only a single, two-drum, water-tube boiler designed by Combustion Engineering in the USA and built under licence in Italy by Franco Tosi; a 'get you home' emergency propulsion system comprised an electric motor on the propeller shaft taking power from a diesel generator. The boiler was designed to operate under balance draught, with two forced and two induced draught fans, generating 2,300lbs of superheated steam per minute at 865psi and

16.3 *Conventionally-powered amphibious cargo ship* Charleston *(LKA-113) fitted with a 22,000-shp geared steam-turbine installation on a single shaft; behind is a conventionally-powered 4,150-ton 'Farragut'-class missile frigate fitted with twin-screw, 85,000shp steam turbine plant. (US Navy)*

915°F. At full power the ships burned 219 tons of coal per day, allowing for a cruising range of 4,000 miles at the service speed of 15 knots.[8]

Probably of even greater interest are another pair of Australian National Line (ANL)-owned coal-fired bulk carriers, the Mitsubishi-built *River Boyne* and *River Embley* as the machinery philosophy differed from that adopted by TNT Bulkships. That company wished to keep the steam plant as simple as possible in order to minimise the loss of condensate and so only the propulsion plant, a single 1,700kW turbo-alternator and key auxiliaries were driven by steam. ANL wished to be independent of oil fuel and steam was employed as much as possible at sea and in port with all electrical power being generated from steam produced by burning coal.[9] The 51,994-gross ton ships were constructed for the ANL specifically to transport bauxite from Weipa in the northeast of Australia to the aluminium refinery at Gladstone in Queensland. After careful consideration of the route, water depth, power requirement and fuel availability, it was decided to install turbines supplied with steam from two coal-fired boilers; ordinary local coal was available at Gladstone and the ships would bunker there for a round trip. Mitsubishi conducted extensive trials with the coal in order to determine its combustion characteristics

and then designed the automatic system of the forced-draught boilers to give the optimum performance without producing smoke. The entire engine room was designed for unmanned operation and the ships were granted Lloyd's Register of Shipping UMS (Unattended Machinery Space) classification.[10]

Each of the two ANL 'River'-class steamers was provided with two Mitsubishi/Combustion Engineering V2M-9S stoker-type boilers which generated steam at 873psi and 895°F, the maximum evaporation rate for each boiler being 1,306lbs per minute; at this rating each boiler would burn 179lbs of coal per minute (115 tons per day). A system of balanced draught was used to enable accurate regulation of combustion under all conditions of steam demand. A major problem with coal-fired boilers is that coal on the grate will continue to burn whereas oil firing can be shut off when steam demand is reduced; the incorporation of an efficient electronic combustion control system, incorporating regulation of the balanced draught fans and coal supply to the stoker, together with a system of steam dumping allowed the boilers to operate on coal firing at all times and for all purposes. Stokers are of the moving grate type on to which is fed coal from the spreader unit which in turn is supplied from a daily hopper; sealed transportation systems take coal

16.4 Nimitz-*class nuclear-powered carrier* Dwight D. Eisenhower *(CVN-69) (US Navy)*

16.5 Sturgeon-*class nuclear-powered submarine* Aspro *(SSN-648); 4,650 tons submerged displacement with a single reactor steam turbine plant developing 15,000shp. (US Navy)*

from the bunker tanks and keep the hoppers supplied. Air supply is regulated both above and below the grate in order to achieve optimum combustion with the minimum of smoke. The ash removal system deals both with ash in the grate and fly ash carried upwards with the combustion gases. At full load when burning callide coal about 1.5 tons of ash per hour are produced, some 70 to 80 per cent of it being bottom ash and the remainder fly ash. The ash may be discharged overboard as a slurry or kept on board for discharge ashore in a dry state.[11]

The turbines fitted in *River Boyne* and her sister are of the Mitsubishi MS21-2 cross-compound type with tandem, articulated, double-reduction helical gearing. Under normal steam conditions the turbines develop 19,000shp to give a service speed of 15.8 knots when the propeller rotates at 80rpm. In contrast to the coal-fired boiler plant, the turbine plant is conventional but reflects years of development by

Mitsubishi engineers to produce a compact and efficient installation which requires the minimum of maintenance. Both HP and LP turbines have impulse and reaction blading while the under-slung condenser has an enlarged capacity to accommodate the surplus steam which is dumped when not required by the propulsion turbine or other systems; a special chamber in the condenser receives dumped steam.[12]

Coal-fired steamships differ from other steamships only in the way that the steam is generated, or rather only in the manner in which heat is produced to generate that steam. As has already been stated, by the late 1980s steam power for ship propulsion could not compete with the internal combustion engine but the internal combustion engine could not effectively burn coal for any reasonable period of time without serious maintenance problems. For similar reasons one other area of commercial ship operation

16.6 Coal-fired, steam-powered bulk carrier River Boyne *(Mitsubishi Heavy Industries)*

remains open to the steam turbine during the 1990s and that is the LNG carrier. Since the 1960s the transportation of liquefied petroleum gas (LPG) and LNG has increased dramatically as the commercial possibilities of such gases have been realised. For reasons which need not be considered here, the burning of LPG in marine plant is neither safe nor satisfactory and so only the LNG carrier needs to be discussed. Such gas, mainly methane, is carried in special tanks at temperatures below $-115°F$ ($-82°C$) and despite good insulation some of the liquefied gas will evaporate during the voyage from the loading terminal to the discharge port. If this 'boil-off' gas is not released it will result in an increase in tank pressure and the potential rupture of the tank. The venting of boil-off methane to the atmosphere is environmentally unfriendly as methane is a 'greenhouse gas' which contributes to global warming. Reliquefying the gas is not considered economical in most cases but methane will burn and may be used as a fuel in a boiler. Methane has a low ignition quality which means that it is difficult to ignite but if a flame already exists any new gas allowed into a combustion chamber will burn readily. That low ignition quality means that methane is not an easy fuel to burn in a diesel engine and, although systems have been developed, they have not yet reached the stage of perfection demanded by marine operators. As a fuel for boilers, however, boil-off methane gas

is ideal as it contains no ash or other substances which cause smoke, corrosion or boiler deterioration; if the boil-off rate is too low the burning of methane may be supplemented by the oil firing of the boiler to obtain the correct steam generation rate.

Many LNG carriers were constructed during the 1970s and fuel arrangements were such that the boilers were essentially arranged for oil firing with boil-off methane gas being used as and when it was available. The amount of liquid fuel required for the boilers varied considerably depending upon atmospheric conditions and at times the boil-off rate could exceed the boiler fuel demand with the consequent need to vent surplus gas. During ballast passage back to the loading port little gas was available although some liquid gas was retained in the tanks in order to ensure that they remained at a temperature low enough to allow for the loading of the next cargo without the need for time-consuming cooling. Throughout the 1970s and into the 1980s the steam turbine remained the sole means of propulsion for LNG carriers because boilers provided the safe means of disposal for boil-off gas. However, by the mid-1980s efforts were directed towards the efficient operation of the system and not simply the safe disposal of methane.

The Japanese engineering giant Mitsubishi was to the fore in development work and in 1989 the first of a new

225

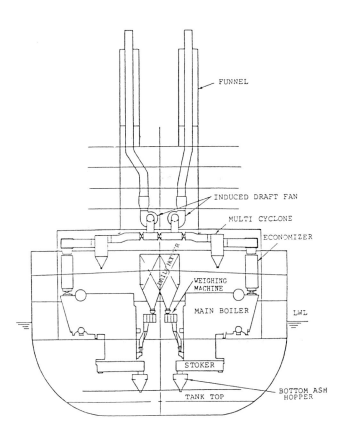

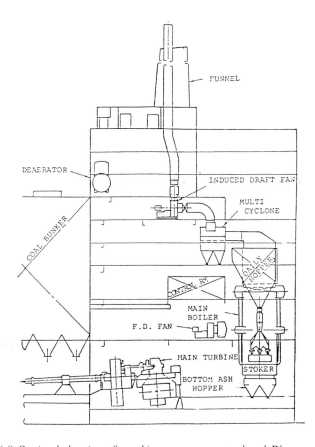

16.7 Sectional drawing of boiler room aboard River Boyne *(Mitsubishi Heavy Industries)*

16.8 Sectional drawing of machinery arrangement aboard River Boyne *(Mitsubishi Heavy Industries)*

generation of LNG carriers, the 125,000m³ capacity vessel *Northwest Sanderling* entered service, this being one of seven ships designed to carry LNG from Australia to Japan. Mitsubishi designers took their approach back to first principles and looked at what the ship was intended to do and then took account of the problems associated with the transportation of that cargo. The fact that boil-off occurred

during passage could not be avoided, but efficient insulation would limit boil-off thus avoiding the wastage of cargo; however, if less gas were available more fuel oil would need to be burned. The preferred situation was to make use of less gas when oil was cheaper than methane but to make full use of methane when oil was more expensive and Mitsubishi arranged for cargo tanks to be fitted with forcing

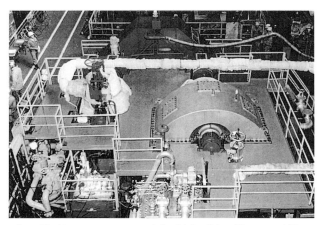

16.9 Mitsubishi coal-fired boiler front showing coal-spreader unit (Mitsubishi Heavy Industries)

16.10 Turbine arrangement used for driving River Boyne *and* River Embley *(Mitsubishi Heavy Industries)*

16.11 Steam-powered LNG carrier Northwest Swift *(Mitsubishi Heavy Industries)*

16.12 Turbine set for Mitsubishi-built LNG carrier with turbine and gearing covers removed   (Mitsubishi Heavy Industries)

16.13 Mitsubishi-built boiler ready for installation in an LNG carrier (Mitsubishi Heavy Industries)

vaporisers which would increase the rate of gas boil-off to meet the needs of the boilers when methane was the cheaper fuel. The boil-off rate of a traditional 125,000m³ LNG carrier is 0.25 per cent per day but for the new generation of Mitsubishi ships it amounted to only 0.15 per cent per day. The four cargo tank *Northwest Sanderling* and her sisters were fitted with two Mitsubishi-built Foster, Wheeler MSD double-drum, water-tube boilers with a maximum evaporation rate of 1,481lbs per minute while operating at 873psi and 960°F: the single set of Mitsubishi cross compound turbines developing 23,000shp at 76rpm. Boilers could operate on boil-off gas alone or on a combination of gas and oil.[13]

In 1990 Mitsubishi introduced the more advanced five cargo tank 137,000m³ LNG carrier *Ekaputra* which had a normal gas boil-off rate of only 0.1 per cent per day. Although the machinery system was similar to that of the 'Northwest'-class ships it was more powerful at 26,500shp, while the two Mitsubishi-designed N-3 water-tube boilers operate at the same steam conditions but with an evaporation rate of 1,830lbs per hour.[14] Further advances came in 1994 when Mitsubishi introduced the four tank 125,000m³ *LNG Vesta*; although the ship was no larger than earlier vessels and the boil-off rate was 0.15 per cent per day the cross compound steam turbine developed 32,000shp at 85rpm with the two Mitsubishi N-4 water-tube boilers evaporating 1,830lbs of steam per hour at 873psi.[15]

Marine steam propulsion during the final decade of the twentieth century has only two real areas of application, the nuclear warship and the liquefied natural gas carrier, and it is only employed in these ships because of the fuel and not because of any superiority over its main rival, the diesel engine. As a means of ship propulsion the steam engine has had its day and though its future is bleak its past is glorious. This book has attempted to relate some of that glory but it would take more than one book to cover the 200-year history of the marine steam engine comprehensively. As coal gave way to oil the balance of maritime power also shifted and Britain, once leader of the maritime world, found itself overtaken by other nations. The same is true for the steam engine as the diesel engine can burn oil more efficiently than any steam plant and the demand for greater efficiency at sea has seen the steam engine relegated to the fringes of marine propulsion. Steam is champion of the seas no more but its reign was one of magnificent achievement, an achievement at which we can only marvel.

References

1 Between 1974 and 1980 the cost of oil rose by 300 per cent compared with a cost of living increase of 230 per cent in Britain and 160 per cent in the USA. R.V. Thompson, 'Techno Economic Evaluation of Propulsion Plant to the Year 2000', *Trans. NECIES*, 1980–1, vol. 97, p.161.

2 J. K. Withrington & D.L. Saunders-Davies, ' The Role of Steam Propulsion Plant in the 1980s', *Bulletin of the Marine Engineering Society in Japan*, vol. 7, no. 4, Dec. 1979, p.16.

3 Y. Suguro, *et al*, 'Performance Improvement Technology for Marine Propulsion Steam Turbines', *Mitsubishi Heavy Industries Technical Review*, vol. 30, no. 1, Feb. 1993, pp. 51–5.

4 Department of Defense/Department of Energy, *United States Naval Nuclear Propulsion Program*, June 1994, pp. 45–50.

5 Ibid., pp. 38–43.

6 The proceeding of the Coal-Fired Ships Conference 1982 held in London gave details of the then state of the market; details of ships built with coal-burning plants were given in *Shipping World & Shipbuilder*, May 1982 and Oct. 1982 also *Marine Propulsion*, Sep. 1980, Oct. 1981, and June 1982.

7 Ibid., June 1982, pp. 26–30

8 'Italcantieri Building Coal-Fired Bulk Carriers', *Shipping World & Shipbuilder*, Oct. 1982; also M. Richards, *Workhorses in Australian Waters*, Turton & Armstrong, Wahroonga, Australia, 1987, pp. 193–4.

9 *Marine Propulsion*, March 1982, pp. 36–7.

10 Mitsubishi Heavy Industries, 'New Generation of Coal-Fired Steamship *River Boyne*', *Shipbuilding Report* No. 206, 1982.

11 M. Sakata and H. Koga 'The New Generation of Coal-fired Ships', Coal-fired Ships Conference, London, 1982; A. Fakugaki, *et al*, 'Design of a New-Generation Coal-Fired Marine Propulsion Plant', *Trans. Society of Naval Architects & Marine Engineers*, vol. 90, 1982, pp. 339–64.

12 M. Sakata and H. Koga, 'New Generation of Coal-fired Ships'.

13 Mitsubishi Heavy Industries, 'A 125,000m³ New Generation LNG Carrier *Northwest Sanderling*', *Shipbuilding Record* No. 37, 1989.

14 Mitsubishi Heavy Industries, '137,000m³ LNG Carrier *Ekaputra*', *Shipbuilding Record* No. 46, 1990.

15 Mitsubishi Heavy Industries, 'A 125,000m³ LNG Carrier for the Indonesian F-Train Project', *Shipbuilding Record* No. 97, 1994.

Glossary

'A'-frame a structure (in the form of a letter A or inverted V for supporting engine cylinders

Air preheater a heat exchanger used for heating the combustion air being supplied to a boiler furnace in order to improve combustion efficiency

Alternating current electric current which varies in strength and polarity (direction) with time; the number of cycles per second is the frequency (measured in hertz)

Alternator an electric machine which generates alternating electric current when rotated by an engine

Attemperator a heat exchanger used to reduce the temperature of steam (usually superheated steam); often acts as an air preheater

Axial turbine a turbine in which the steam flows from inlet to outlet in a direction parallel with the axis of the turbine rotor

Balanced draught a system of air supply to a boiler employing both induced draught and forced draught

Bedplate the base structure on which an engine frame is erected; the bedplate is bolted to the structure of the ship

Bled steam steam taken from some point in an engine before the exhaust in order to provide heating or do useful work elsewhere

Blue Riband an award given to a passenger ship setting a new record for the fastest crossing of the Atlantic Ocean

Bottom end bearing the bearing which attaches a cylinder connecting rod to the crankshaft

Box boiler a low-pressure boiler of box shape; usually of the flue type but sometimes of tubular form

Brake horse power a measure of the output power of an engine measured by attaching a brake mechanism to the output shaft

Camshaft a shaft, driven by the engine, by which means valves may be operated through a system of levers moved by circular discs or cams attached to the camshaft

Cavitation erosion or wear damage to the surface of propeller blades due to the formation and breaking of vacuum pockets caused by high-speed rotation

Centrifugal pump a pump which employs a rotating impeller to bring about pressure increase rather than a reciprocating piston; such pumps can deal with large volumes of water at relatively low pressures

Classification society an independent organisation which inspects ships and machinery at the planning stage, during construction at periodic intervals, and during operation in order to ensure that the ship and its equipment are maintained to an approved standard; Lloyd's Register of Shipping, the American Bureau of Shipping and Det Norske Veritas are three such organisations

Clinker solid, incombustible material which forms on the grates of coal-burning furnaces resulting in restricted passage for air through the furnace firebars

Closed stokehold a system of forced draught whereby air is supplied to an enclosed stokehold which is then under pressure; entry to the stokehold must be by means of an airlock

Compounding a system in which steam is expanded in two cylinders thus restricting the pressure and temperature drop which takes place at each stage

Condenser a device which changes steam into water; employed in conjunction with a steam engine in order to reduce the back pressure on the engine and so enable the steam to be expanded to a lower pressure

Corrugated furnace a boiler furnace which is has corrugated walls rather than being a plain cylinder; the corrugations provide for additional strength from the same thickness of material, allowing higher pressures to be withstood

Crankshaft a stepped shaft of an engine with the connecting rods from the cylinders being attached to the cranks or stepped sections

Crosshead the attachment point of the piston rod and the connecting rod where reciprocating motion of the piston is translated into oscillating motion at the connecting rod; usually a guide arrangement is provided at the crosshead in order to keep the motion of the piston in a straight line

Curtis wheel an impulse turbine wheel containing two or sometimes more impulse stages; often employed before reaction blading on a turbine

Deaerator a device used to remove dissolved gases from boiler feed water before it is pumped into the boiler; generally heating is employed

Direct current electric current in which the polarity remains the same

Distiller a device used for obtaining fresh water from sea water by boiling it to produce vapour and subsequently condensing the vapour

Donkey boiler an auxiliary boiler used for generating steam to supply donkey engines when required for use in port; subsequently the auxiliary boiler on any ship became known as the donkey boiler

Donkey engine an auxiliary engine used for driving pumps on early steamships

Double-ended boiler a fire tube boiler with furnaces at each end

Double flow turbine a turbine in which the steam enters at the middle of the casing and flows in both directions to the ends of the casing

Dynamo an electrical generator of direct current

Eccentric a circular disc fitted off-centre to a shaft by which a reciprocating motion may be imparted to a valve through a suitable eccentric strap and linkage

End tightening a method of sealing the tips of turbine blading by the use of projections at the blade tips; these projections having a fine clearance against the turbine casing

Feed heater a heater used for raising the temperature of water being pumped into the boiler thus improving operating efficiency as the boiler needs to impart less heat to raise the temperature to boiling temperature

Feed pump a pump used for supplying water to the boiler; aboard early steamships feed pumps were engine driven but subsequently independent steam-driven pumps were developed

Fluid clutch (Fottinger transformer) a device employing hydraulic means to make and break the connection between the engine and the output shaft or gearbox

Forced draught a system whereby combustion air is supplied to the boiler under pressure thus allowing for more rapid combustion of coal from a smaller grate area

Flue boiler a boiler employing rectangular flues through which hot combustion gases flow while imparting heat to the boiler water

Fly ash fine ash particles from the combustion of coal; the particles passed through the boiler with the hot gases and could pass out the funnel or build up in the boiler or uptakes

Furnace the part of a boiler in which the fuel is burned

Generator an electrical machine which produces electric current when rotated by an engine

Grate the part of a furnace on which coal is burned

Gland a seal arrangement through which a moving shaft or rod passes; this may be a reciprocating rod such as a piston rod or a rotating shaft such as a propeller shaft

Hot well the tank or container which holds hot water discharged from the condenser before it is taken by the feed pump for use in the boiler

Howden system a system of forced draught which employs trunking to supply heated combustion air under pressure direct to the furnace

Hydrogen peroxide propulsion a system of steam-turbine propulsion which does not require atmospheric oxygen but relies upon the decomposition of hydrogen peroxide to produce heat and oxygen in which fuel may be burned

Impulse turbine a turbine which relies upon the impact of steam against the blades to bring about rotation of the turbine disc

Incandescent lamp an electric lamp which provides illumination by the passage of an electric current through the filament

Indicated horse power (ihp) the power actually developed in an engine cylinder; it may be calculated using the equation Horse Power = Mean Cylinder pressure (psi) x piston area (in^2) x piston stroke (ft) x rpm x $1/33,000$

Induced draught a means by which increased air supply to a boiler furnace is produced by a suction fan acting on the flue gases to draw air through the furnace

Induction motor an alternating current electric motor which works because a magnetic field is induced in the windings rather than brought about by the passage of an applied electric current

Jet condenser a device in which exhaust steam is condensed by coming into contact with a jet of cold water sprayed into the condensing chamber

Ljungstrom air heater an air heater which uses waste heat in the flue gases to heat a series of metal plates which subsequently rotate in the air flow passage and impart their heat to combustion air passing to the furnace

Ljungstrom radial turbine a turbine which has no static blades; steam enters at the rotor centre and flows radially outwards; a compact turbine with two shafts rotating in opposite directions

Natural draught the system by which air is drawn through a furnace of a boiler by the draught caused by the funnel; a taller funnel allows for a stronger natural draught

Nominal horse power (nhp) a value of engine power calculated from engine dimensions and steam pressure; it bears no real relationship to the actual power developed by an engine but was an early method by which engines could be compared.

Open stokehold a system of forced draught in which the air is sent direct to the furnaces allowing the stokeholds to be open to the atmosphere

Parallel motion mechanism a system of linkages which allows a piston rod or valve rod to maintain movement parallel to the axis of a cylinder without the need for guides

Partial admission an arrangement in a steam turbine which allows steam entry to the turbine through certain nozzles around the circumference but not 360° admission; partial admission improves steam consumption with impulse turbines

Phosphor-bronze an alloy of copper, tin and a small

amount of phosphorus; a strong material used for gear wheels, valves and other marine engineering parts

Pinion   the shaft with the drive gear wheel which is in contact with the main gear wheel; for single reduction gearing the pinions are driven by the turbines

Piston valve   a valve used for directing steam to and exhaust from an engine cylinder; the valve was in the form of a double piston working in a cylindrical valve chest; piston valves allowed for a large valve area without high forces between the valve and the valve chest

Poppet valve   a cylinder valve of mushroom shape to allow the passage of live steam or exhaust; used mainly for internal combustion engines rather than steam engines

Priming [of a boiler]   the carry-over of water droplets into the steam lines to the engine; often caused by high water level in the boiler or an excess of certain chemicals

Quadruple expansion   the expansion of steam in four separate stages in a reciprocating engine or a turbine

Radial turbine   a turbine in which steam flow is radial rather than axial (*see* Ljungstrom radial turbine)

Raw feed water   feed water taken direct from a tank and so containing salts which may cause corrosion or scale formation

Reaction turbine   a turbine in which blade movement and hence rotation is caused by the reaction effect of steam leaving the nozzle created by a pair of adjacent rotating blades; the blades are shaped so that they create a nozzle when mounted next to each other in the turbine wheel. The reaction effect is similar to that obtained from water issuing from a rotary garden sprayer. [*see* fig. 11.1 in Chapter 11]

Reduction gearing   a system of gearing whereby the high rotational speed of a turbine is reduced to a much lower value for turning a propeller

Safety valve   a valve fitted to a boiler shell in the steam space; the valve is generally spring loaded and will lift at a preset pressure thus releasing steam and preventing boiler damage through over-pressure

Saturated steam   steam which contains all of its latent heat but no superheat; it is dry and so has no water droplets

Scotch boiler   a cylindrical tubular boiler with two to four cylindrical furnaces passing to combustion chambers and return tubes

Shaft horse power (shp)   the output power of a turbine; essentially the same as brake horse power

Shrouds   circumferential strips fitted to turbine blades at their tips in order to minimise vibration by holding blades together; also assists in minimising steam leakage at the blade tips

Simple expansion   expansion of steam in a single cylinder

Slide valve   a valve used for regulating steam flow to and from a reciprocating engine cylinder; the valve is held against a flat surface by steam pressure and is actuated by a system of linkages and eccentrics

Smokebox   the flue gas outlet from a tubular boiler; gases pass from the tubes into the common space called the smokebox and then up the funnel

Steam jacket   a space surrounding an engine cylinder which is heated by steam in order to minimise condensation in the engine cylinder

Steam receiver   a space between two cylinders of a multi-expansion engine into which steam flows on passage between the cylinders

Stephenson link motion   a system of linkages for operating cylinder valves; it employs two eccentrics, one ahead and one astern, the valve motion being obtained from movement of these

Stern tube   the tube through which the propeller shaft passes out of the ship; it is provided with a bearing surface and a gland for sealing

Superheated steam   steam which is raised in temperature above the temperature at which it is generated; superheated steam has more energy per unit mass than saturated steam but it is dry and so some lubrication needs to be provided in reciprocating engines

Surface condenser   a device in which steam is condensed without coming into contact with the condensing circulating water; generally water flows through tubes and the steam surrounds them

Synchronous electric motor   an electric motor whose speed is related directly to the frequency of the alternating current supply

Thrust block   the device through which the thrust of the propeller acting along the shaft is transferred to the structure of the ship

Triple expansion   the expansion of steam in three distinct stages

Trunnion   a pivot of an oscillating engine through which steam may also pass

Tubular boiler   a boiler in which heat transfer from gas to water takes place through small diameter tubes rather than large flues; in a fire-tube boiler the gas flows through the tubes whereas in a water-tube boiler the water is contained in the tubes

Turbine nozzle   a device through which steam is directed on to turbine blades; nozzles allow for steam pressure reduction with an accompanying increase in velocity

Turbo-alternator   a turbine-driven electric machine which generates alternating current

Turbo-generator   a turbine driven electric machine which generates direct current

Turbo-electric propulsion   a system of ship propulsion in which turbines are used to generate electricity (AC or

DC) and this electrical power is then used to turn an electric motor or motors connected to the propeller shaft(s)

Turn-down-ratio the arrangement whereby the fuel burned in a boiler may be regulated by either reducing oil quantity to specific burners or shutting down specific burners

Vortex separator a device for separating water particles from steam by giving the mixture of steam and droplets a rotation thus forcing the droplets to the outside of the separator

Water-tube boiler a boiler in which the water is contained in a series of tubes and the combustion gases flow around them

Wrapperitis a problem of leakage with early Yarrow water-tube boilers due to the joint in the 'D'-shaped water drums

Yarrow-Schlick-Tweedy a system of balancing four-cylinder reciprocating engines through a specific arrangement of crank angles, distances between cranks and weights on cranks

General Index

Index of Ships

This index is organised with merchantships first, then by national navy. Numbers in *italic* indicate illustrations.